Toshiaki Iwashiro

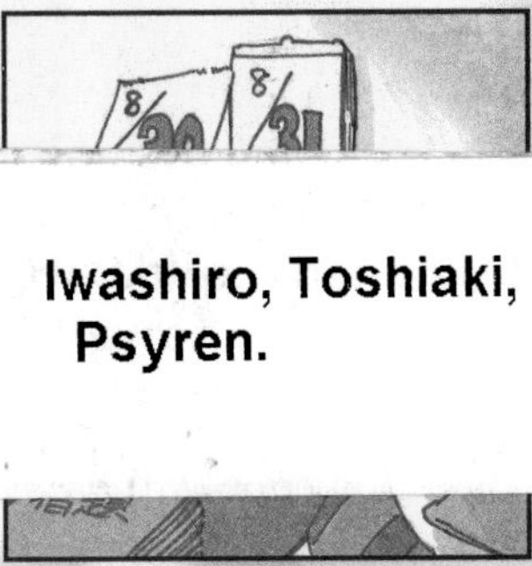

For a disorganized person like me, drawing a manga for a weekly publication has been nothing short of a miracle.

I lean heavily on a lot of people!

Toshiaki Iwashiro was born December 11, 1977, in Tokyo and has the blood type of A. His debut manga was the popular *Mieru Hito*, which ran from 2005 to 2007 in Japan in *Weekly Shonen Jump*, where *Psyren* was also serialized.

PSYREN VOL. 4
SHONEN JUMP Manga Edition

STORY AND ART BY TOSHIAKI IWASHIRO

Translation/Camellia Nieh
Lettering/Annaliese Christman
Design/Sam Elzway, Matt Hinrichs
Editors/Joel Enos, Carrie Shepherd

Printed in the U.S.A.

Published by VIZ Media, LLC
P.O. Box 77010
San Francisco, CA 94107

10 9 8 7 6 5 4 3 2 1
First printing, May 2012

www.viz.com

PARENTAL ADVISORY
PSYREN is rated T for Teen and is
recommended for ages 13 and up.
This volume contains fantasy violence.
ratings.viz.com

THE WORLD'S
MOST POPULAR MANGA
www.shonenjump.com

SHONEN JUMP MANGA EDITION

4

MELZEZ DOOR

Story and Art by
Toshiaki Iwashiro

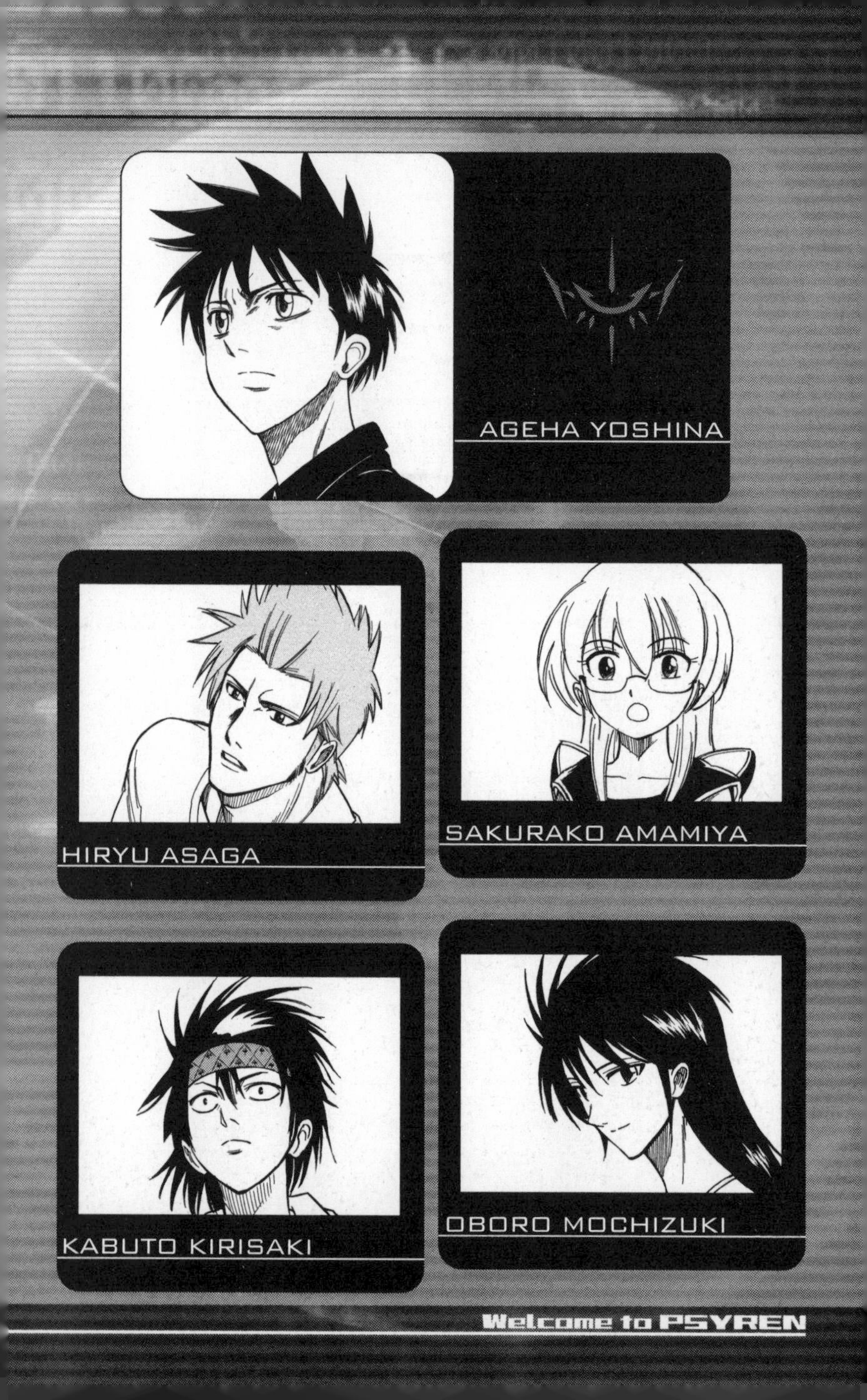
AGEHA YOSHINA
SAKURAKO AMAMIYA
HIRYU ASAGA
OBORO MOCHIZUKI
KABUTO KIRISAKI

Characters

NEMESIS Q

MATSURI YAGUMO

ELMORE TENJUIN

Story

HIGH SCHOOLER AGEHA YOSHINA HAPPENS UPON A RED TELEPHONE CARD EMBLAZONED WITH THE WORD PSYREN. SUSPECTING A LINK BETWEEN THE DISAPPEARANCE OF HIS CHILDHOOD FRIEND SAKURAKO AMAMIYA AND THE URBAN LEGEND OF THE PSYREN SECRET SOCIETY, AGEHA DECIDES TO USE THE CARD AND FINDS HIMSELF CAUGHT UP IN THE LIFE-OR-DEATH GAME OF THE BIZARRE PSYREN WORLD.

ON THEIR SECOND VISIT TO PSYREN, AGEHA AND COMPANY ARE ATTACKED BY A MYSTERIOUS SNIPER AND A GIANT WORM. THE SNIPER TURNS OUT TO BE TATSUO, THE LONG-LOST FRIEND AGEHA'S COMPATRIOT HIRYU HAS BEEN SEARCHING FOR. AFTER A FEROCIOUS BATTLE TATSUO REGAINS HIS MEMORY AND HELPS AGEHA AND FRIENDS RETURN HOME. ONLY THEN DO THEY REALIZE THAT TATSUO HAS STAYED BEHIND IN PSYREN ALONE...

PSYREN

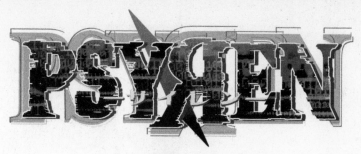

VOL. 4
MELZEZ DOOR

CONTENTS

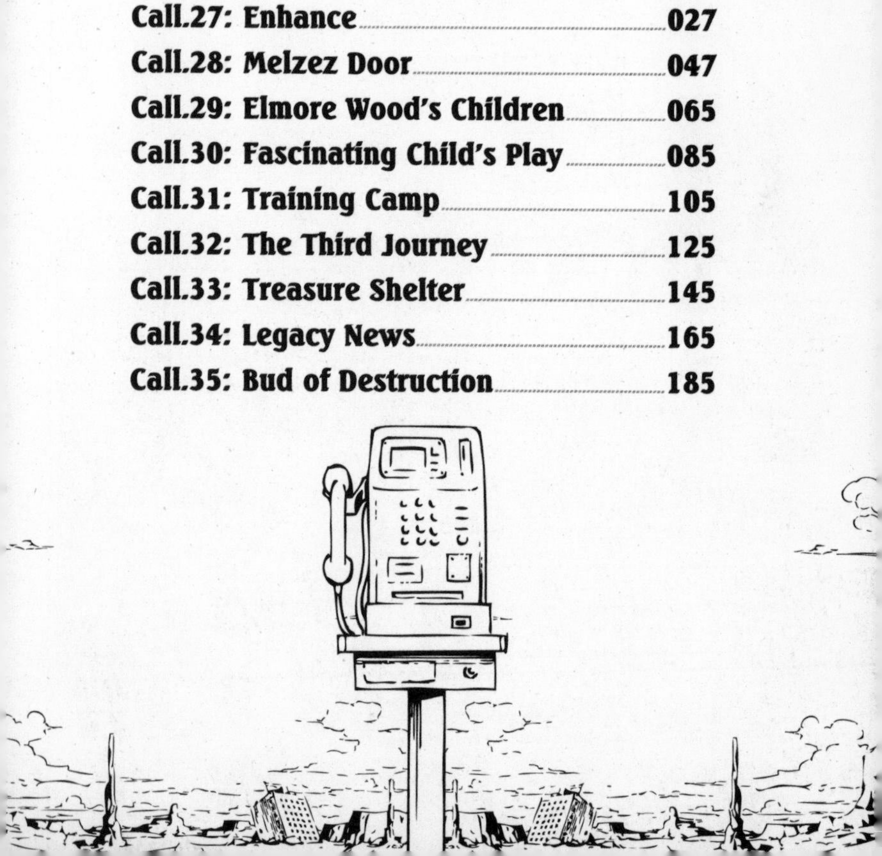

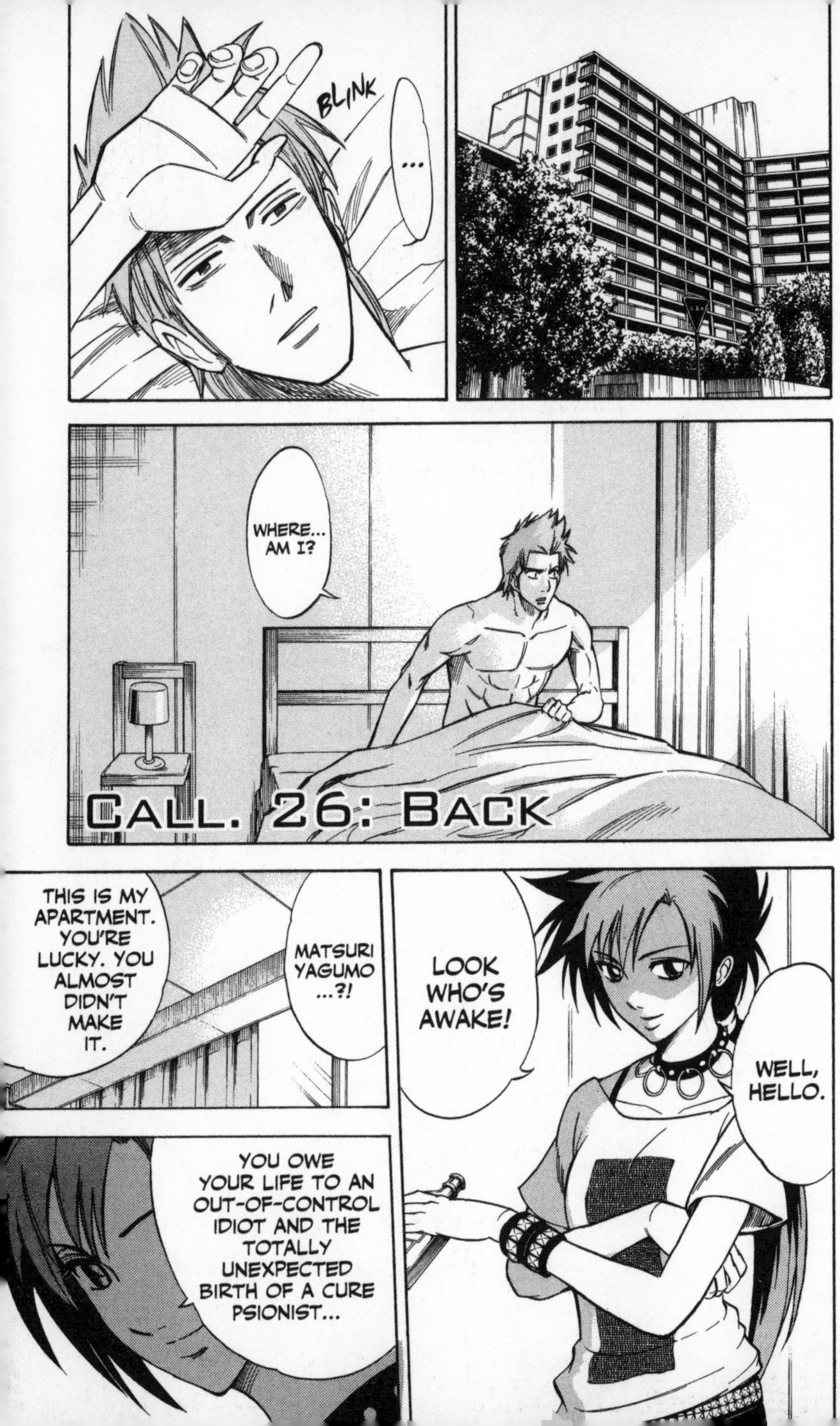
BLINK
...
WHERE... AM I?
CALL. 26: BACK
WELL, HELLO.
LOOK WHO'S AWAKE!
MATSURI YAGUMO ...?!
THIS IS MY APARTMENT. YOU'RE LUCKY. YOU ALMOST DIDN'T MAKE IT.
YOU OWE YOUR LIFE TO AN OUT-OF-CONTROL IDIOT AND THE TOTALLY UNEXPECTED BIRTH OF A CURE PSIONIST...

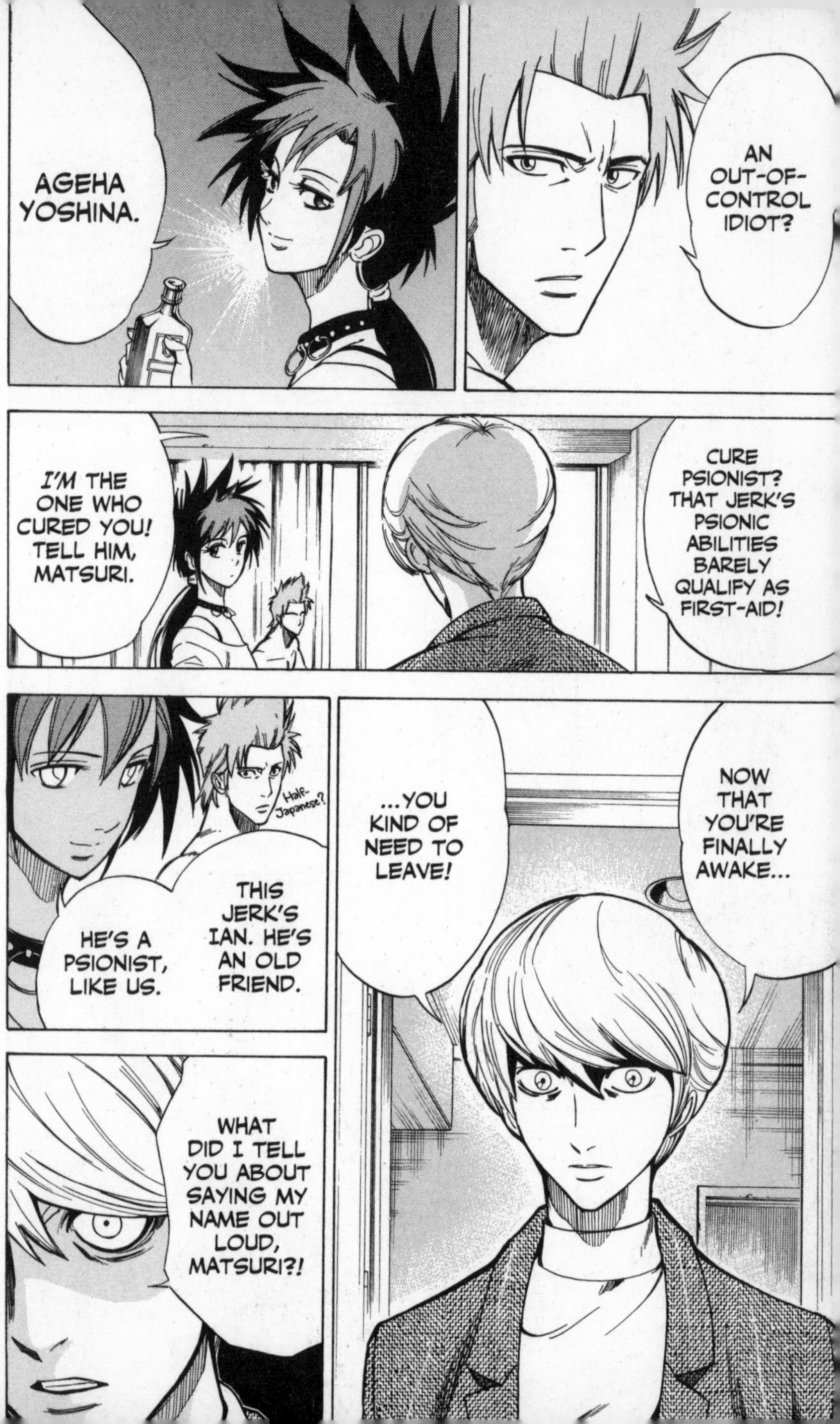
AN OUT-OF-CONTROL IDIOT?
AGEHA YOSHINA.
CURE PSIONIST? THAT JERK'S PSIONIC ABILITIES BARELY QUALIFY AS FIRST-AID!
I'M THE ONE WHO CURED YOU! TELL HIM, MATSURI.
NOW THAT YOU'RE FINALLY AWAKE...
...YOU KIND OF NEED TO LEAVE!
Half-Japanese?
THIS JERK'S IAN. HE'S AN OLD FRIEND.
HE'S A PSIONIST, LIKE US.
WHAT DID I TELL YOU ABOUT SAYING MY NAME OUT LOUD, MATSURI?!

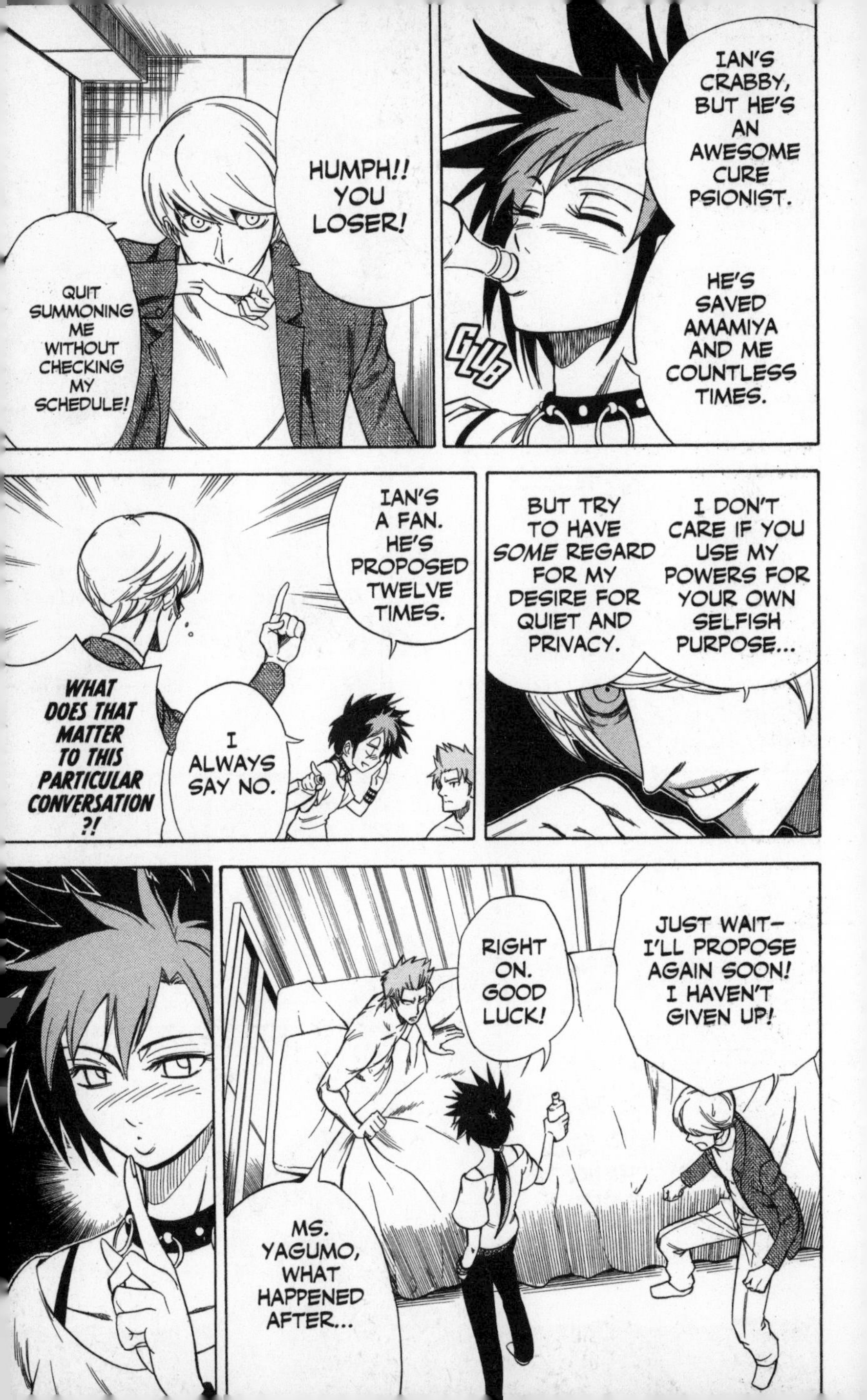
IAN'S CRABBY, BUT HE'S AN AWESOME CURE PSIONIST.
HE'S SAVED AMAMIYA AND ME COUNTLESS TIMES.
GLUB
HUMPH!! YOU LOSER!
QUIT SUMMONING ME WITHOUT CHECKING MY SCHEDULE!
I DON'T CARE IF YOU USE MY POWERS FOR YOUR OWN SELFISH PURPOSE...
BUT TRY TO HAVE *SOME* REGARD FOR MY DESIRE FOR QUIET AND PRIVACY.
IAN'S A FAN. HE'S PROPOSED TWELVE TIMES.
I ALWAYS SAY NO.
WHAT DOES THAT MATTER TO THIS PARTICULAR CONVERSATION ?!
JUST WAIT— I'LL PROPOSE AGAIN SOON! I HAVEN'T GIVEN UP!
RIGHT ON. GOOD LUCK!
MS. YAGUMO, WHAT HAPPENED AFTER...

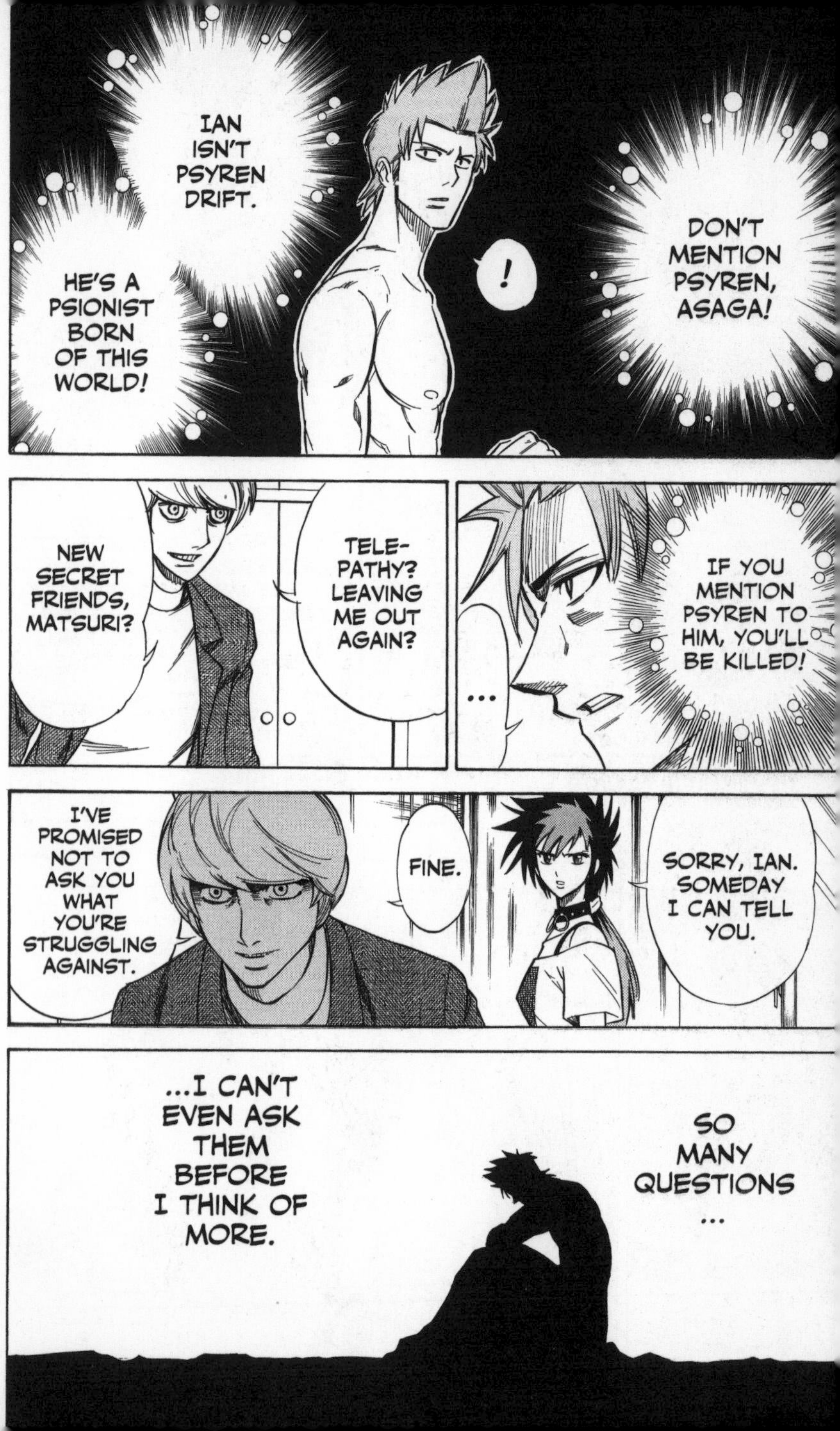
DON'T MENTION PSYREN, ASAGA!
!
IAN ISN'T PSYREN DRIFT.
HE'S A PSIONIST BORN OF THIS WORLD!
IF YOU MENTION PSYREN TO HIM, YOU'LL BE KILLED!
...
TELE-PATHY? LEAVING ME OUT AGAIN?
NEW SECRET FRIENDS, MATSURI?
SORRY, IAN. SOMEDAY I CAN TELL YOU.
FINE.
I'VE PROMISED NOT TO ASK YOU WHAT YOU'RE STRUGGLING AGAINST.
SO MANY QUESTIONS...
...I CAN'T EVEN ASK THEM BEFORE I THINK OF MORE.

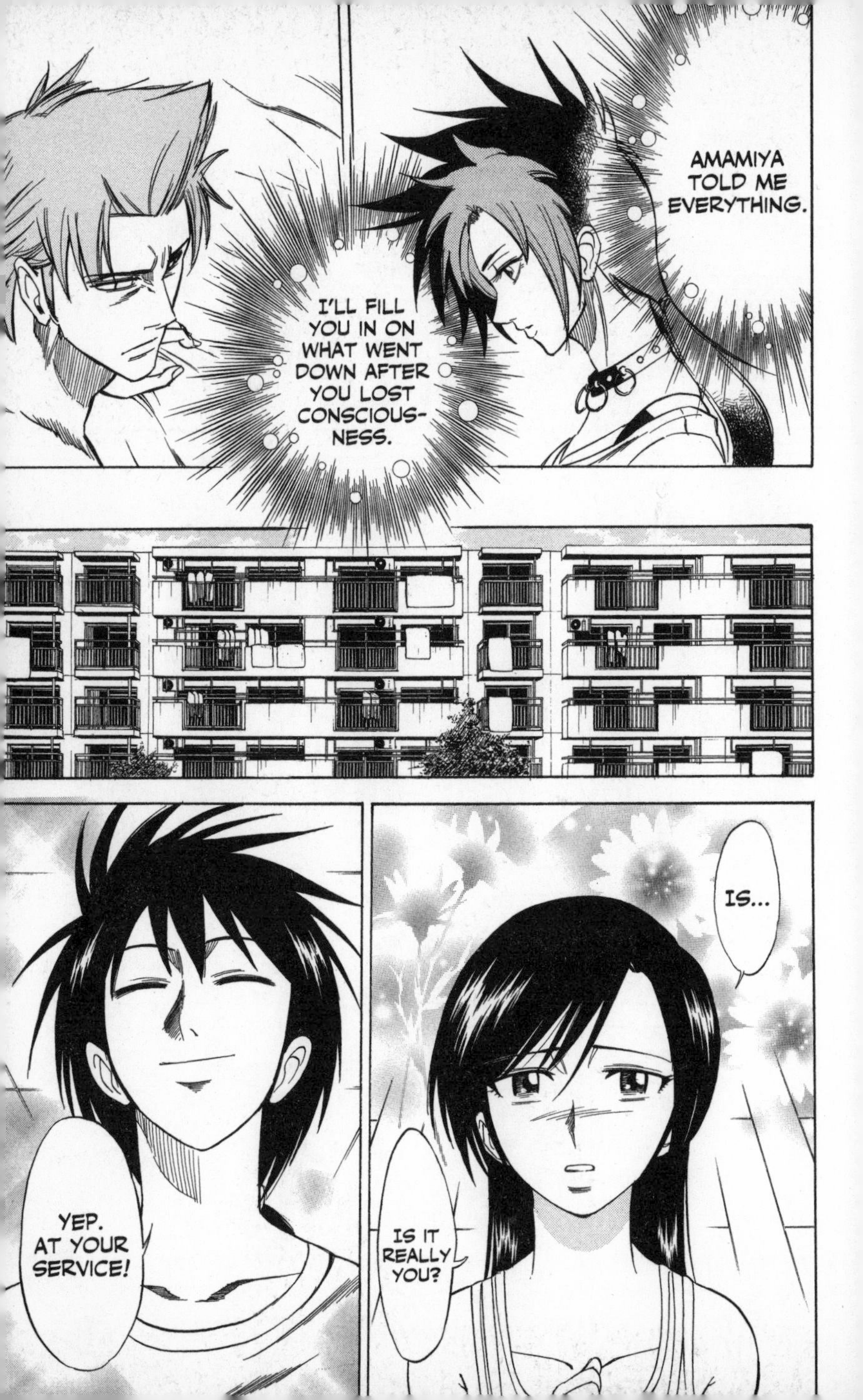
AMAMIYA TOLD ME EVERYTHING.
I'LL FILL YOU IN ON WHAT WENT DOWN AFTER YOU LOST CONSCIOUS-NESS.
IS...
IS IT REALLY YOU?
YEP. AT YOUR SERVICE!

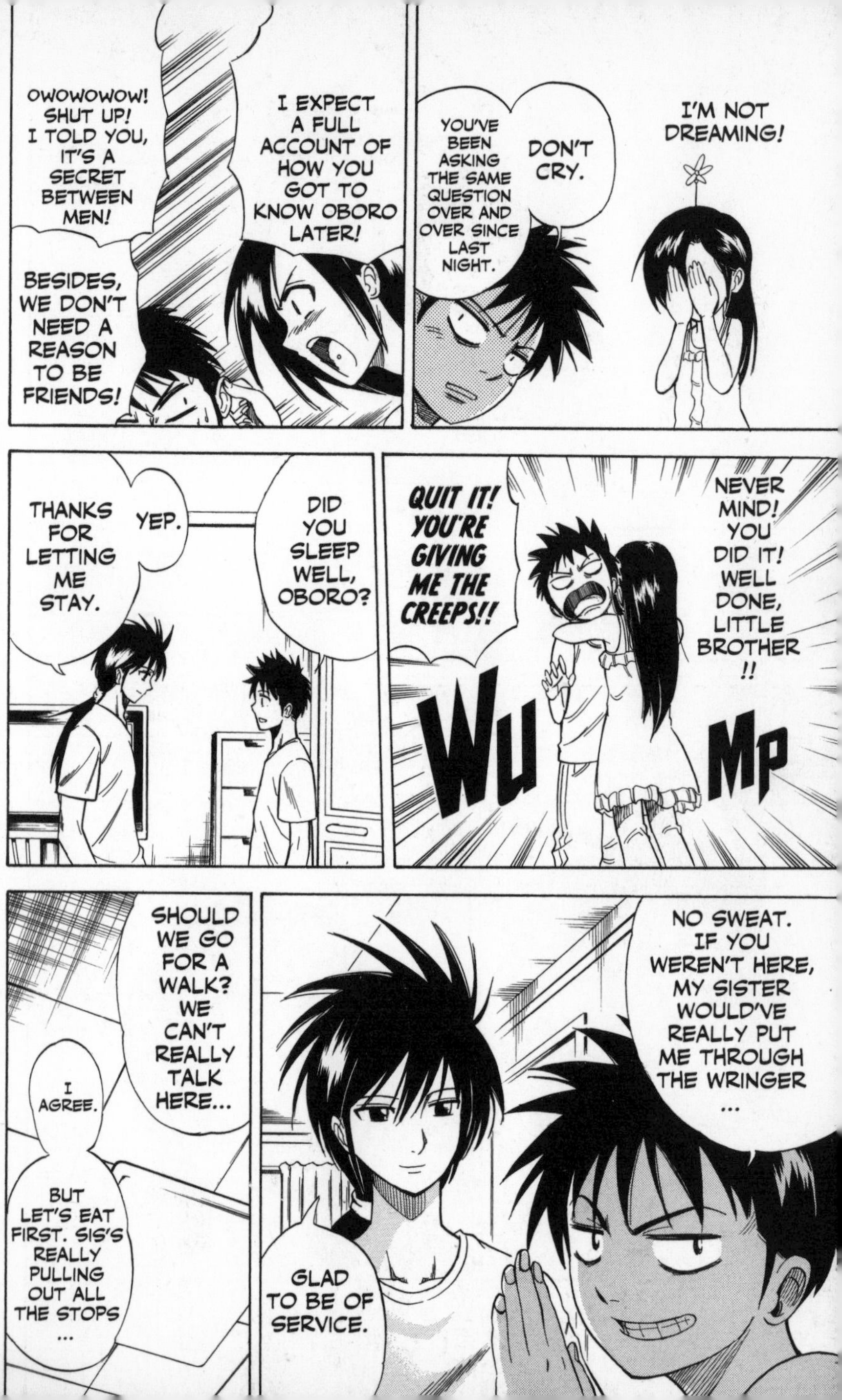
I'M NOT DREAMING!
DON'T CRY.
YOU'VE BEEN ASKING THE SAME QUESTION OVER AND OVER SINCE LAST NIGHT.
I EXPECT A FULL ACCOUNT OF HOW YOU GOT TO KNOW OBORO LATER!
OWOWOWOW! SHUT UP! I TOLD YOU, IT'S A SECRET BETWEEN MEN!
BESIDES, WE DON'T NEED A REASON TO BE FRIENDS!
NEVER MIND! YOU DID IT! WELL DONE, LITTLE BROTHER!!
QUIT IT! YOU'RE GIVING ME THE CREEPS!!
WUMP
DID YOU SLEEP WELL, OBORO?
YEP.
THANKS FOR LETTING ME STAY.
NO SWEAT. IF YOU WEREN'T HERE, MY SISTER WOULD'VE REALLY PUT ME THROUGH THE WRINGER...
GLAD TO BE OF SERVICE.
SHOULD WE GO FOR A WALK? WE CAN'T REALLY TALK HERE...
I AGREE.
BUT LET'S EAT FIRST. SIS'S REALLY PULLING OUT ALL THE STOPS...

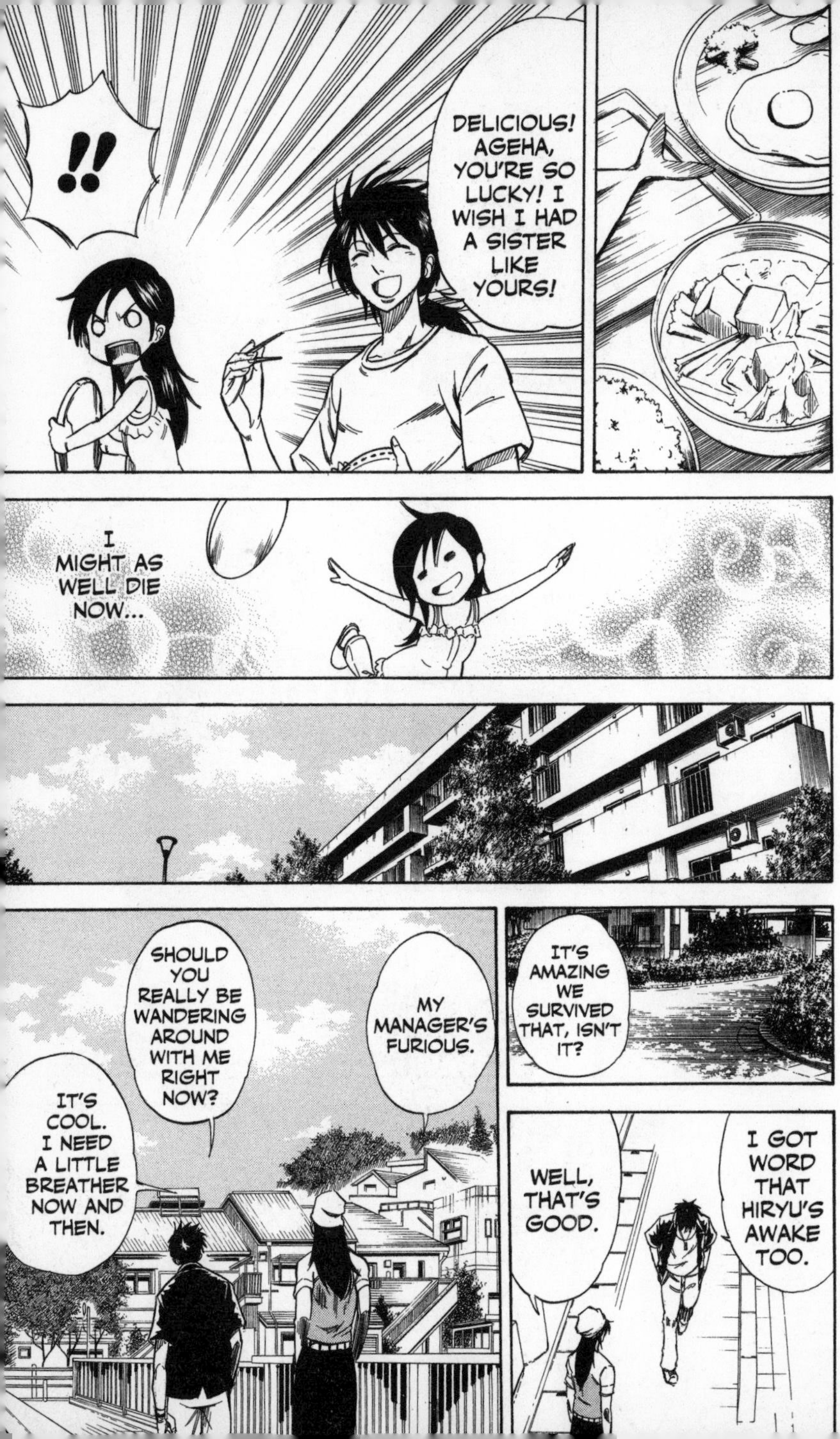
DELICIOUS! AGEHA, YOU'RE SO LUCKY! I WISH I HAD A SISTER LIKE YOURS!
!!
I MIGHT AS WELL DIE NOW...
IT'S AMAZING WE SURVIVED THAT, ISN'T IT?
I GOT WORD THAT HIRYU'S AWAKE TOO.
WELL, THAT'S GOOD.
MY MANAGER'S FURIOUS.
SHOULD YOU REALLY BE WANDERING AROUND WITH ME RIGHT NOW?
IT'S COOL. I NEED A LITTLE BREATHER NOW AND THEN.

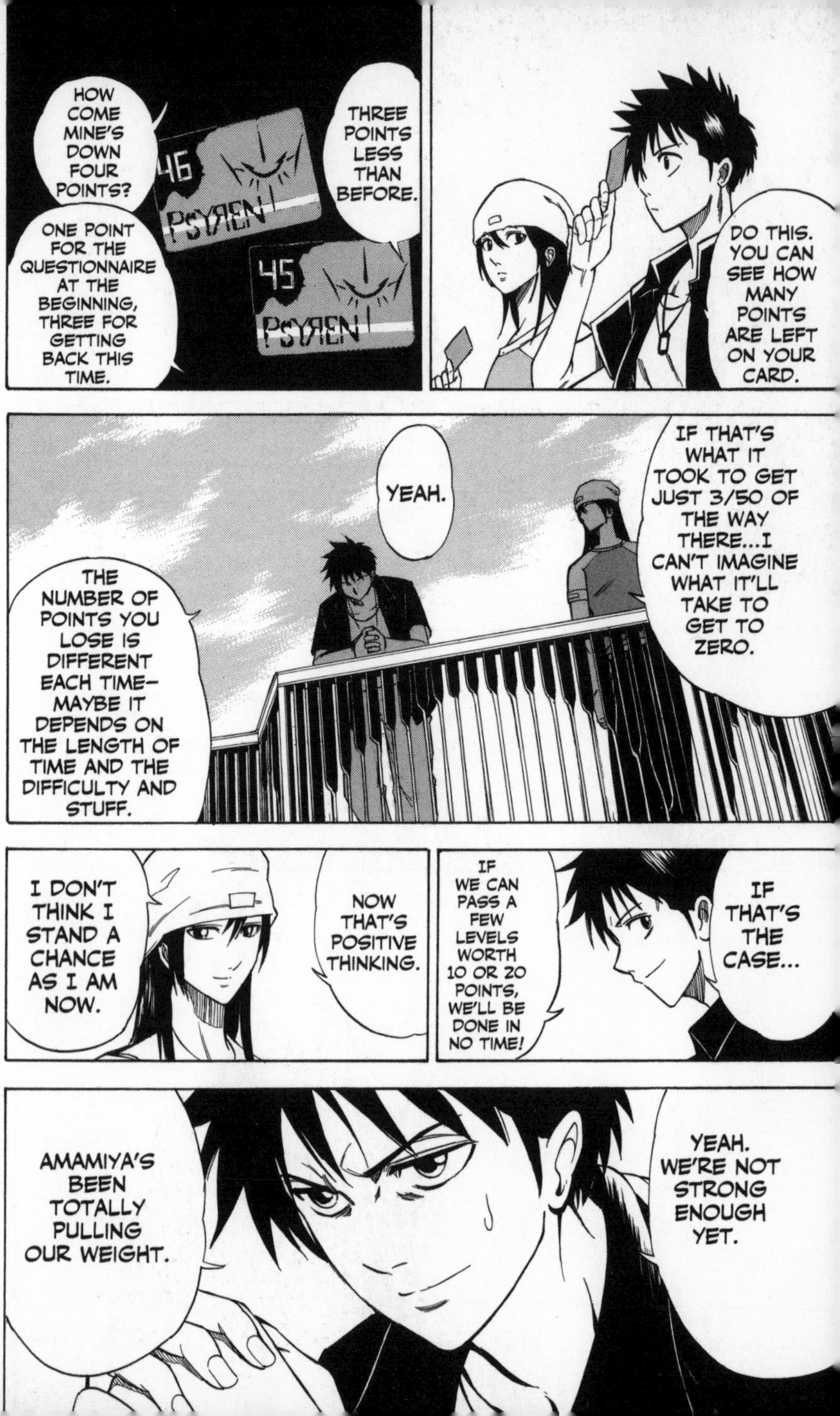
DO THIS. YOU CAN SEE HOW MANY POINTS ARE LEFT ON YOUR CARD.
THREE POINTS LESS THAN BEFORE.
HOW COME MINE'S DOWN FOUR POINTS?
46 PSYREN
45 PSYREN
ONE POINT FOR THE QUESTIONNAIRE AT THE BEGINNING, THREE FOR GETTING BACK THIS TIME.
IF THAT'S WHAT IT TOOK TO GET JUST 3/50 OF THE WAY THERE...I CAN'T IMAGINE WHAT IT'LL TAKE TO GET TO ZERO.
YEAH.
THE NUMBER OF POINTS YOU LOSE IS DIFFERENT EACH TIME—MAYBE IT DEPENDS ON THE LENGTH OF TIME AND THE DIFFICULTY AND STUFF.
IF THAT'S THE CASE...
IF WE CAN PASS A FEW LEVELS WORTH 10 OR 20 POINTS, WE'LL BE DONE IN NO TIME!
NOW THAT'S POSITIVE THINKING.
I DON'T THINK I STAND A CHANCE AS I AM NOW.
YEAH. WE'RE NOT STRONG ENOUGH YET.
AMAMIYA'S BEEN TOTALLY PULLING OUR WEIGHT.

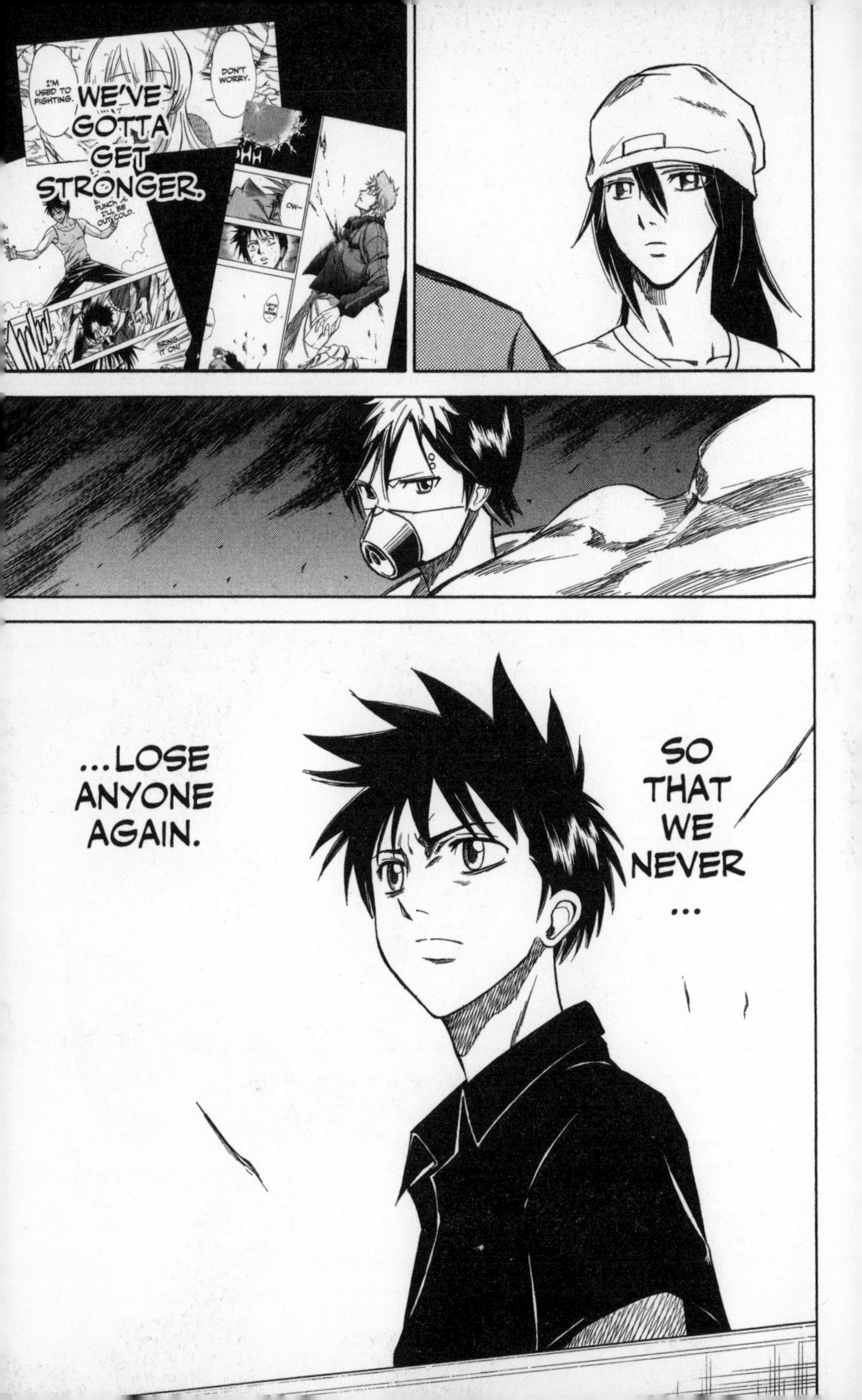
DON'T WORRY.
I'M USED TO FIGHTING.
OW-
BRING IT ON!
WE'VE GOTTA GET STRONGER.
SO THAT WE NEVER ...
...LOSE ANYONE AGAIN.

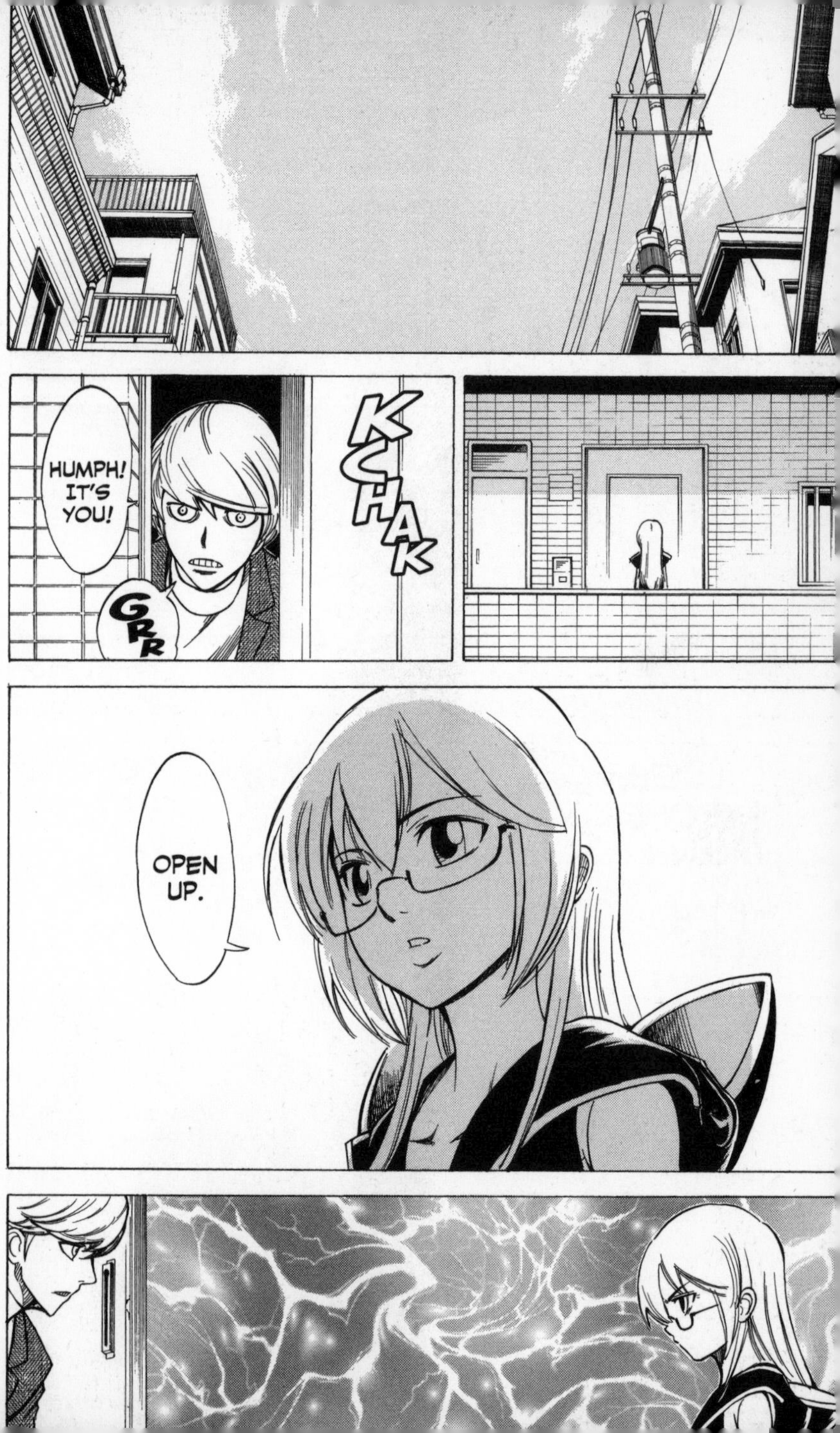
KCHAK
HUMPH! IT'S YOU!
GRR
OPEN UP.

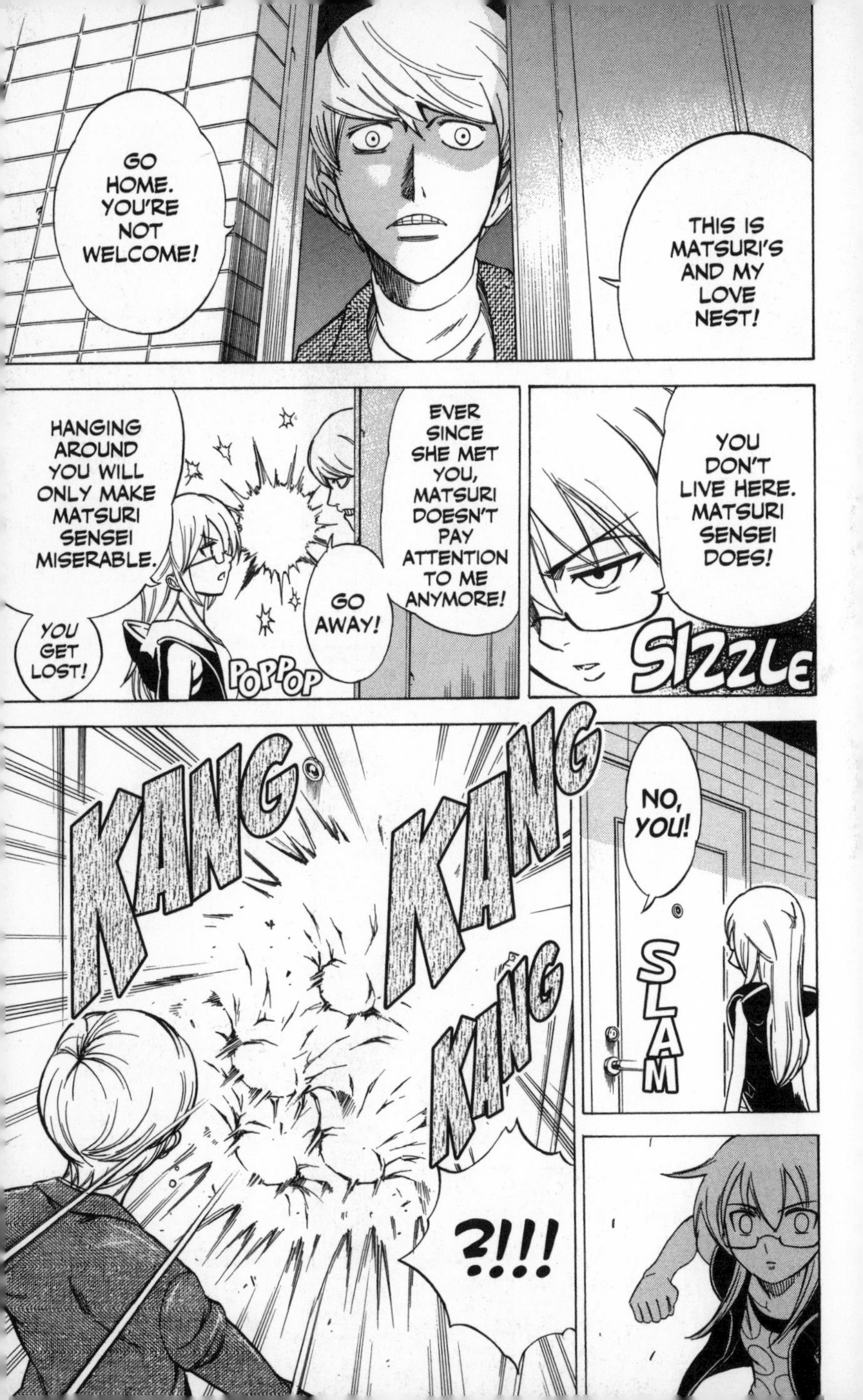
THIS IS MATSURI'S AND MY LOVE NEST!
GO HOME. YOU'RE NOT WELCOME!
YOU DON'T LIVE HERE. MATSURI SENSEI DOES!
SIZZLE
EVER SINCE SHE MET YOU, MATSURI DOESN'T PAY ATTENTION TO ME ANYMORE!
GO AWAY!
POPPOP
HANGING AROUND YOU WILL ONLY MAKE MATSURI SENSEI MISERABLE.
YOU GET LOST!
NO, YOU!
SLAM
KANG
KANG
KANG
?!!!

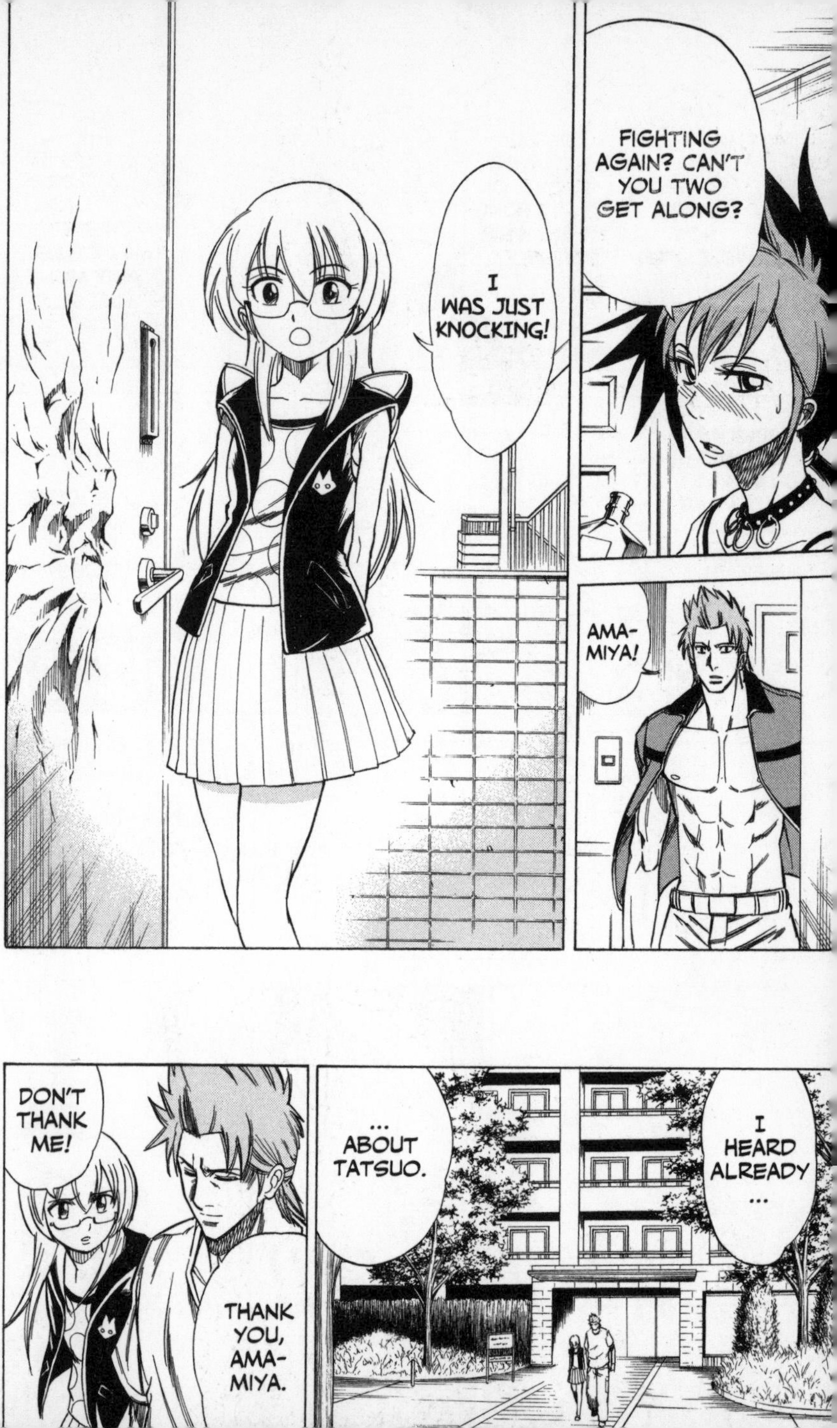
FIGHTING AGAIN? CAN'T YOU TWO GET ALONG?
AMA-MIYA!
I WAS JUST KNOCKING!
I HEARD ALREADY ...
... ABOUT TATSUO.
THANK YOU, AMA-MIYA.
DON'T THANK ME!

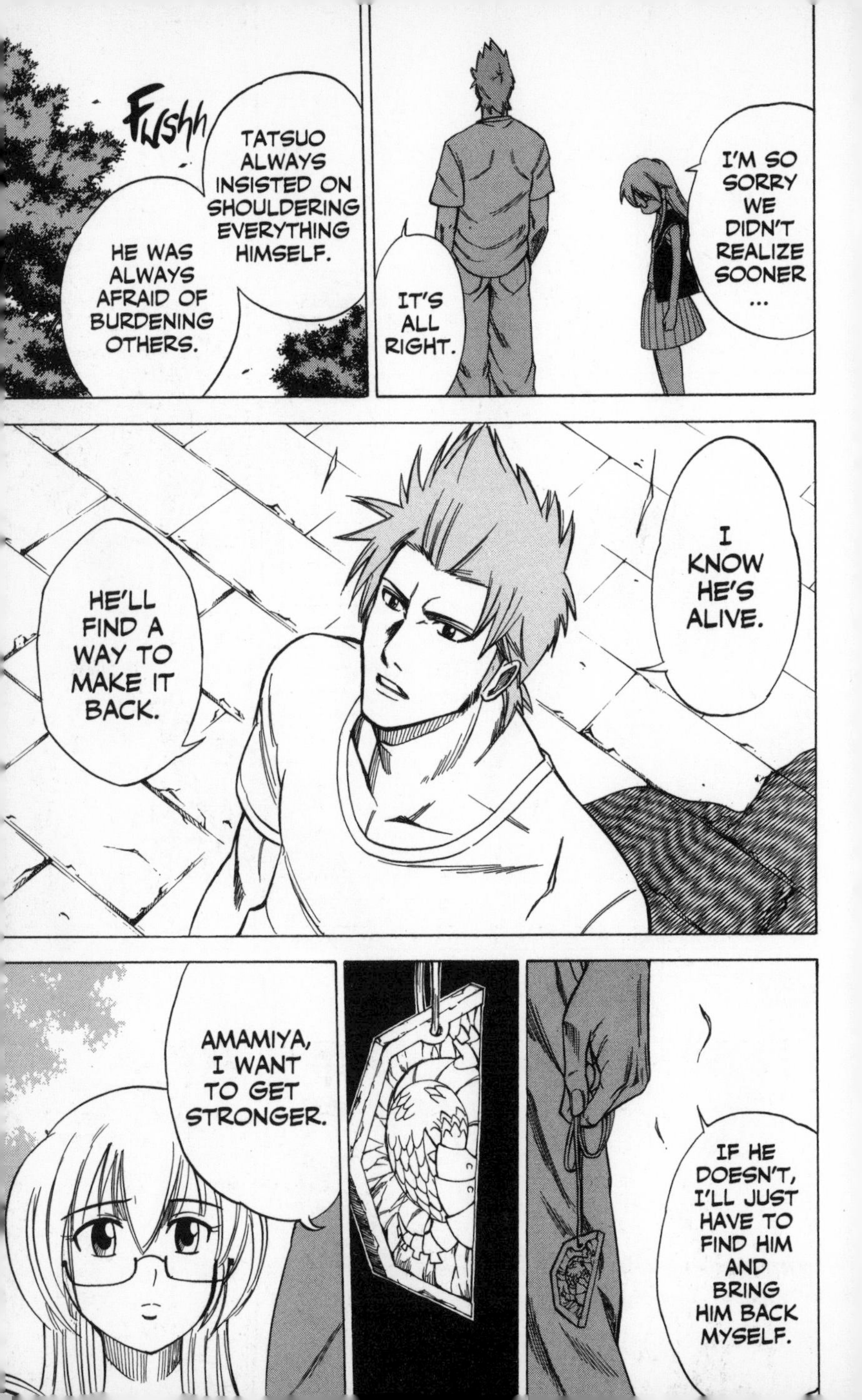
I'M SO SORRY WE DIDN'T REALIZE SOONER...
IT'S ALL RIGHT.
TATSUO ALWAYS INSISTED ON SHOULDERING EVERYTHING HIMSELF.
FWSHH
HE WAS ALWAYS AFRAID OF BURDENING OTHERS.
I KNOW HE'S ALIVE.
HE'LL FIND A WAY TO MAKE IT BACK.
IF HE DOESN'T, I'LL JUST HAVE TO FIND HIM AND BRING HIM BACK MYSELF.
AMAMIYA, I WANT TO GET STRONGER.

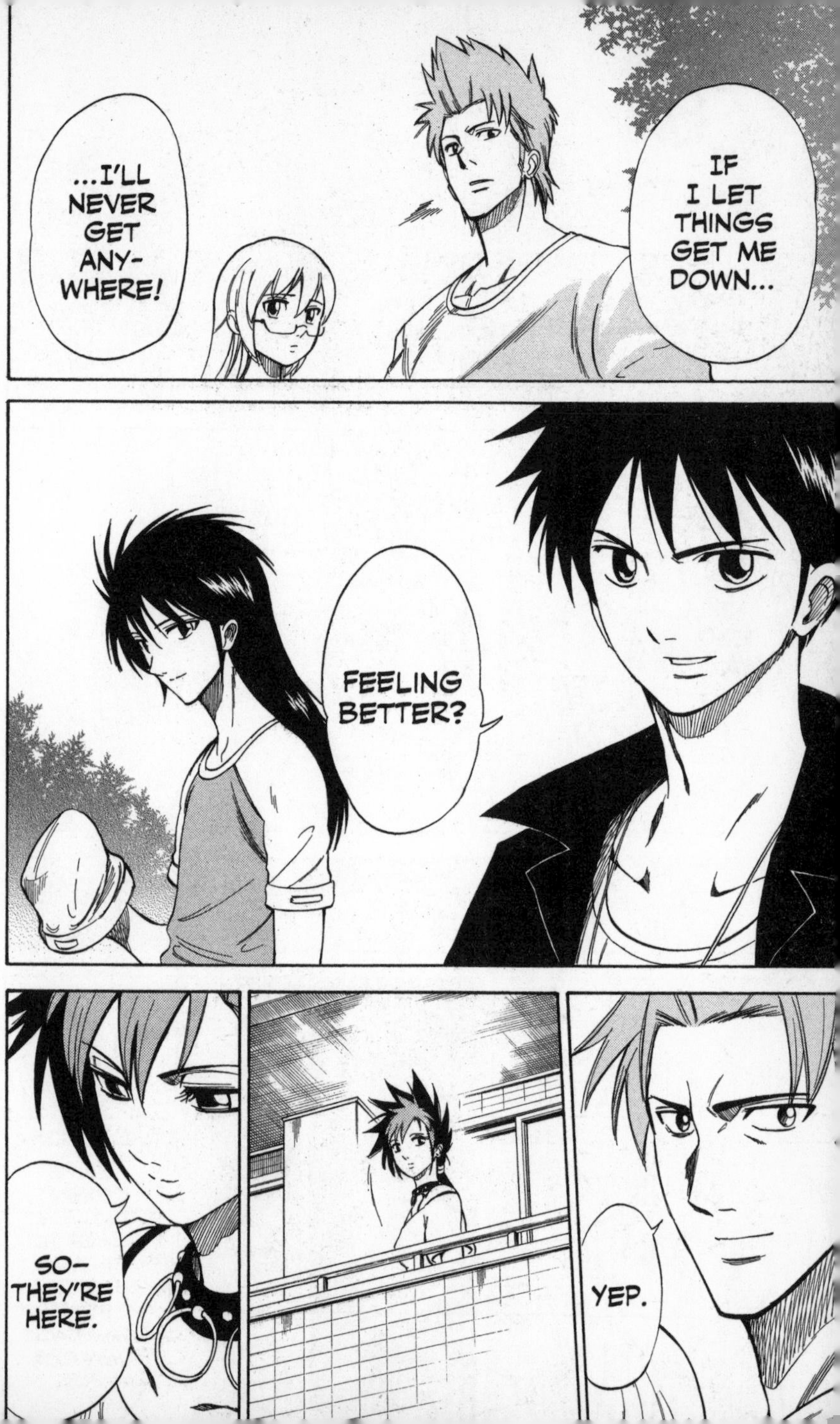
IF I LET THINGS GET ME DOWN...
...I'LL NEVER GET ANY-WHERE!
FEELING BETTER?
YEP.
SO— THEY'RE HERE.

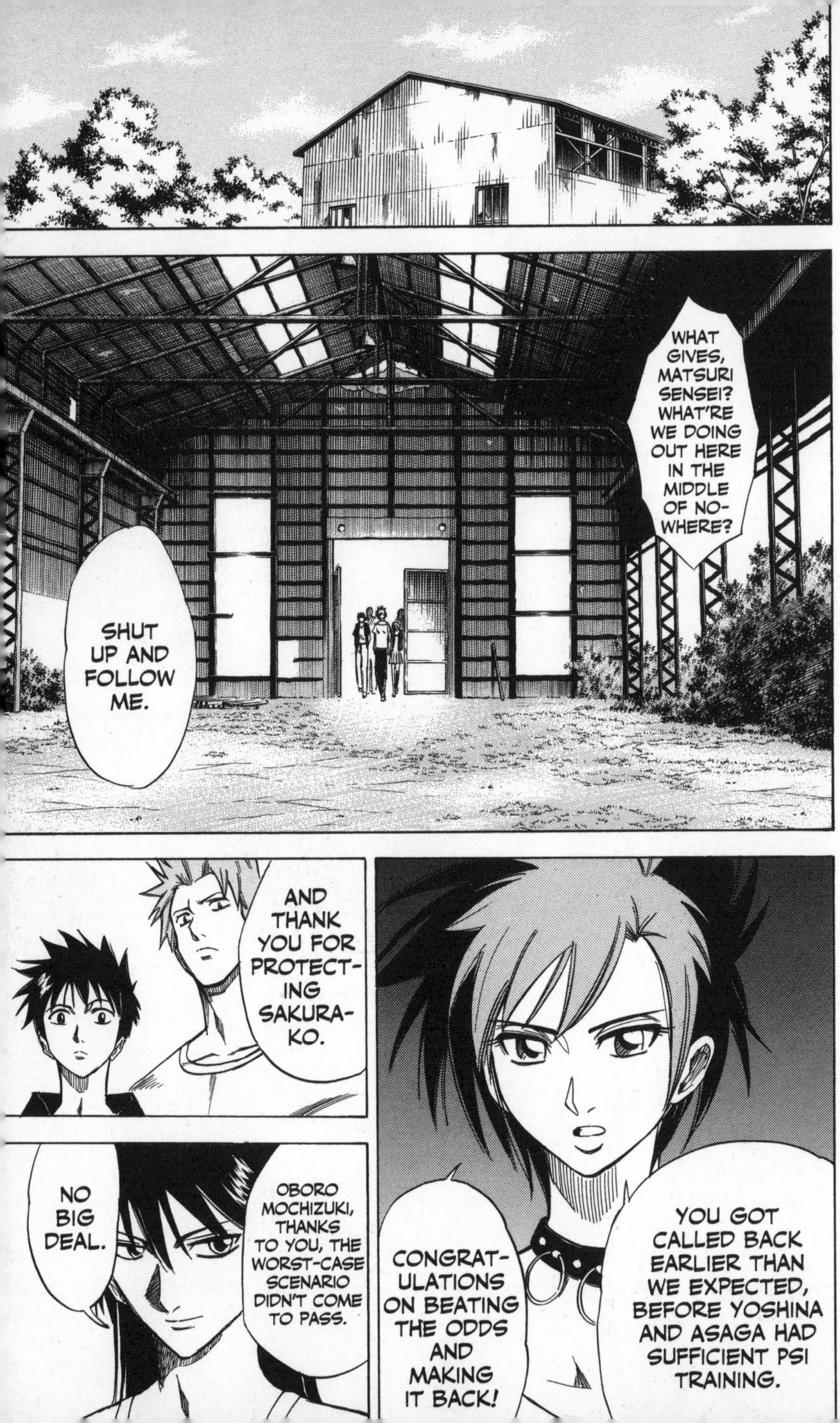
WHAT GIVES, MATSURI SENSEI? WHAT'RE WE DOING OUT HERE IN THE MIDDLE OF NO-WHERE?
SHUT UP AND FOLLOW ME.
YOU GOT CALLED BACK EARLIER THAN WE EXPECTED, BEFORE YOSHINA AND ASAGA HAD SUFFICIENT PSI TRAINING.
CONGRAT-ULATIONS ON BEATING THE ODDS AND MAKING IT BACK!
AND THANK YOU FOR PROTECT-ING SAKURA-KO.
OBORO MOCHIZUKI, THANKS TO YOU, THE WORST-CASE SCENARIO DIDN'T COME TO PASS.
NO BIG DEAL.

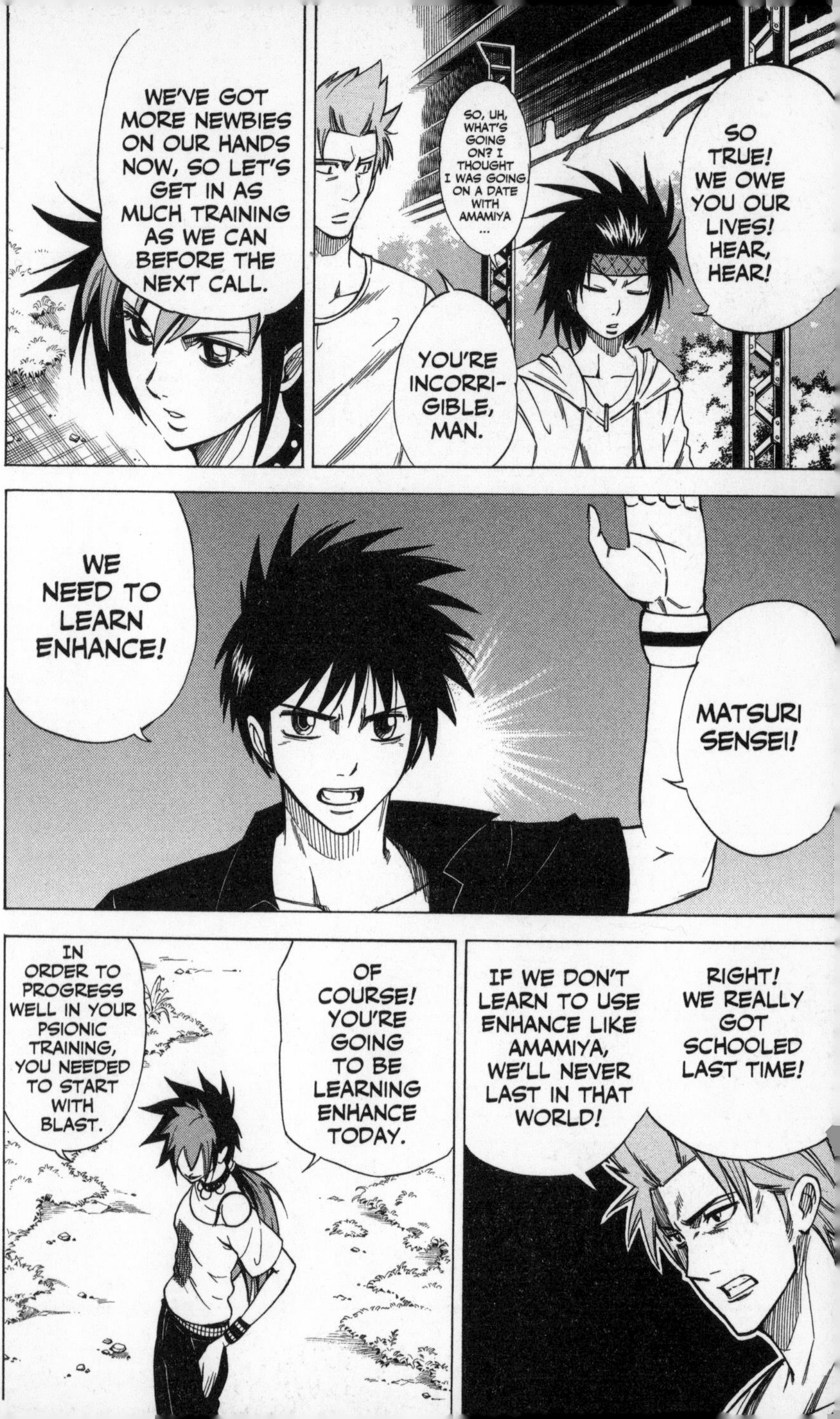
SO TRUE! WE OWE YOU OUR LIVES! HEAR, HEAR!
SO, UH, WHAT'S GOING ON? I THOUGHT I WAS GOING ON A DATE WITH AMAMIYA ...
YOU'RE INCORRI-GIBLE, MAN.
WE'VE GOT MORE NEWBIES ON OUR HANDS NOW, SO LET'S GET IN AS MUCH TRAINING AS WE CAN BEFORE THE NEXT CALL.
MATSURI SENSEI!
WE NEED TO LEARN ENHANCE!
RIGHT! WE REALLY GOT SCHOOLED LAST TIME!
IF WE DON'T LEARN TO USE ENHANCE LIKE AMAMIYA, WE'LL NEVER LAST IN THAT WORLD!
OF COURSE! YOU'RE GOING TO BE LEARNING ENHANCE TODAY.
IN ORDER TO PROGRESS WELL IN YOUR PSIONIC TRAINING, YOU NEEDED TO START WITH BLAST.

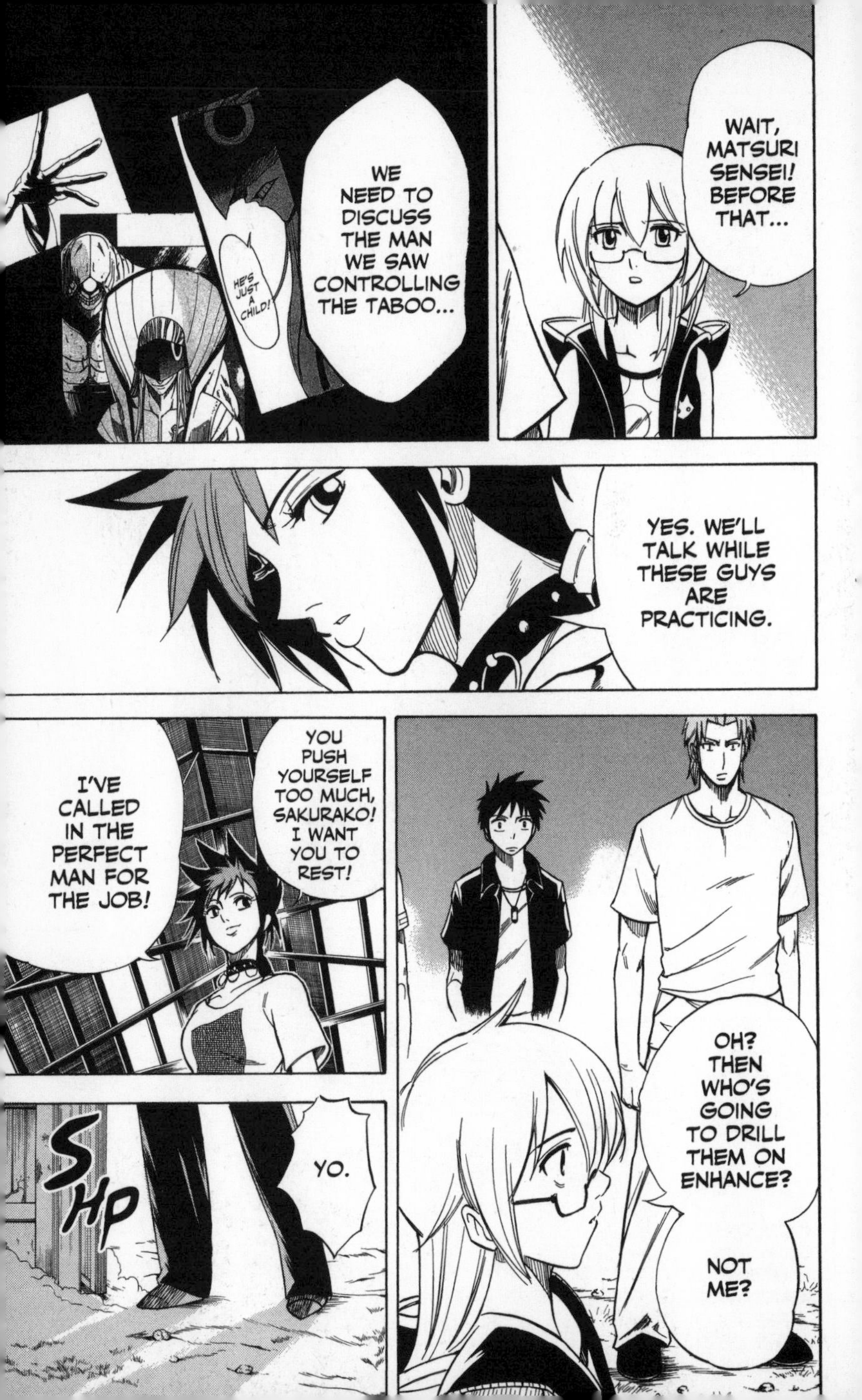
WAIT, MATSURI SENSEI! BEFORE THAT...
WE NEED TO DISCUSS THE MAN WE SAW CONTROLLING THE TABOO...
HE'S JUST A CHILD!
YES. WE'LL TALK WHILE THESE GUYS ARE PRACTICING.
OH? THEN WHO'S GOING TO DRILL THEM ON ENHANCE?
NOT ME?
YOU PUSH YOURSELF TOO MUCH, SAKURAKO! I WANT YOU TO REST!
I'VE CALLED IN THE PERFECT MAN FOR THE JOB!
YO.
SHP

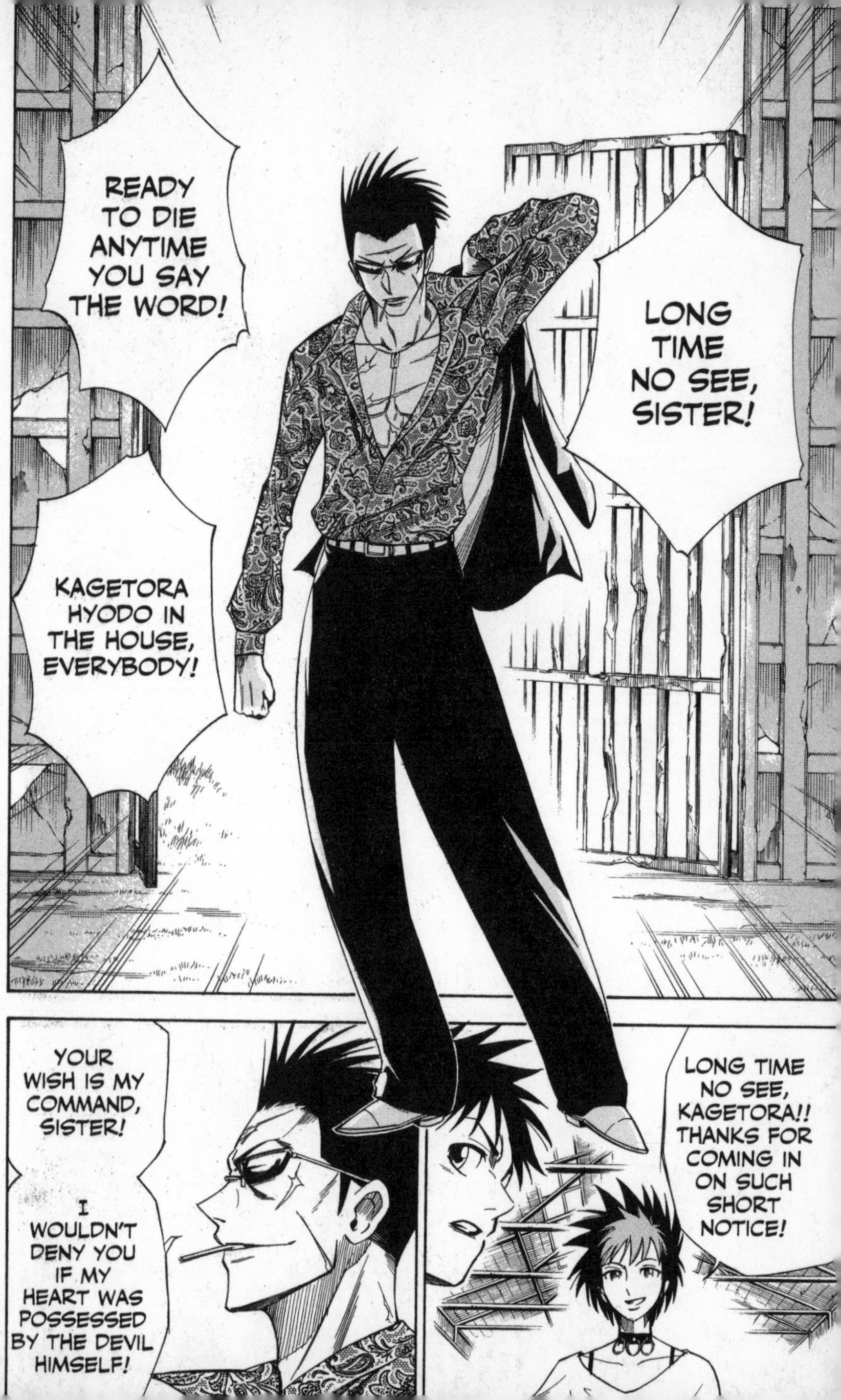
LONG TIME NO SEE, SISTER!
READY TO DIE ANYTIME YOU SAY THE WORD!
KAGETORA HYODO IN THE HOUSE, EVERYBODY!
LONG TIME NO SEE, KAGETORA!! THANKS FOR COMING IN ON SUCH SHORT NOTICE!
YOUR WISH IS MY COMMAND, SISTER!
I WOULDN'T DENY YOU IF MY HEART WAS POSSESSED BY THE DEVIL HIMSELF!

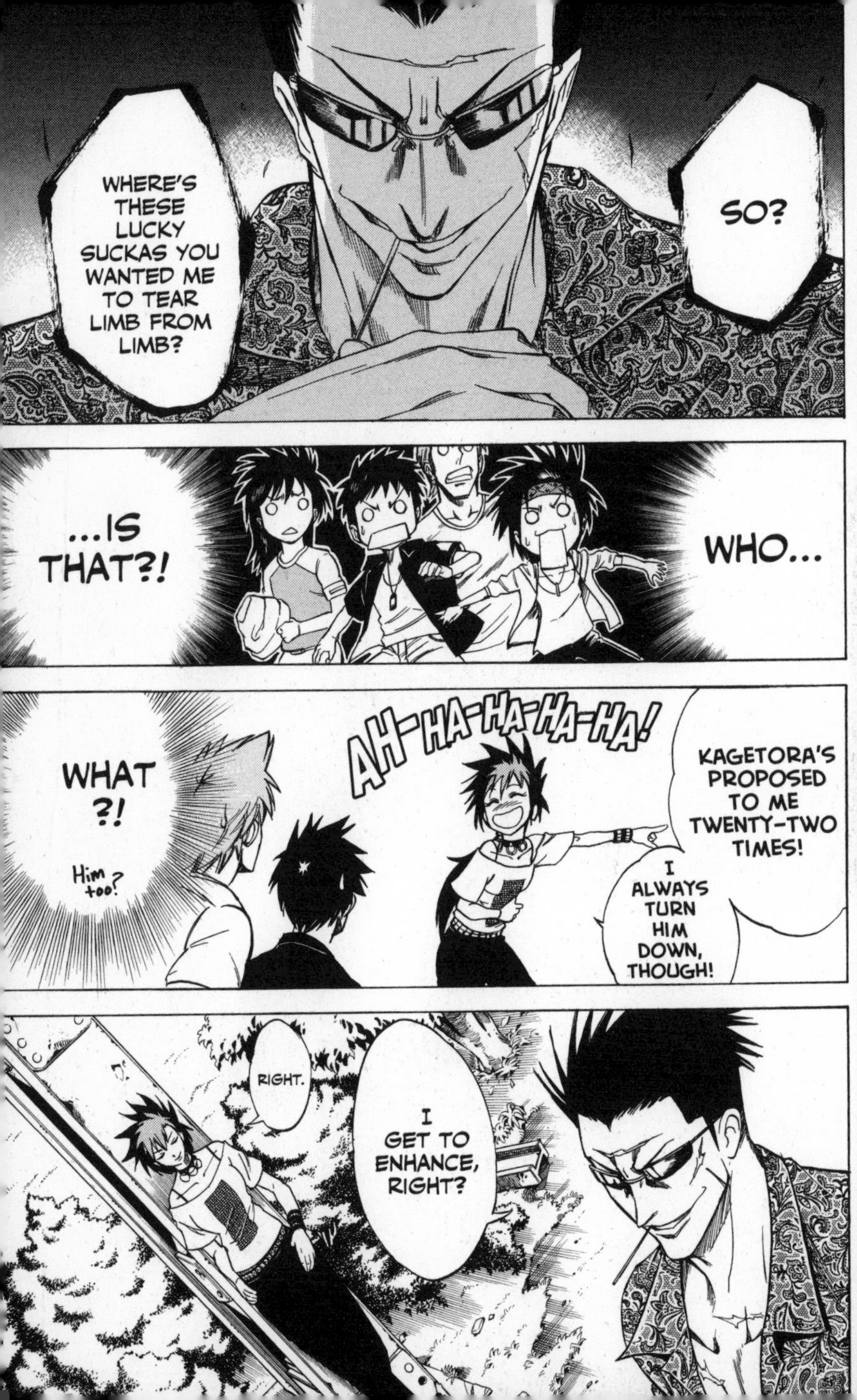
SO?
WHERE'S THESE LUCKY SUCKAS YOU WANTED ME TO TEAR LIMB FROM LIMB?
WHO...
...IS THAT?!
KAGETORA'S PROPOSED TO ME TWENTY-TWO TIMES!
AH-HA-HA-HA-HA!
I ALWAYS TURN HIM DOWN, THOUGH!
WHAT?!
Him too?
I GET TO ENHANCE, RIGHT?
RIGHT.

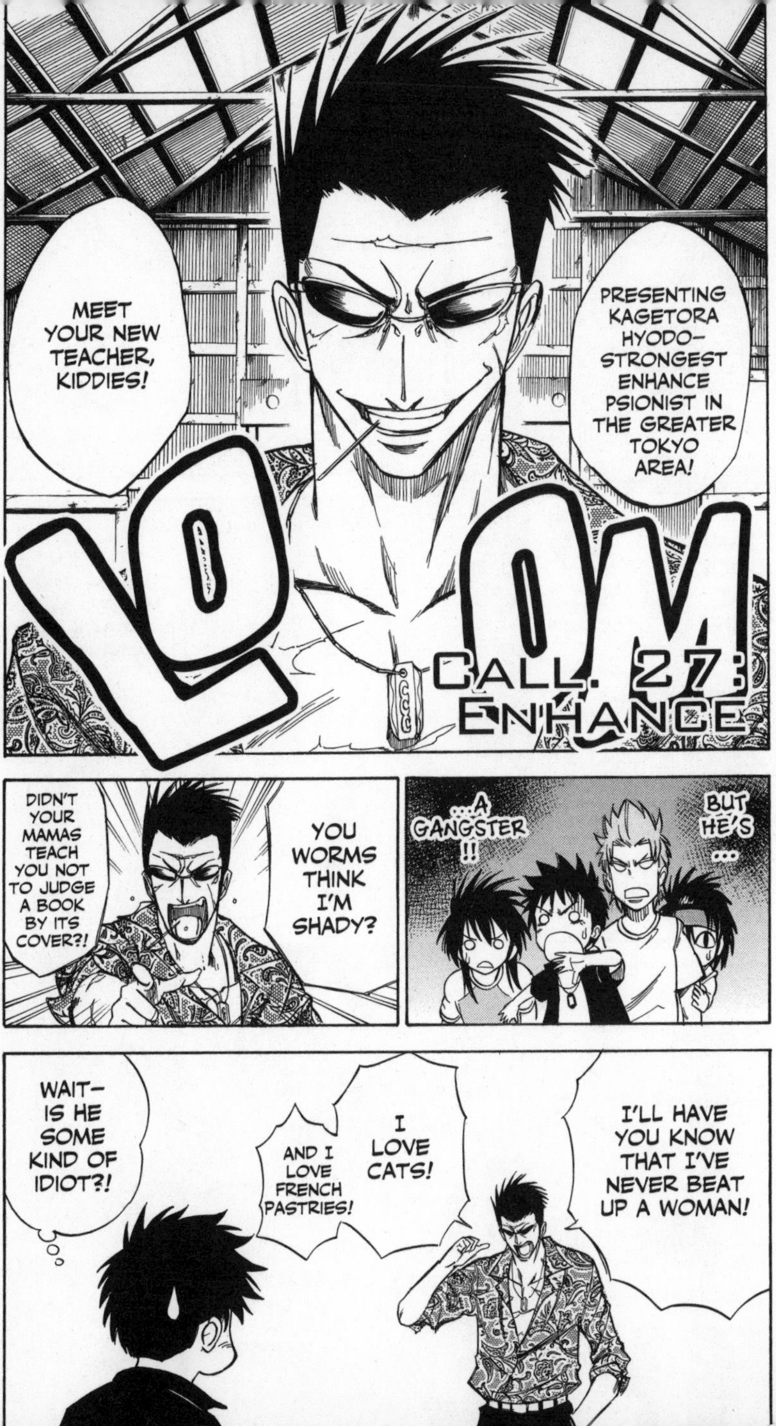
PRESENTING KAGETORA HYODO—STRONGEST ENHANCE PSIONIST IN THE GREATER TOKYO AREA!
MEET YOUR NEW TEACHER, KIDDIES!
LOOM
CALL. 27: ENHANCE
BUT HE'S ...
...A GANGSTER !!
YOU WORMS THINK I'M SHADY?
DIDN'T YOUR MAMAS TEACH YOU NOT TO JUDGE A BOOK BY ITS COVER?!
I'LL HAVE YOU KNOW THAT I'VE NEVER BEAT UP A WOMAN!
I LOVE CATS!
AND I LOVE FRENCH PASTRIES!
WAIT— IS HE SOME KIND OF IDIOT?!

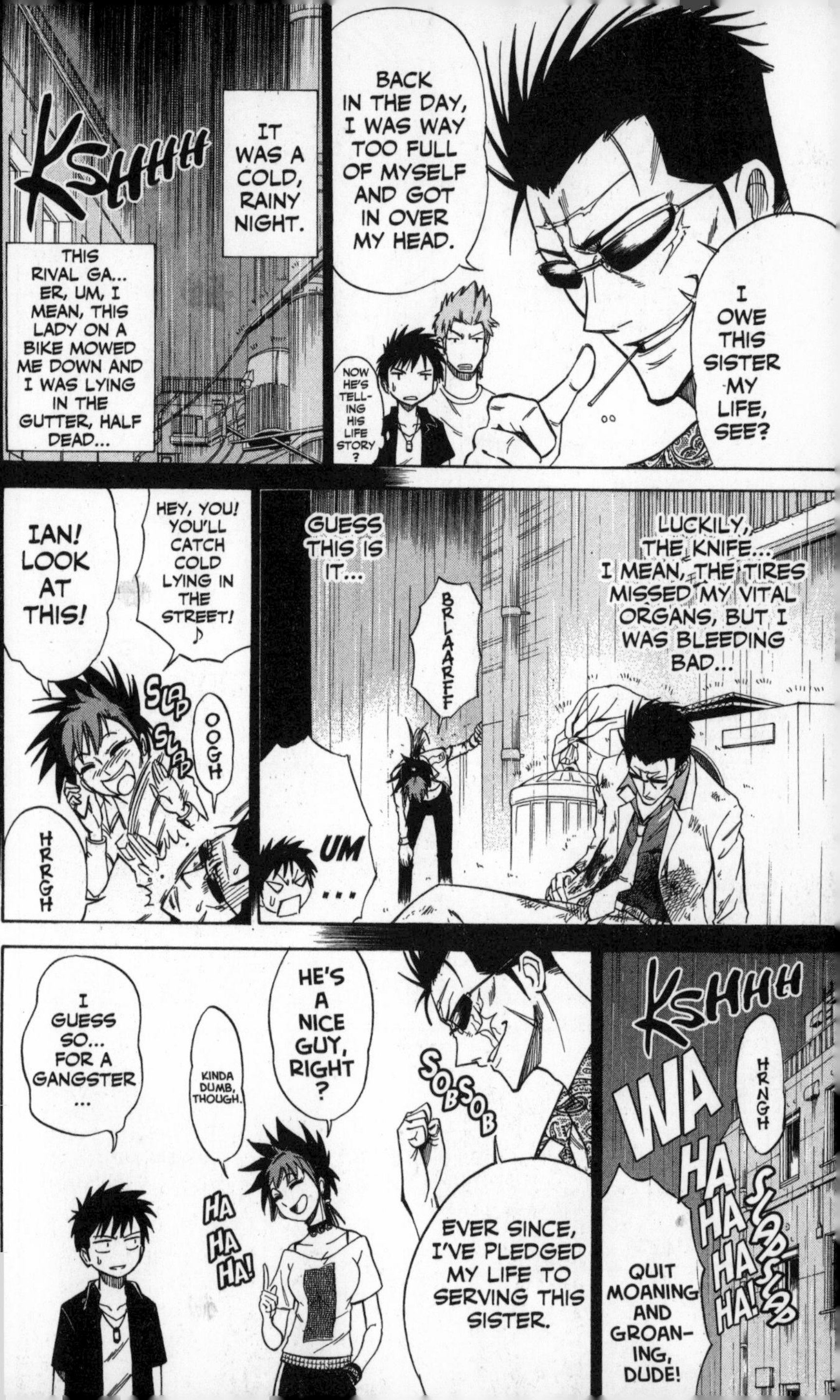
I OWE THIS SISTER MY LIFE, SEE?
BACK IN THE DAY, I WAS WAY TOO FULL OF MYSELF AND GOT IN OVER MY HEAD.
NOW HE'S TELLING HIS LIFE STORY?
KSHHH
IT WAS A COLD, RAINY NIGHT.
THIS RIVAL GA... ER, UM, I MEAN, THIS LADY ON A BIKE MOWED ME DOWN AND I WAS LYING IN THE GUTTER, HALF DEAD...
LUCKILY, THE KNIFE... I MEAN, THE TIRES MISSED MY VITAL ORGANS, BUT I WAS BLEEDING BAD...
GUESS THIS IS IT...
BRLAARFF
UM...
HEY, YOU! YOU'LL CATCH COLD LYING IN THE STREET! ♪
IAN! LOOK AT THIS!
SLAP SLAP
OOGH
HRRGH
KSHHH
HRNGH
WA HA HA HA HA!
QUIT MOANING AND GROANING, DUDE!
SOB SOB
EVER SINCE, I'VE PLEDGED MY LIFE TO SERVING THIS SISTER.
HE'S A NICE GUY, RIGHT?
KINDA DUMB, THOUGH.
HA HA HA!
I GUESS SO... FOR A GANGSTER...

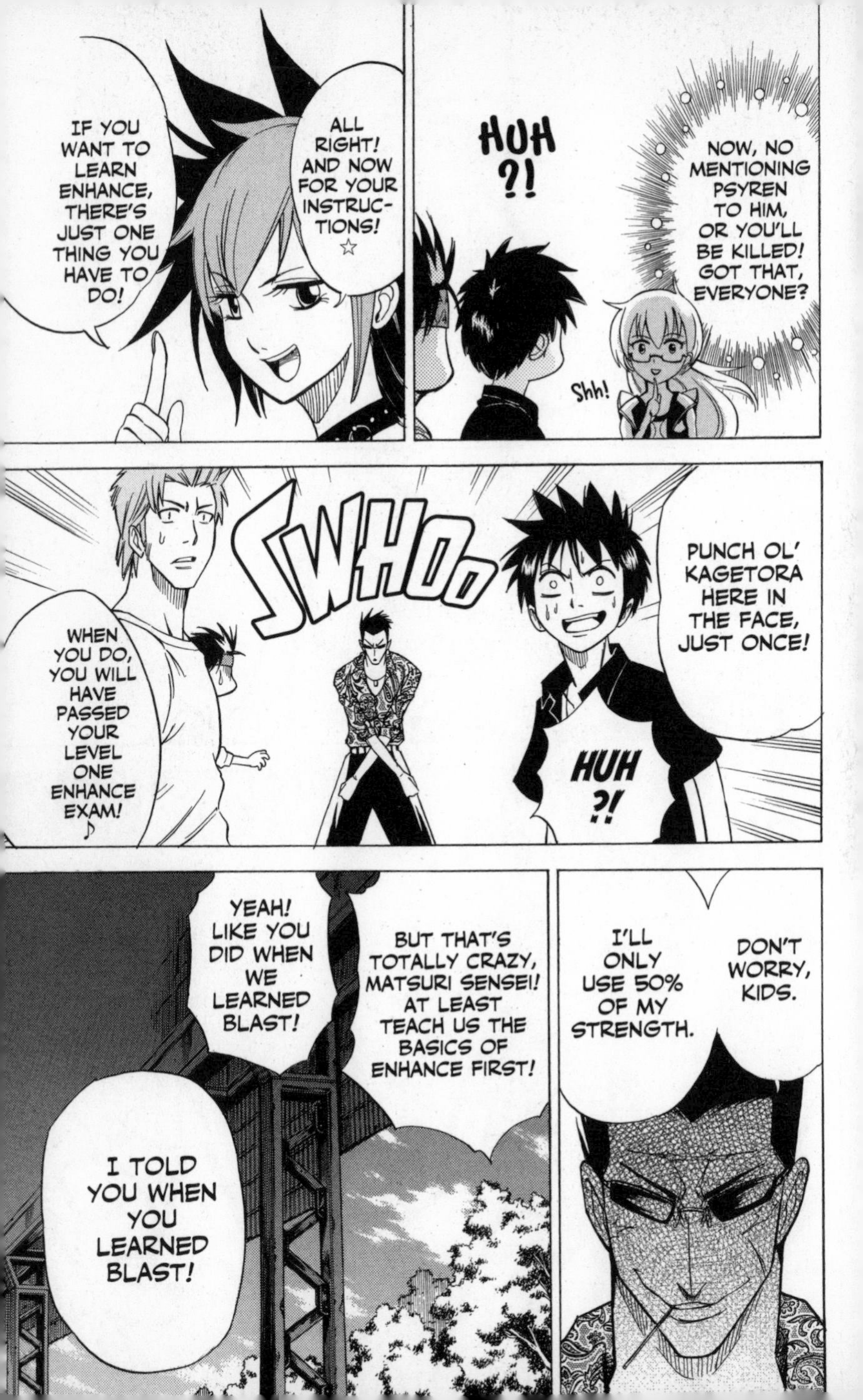
NOW, NO MENTIONING PSYREN TO HIM, OR YOU'LL BE KILLED! GOT THAT, EVERYONE?
Shh!
HUH ?!
ALL RIGHT! AND NOW FOR YOUR INSTRUC- TIONS! ☆
IF YOU WANT TO LEARN ENHANCE, THERE'S JUST ONE THING YOU HAVE TO DO!
PUNCH OL' KAGETORA HERE IN THE FACE, JUST ONCE!
HUH ?!
SWHOO
WHEN YOU DO, YOU WILL HAVE PASSED YOUR LEVEL ONE ENHANCE EXAM! ♪
DON'T WORRY, KIDS.
I'LL ONLY USE 50% OF MY STRENGTH.
BUT THAT'S TOTALLY CRAZY, MATSURI SENSEI! AT LEAST TEACH US THE BASICS OF ENHANCE FIRST!
YEAH! LIKE YOU DID WHEN WE LEARNED BLAST!
I TOLD YOU WHEN YOU LEARNED BLAST!

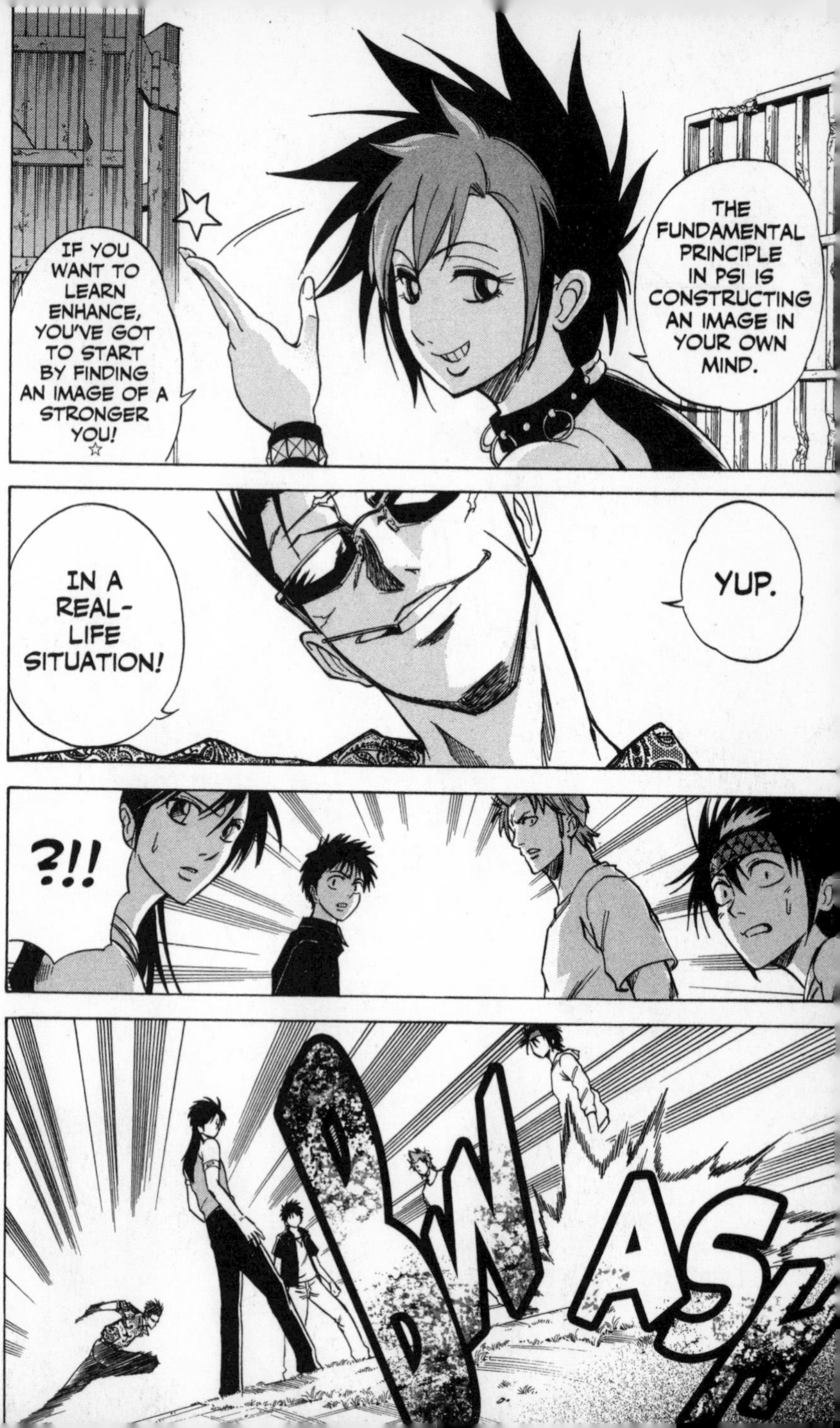
THE FUNDAMENTAL PRINCIPLE IN PSI IS CONSTRUCTING AN IMAGE IN YOUR OWN MIND.
IF YOU WANT TO LEARN ENHANCE, YOU'VE GOT TO START BY FINDING AN IMAGE OF A STRONGER YOU! ☆
YUP.
IN A REAL-LIFE SITUATION!
?!!
DWAS

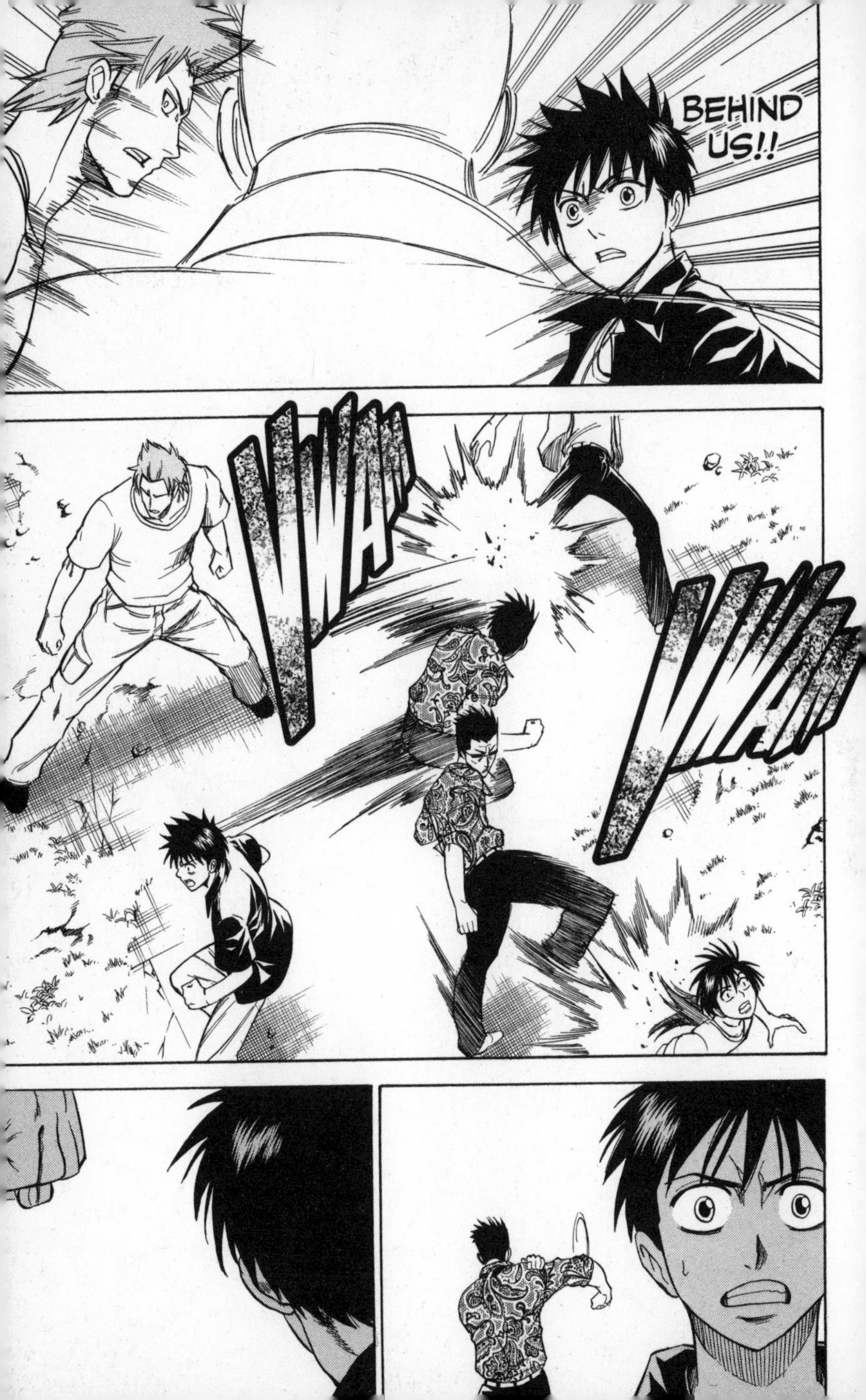
BEHIND US!!
VWAM
VWAM

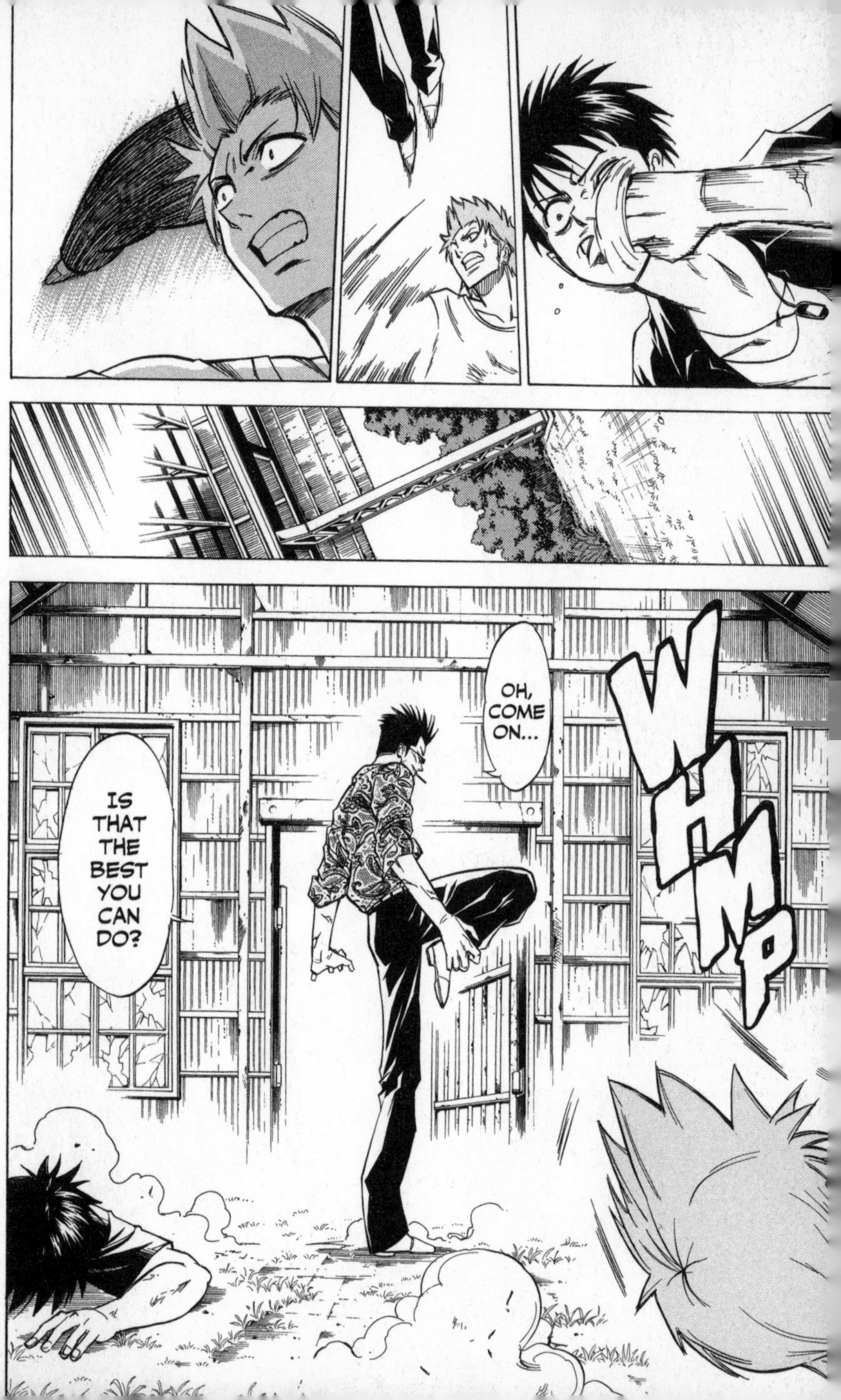
WHMP
OH, COME ON...
IS THAT THE BEST YOU CAN DO?

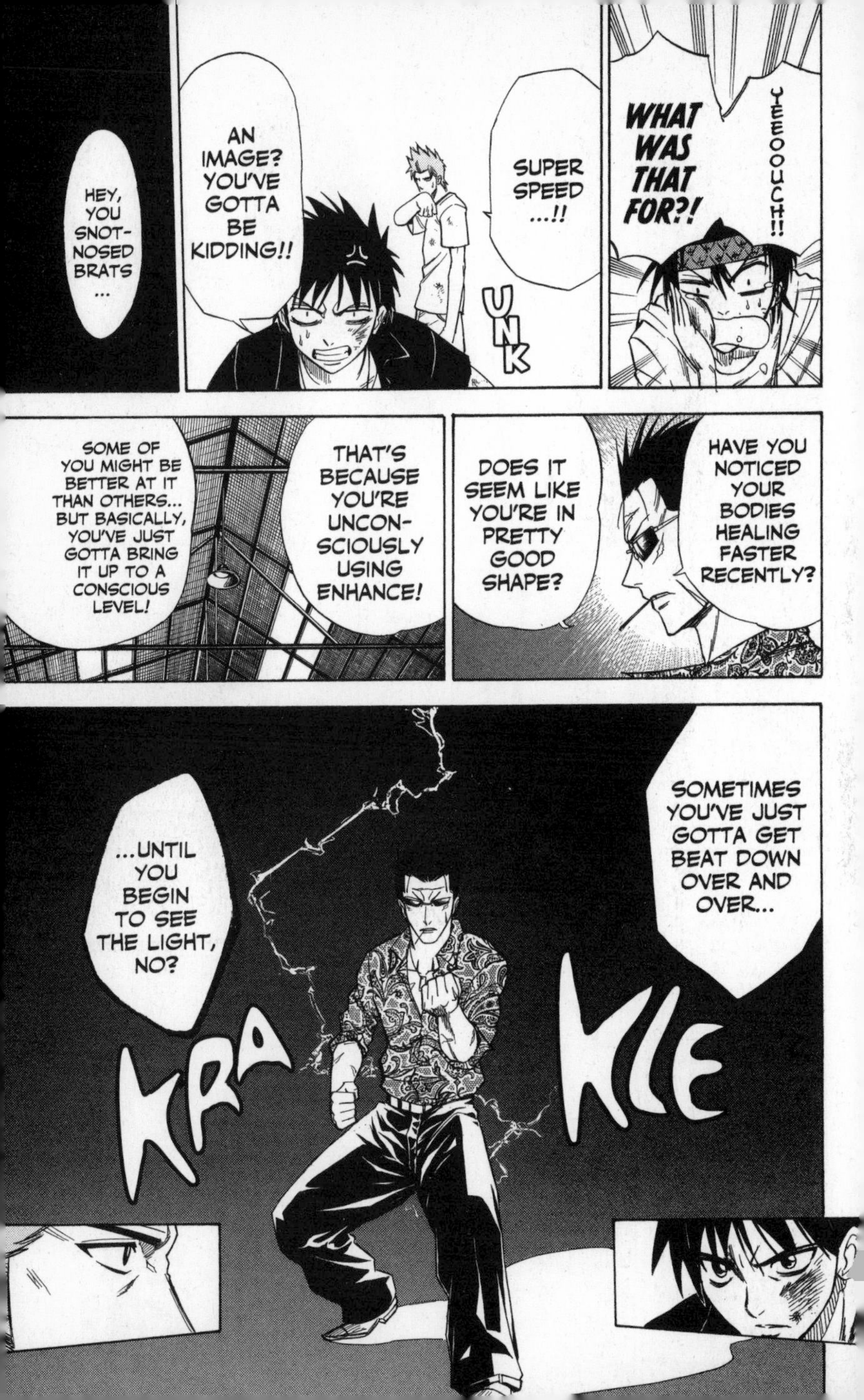
YEEOOUCH!!
WHAT WAS THAT FOR?!
SUPER SPEED ...!!
UNK
AN IMAGE? YOU'VE GOTTA BE KIDDING!!
HEY, YOU SNOT-NOSED BRATS ...
HAVE YOU NOTICED YOUR BODIES HEALING FASTER RECENTLY?
DOES IT SEEM LIKE YOU'RE IN PRETTY GOOD SHAPE?
THAT'S BECAUSE YOU'RE UNCONSCIOUSLY USING ENHANCE!
SOME OF YOU MIGHT BE BETTER AT IT THAN OTHERS... BUT BASICALLY, YOU'VE JUST GOTTA BRING IT UP TO A CONSCIOUS LEVEL!
SOMETIMES YOU'VE JUST GOTTA GET BEAT DOWN OVER AND OVER...
KRA KLE
...UNTIL YOU BEGIN TO SEE THE LIGHT, NO?

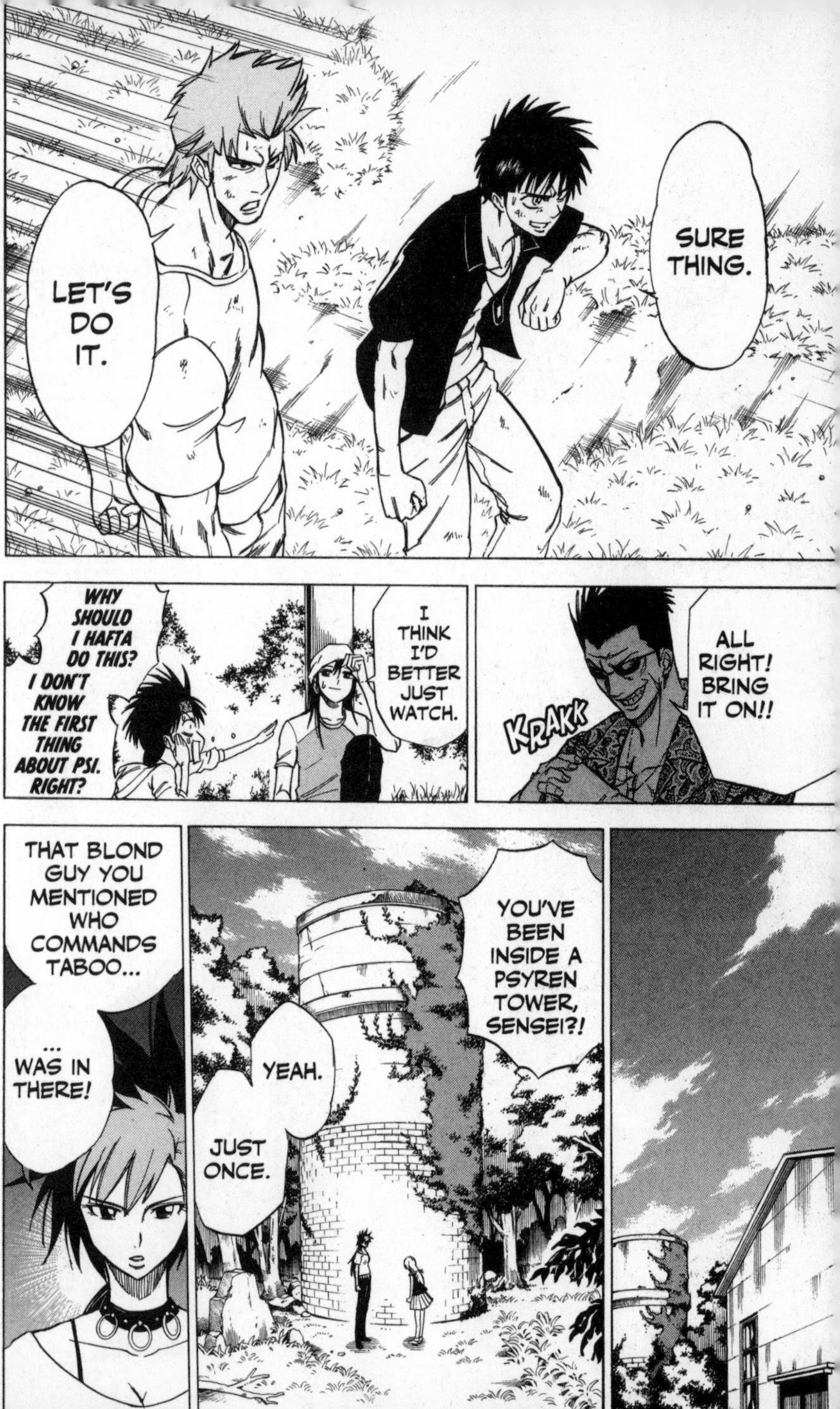
SURE THING.
LET'S DO IT.
ALL RIGHT! BRING IT ON!!
KRAKK
I THINK I'D BETTER JUST WATCH.
WHY SHOULD I HAFTA DO THIS? I DON'T KNOW THE FIRST THING ABOUT PSI. RIGHT?
YOU'VE BEEN INSIDE A PSYREN TOWER, SENSEI?!
YEAH.
JUST ONCE.
THAT BLOND GUY YOU MENTIONED WHO COMMANDS TABOO...
... WAS IN THERE!

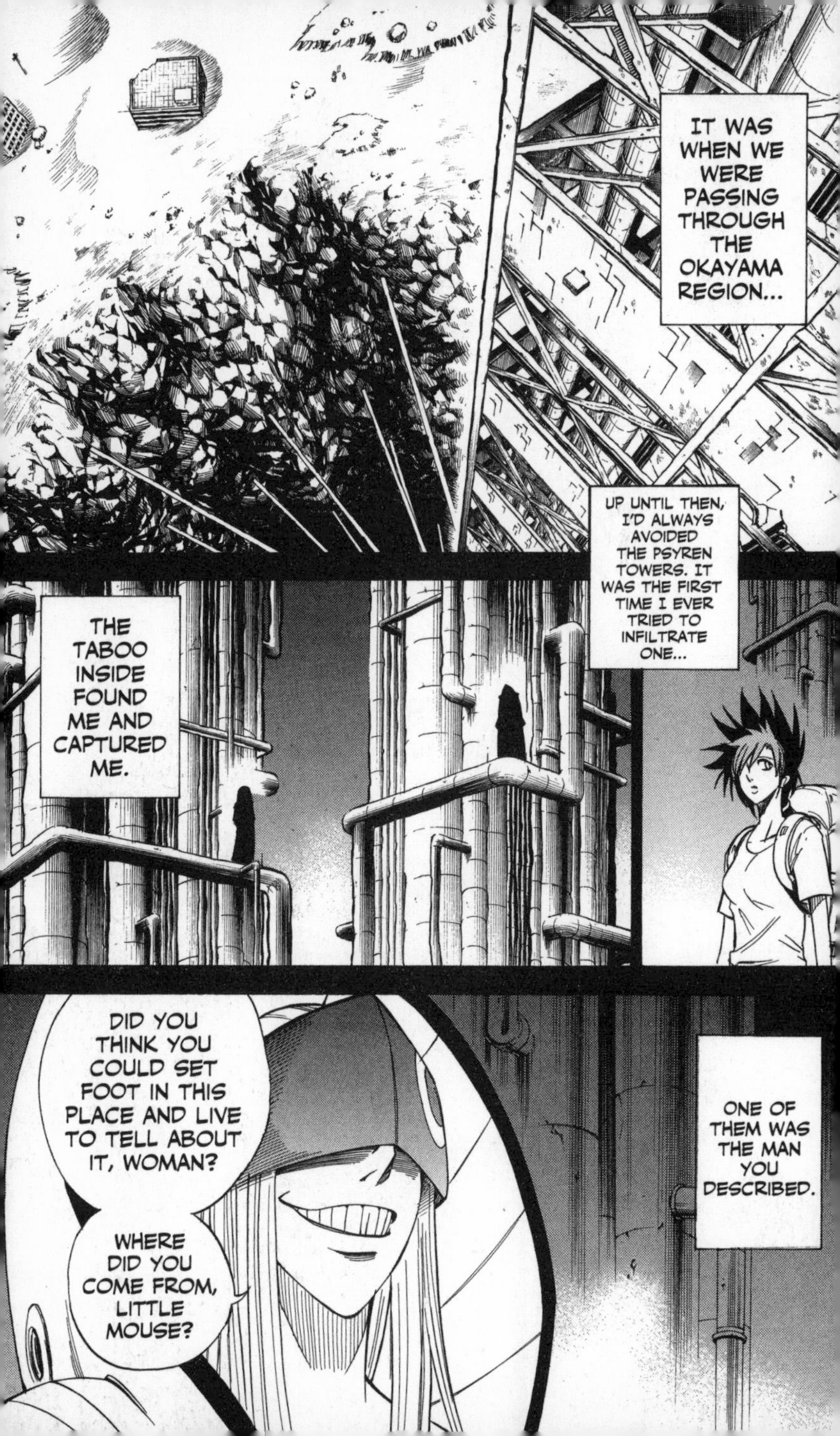
IT WAS WHEN WE WERE PASSING THROUGH THE OKAYAMA REGION...
UP UNTIL THEN, I'D ALWAYS AVOIDED THE PSYREN TOWERS. IT WAS THE FIRST TIME I EVER TRIED TO INFILTRATE ONE...
THE TABOO INSIDE FOUND ME AND CAPTURED ME.
ONE OF THEM WAS THE MAN YOU DESCRIBED.
DID YOU THINK YOU COULD SET FOOT IN THIS PLACE AND LIVE TO TELL ABOUT IT, WOMAN?
WHERE DID YOU COME FROM, LITTLE MOUSE?

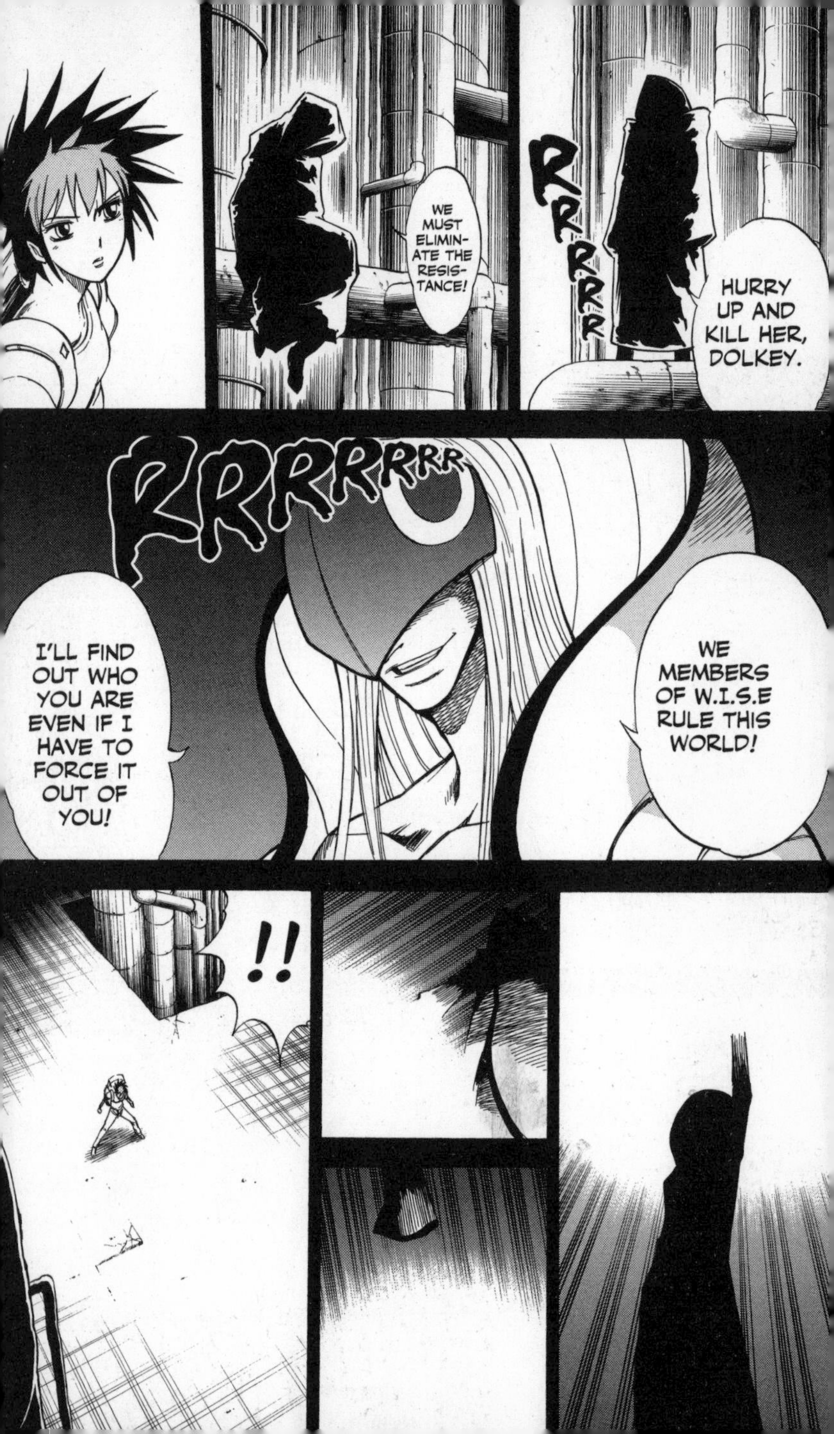
RRRRR
HURRY UP AND KILL HER, DOLKEY.
WE MUST ELIMINATE THE RESISTANCE!
RRRRRRR
WE MEMBERS OF W.I.S.E RULE THIS WORLD!
I'LL FIND OUT WHO YOU ARE EVEN IF I HAVE TO FORCE IT OUT OF YOU!
!!

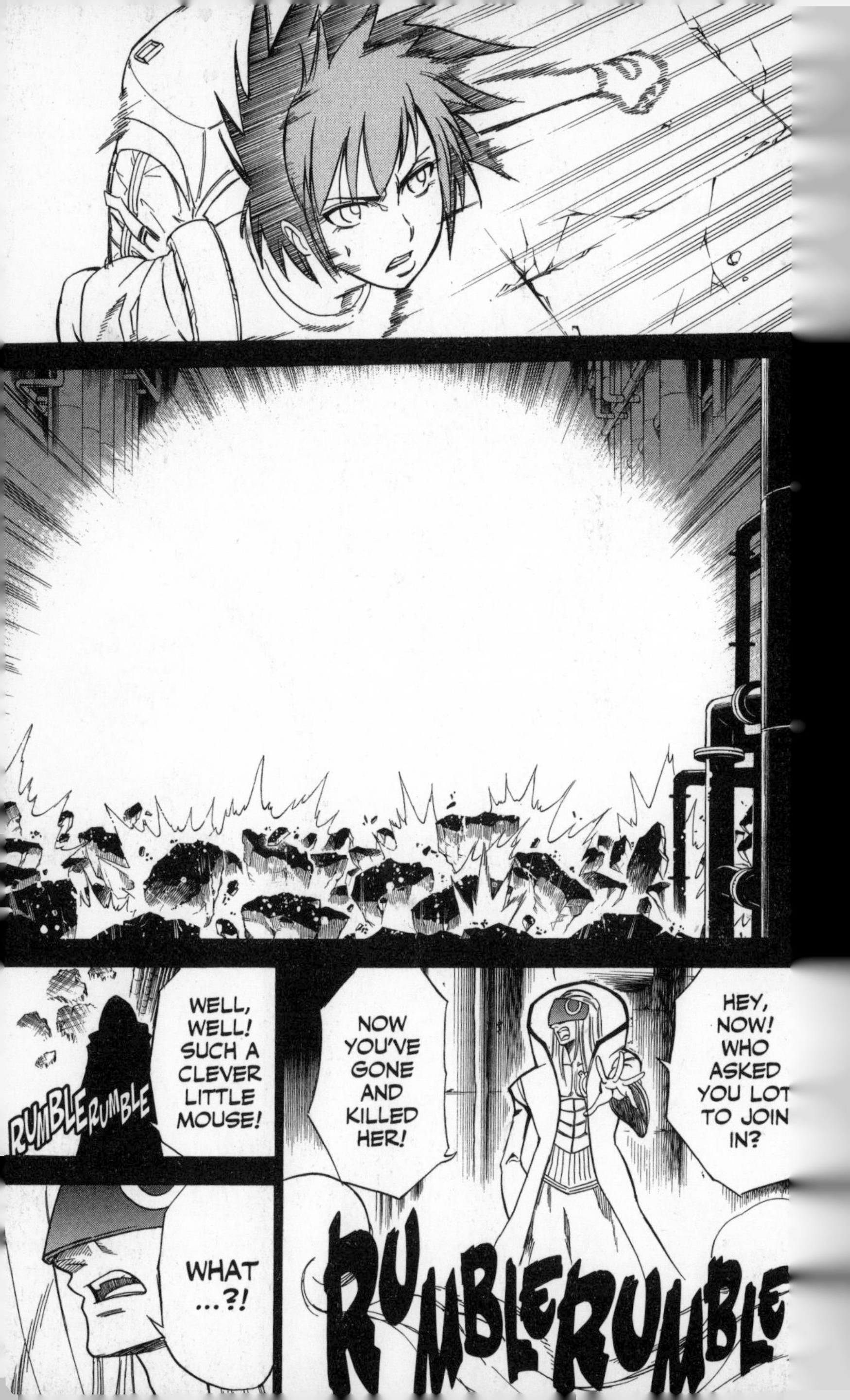
HEY, NOW! WHO ASKED YOU LOT TO JOIN IN?
NOW YOU'VE GONE AND KILLED HER!
RUMBLERUMBLE
WELL, WELL! SUCH A CLEVER LITTLE MOUSE!
RUMBLERUMBLE
WHAT ...?!

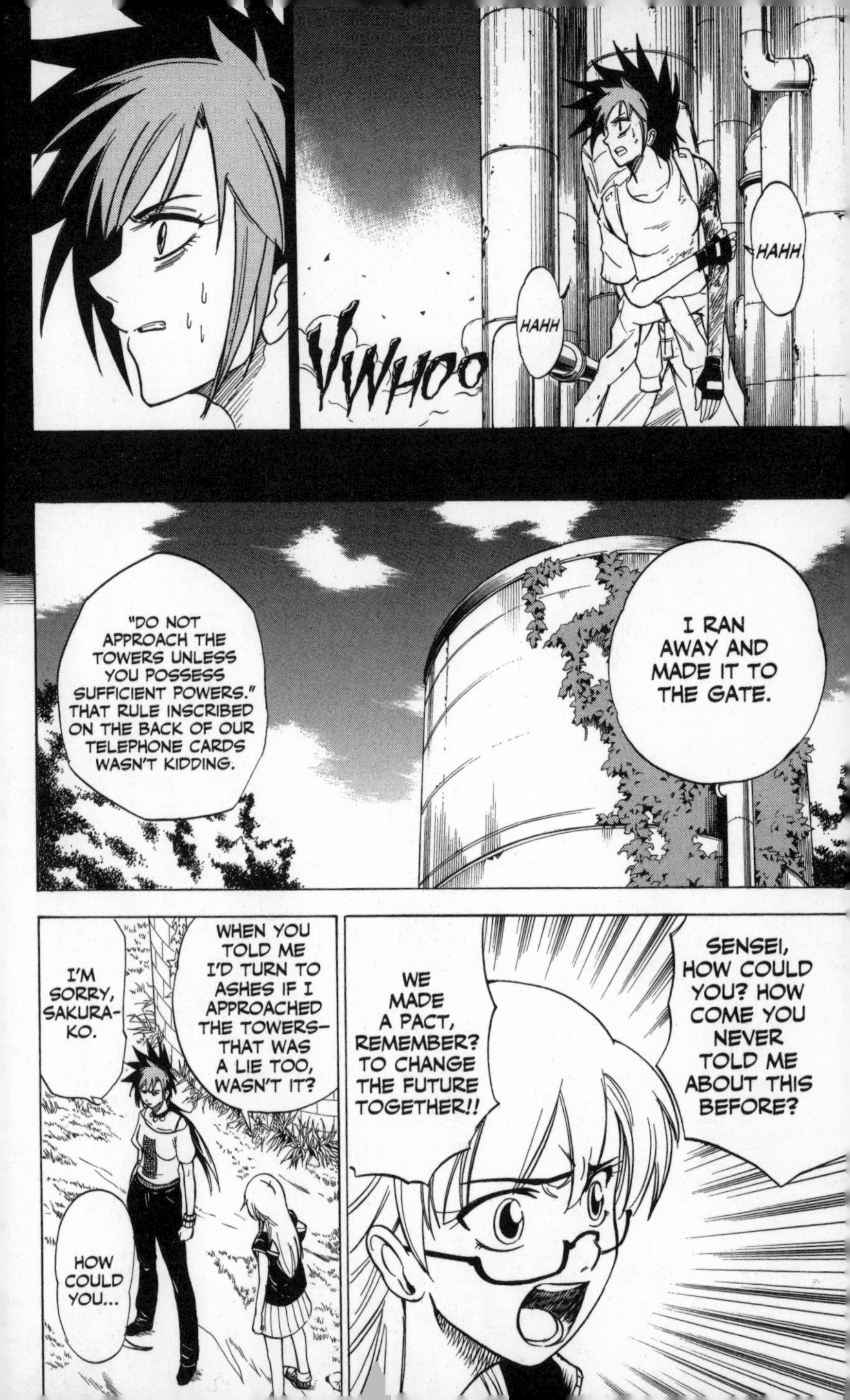
HAHH
HAHH
VWHOO
I RAN AWAY AND MADE IT TO THE GATE.
"DO NOT APPROACH THE TOWERS UNLESS YOU POSSESS SUFFICIENT POWERS." THAT RULE INSCRIBED ON THE BACK OF OUR TELEPHONE CARDS WASN'T KIDDING.
SENSEI, HOW COULD YOU? HOW COME YOU NEVER TOLD ME ABOUT THIS BEFORE?
WE MADE A PACT, REMEMBER? TO CHANGE THE FUTURE TOGETHER!!
WHEN YOU TOLD ME I'D TURN TO ASHES IF I APPROACHED THE TOWERS—THAT WAS A LIE TOO, WASN'T IT?
I'M SORRY, SAKURA-KO.
HOW COULD YOU...

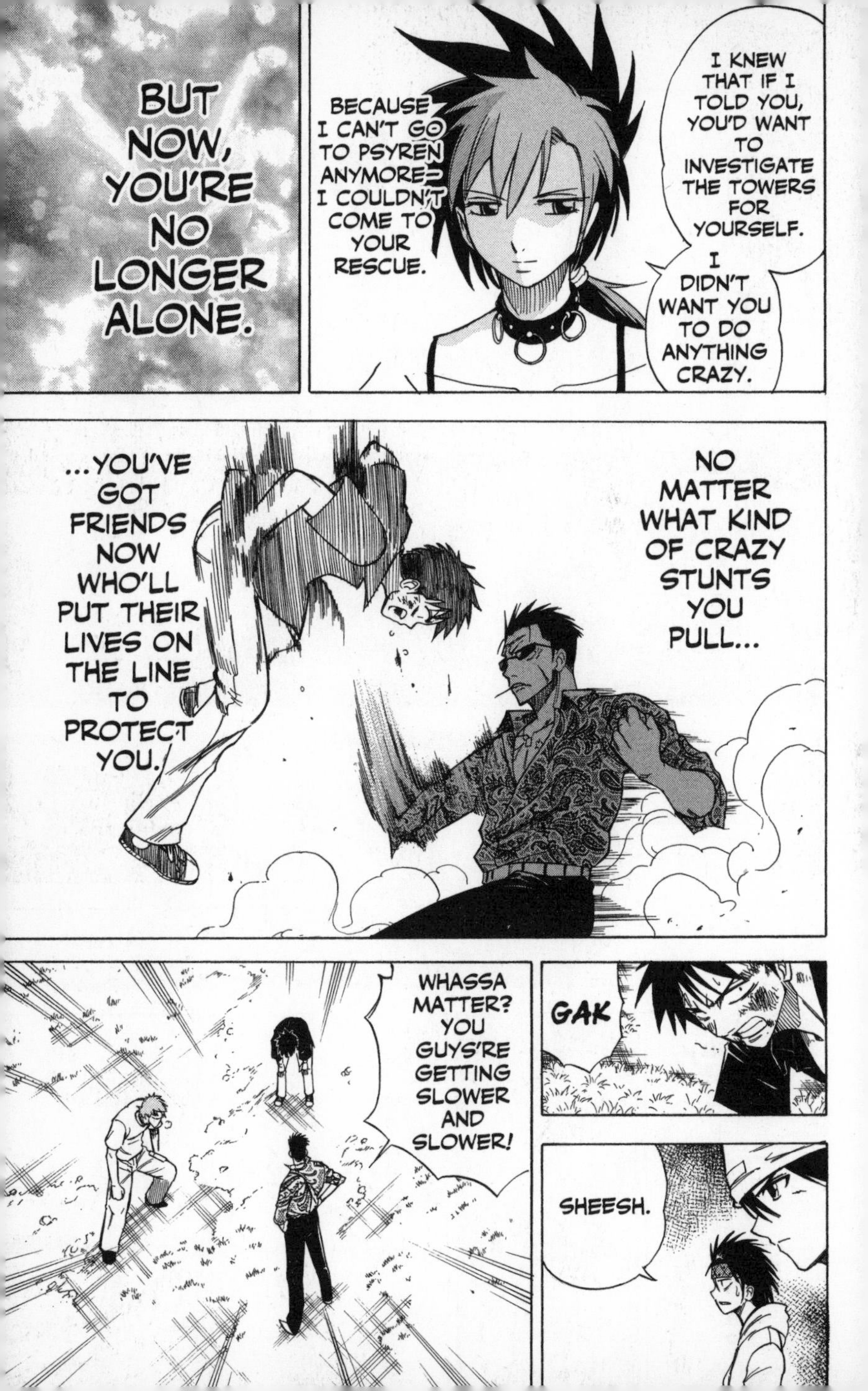
I KNEW THAT IF I TOLD YOU, YOU'D WANT TO INVESTIGATE THE TOWERS FOR YOURSELF.
I DIDN'T WANT YOU TO DO ANYTHING CRAZY.
BECAUSE I CAN'T GO TO PSYREN ANYMORE— I COULDN'T COME TO YOUR RESCUE.
BUT NOW, YOU'RE NO LONGER ALONE.
NO MATTER WHAT KIND OF CRAZY STUNTS YOU PULL...
...YOU'VE GOT FRIENDS NOW WHO'LL PUT THEIR LIVES ON THE LINE TO PROTECT YOU.
GAK
SHEESH.
WHASSA MATTER? YOU GUYS'RE GETTING SLOWER AND SLOWER!

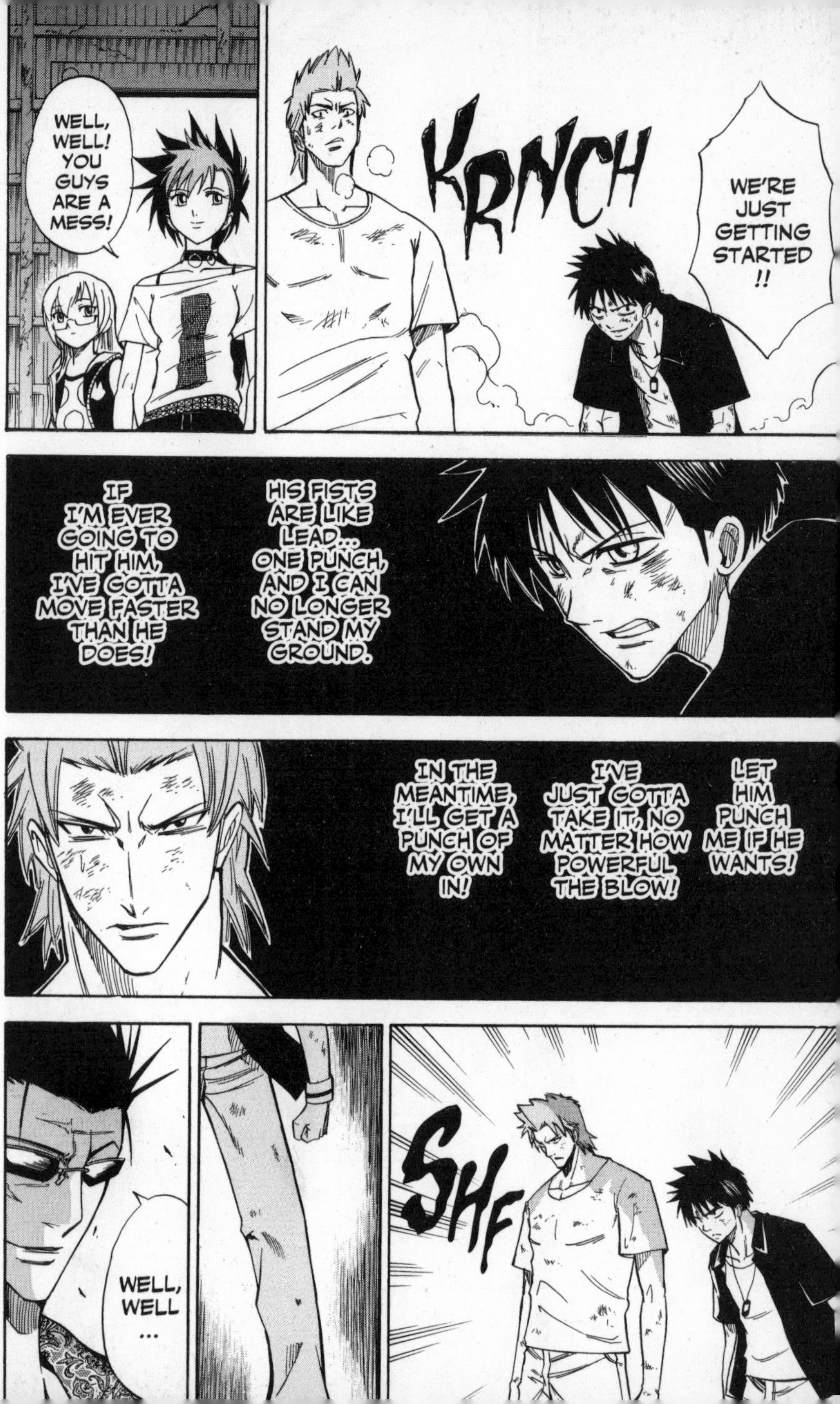
WE'RE JUST GETTING STARTED !!
KRNCH
WELL, WELL! YOU GUYS ARE A MESS!
HIS FISTS ARE LIKE LEAD... ONE PUNCH, AND I CAN NO LONGER STAND MY GROUND.
IF I'M EVER GOING TO HIT HIM, I'VE GOTTA MOVE FASTER THAN HE DOES!
LET HIM PUNCH ME IF HE WANTS!
I'VE JUST GOTTA TAKE IT, NO MATTER HOW POWERFUL THE BLOW!
IN THE MEANTIME, I'LL GET A PUNCH OF MY OWN IN!
SHF
WELL, WELL ...

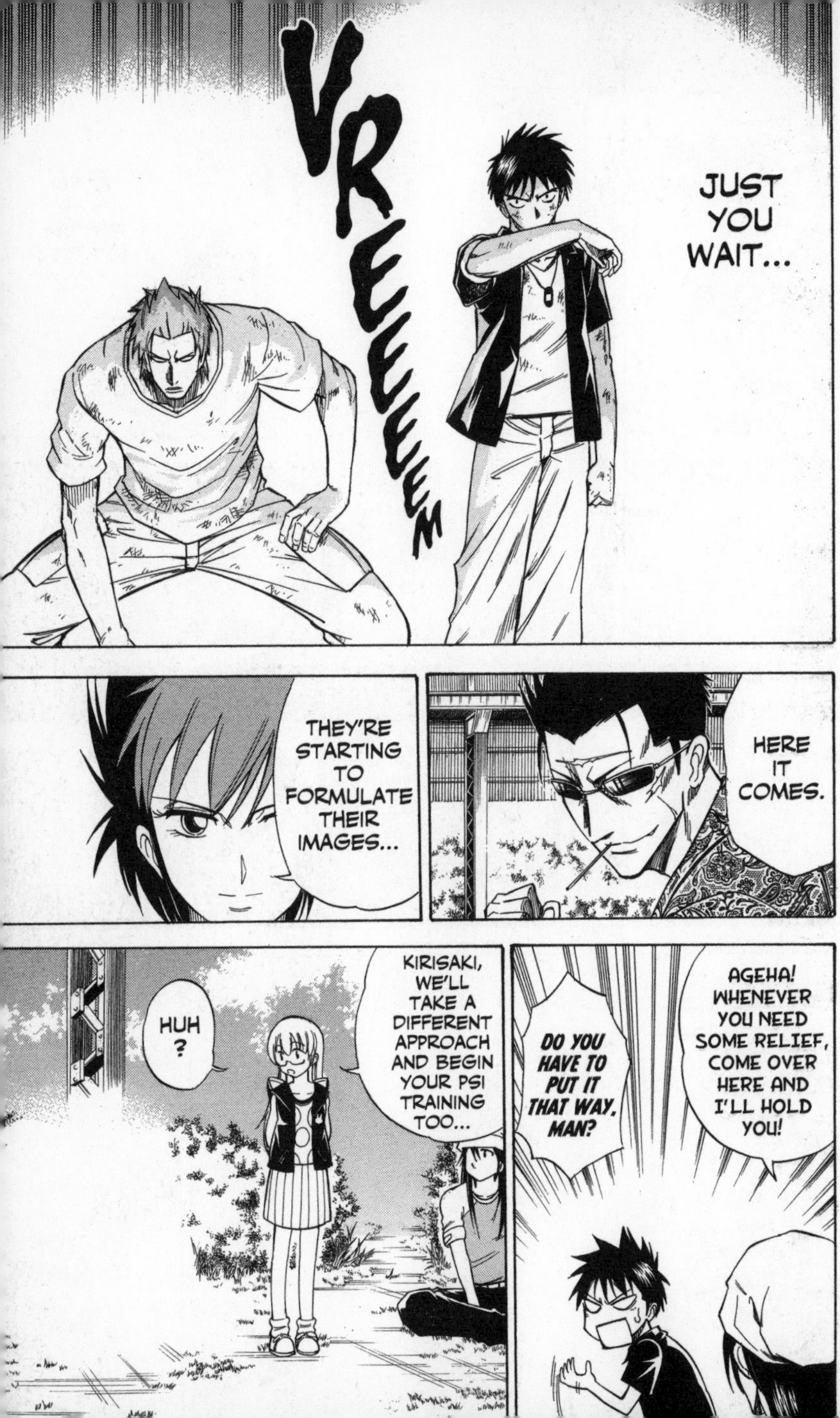
JUST YOU WAIT...
VREEEEEM
HERE IT COMES.
THEY'RE STARTING TO FORMULATE THEIR IMAGES...
AGEHA! WHENEVER YOU NEED SOME RELIEF, COME OVER HERE AND I'LL HOLD YOU!
DO YOU HAVE TO PUT IT THAT WAY, MAN?
KIRISAKI, WE'LL TAKE A DIFFERENT APPROACH AND BEGIN YOUR PSI TRAINING TOO...
HUH?

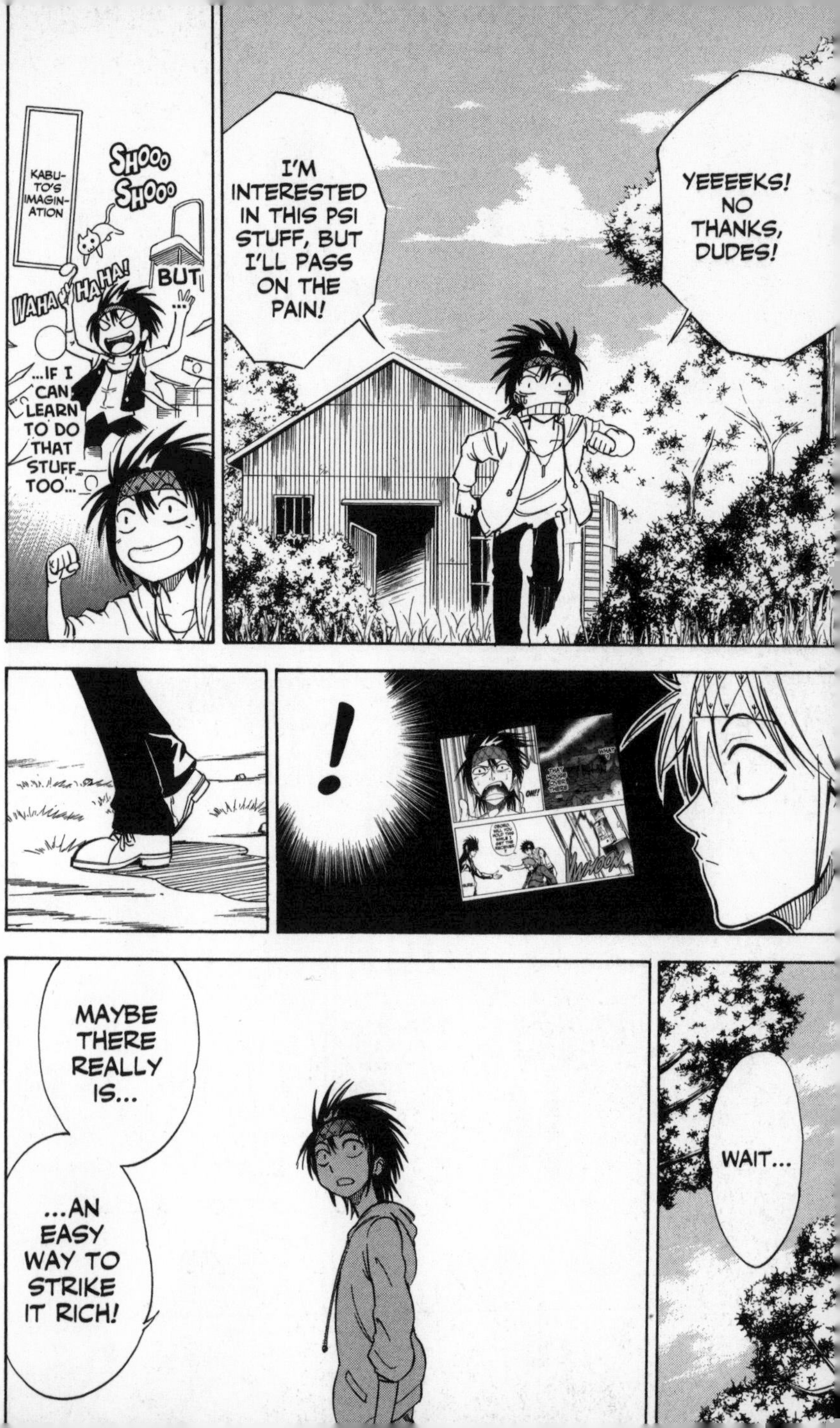
YEEEEKS! NO THANKS, DUDES!
I'M INTERESTED IN THIS PSI STUFF, BUT I'LL PASS ON THE PAIN!
KABU-TO'S IMAGINATION
SHOOO SHOOO
BUT...
WAHAHAHA!
...IF I CAN LEARN TO DO THAT STUFF TOO...
!
WAIT...
MAYBE THERE REALLY IS...
...AN EASY WAY TO STRIKE IT RICH!

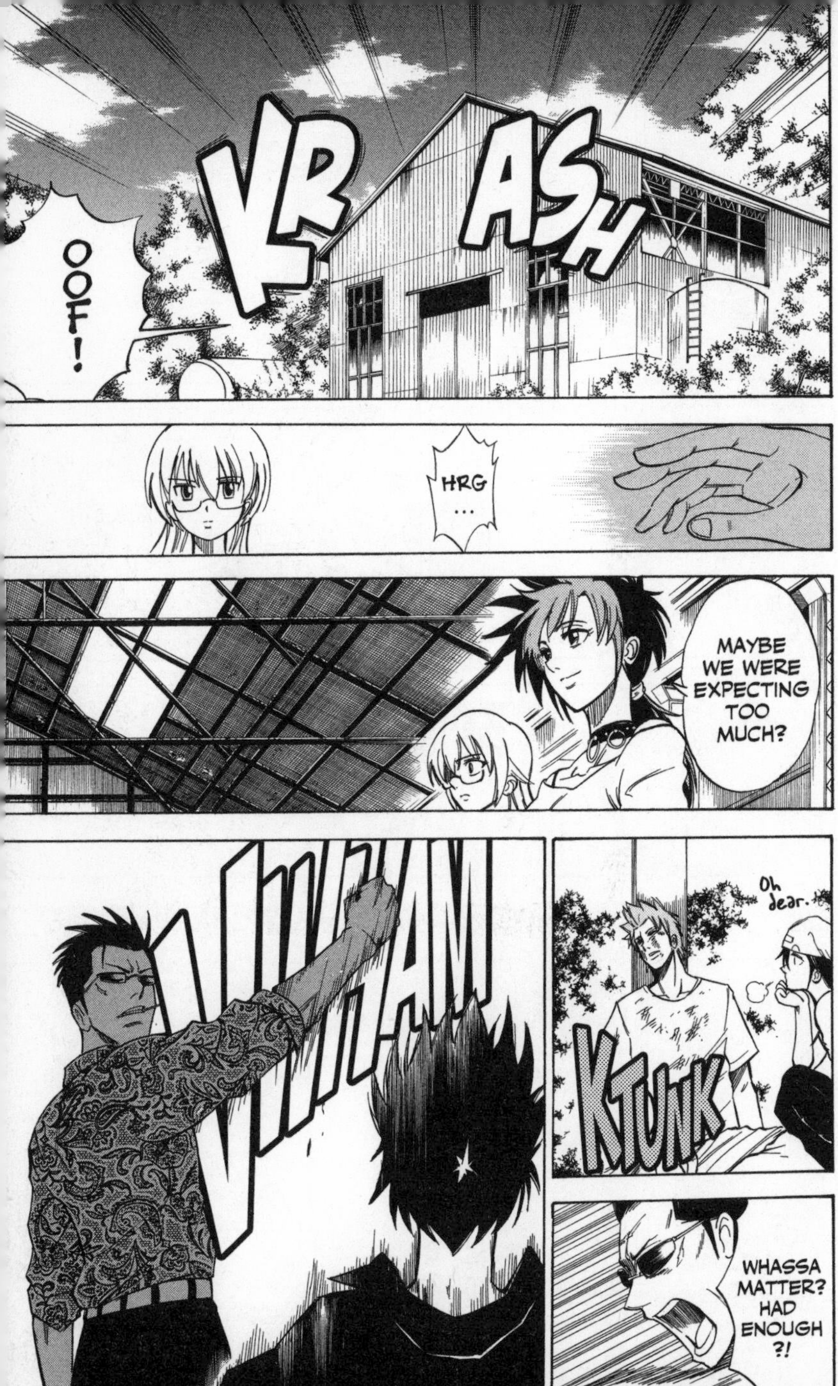
KRASH
OOF!
HRG ...
MAYBE WE WERE EXPECTING TOO MUCH?
Oh dear.
KTUNK
WHASSA MATTER? HAD ENOUGH ?!
WHAM

OH...

...NO.

YOSHINA
!!

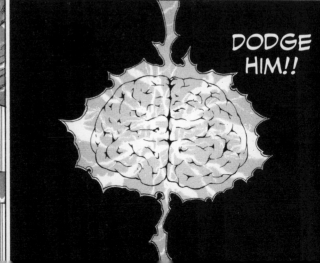

DODGE
HIM!!

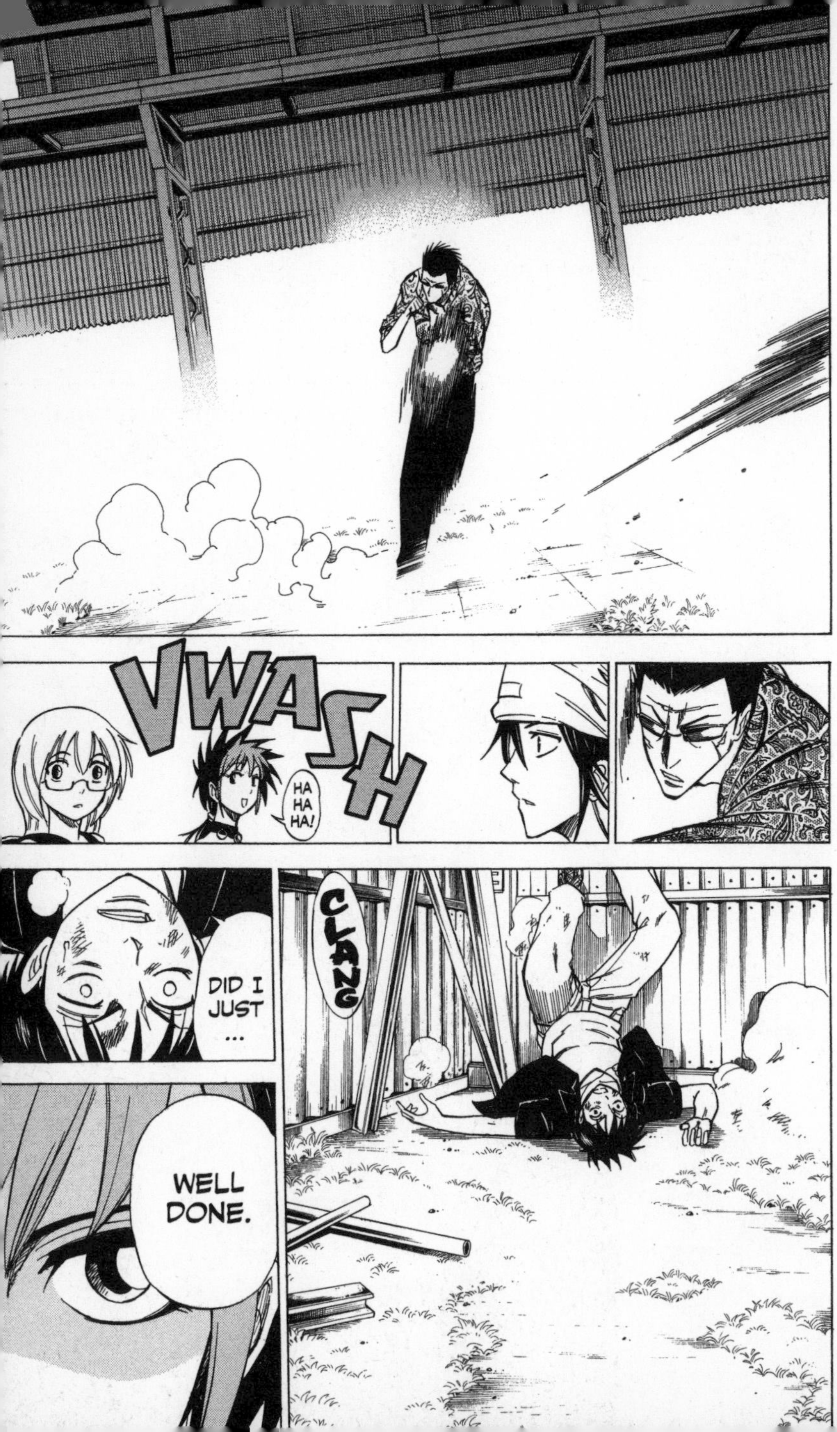
VWASH
HA HA HA!
CLANG
DID I JUST ...
WELL DONE.

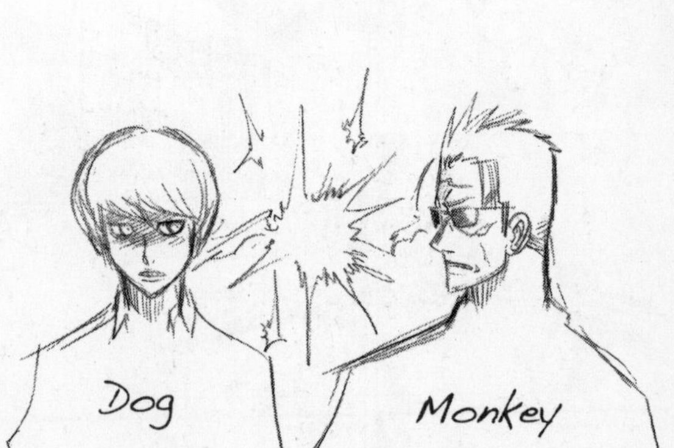

Dog
Monkey

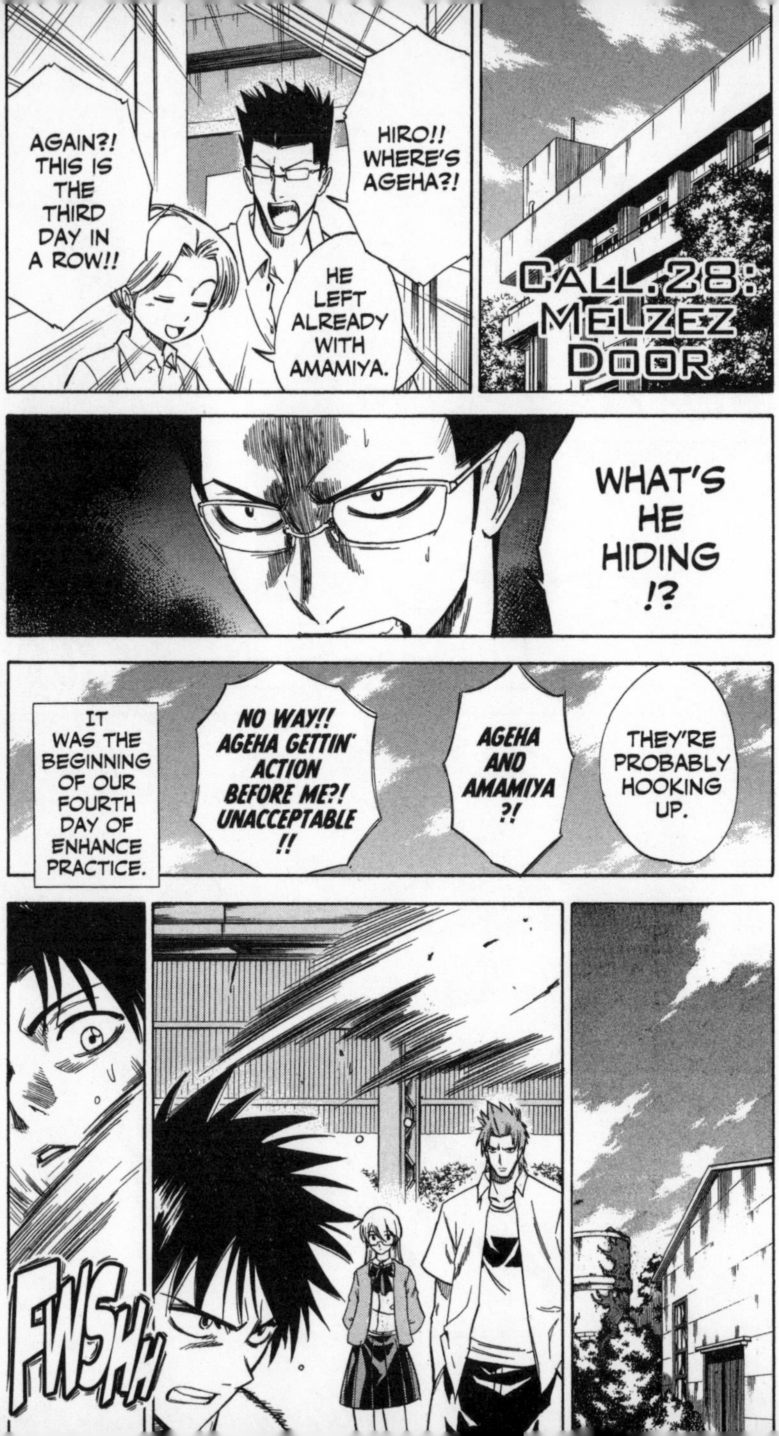
CALL.28: MELZEZ DOOR
HIRO!! WHERE'S AGEHA?!
HE LEFT ALREADY WITH AMAMIYA.
AGAIN?! THIS IS THE THIRD DAY IN A ROW!!
WHAT'S HE HIDING !?
THEY'RE PROBABLY HOOKING UP.
AGEHA AND AMAMIYA ?!
NO WAY!! AGEHA GETTIN' ACTION BEFORE ME?! UNACCEPTABLE !!
IT WAS THE BEGINNING OF OUR FOURTH DAY OF ENHANCE PRACTICE.
FWSHH

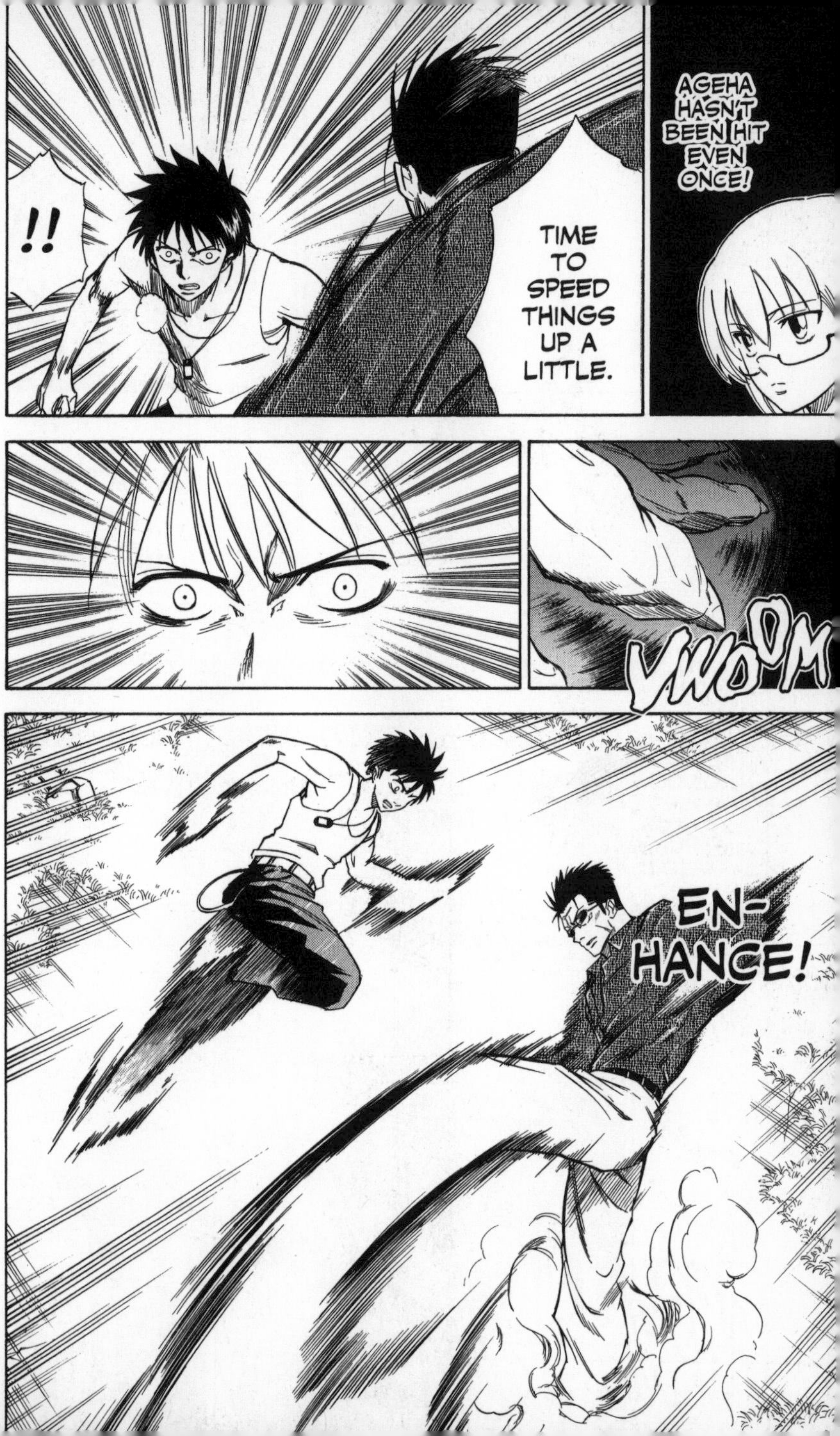
AGEHA HASN'T BEEN HIT EVEN ONCE!
TIME TO SPEED THINGS UP A LITTLE.
!!
VWOOM
EN-HANCE!

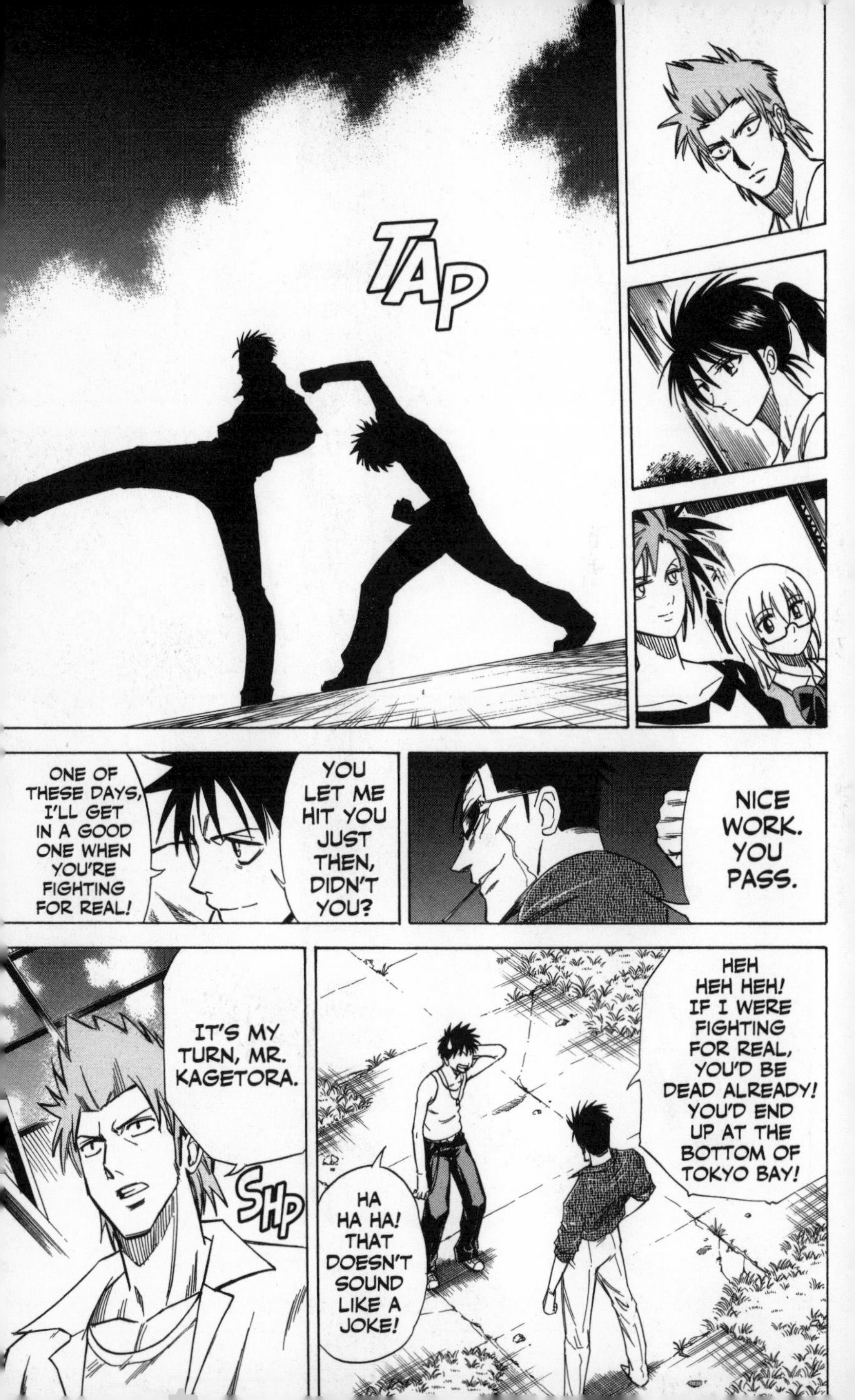
TAP
NICE WORK. YOU PASS.
YOU LET ME HIT YOU JUST THEN, DIDN'T YOU?
ONE OF THESE DAYS, I'LL GET IN A GOOD ONE WHEN YOU'RE FIGHTING FOR REAL!
HEH HEH HEH! IF I WERE FIGHTING FOR REAL, YOU'D BE DEAD ALREADY! YOU'D END UP AT THE BOTTOM OF TOKYO BAY!
HA HA HA! THAT DOESN'T SOUND LIKE A JOKE!
IT'S MY TURN, MR. KAGETORA.
SHP

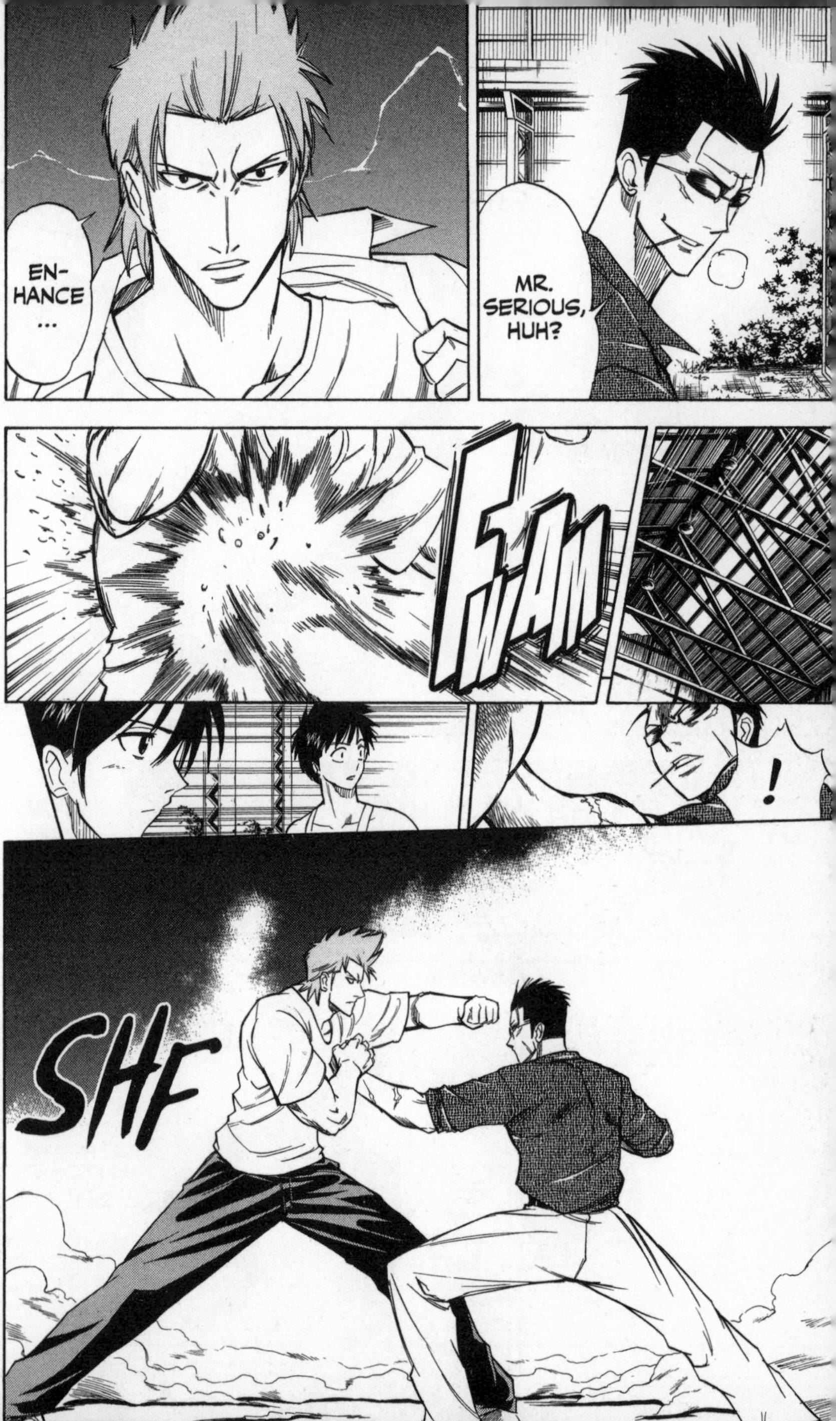
MR. SERIOUS, HUH?
EN-HANCE...
FWAM
!
SHF

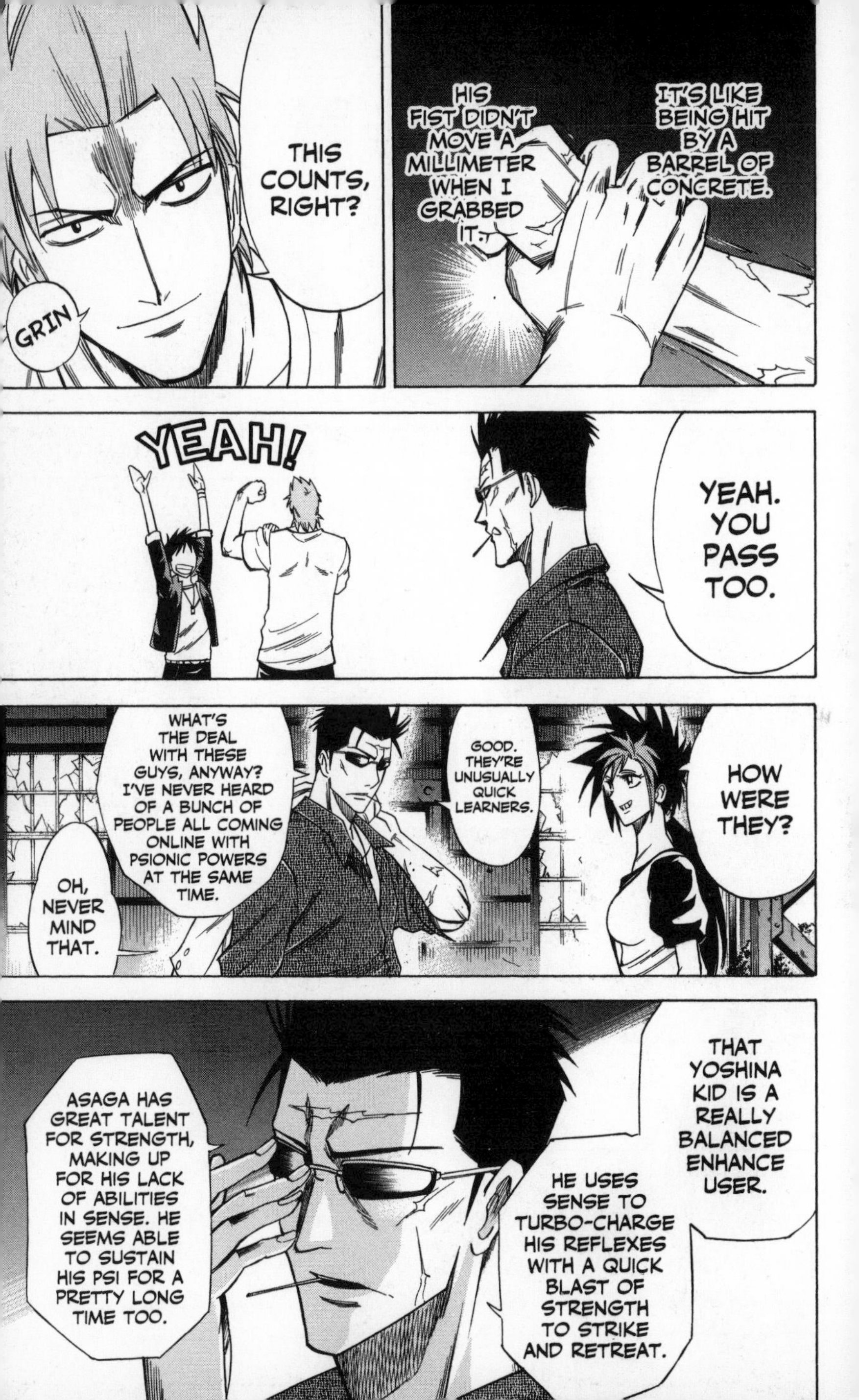
IT'S LIKE BEING HIT BY A BARREL OF CONCRETE.
HIS FIST DIDN'T MOVE A MILLIMETER WHEN I GRABBED IT.
THIS COUNTS, RIGHT?
GRIN
YEAH. YOU PASS TOO.
YEAH!
HOW WERE THEY?
GOOD. THEY'RE UNUSUALLY QUICK LEARNERS.
WHAT'S THE DEAL WITH THESE GUYS, ANYWAY? I'VE NEVER HEARD OF A BUNCH OF PEOPLE ALL COMING ONLINE WITH PSIONIC POWERS AT THE SAME TIME.
OH, NEVER MIND THAT.
THAT YOSHINA KID IS A REALLY BALANCED ENHANCE USER.
HE USES SENSE TO TURBO-CHARGE HIS REFLEXES WITH A QUICK BLAST OF STRENGTH TO STRIKE AND RETREAT.
ASAGA HAS GREAT TALENT FOR STRENGTH, MAKING UP FOR HIS LACK OF ABILITIES IN SENSE. HE SEEMS ABLE TO SUSTAIN HIS PSI FOR A PRETTY LONG TIME TOO.

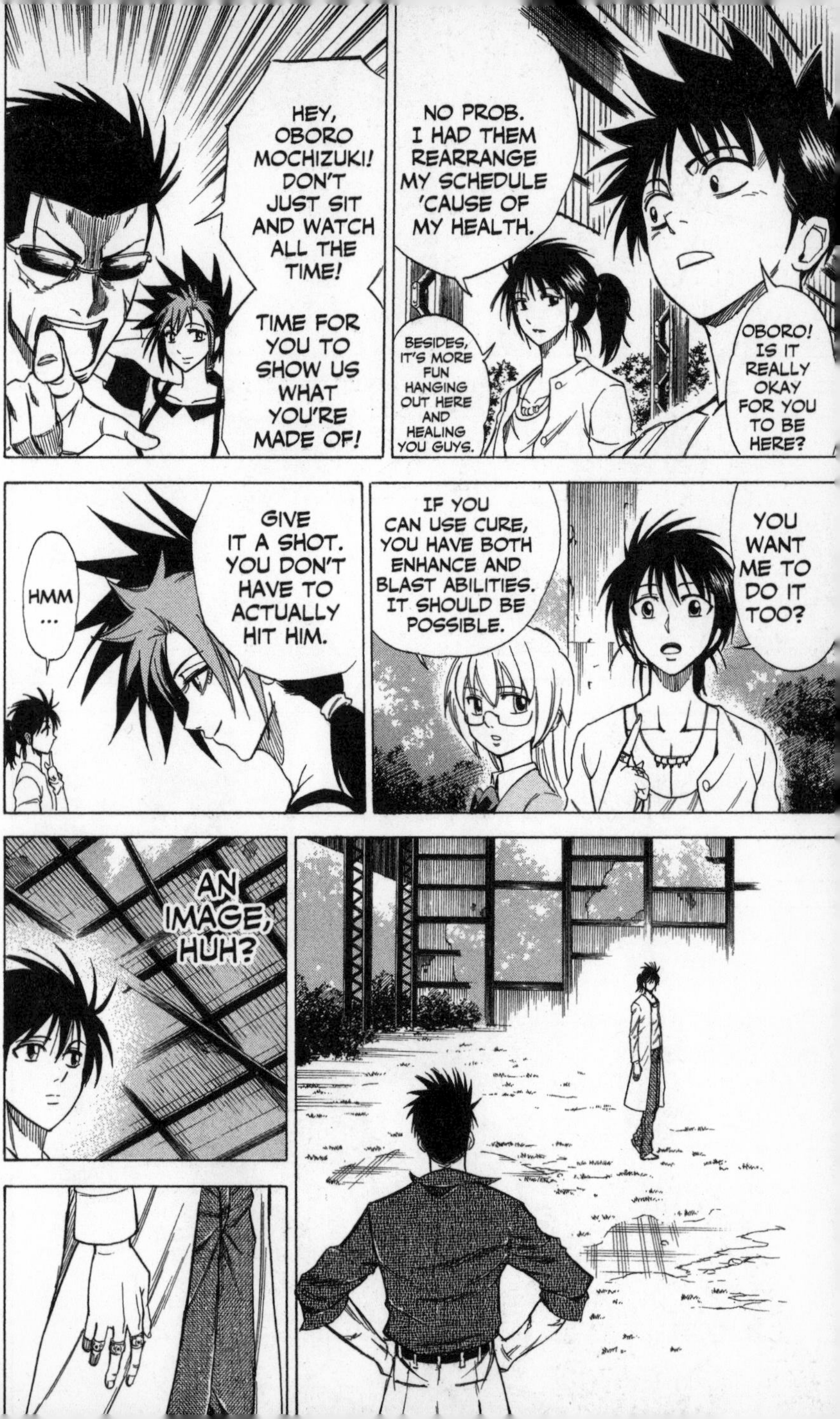
OBORO! IS IT REALLY OKAY FOR YOU TO BE HERE?
NO PROB. I HAD THEM REARRANGE MY SCHEDULE 'CAUSE OF MY HEALTH.
BESIDES, IT'S MORE FUN HANGING OUT HERE AND HEALING YOU GUYS.
HEY, OBORO MOCHIZUKI! DON'T JUST SIT AND WATCH ALL THE TIME!
TIME FOR YOU TO SHOW US WHAT YOU'RE MADE OF!
YOU WANT ME TO DO IT TOO?
IF YOU CAN USE CURE, YOU HAVE BOTH ENHANCE AND BLAST ABILITIES. IT SHOULD BE POSSIBLE.
GIVE IT A SHOT. YOU DON'T HAVE TO ACTUALLY HIT HIM.
HMM...
AN IMAGE, HUH?

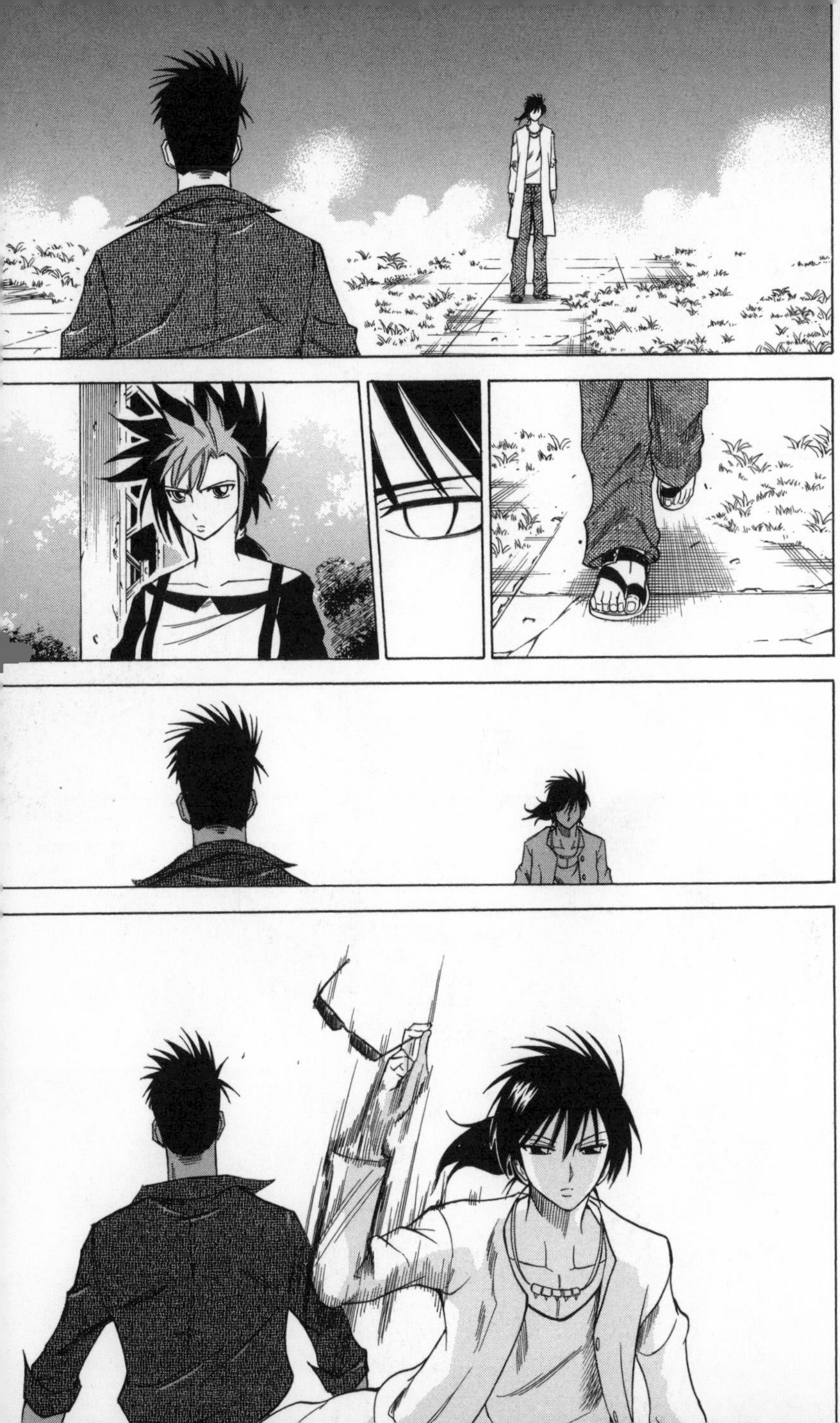

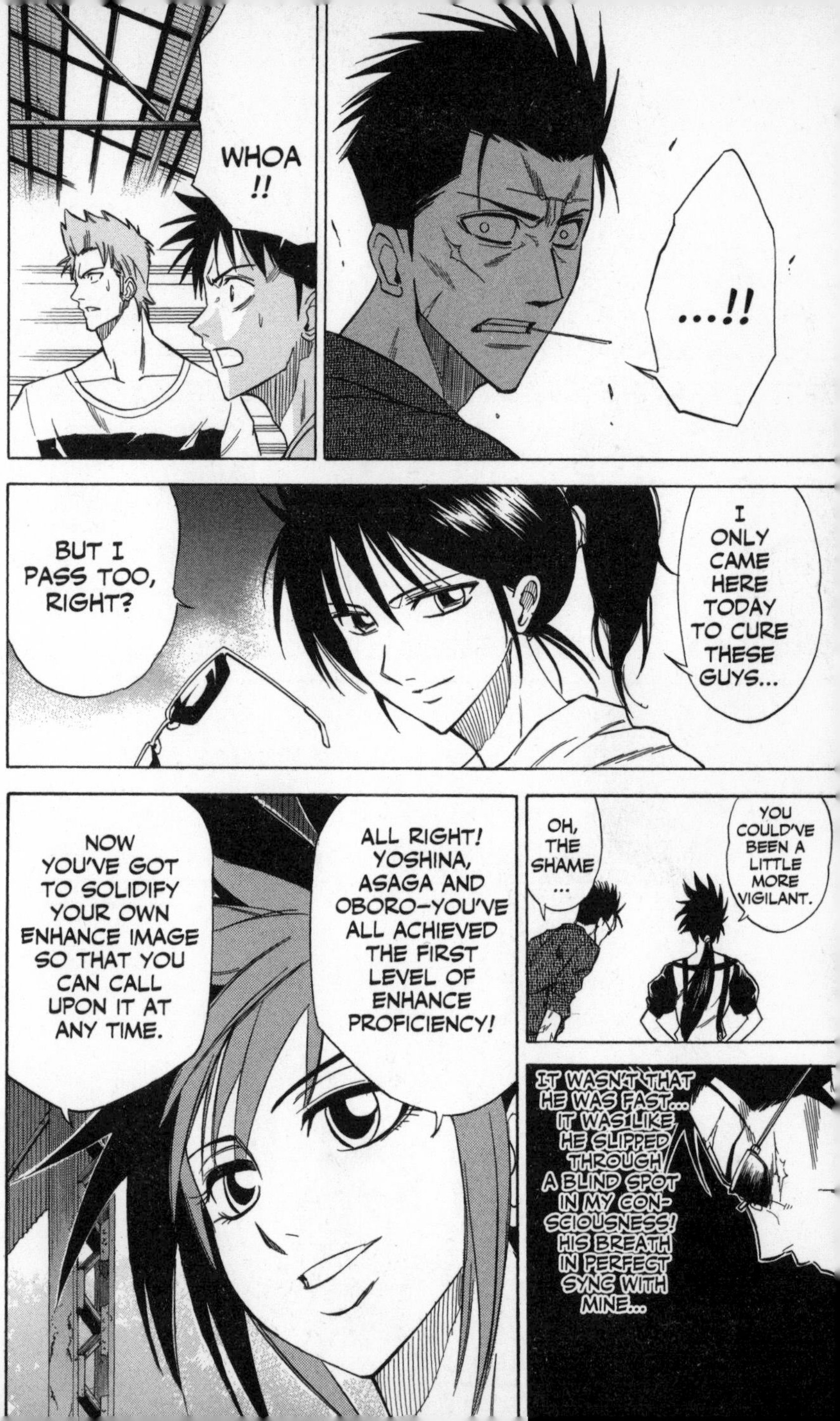
...!!
WHOA !!
I ONLY CAME HERE TODAY TO CURE THESE GUYS...
BUT I PASS TOO, RIGHT?
YOU COULD'VE BEEN A LITTLE MORE VIGILANT.
OH, THE SHAME ...
IT WASN'T THAT HE WAS FAST... IT WAS LIKE HE SLIPPED THROUGH A BLIND SPOT IN MY CONSCIOUSNESS! HIS BREATH IN PERFECT SYNC WITH MINE...
ALL RIGHT! YOSHINA, ASAGA AND OBORO—YOU'VE ALL ACHIEVED THE FIRST LEVEL OF ENHANCE PROFICIENCY!
NOW YOU'VE GOT TO SOLIDIFY YOUR OWN ENHANCE IMAGE SO THAT YOU CAN CALL UPON IT AT ANY TIME.

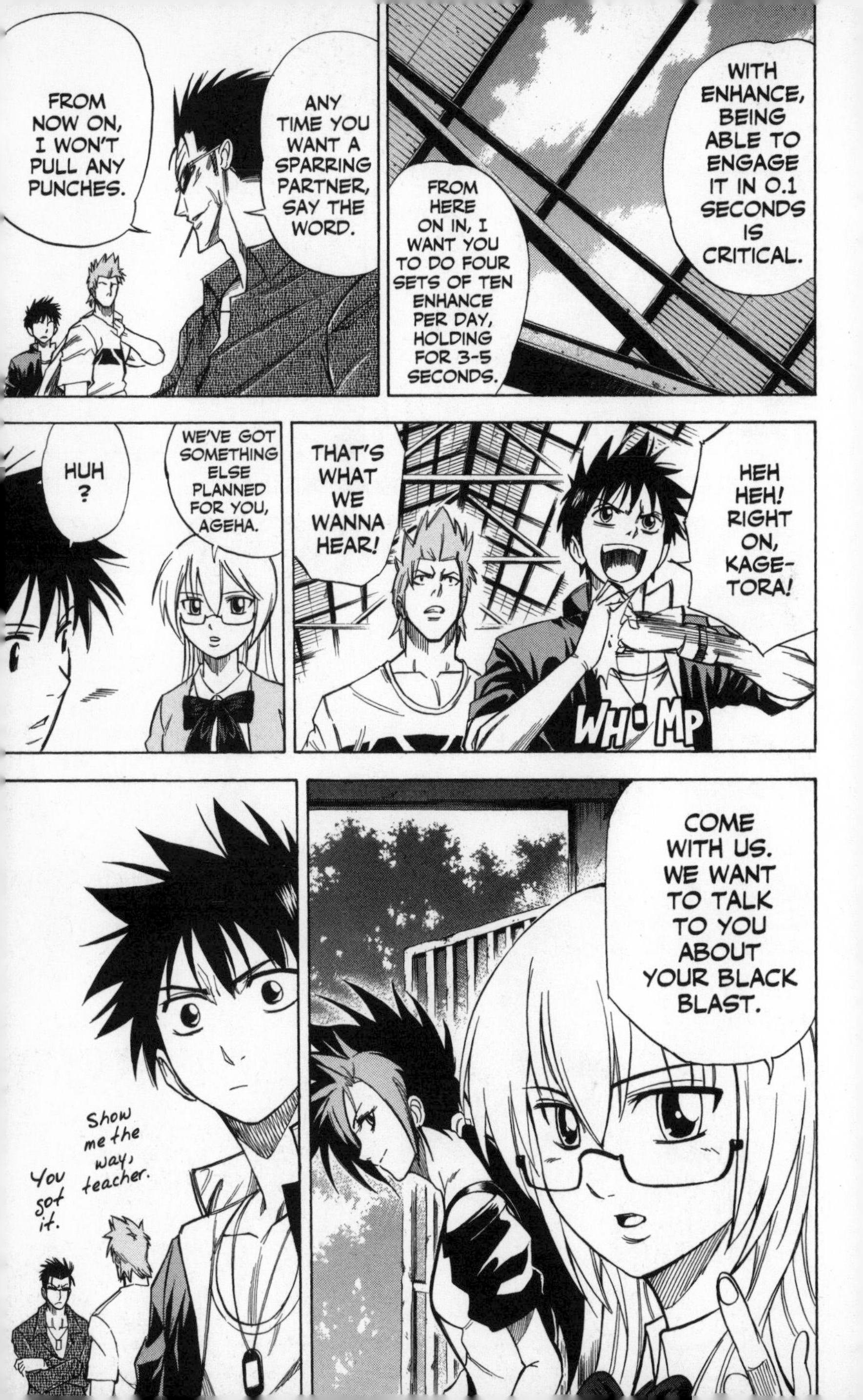
WITH ENHANCE, BEING ABLE TO ENGAGE IT IN 0.1 SECONDS IS CRITICAL.
FROM HERE ON IN, I WANT YOU TO DO FOUR SETS OF TEN ENHANCE PER DAY, HOLDING FOR 3-5 SECONDS.
ANY TIME YOU WANT A SPARRING PARTNER, SAY THE WORD.
FROM NOW ON, I WON'T PULL ANY PUNCHES.
HEH HEH! RIGHT ON, KAGE-TORA!
THAT'S WHAT WE WANNA HEAR!
WHOMP
WE'VE GOT SOMETHING ELSE PLANNED FOR YOU, AGEHA.
HUH?
COME WITH US. WE WANT TO TALK TO YOU ABOUT YOUR BLACK BLAST.
Show me the way, teacher.
You got it.

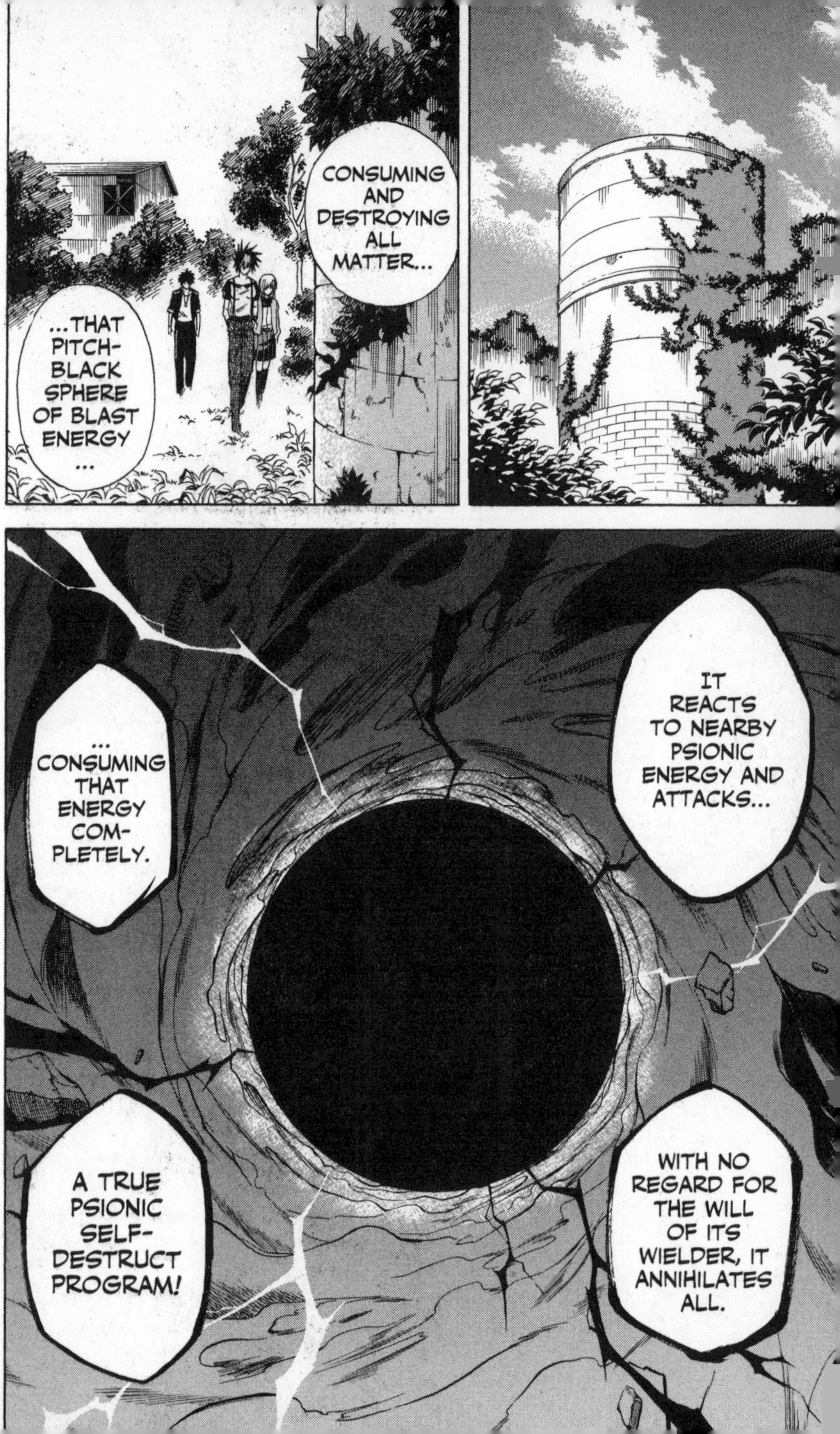
CONSUMING AND DESTROYING ALL MATTER...
...THAT PITCH-BLACK SPHERE OF BLAST ENERGY ...
IT REACTS TO NEARBY PSIONIC ENERGY AND ATTACKS...
...CONSUMING THAT ENERGY COM-PLETELY.
WITH NO REGARD FOR THE WILL OF ITS WIELDER, IT ANNIHILATES ALL.
A TRUE PSIONIC SELF-DESTRUCT PROGRAM!

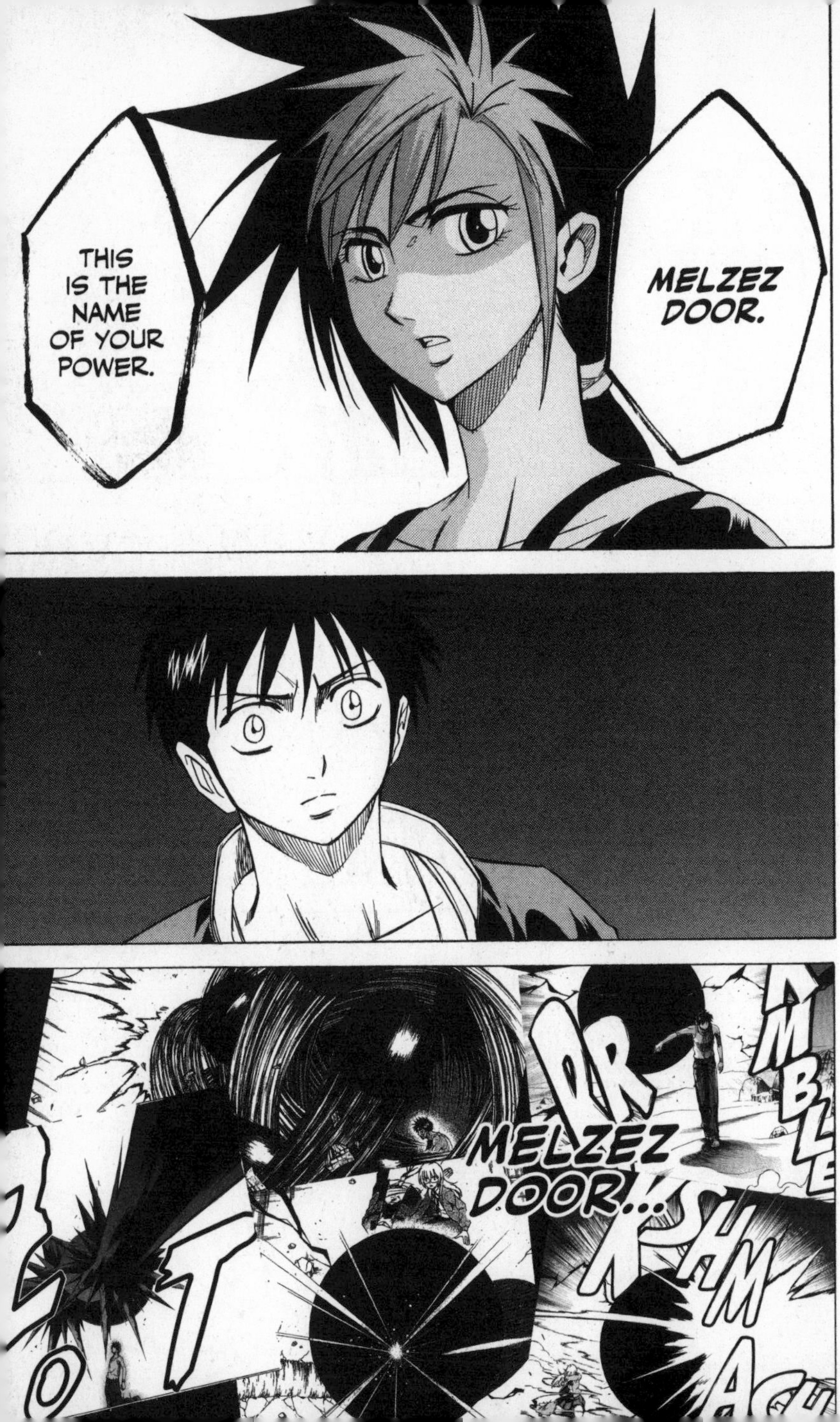
MELZEZ DOOR.
THIS IS THE NAME OF YOUR POWER.
MELZEZ DOOR...!

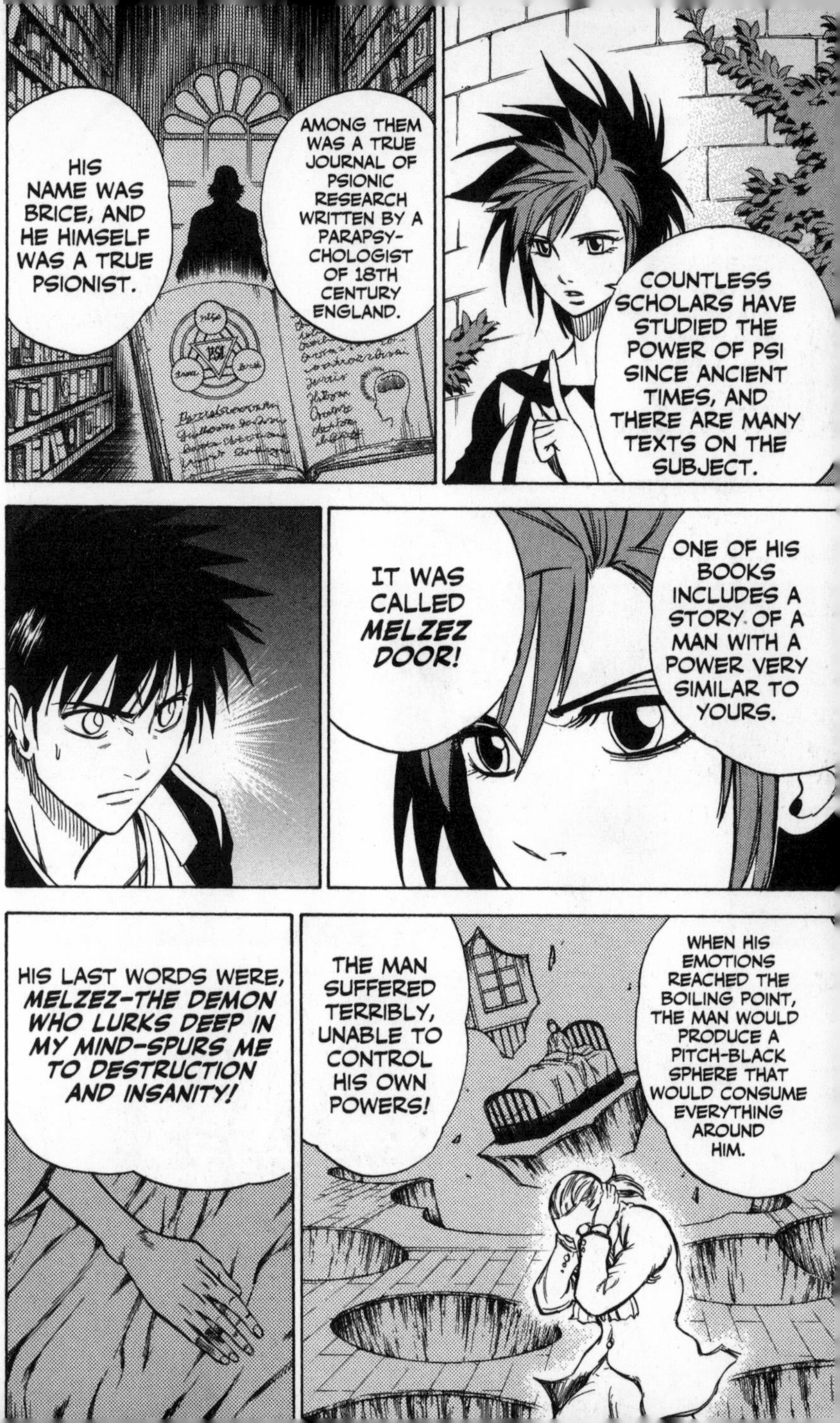
COUNTLESS SCHOLARS HAVE STUDIED THE POWER OF PSI SINCE ANCIENT TIMES, AND THERE ARE MANY TEXTS ON THE SUBJECT.
AMONG THEM WAS A TRUE JOURNAL OF PSIONIC RESEARCH WRITTEN BY A PARAPSY-CHOLOGIST OF 18TH CENTURY ENGLAND.
HIS NAME WAS BRICE, AND HE HIMSELF WAS A TRUE PSIONIST.
ONE OF HIS BOOKS INCLUDES A STORY OF A MAN WITH A POWER VERY SIMILAR TO YOURS.
IT WAS CALLED *MELZEZ DOOR*!
WHEN HIS EMOTIONS REACHED THE BOILING POINT, THE MAN WOULD PRODUCE A PITCH-BLACK SPHERE THAT WOULD CONSUME EVERYTHING AROUND HIM.
THE MAN SUFFERED TERRIBLY, UNABLE TO CONTROL HIS OWN POWERS!
HIS LAST WORDS WERE, *MELZEZ–THE DEMON WHO LURKS DEEP IN MY MIND–SPURS ME TO DESTRUCTION AND INSANITY!*

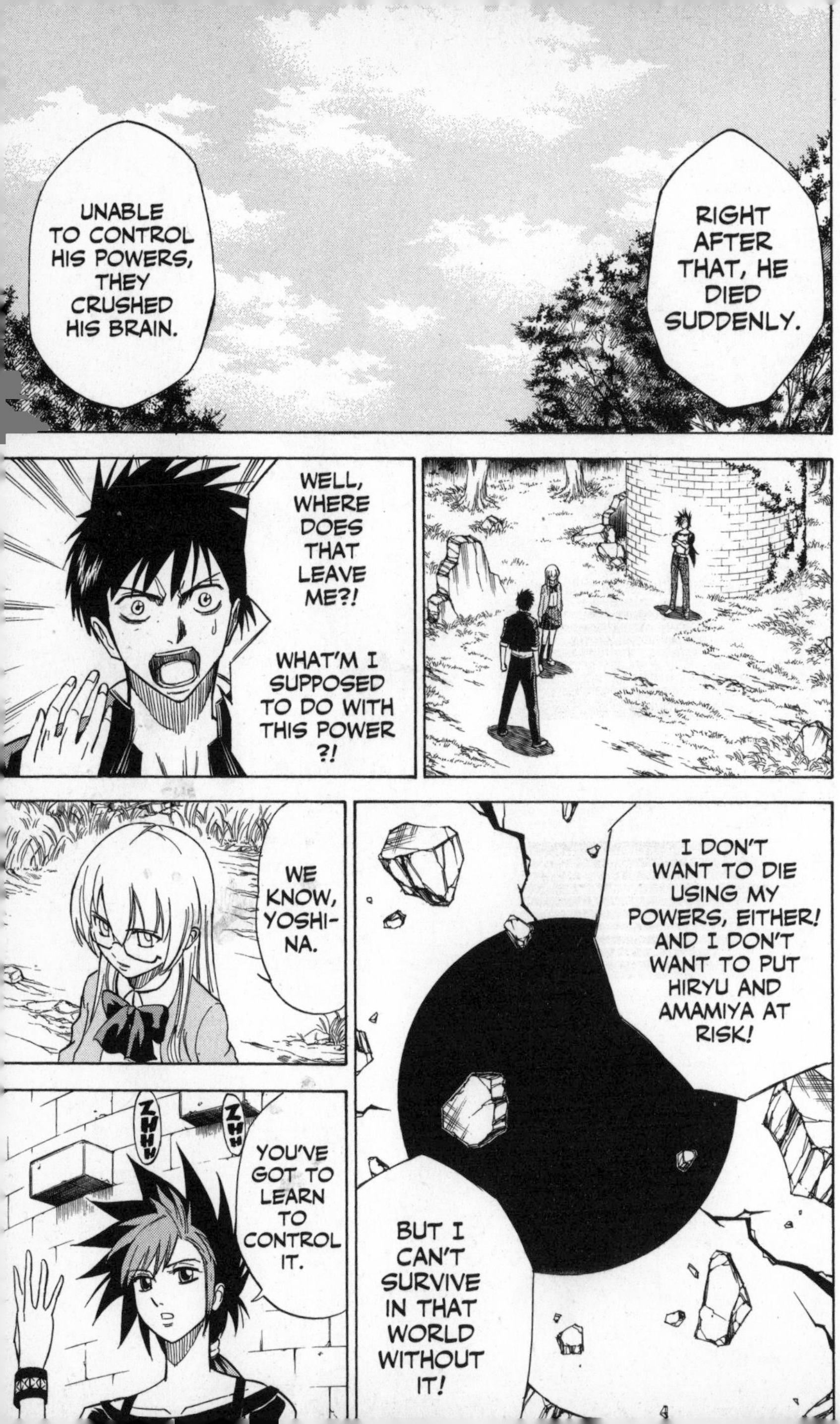
RIGHT AFTER THAT, HE DIED SUDDENLY.
UNABLE TO CONTROL HIS POWERS, THEY CRUSHED HIS BRAIN.
WELL, WHERE DOES THAT LEAVE ME?!
WHAT'M I SUPPOSED TO DO WITH THIS POWER ?!
I DON'T WANT TO DIE USING MY POWERS, EITHER! AND I DON'T WANT TO PUT HIRYU AND AMAMIYA AT RISK!
BUT I CAN'T SURVIVE IN THAT WORLD WITHOUT IT!
WE KNOW, YOSHINA.
ZHHH
ZHHH
YOU'VE GOT TO LEARN TO CONTROL IT.

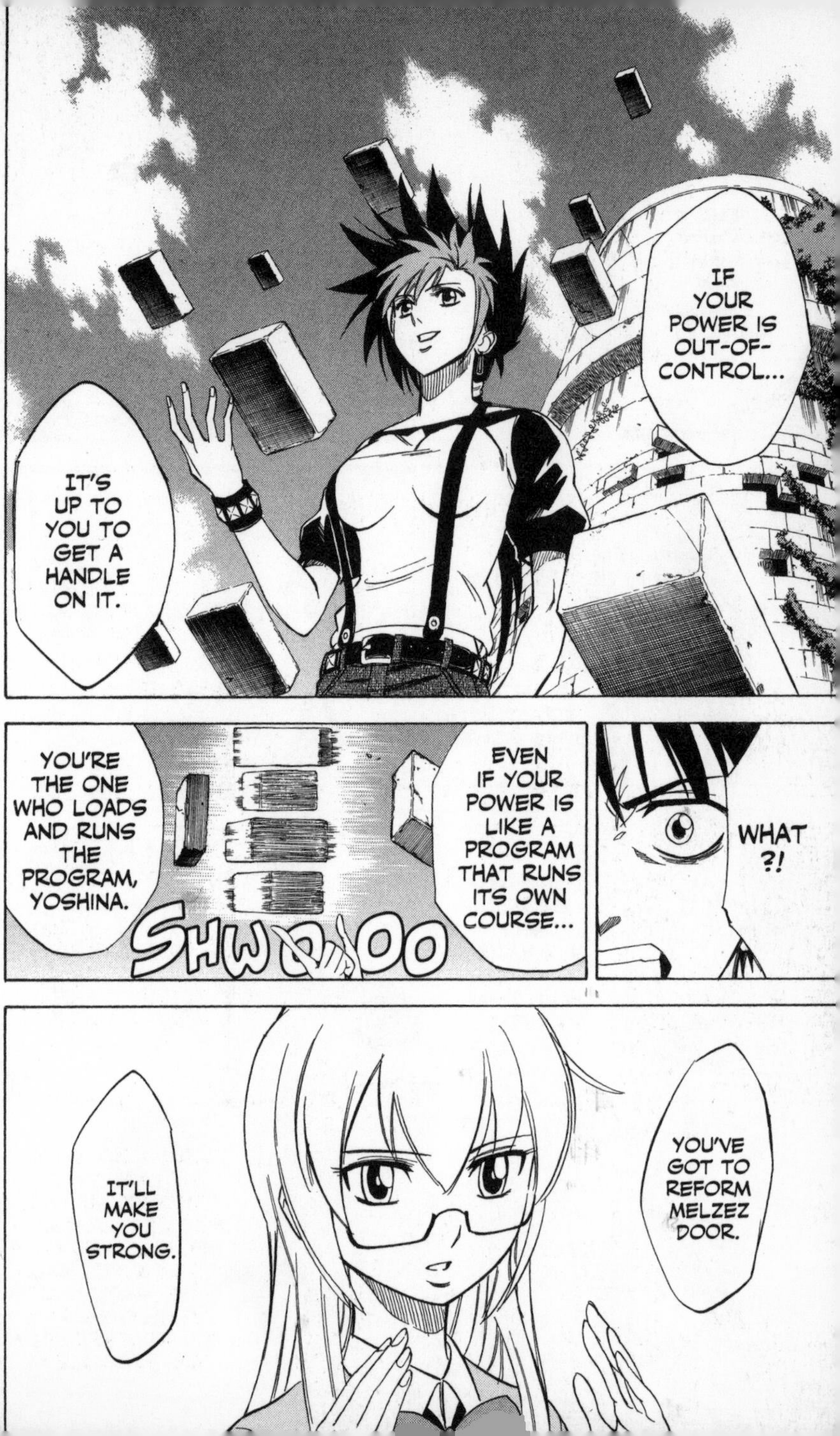
IF YOUR POWER IS OUT-OF-CONTROL...
IT'S UP TO YOU TO GET A HANDLE ON IT.
WHAT?!
EVEN IF YOUR POWER IS LIKE A PROGRAM THAT RUNS ITS OWN COURSE...
YOU'RE THE ONE WHO LOADS AND RUNS THE PROGRAM, YOSHINA.
YOU'VE GOT TO REFORM MELZEZ DOOR.
IT'LL MAKE YOU STRONG.

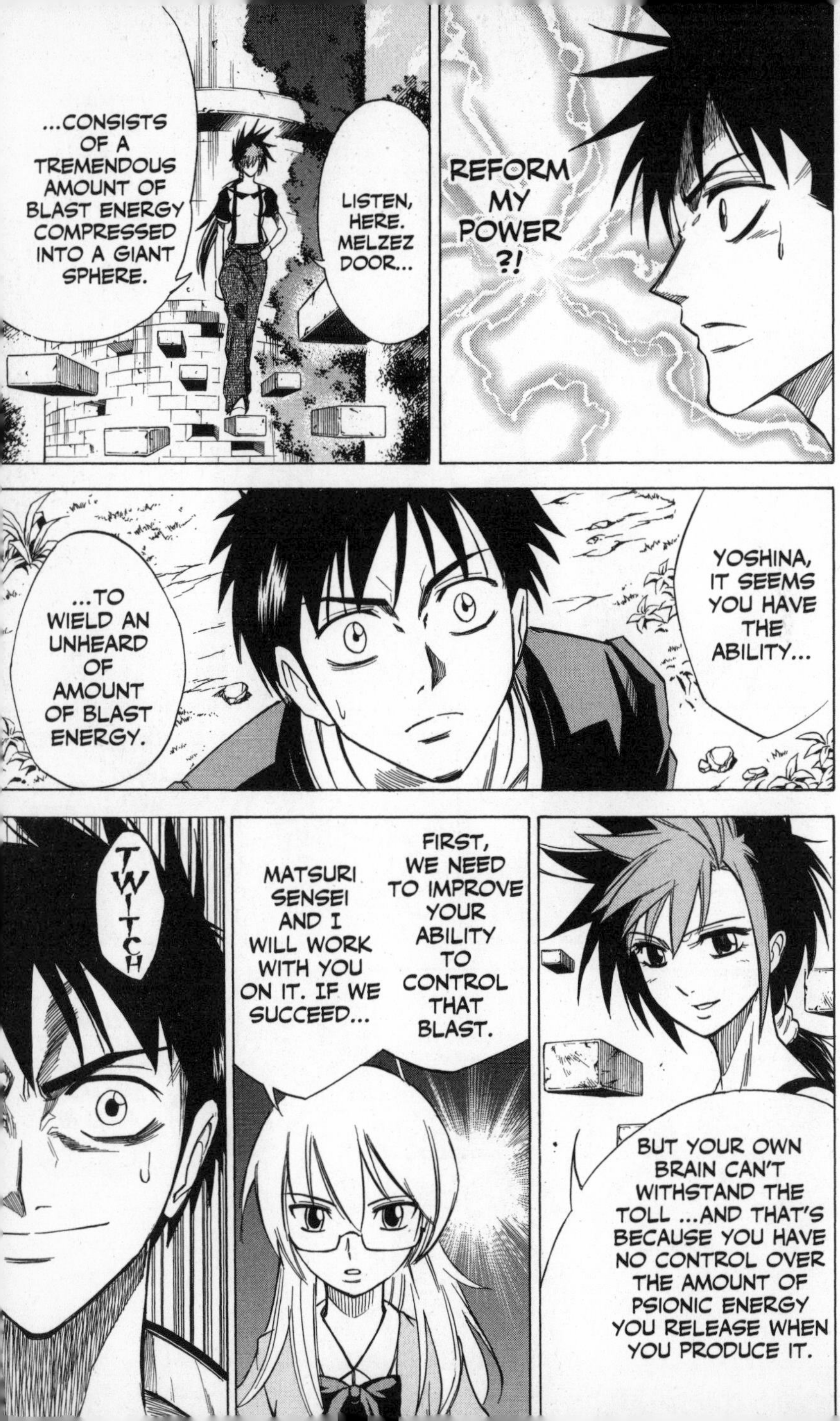
REFORM MY POWER ?!
LISTEN, HERE. MELZEZ DOOR...
...CONSISTS OF A TREMENDOUS AMOUNT OF BLAST ENERGY COMPRESSED INTO A GIANT SPHERE.
YOSHINA, IT SEEMS YOU HAVE THE ABILITY...
...TO WIELD AN UNHEARD OF AMOUNT OF BLAST ENERGY.
BUT YOUR OWN BRAIN CAN'T WITHSTAND THE TOLL ...AND THAT'S BECAUSE YOU HAVE NO CONTROL OVER THE AMOUNT OF PSIONIC ENERGY YOU RELEASE WHEN YOU PRODUCE IT.
FIRST, WE NEED TO IMPROVE YOUR ABILITY TO CONTROL THAT BLAST.
MATSURI SENSEI AND I WILL WORK WITH YOU ON IT. IF WE SUCCEED...
TWITCH

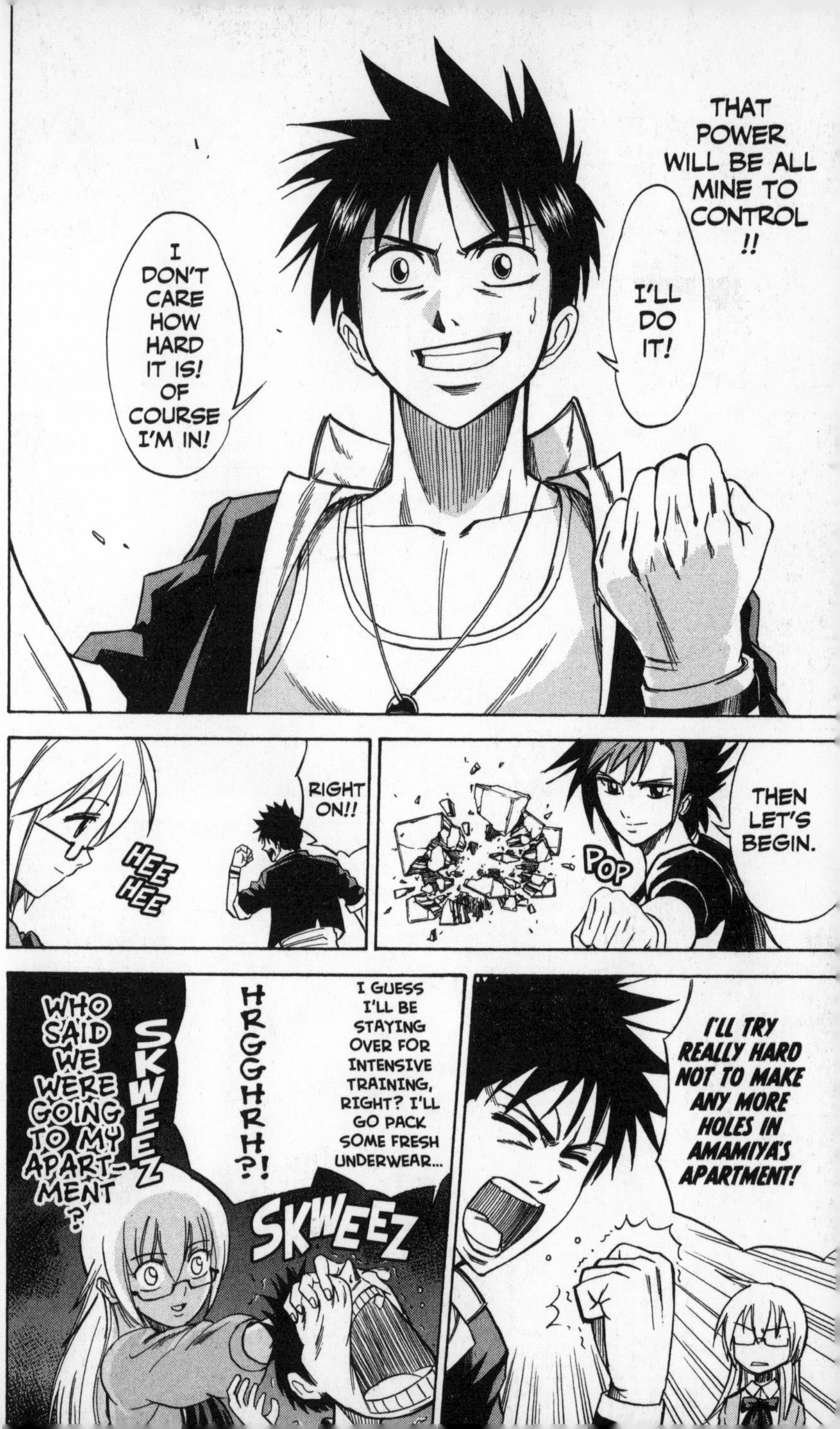
THAT POWER WILL BE ALL MINE TO CONTROL!!
I'LL DO IT!
I DON'T CARE HOW HARD IT IS! OF COURSE I'M IN!
THEN LET'S BEGIN.
POP
RIGHT ON!!
HEE HEE
I'LL TRY REALLY HARD NOT TO MAKE ANY MORE HOLES IN AMAMIYA'S APARTMENT!
I GUESS I'LL BE STAYING OVER FOR INTENSIVE TRAINING, RIGHT? I'LL GO PACK SOME FRESH UNDERWEAR...
HRGGHRH?!
SKWEEZ
WHO SAID WE WERE GOING TO MY APART-MENT?
SKWEEZ

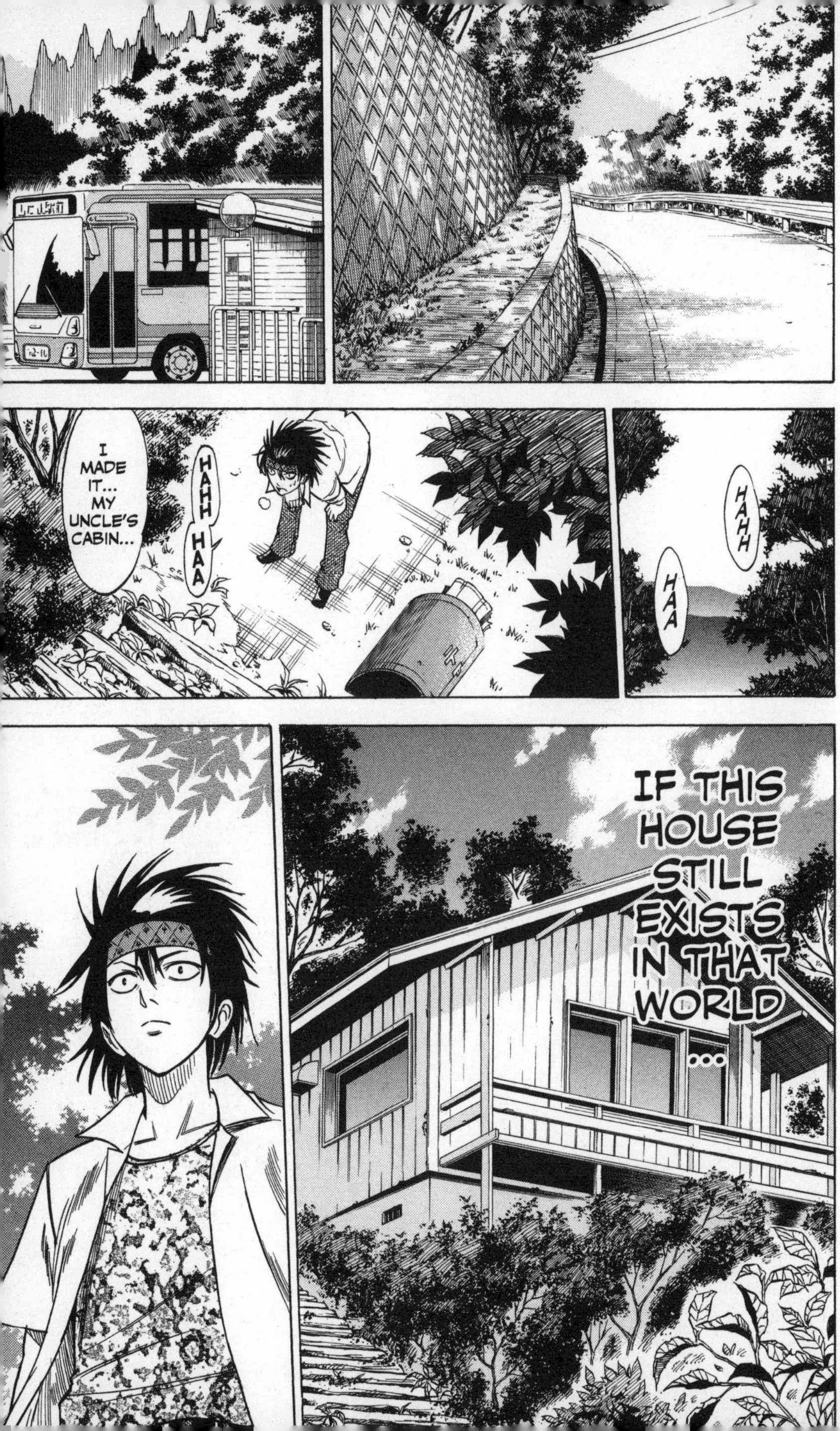
HAHH
HAA
HAHH HAA
I MADE IT... MY UNCLE'S CABIN...
IF THIS HOUSE STILL EXISTS IN THAT WORLD...

Mutters and mumblings...

SOMETIMES I THINK ABOUT HAVING CHARACTERS FROM
MIERU HITO APPEAR IN *PSYREN*...BUT IT JUST NEVER WORKS
OUT. THE CHARACTERS IN *MIERU HITO* ARE JUST TOO EVIL
FOR *PSYREN!* AND THE WHOLE GUIDE/GHOST THING IS A
FUNDAMENTAL PROBLEM ANYWAY. BUT I WOULD'VE LIKED
CHARACTERS LIKE HIKAGURA TO GET A LITTLE MORE
ACTION...

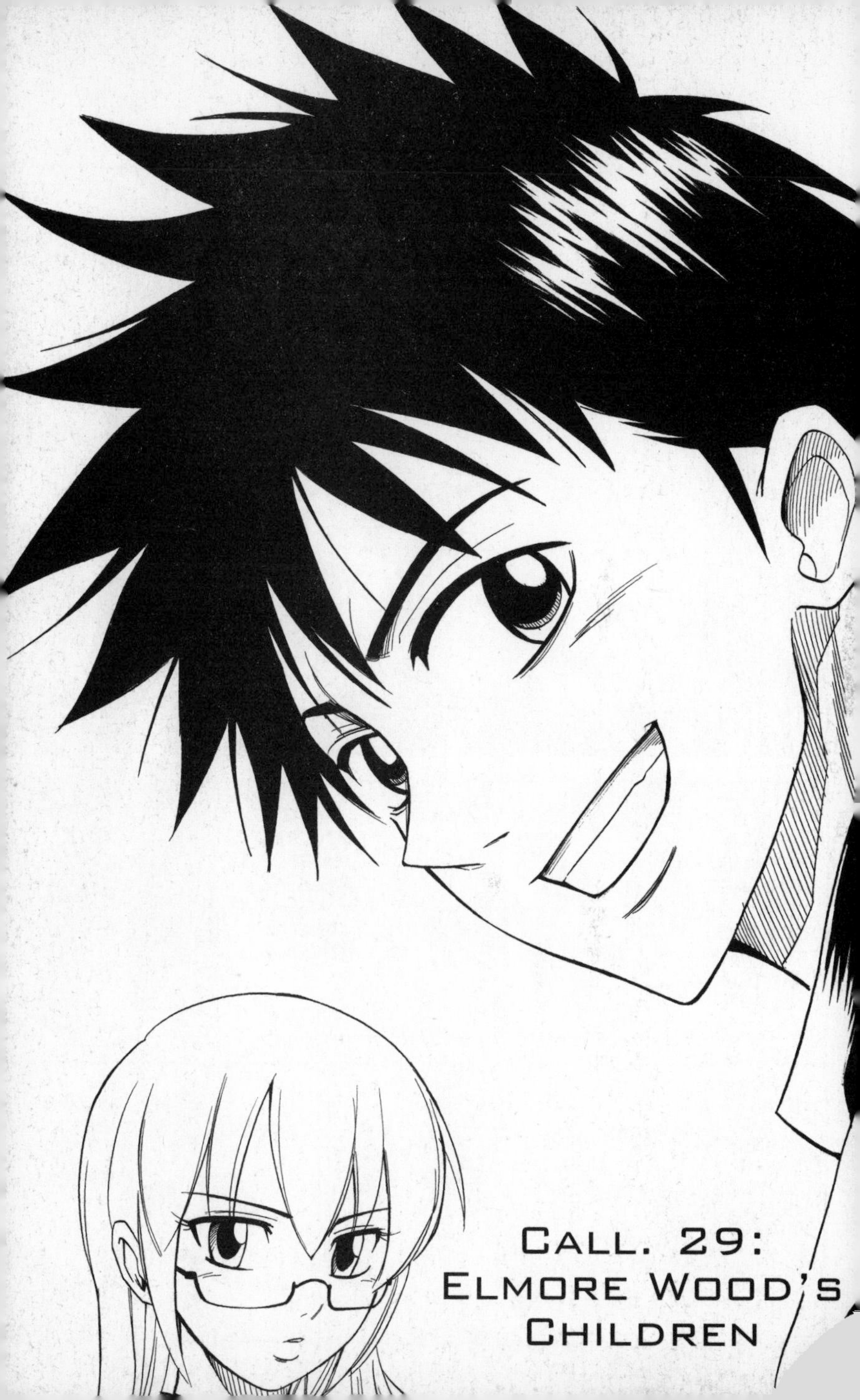

Call. 29: Elmore Wood's Children

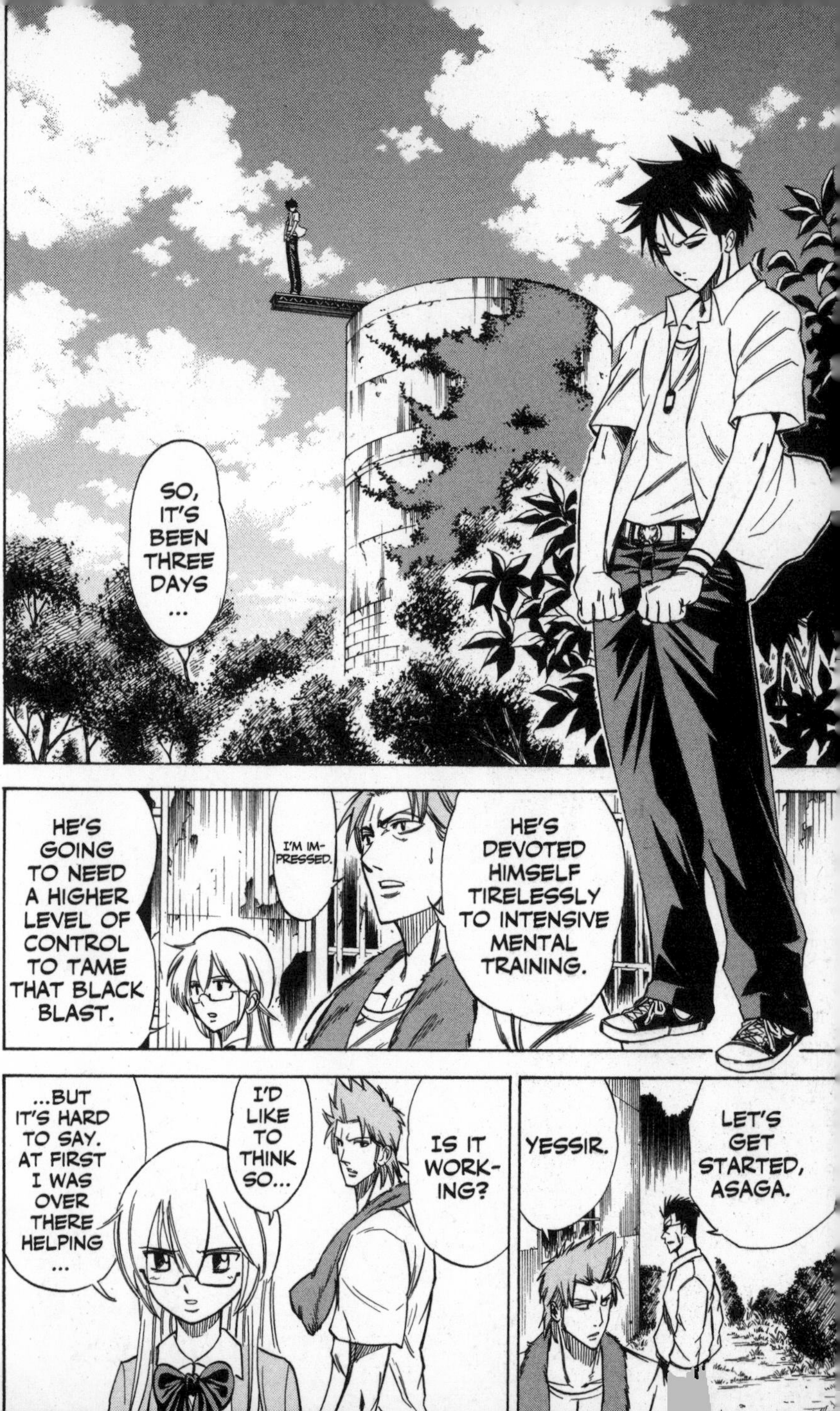
SO, IT'S BEEN THREE DAYS...
HE'S DEVOTED HIMSELF TIRELESSLY TO INTENSIVE MENTAL TRAINING.
I'M IM-PRESSED.
HE'S GOING TO NEED A HIGHER LEVEL OF CONTROL TO TAME THAT BLACK BLAST.
LET'S GET STARTED, ASAGA.
YESSIR.
IS IT WORK-ING?
I'D LIKE TO THINK SO...
...BUT IT'S HARD TO SAY. AT FIRST I WAS OVER THERE HELPING...

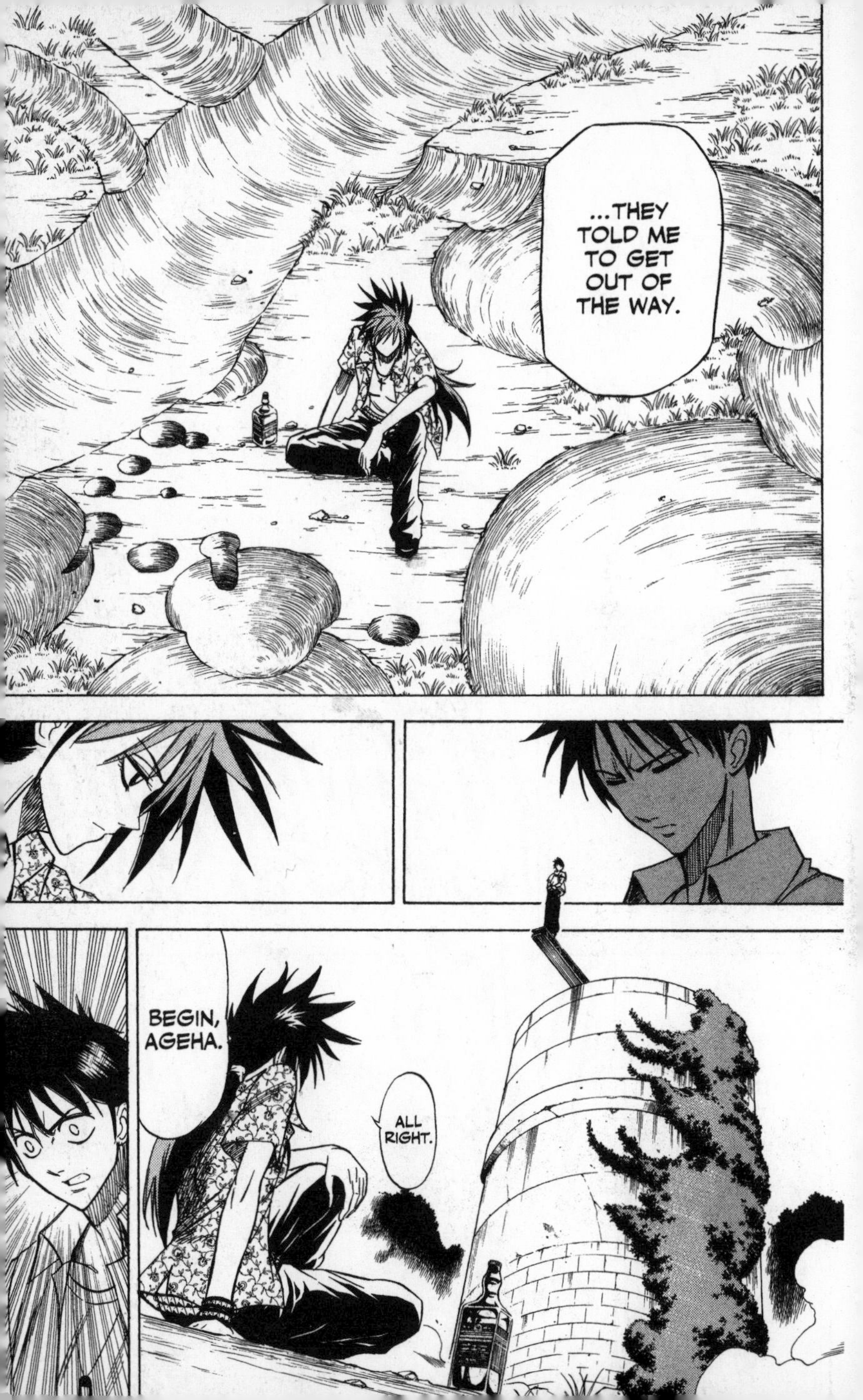
...THEY TOLD ME TO GET OUT OF THE WAY.
BEGIN, AGEHA.
ALL RIGHT.

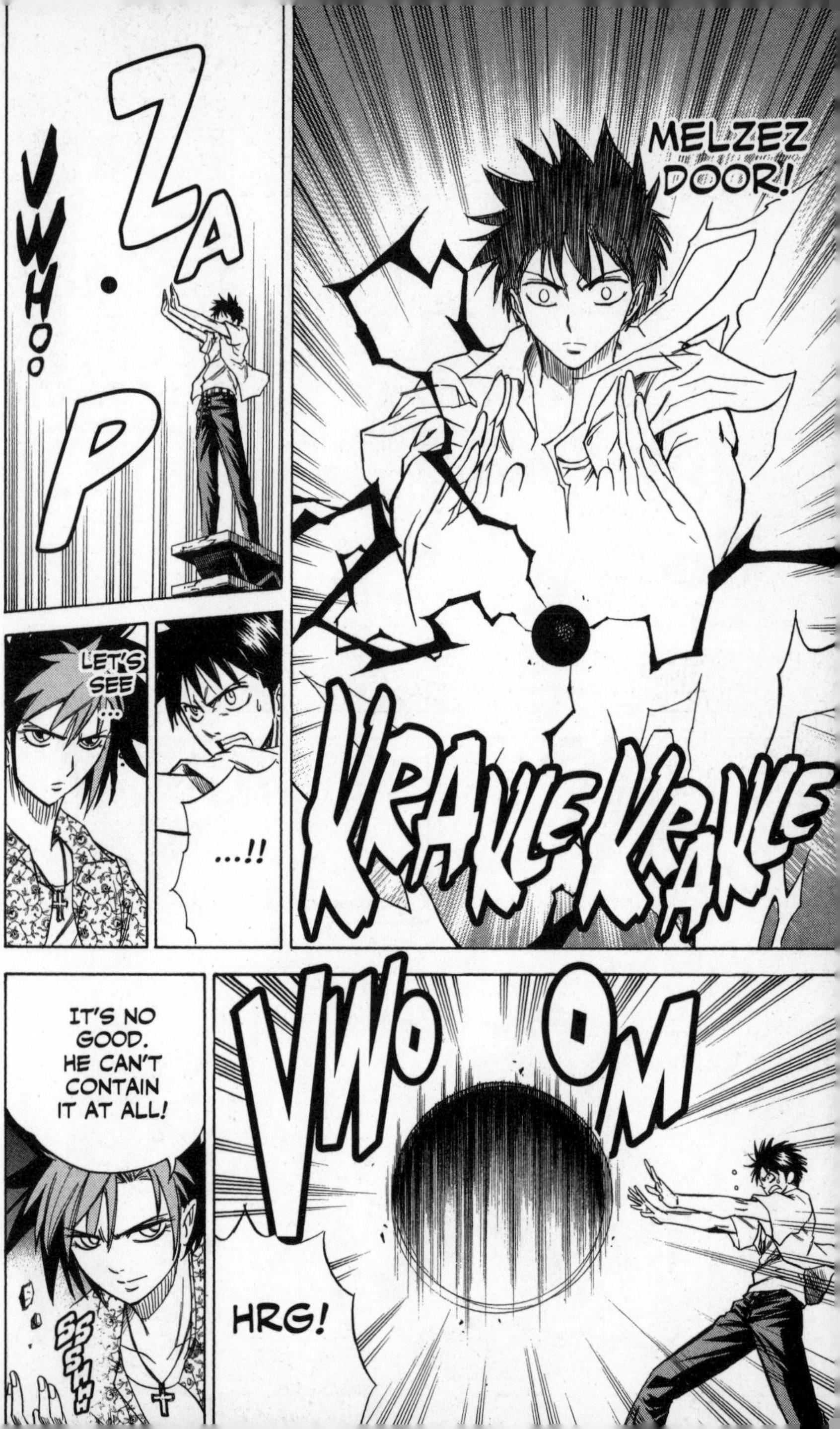
MELZEZ DOOR!
KRACKLE KRACKLE
ZAP
VWHOOO
...!!
LET'S SEE...
VWOOM
HRG!
IT'S NO GOOD. HE CAN'T CONTAIN IT AT ALL!
SSSHH

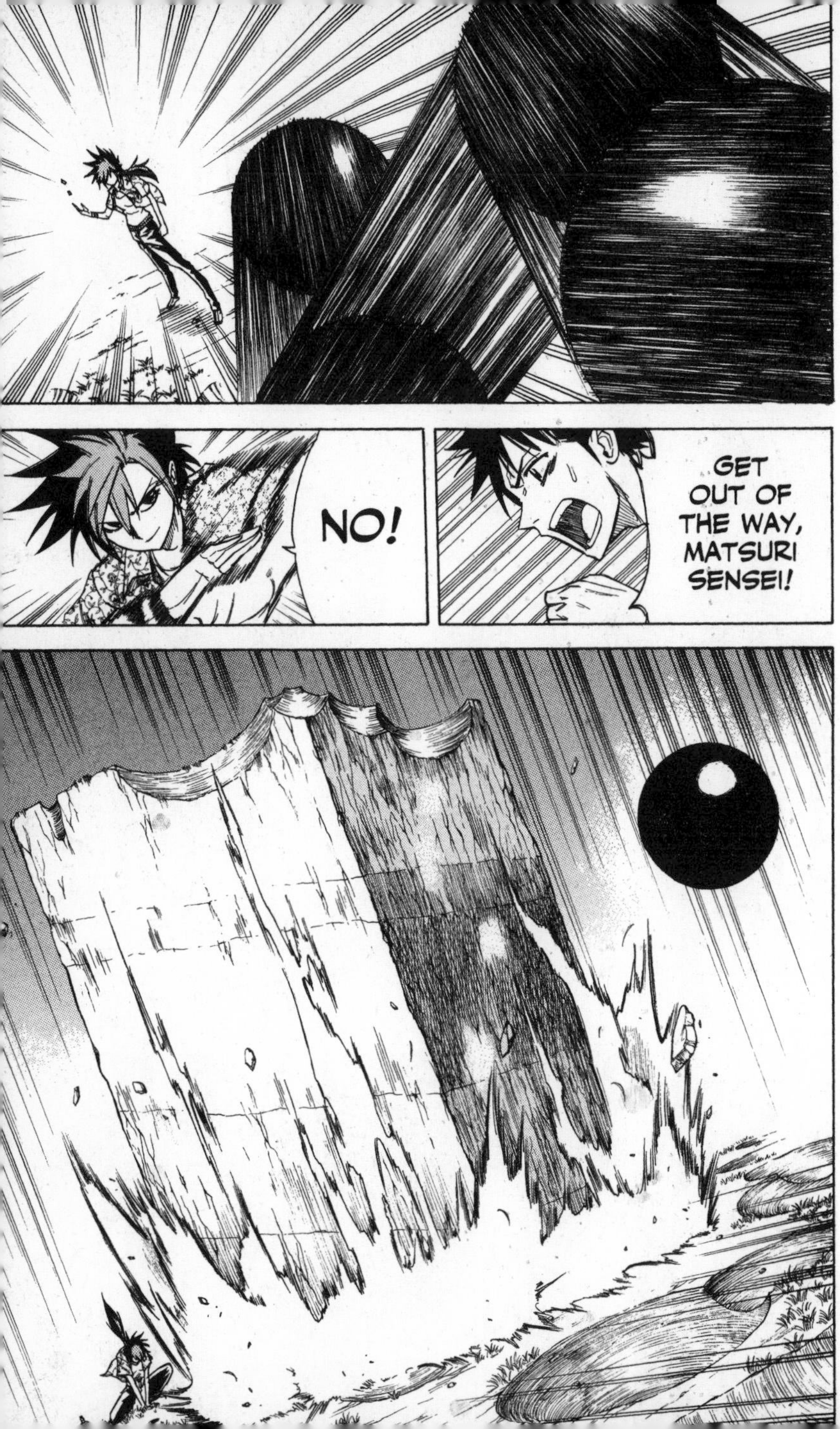
GET OUT OF THE WAY, MATSURI SENSEI!
NO!

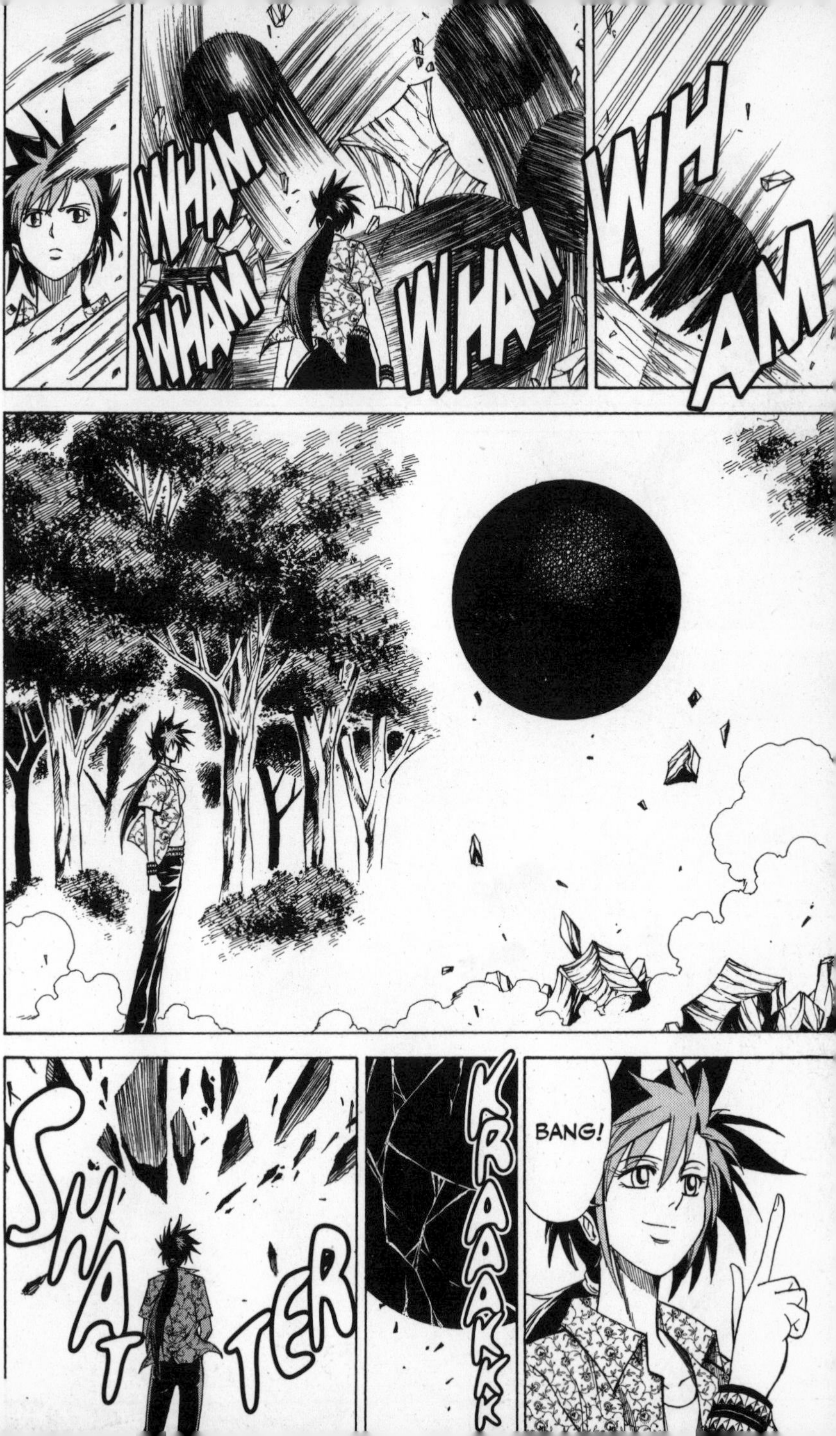
WH
AM
WHAM
WHAM
WHAM
BANG!
KRAAAAKK
SHATTER

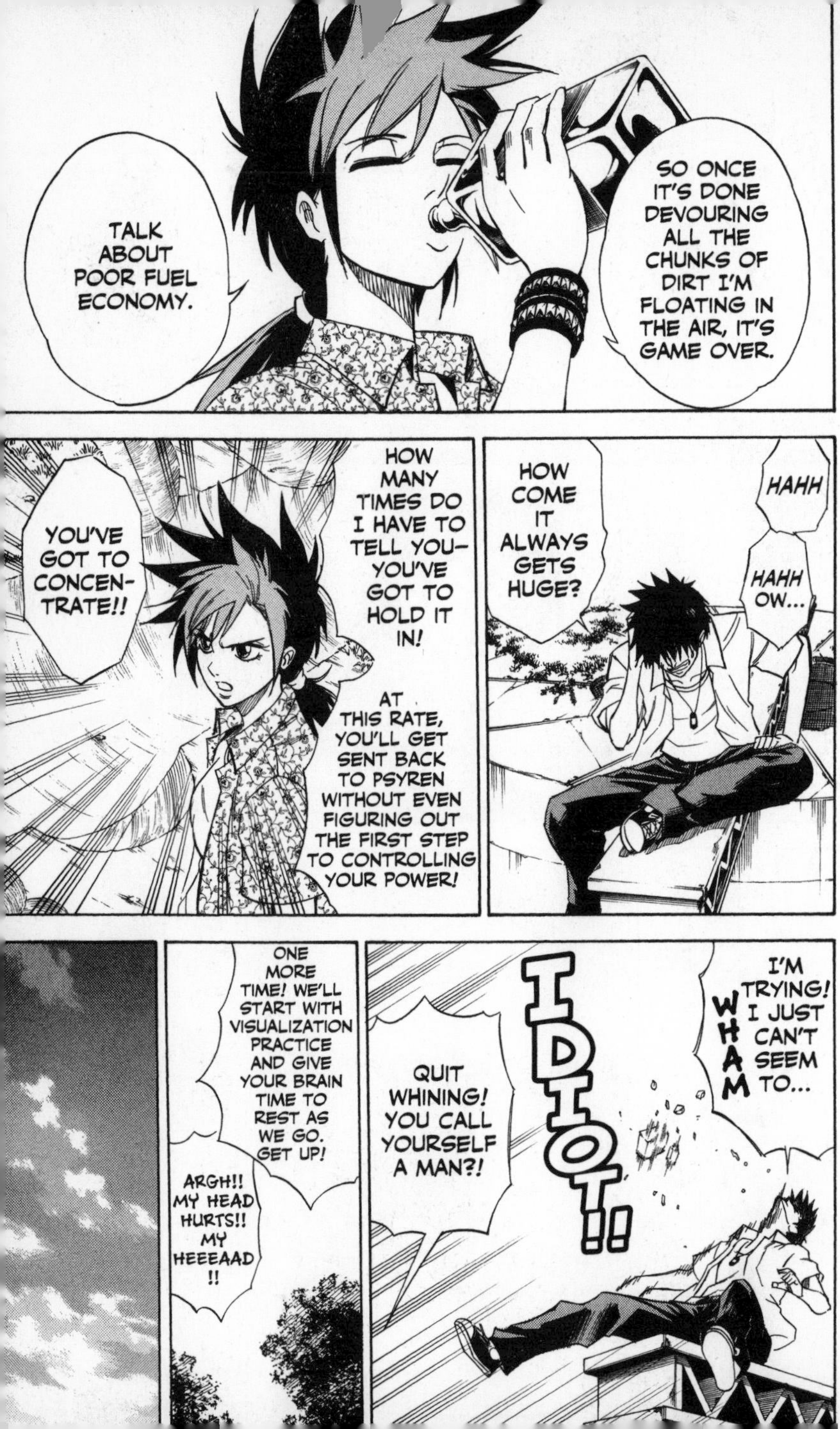
SO ONCE IT'S DONE DEVOURING ALL THE CHUNKS OF DIRT I'M FLOATING IN THE AIR, IT'S GAME OVER.
TALK ABOUT POOR FUEL ECONOMY.
HAHH
HAHH OW...
HOW COME IT ALWAYS GETS HUGE?
HOW MANY TIMES DO I HAVE TO TELL YOU-YOU'VE GOT TO HOLD IT IN!
YOU'VE GOT TO CONCENTRATE!!
AT THIS RATE, YOU'LL GET SENT BACK TO PSYREN WITHOUT EVEN FIGURING OUT THE FIRST STEP TO CONTROLLING YOUR POWER!
I'M TRYING! I JUST CAN'T SEEM TO...
WHAM
IDIOT!!
QUIT WHINING! YOU CALL YOURSELF A MAN?!
ONE MORE TIME! WE'LL START WITH VISUALIZATION PRACTICE AND GIVE YOUR BRAIN TIME TO REST AS WE GO. GET UP!
ARGH!! MY HEAD HURTS!! MY HEEEAAD !!

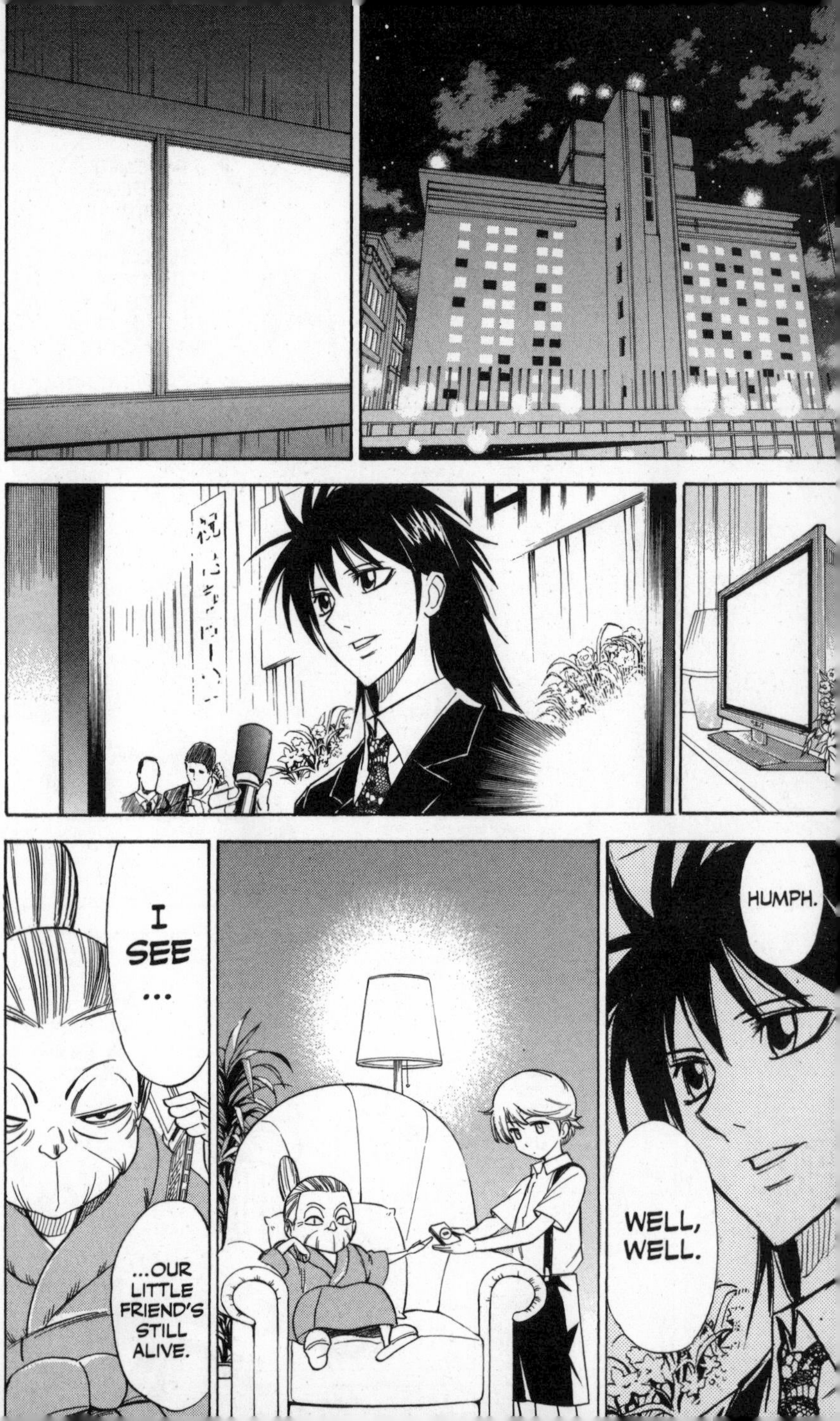
HUMPH.
WELL, WELL.
I SEE...
...OUR LITTLE FRIEND'S STILL ALIVE.

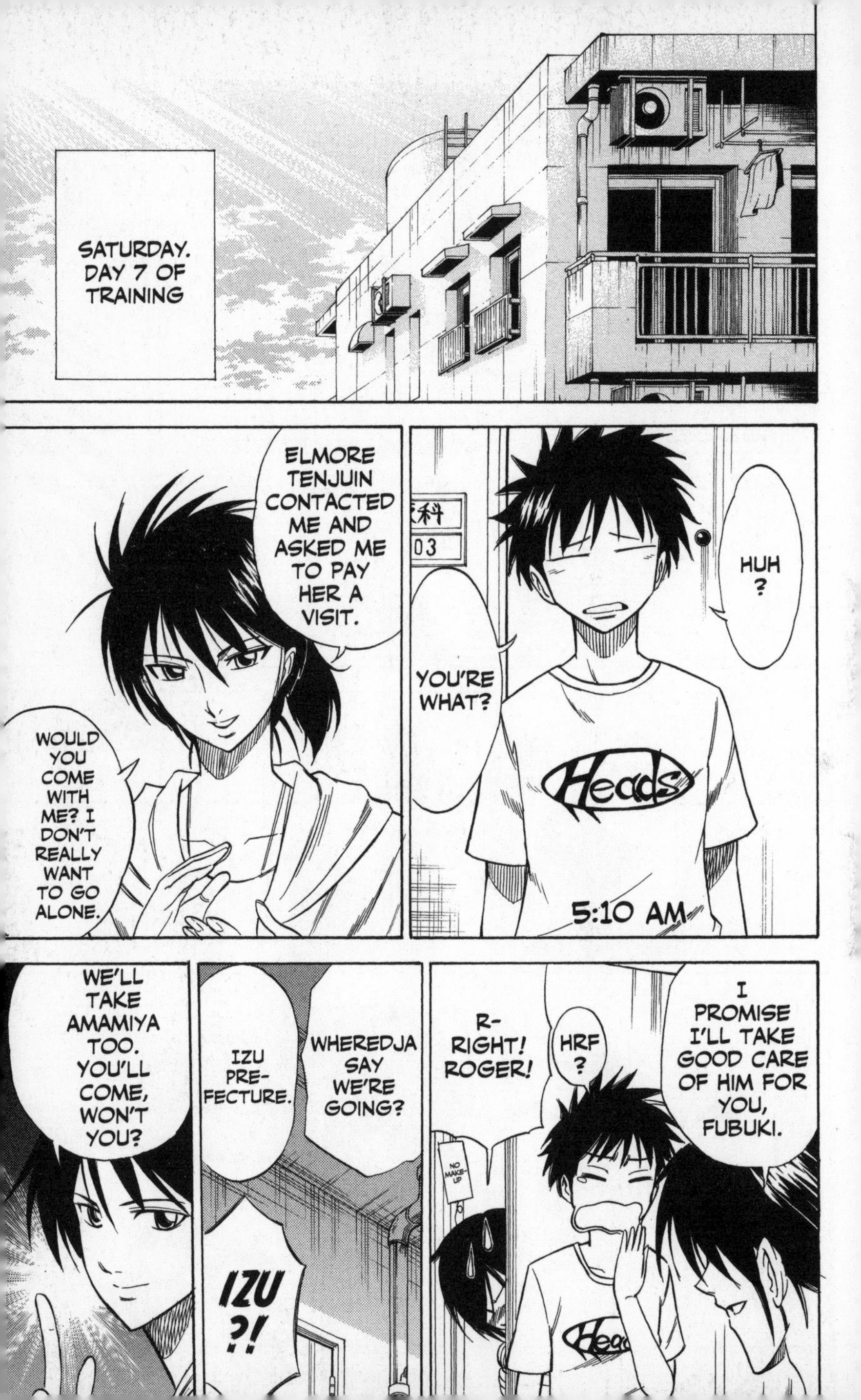
SATURDAY. DAY 7 OF TRAINING
HUH?
YOU'RE WHAT?
Heads
5:10 AM
ELMORE TENJUIN CONTACTED ME AND ASKED ME TO PAY HER A VISIT.
WOULD YOU COME WITH ME? I DON'T REALLY WANT TO GO ALONE.
I PROMISE I'LL TAKE GOOD CARE OF HIM FOR YOU, FUBUKI.
HRF?
R-RIGHT! ROGER!
NO MAKE-UP
WHEREDJA SAY WE'RE GOING?
IZU PRE-FECTURE.
IZU?!
WE'LL TAKE AMAMIYA TOO. YOU'LL COME, WON'T YOU?

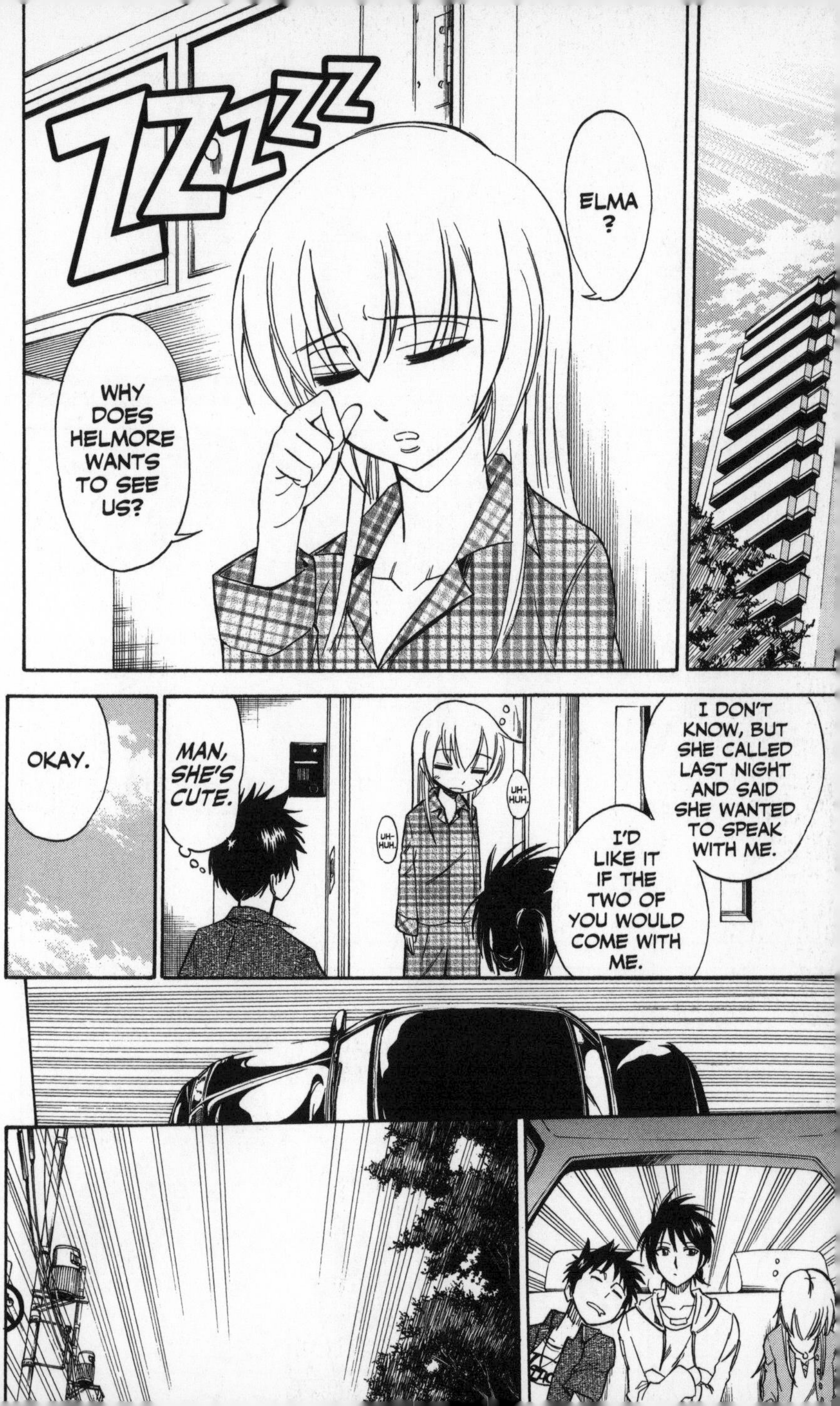
ELMA?
ZZZZZZ
WHY DOES HELMORE WANTS TO SEE US?
I DON'T KNOW, BUT SHE CALLED LAST NIGHT AND SAID SHE WANTED TO SPEAK WITH ME.
I'D LIKE IT IF THE TWO OF YOU WOULD COME WITH ME.
UH-HUH.
UH-HUH.
MAN, SHE'S CUTE.
OKAY.

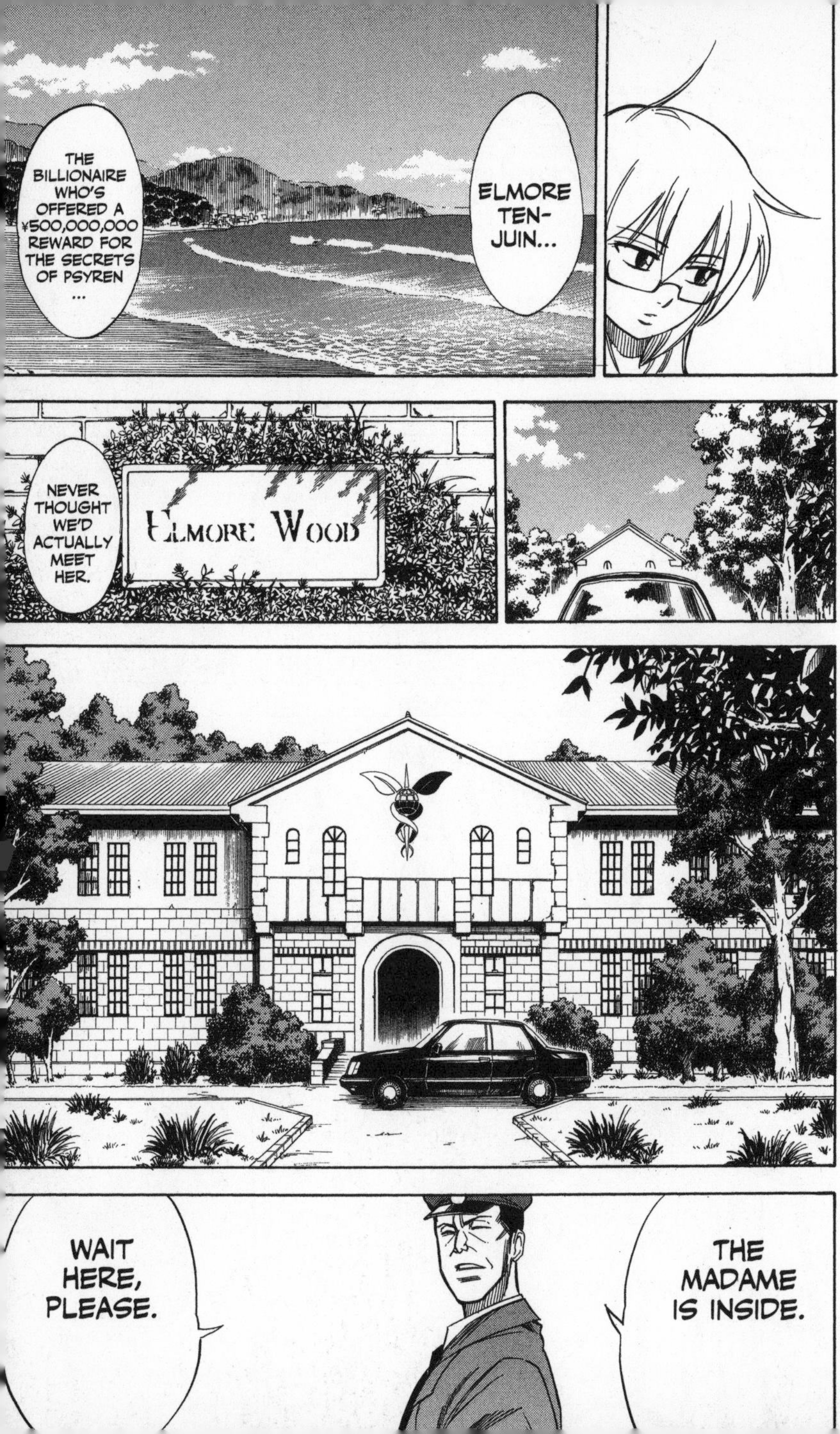
ELMORE TEN-JUIN...
THE BILLIONAIRE WHO'S OFFERED A ¥500,000,000 REWARD FOR THE SECRETS OF PSYREN ...
ELMORE WOOD
NEVER THOUGHT WE'D ACTUALLY MEET HER.
THE MADAME IS INSIDE.
WAIT HERE, PLEASE.

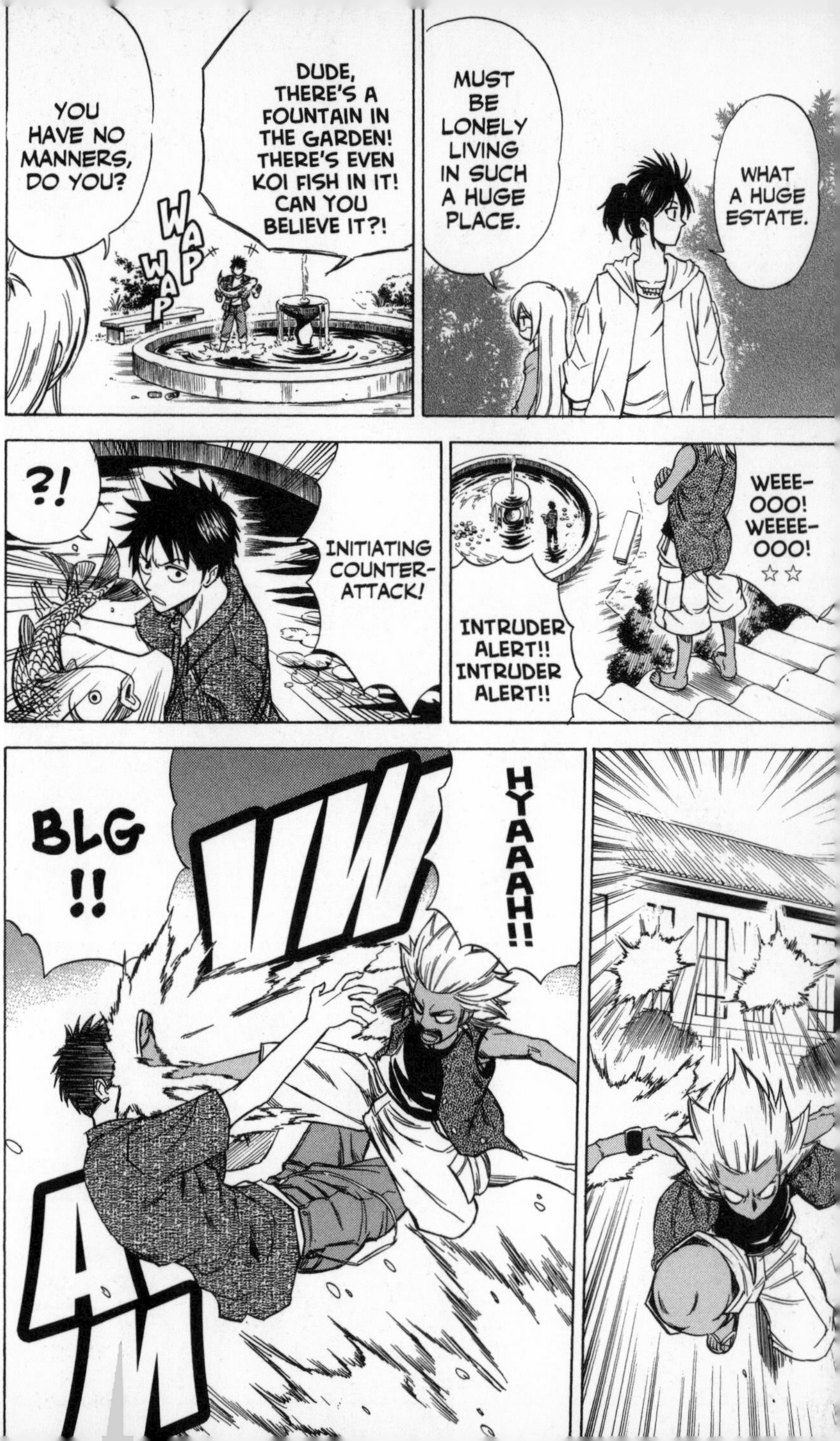
WHAT A HUGE ESTATE.
MUST BE LONELY LIVING IN SUCH A HUGE PLACE.
DUDE, THERE'S A FOUNTAIN IN THE GARDEN! THERE'S EVEN KOI FISH IN IT! CAN YOU BELIEVE IT?!
WAP WAP
YOU HAVE NO MANNERS, DO YOU?
WEEE-OOO! WEEEE-OOO! ☆☆
INTRUDER ALERT!! INTRUDER ALERT!!
INITIATING COUNTER-ATTACK!
?!
HYAAAAH!!
WHAM
BLG !!

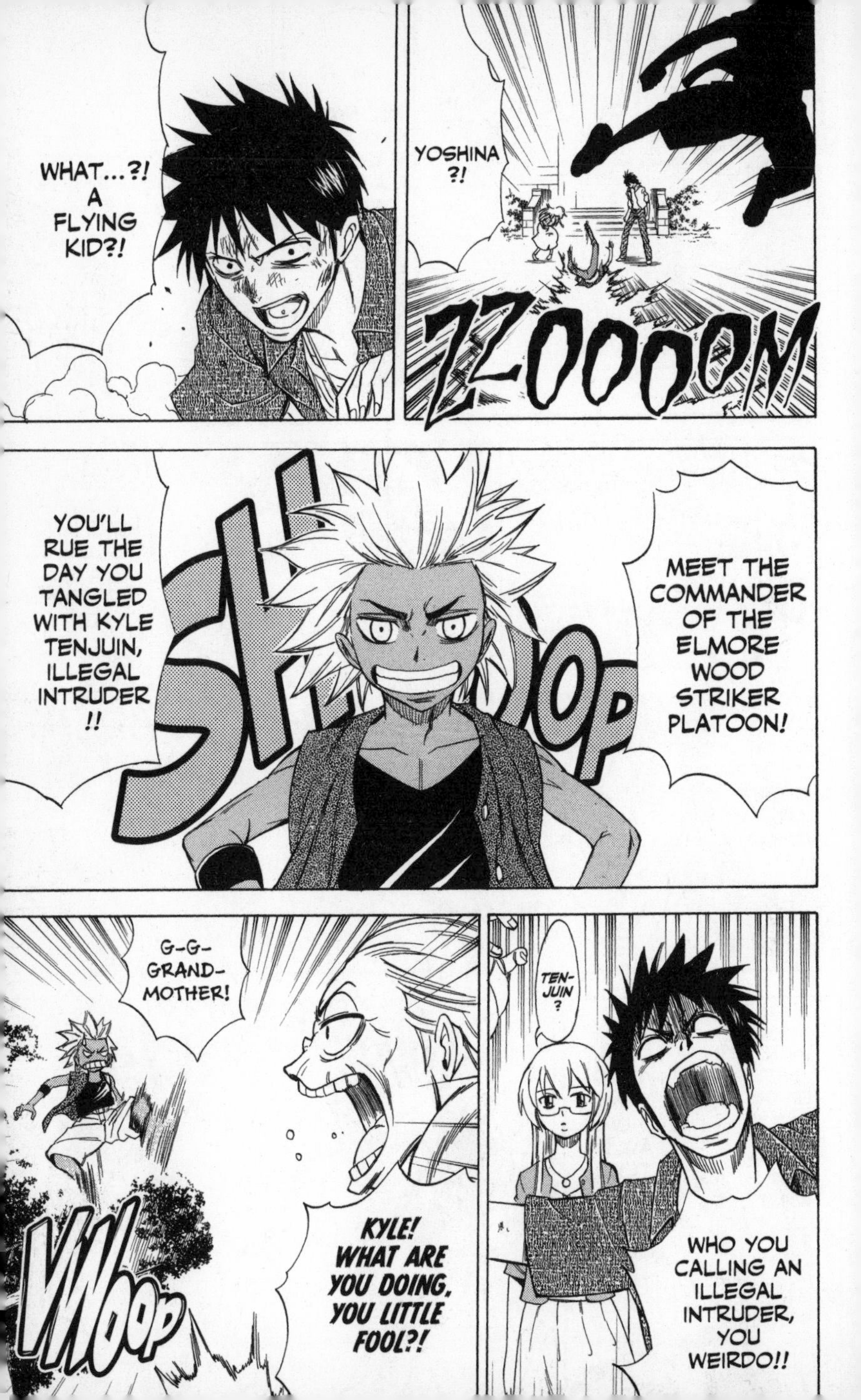
YOSHINA ?!
ZZOOOOM
WHAT...?! A FLYING KID?!
MEET THE COMMANDER OF THE ELMORE WOOD STRIKER PLATOON!
YOU'LL RUE THE DAY YOU TANGLED WITH KYLE TENJUIN, ILLEGAL INTRUDER !!
TEN-JUIN ?
WHO YOU CALLING AN ILLEGAL INTRUDER, YOU WEIRDO!!
G-G-GRAND-MOTHER!
KYLE! WHAT ARE YOU DOING, YOU LITTLE FOOL?!
VVWOOP

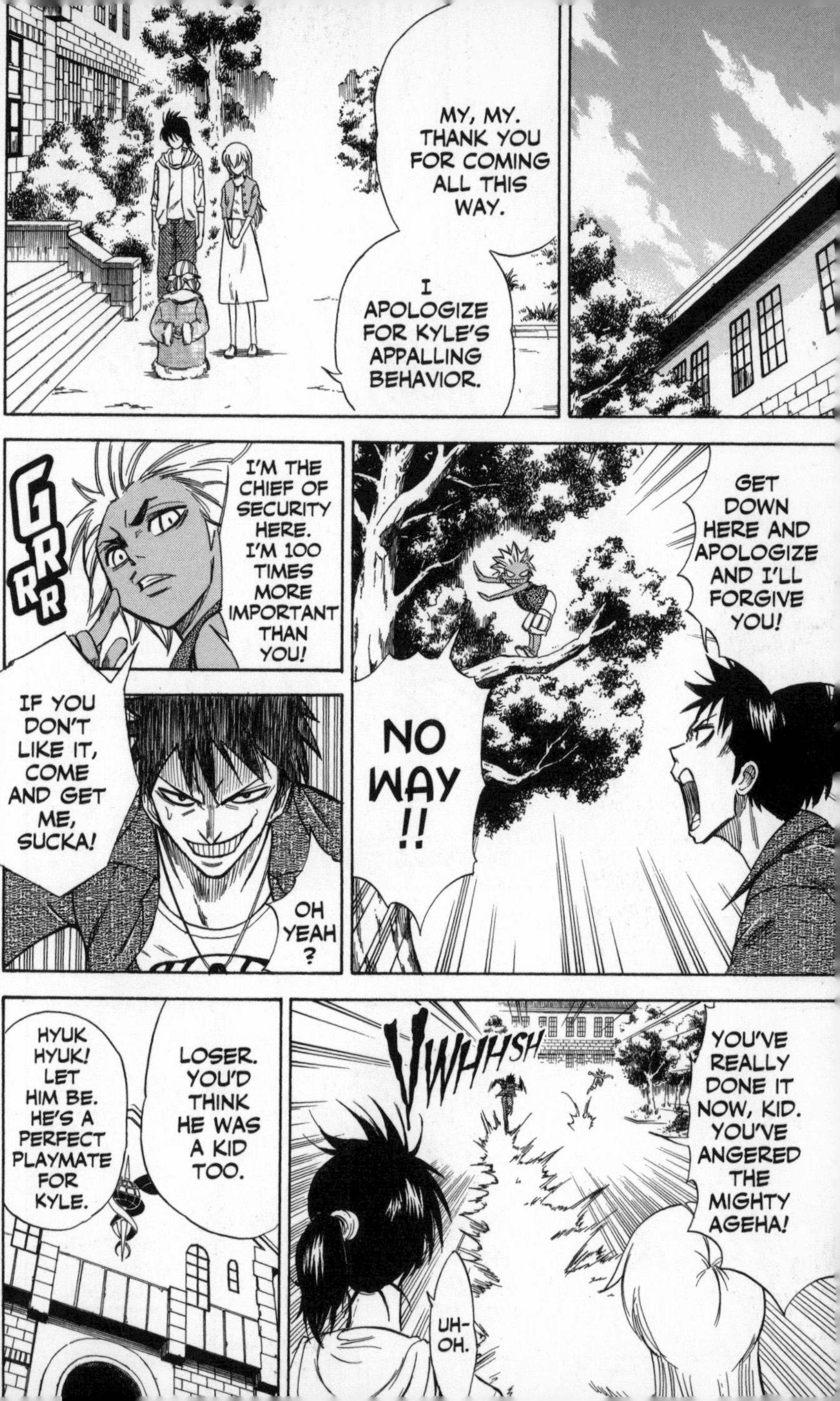
MY, MY. THANK YOU FOR COMING ALL THIS WAY.
I APOLOGIZE FOR KYLE'S APPALLING BEHAVIOR.
GET DOWN HERE AND APOLOGIZE AND I'LL FORGIVE YOU!
NO WAY!!
GRRR
I'M THE CHIEF OF SECURITY HERE. I'M 100 TIMES MORE IMPORTANT THAN YOU!
IF YOU DON'T LIKE IT, COME AND GET ME, SUCKA!
OH YEAH?
YOU'VE REALLY DONE IT NOW, KID. YOU'VE ANGERED THE MIGHTY AGEHA!
VWHHSH
UH-OH.
LOSER. YOU'D THINK HE WAS A KID TOO.
HYUK HYUK! LET HIM BE. HE'S A PERFECT PLAYMATE FOR KYLE.

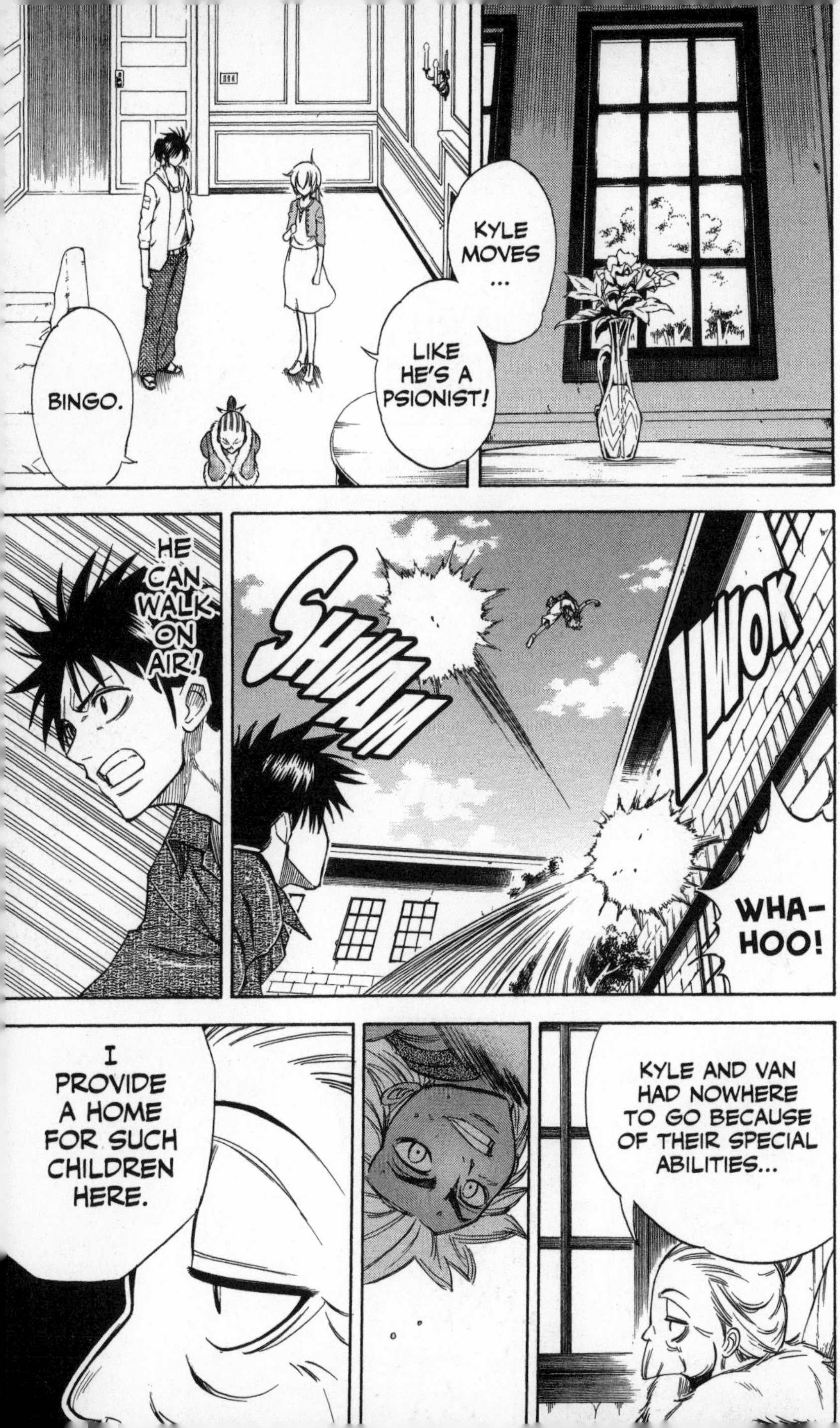
KYLE MOVES ...
LIKE HE'S A PSIONIST!
BINGO.
VWOK
WHA-HOO!
SHWAM
HE CAN WALK ON AIR!
KYLE AND VAN HAD NOWHERE TO GO BECAUSE OF THEIR SPECIAL ABILITIES...
I PROVIDE A HOME FOR SUCH CHILDREN HERE.

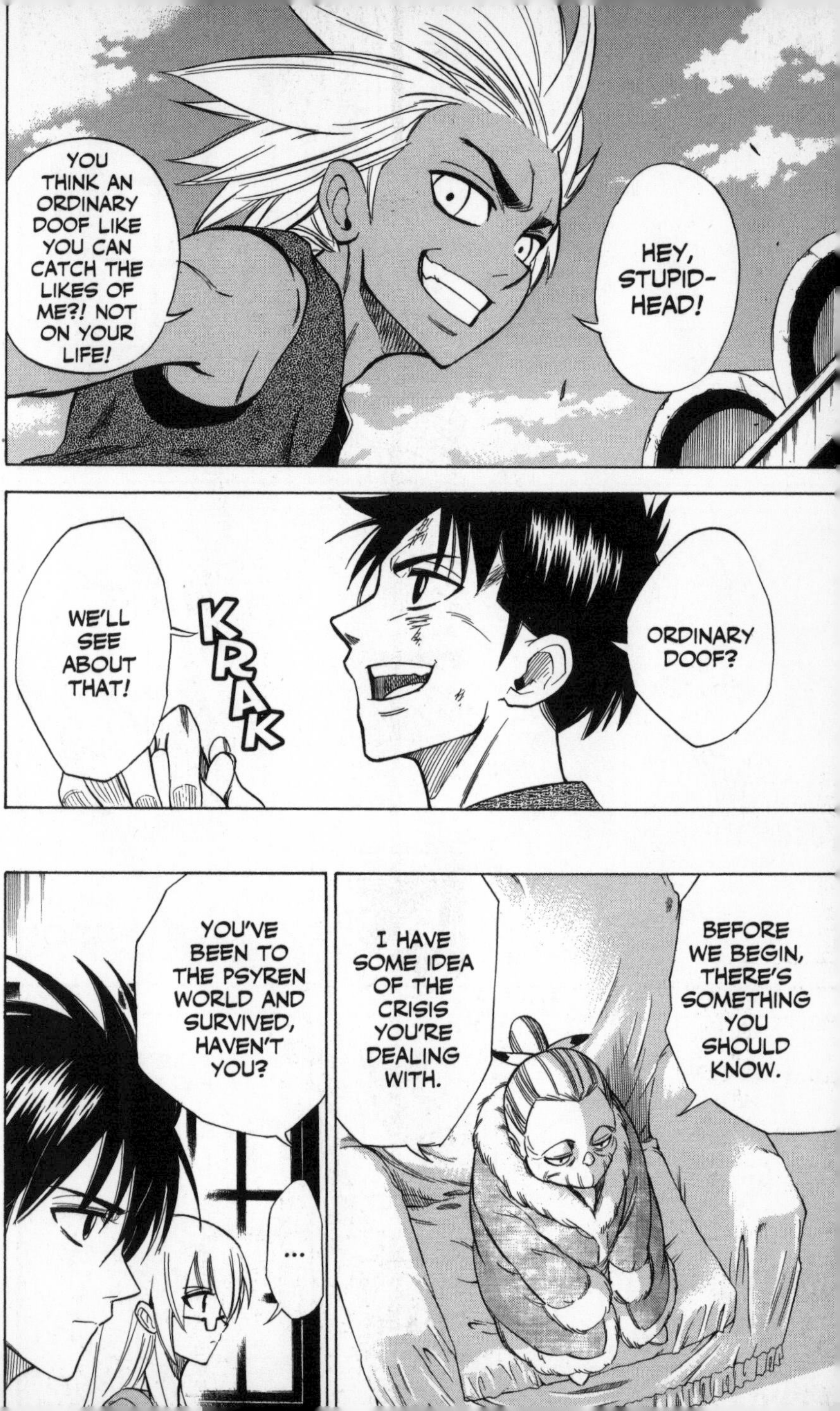
HEY, STUPID-HEAD!
YOU THINK AN ORDINARY DOOF LIKE YOU CAN CATCH THE LIKES OF ME?! NOT ON YOUR LIFE!
ORDINARY DOOF?
KRAK
WE'LL SEE ABOUT THAT!
BEFORE WE BEGIN, THERE'S SOMETHING YOU SHOULD KNOW.
I HAVE SOME IDEA OF THE CRISIS YOU'RE DEALING WITH.
YOU'VE BEEN TO THE PSYREN WORLD AND SURVIVED, HAVEN'T YOU?
...

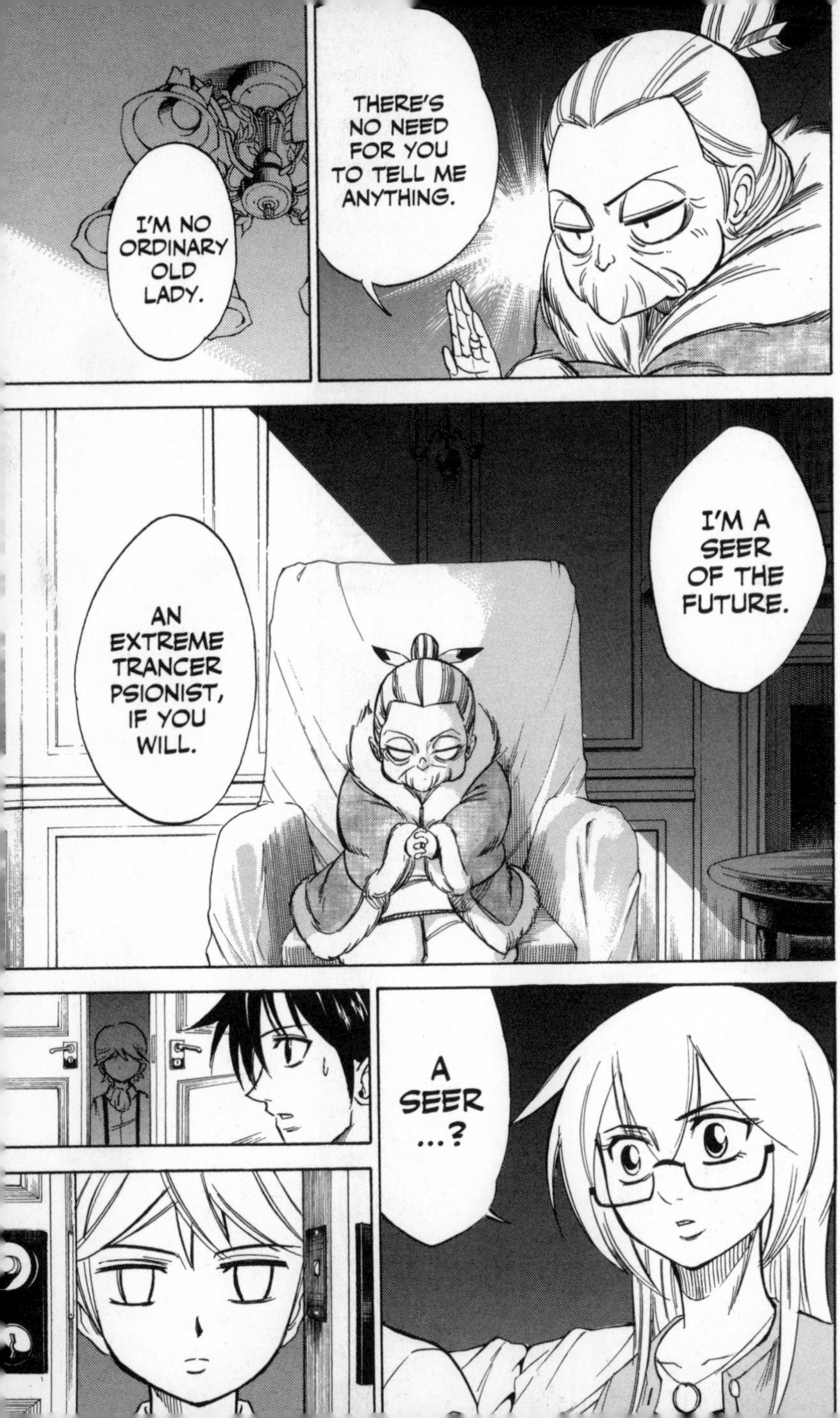
THERE'S NO NEED FOR YOU TO TELL ME ANYTHING.
I'M NO ORDINARY OLD LADY.
I'M A SEER OF THE FUTURE.
AN EXTREME TRANCER PSIONIST, IF YOU WILL.
A SEER ...?

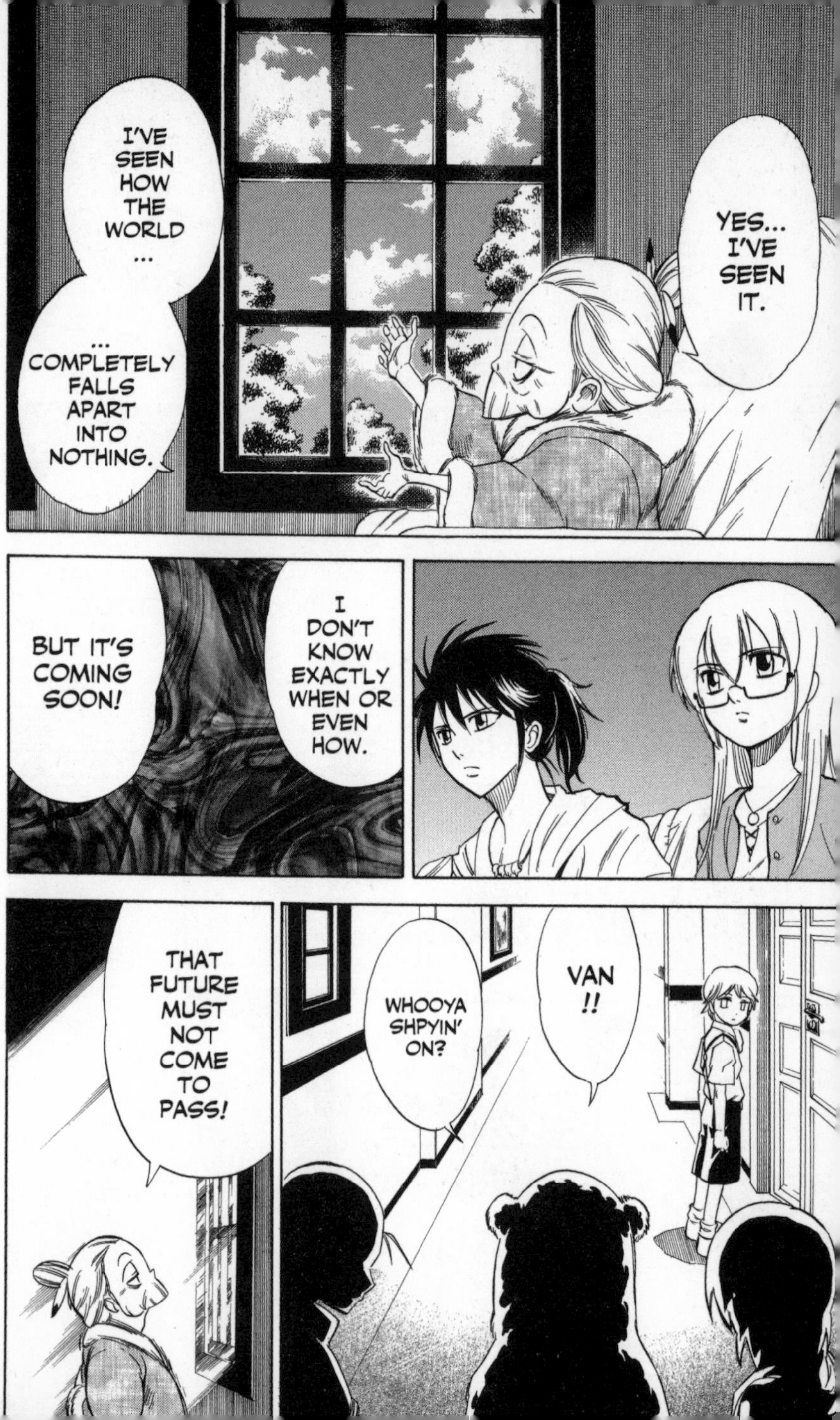
YES... I'VE SEEN IT.
I'VE SEEN HOW THE WORLD ...
... COMPLETELY FALLS APART INTO NOTHING.
I DON'T KNOW EXACTLY WHEN OR EVEN HOW.
BUT IT'S COMING SOON!
VAN !!
WHOOYA SHPYIN' ON?
THAT FUTURE MUST NOT COME TO PASS!

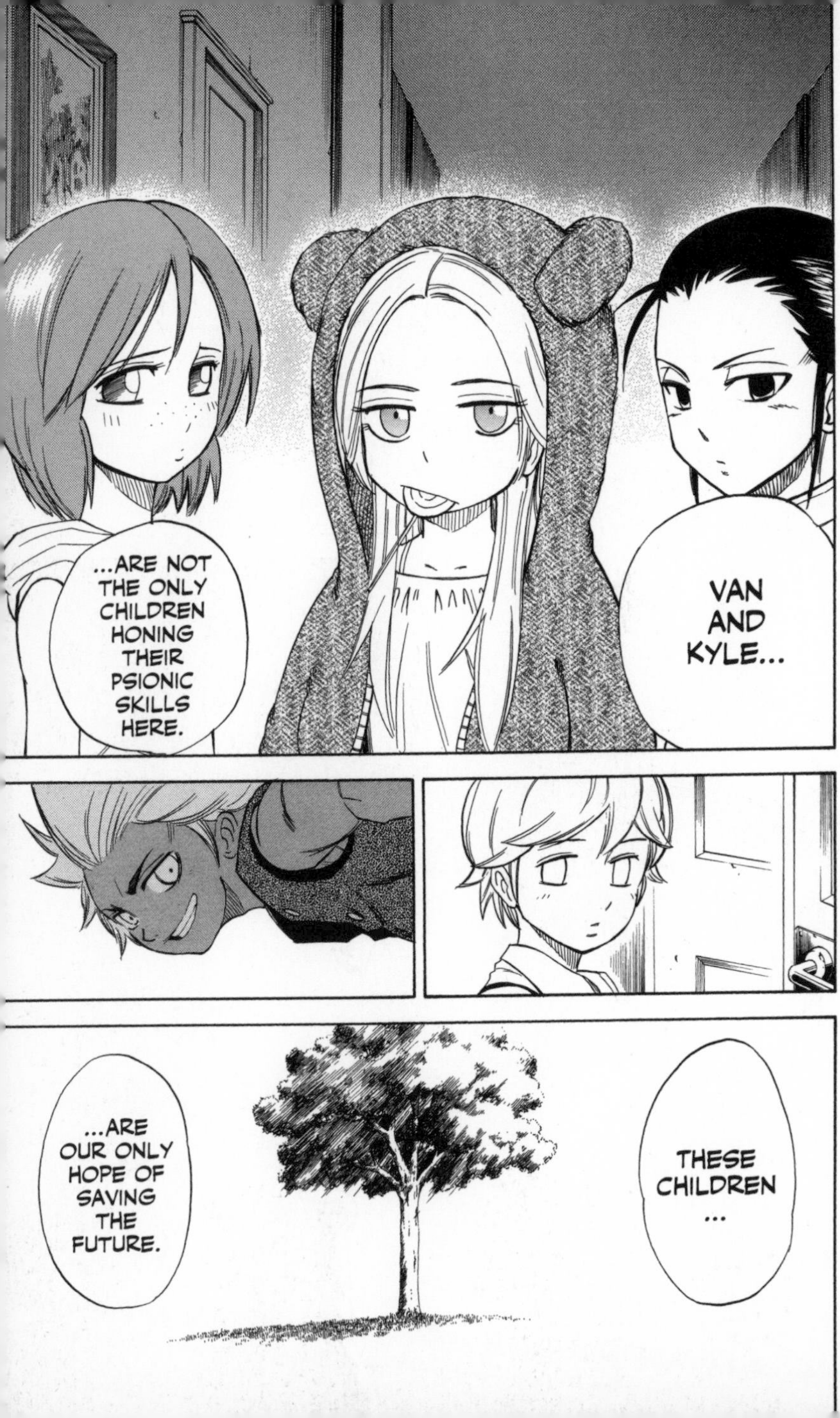
VAN AND KYLE...
...ARE NOT THE ONLY CHILDREN HONING THEIR PSIONIC SKILLS HERE.
THESE CHILDREN ...
...ARE OUR ONLY HOPE OF SAVING THE FUTURE.

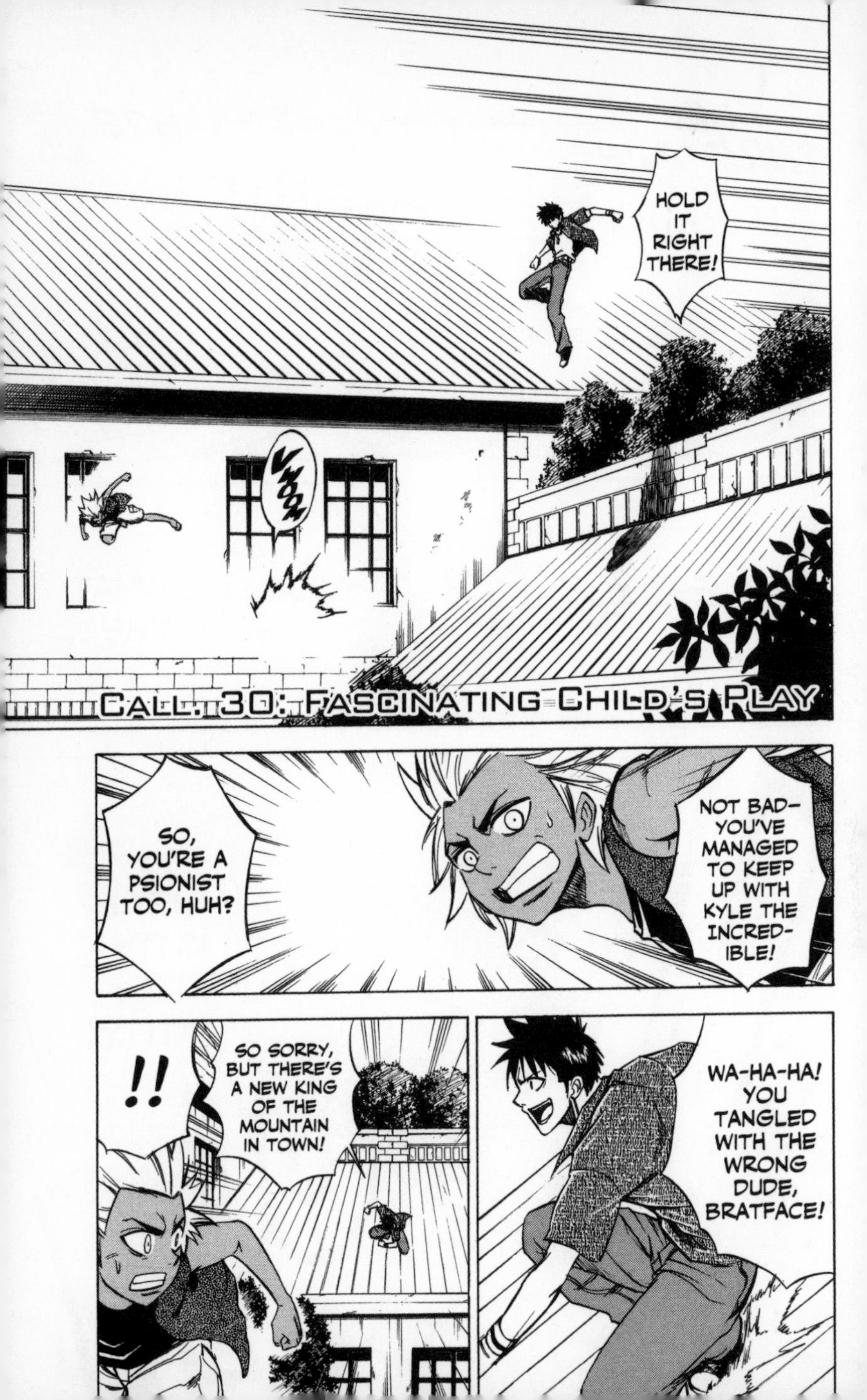
HOLD IT RIGHT THERE!
VWOOM
CALL. 30: FASCINATING CHILD'S PLAY
NOT BAD—YOU'VE MANAGED TO KEEP UP WITH KYLE THE INCREDIBLE!
SO, YOU'RE A PSIONIST TOO, HUH?
WA-HA-HA! YOU TANGLED WITH THE WRONG DUDE, BRATFACE!
SO SORRY, BUT THERE'S A NEW KING OF THE MOUNTAIN IN TOWN!
!!

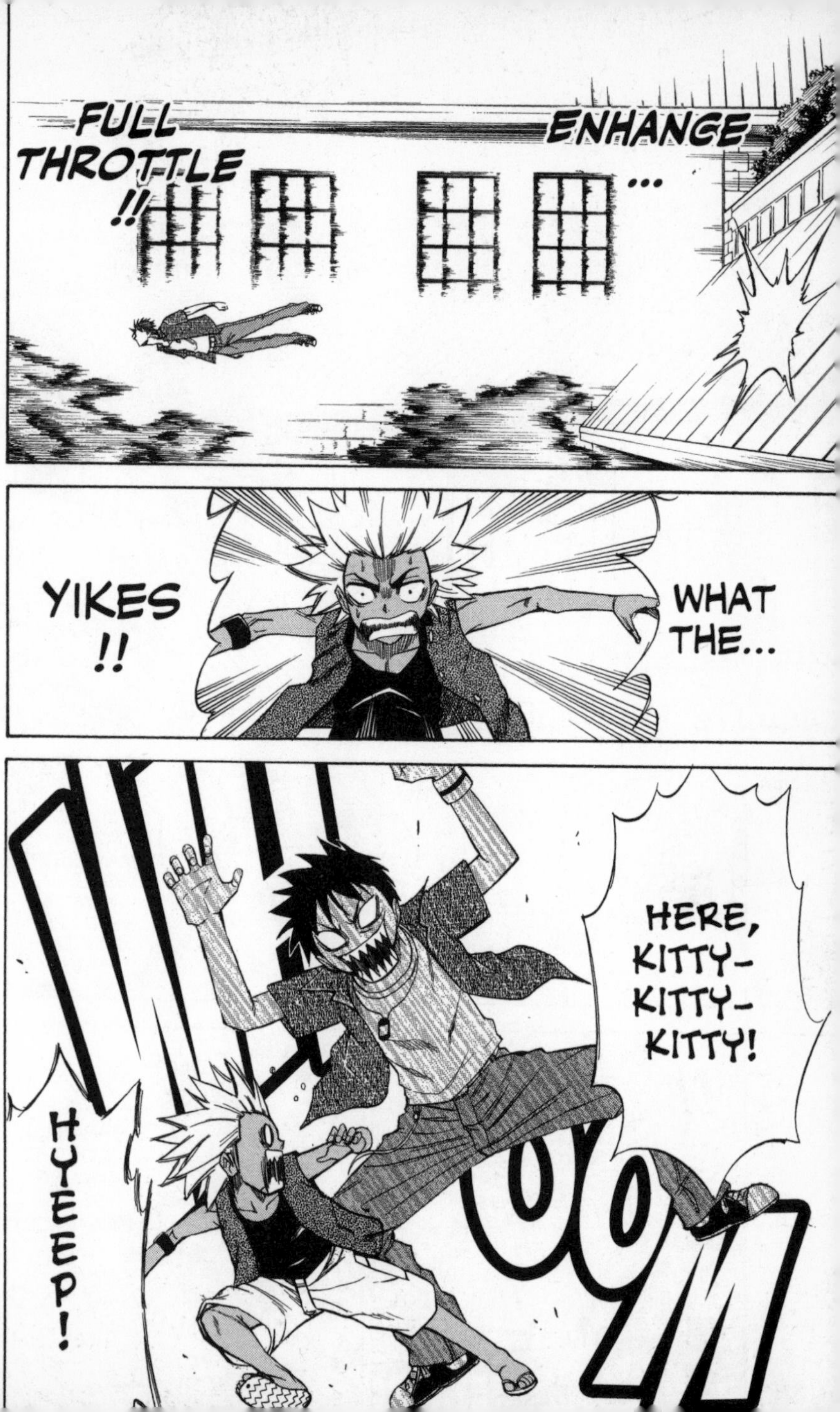
ENHANCE...
FULL THROTTLE!!
WHAT THE...
YIKES!!
HERE, KITTY-KITTY-KITTY!
HYEEEP!

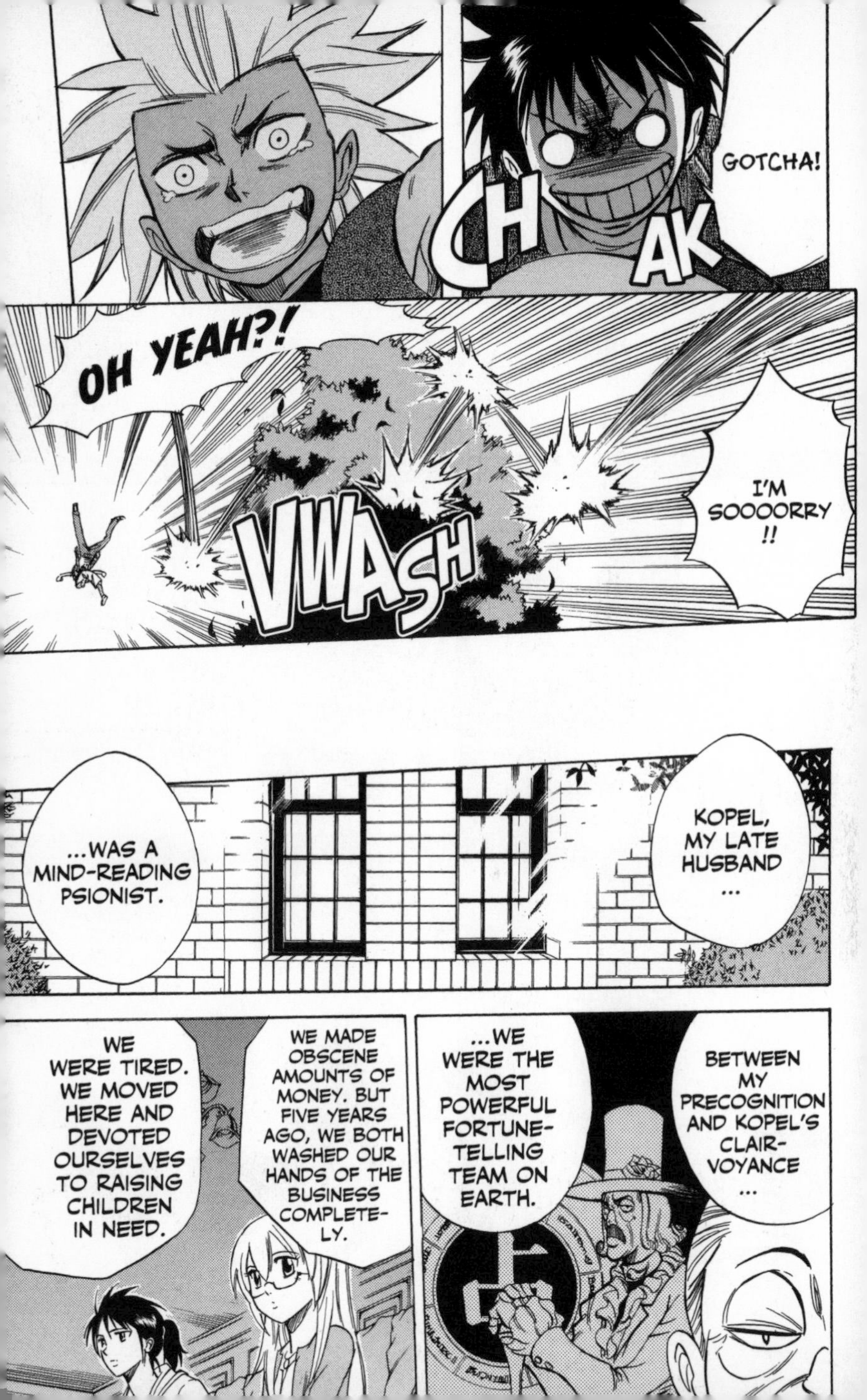
GOTCHA!
CHAK
I'M SOOOORRY!!
VWASH
OH YEAH?!
KOPEL, MY LATE HUSBAND...
...WAS A MIND-READING PSIONIST.
BETWEEN MY PRECOGNITION AND KOPEL'S CLAIR-VOYANCE...
...WE WERE THE MOST POWERFUL FORTUNE-TELLING TEAM ON EARTH.
WE MADE OBSCENE AMOUNTS OF MONEY. BUT FIVE YEARS AGO, WE BOTH WASHED OUR HANDS OF THE BUSINESS COMPLETE-LY.
WE WERE TIRED. WE MOVED HERE AND DEVOTED OURSELVES TO RAISING CHILDREN IN NEED.

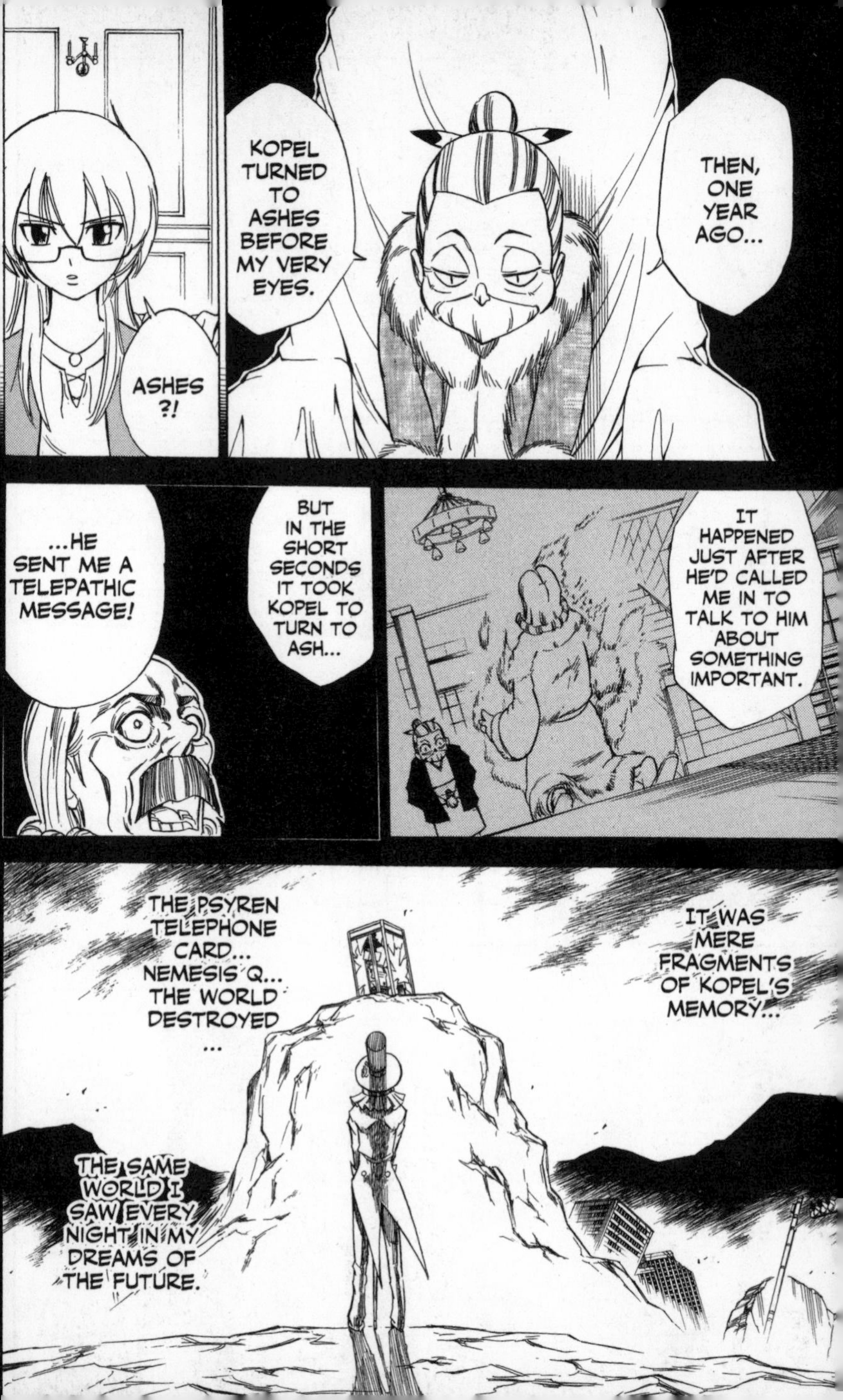
THEN, ONE YEAR AGO...
KOPEL TURNED TO ASHES BEFORE MY VERY EYES.
ASHES ?!
IT HAPPENED JUST AFTER HE'D CALLED ME IN TO TALK TO HIM ABOUT SOMETHING IMPORTANT.
BUT IN THE SHORT SECONDS IT TOOK KOPEL TO TURN TO ASH...
...HE SENT ME A TELEPATHIC MESSAGE!
IT WAS MERE FRAGMENTS OF KOPEL'S MEMORY...
THE PSYREN TELEPHONE CARD... NEMESIS Q... THE WORLD DESTROYED ...
THE SAME WORLD I SAW EVERY NIGHT IN MY DREAMS OF THE FUTURE.

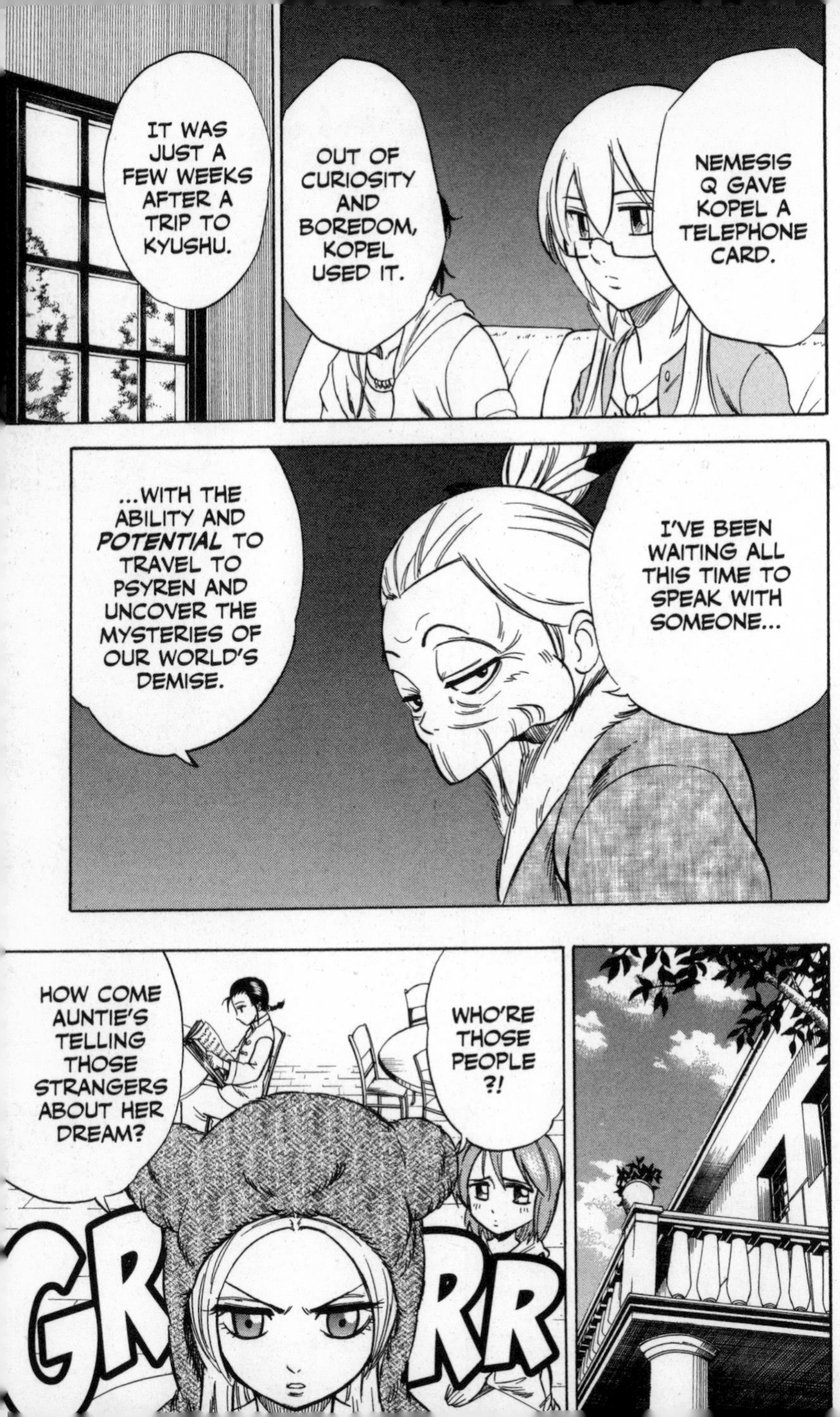
NEMESIS Q GAVE KOPEL A TELEPHONE CARD.
OUT OF CURIOSITY AND BOREDOM, KOPEL USED IT.
IT WAS JUST A FEW WEEKS AFTER A TRIP TO KYUSHU.
I'VE BEEN WAITING ALL THIS TIME TO SPEAK WITH SOMEONE...
...WITH THE ABILITY AND *POTENTIAL* TO TRAVEL TO PSYREN AND UNCOVER THE MYSTERIES OF OUR WORLD'S DEMISE.
WHO'RE THOSE PEOPLE?!
HOW COME AUNTIE'S TELLING THOSE STRANGERS ABOUT HER DREAM?
GR RR

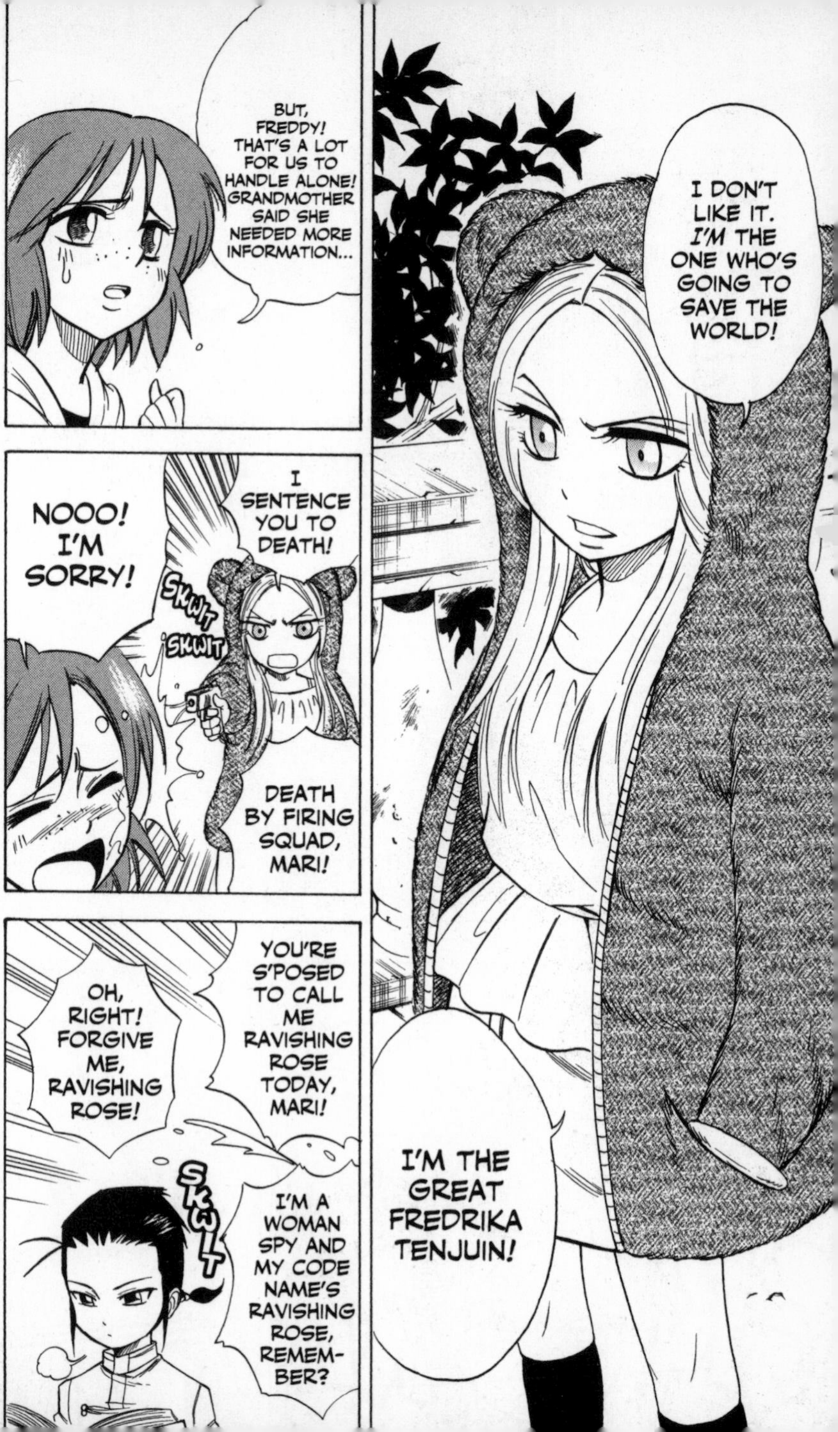
I DON'T LIKE IT. *I'M* THE ONE WHO'S GOING TO SAVE THE WORLD!
I'M THE GREAT FREDRIKA TENJUIN!
BUT, FREDDY! THAT'S A LOT FOR US TO HANDLE ALONE! GRANDMOTHER SAID SHE NEEDED MORE INFORMATION...
I SENTENCE YOU TO DEATH!
SKWIT
SKWIT
DEATH BY FIRING SQUAD, MARI!
NOOO! I'M SORRY!
YOU'RE S'POSED TO CALL ME RAVISHING ROSE TODAY, MARI!
OH, RIGHT! FORGIVE ME, RAVISHING ROSE!
SKWIT
I'M A WOMAN SPY AND MY CODE NAME'S RAVISHING ROSE, REMEMBER?

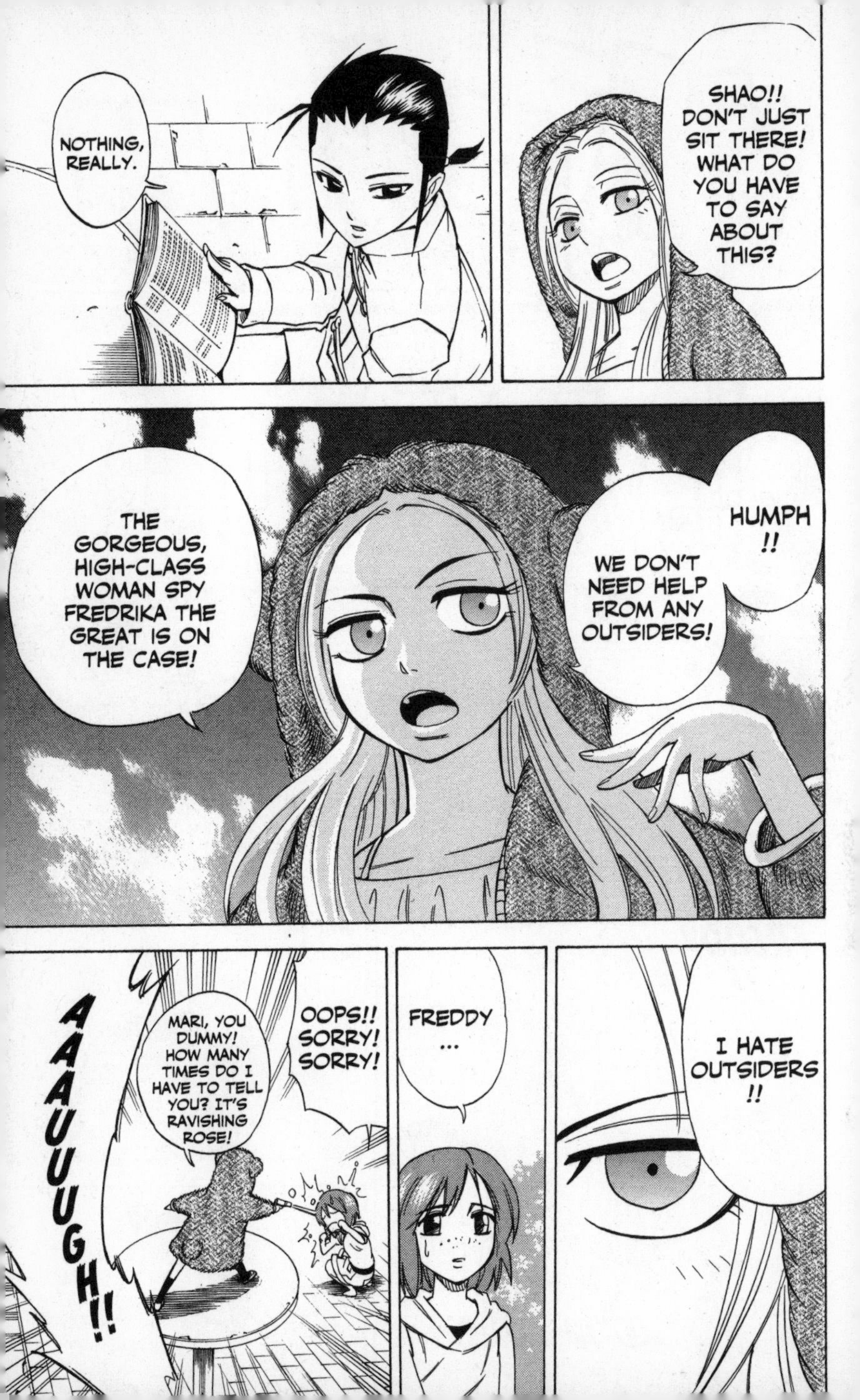
SHAO!! DON'T JUST SIT THERE! WHAT DO YOU HAVE TO SAY ABOUT THIS?
NOTHING, REALLY.
HUMPH !!
WE DON'T NEED HELP FROM ANY OUTSIDERS!
THE GORGEOUS, HIGH-CLASS WOMAN SPY FREDRIKA THE GREAT IS ON THE CASE!
I HATE OUTSIDERS !!
FREDDY ...
OOPS!! SORRY! SORRY!
MARI, YOU DUMMY! HOW MANY TIMES DO I HAVE TO TELL YOU? IT'S RAVISHING ROSE!
AAAUUUGH!!

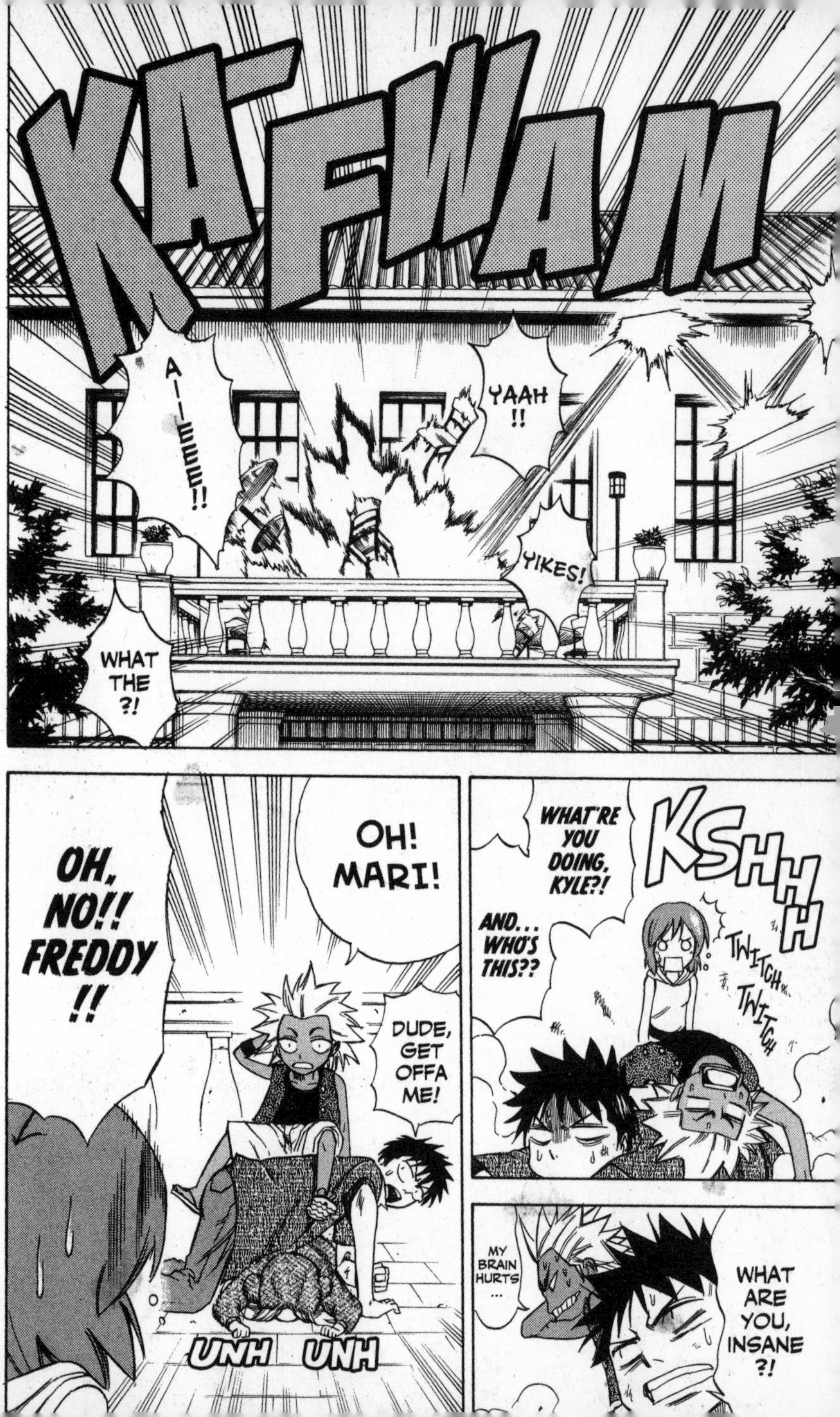
KA-FWAM
YAAH!!
A-IIEEEE!!
YIKES!
WHAT THE?!
KSHHHH
WHAT'RE YOU DOING, KYLE?!
TWITCH TWITCH
AND... WHO'S THIS??
WHAT ARE YOU, INSANE?!
MY BRAIN HURTS...
OH! MARI!
DUDE, GET OFFA ME!
OH, NO!! FREDDY!!
UNH UNH

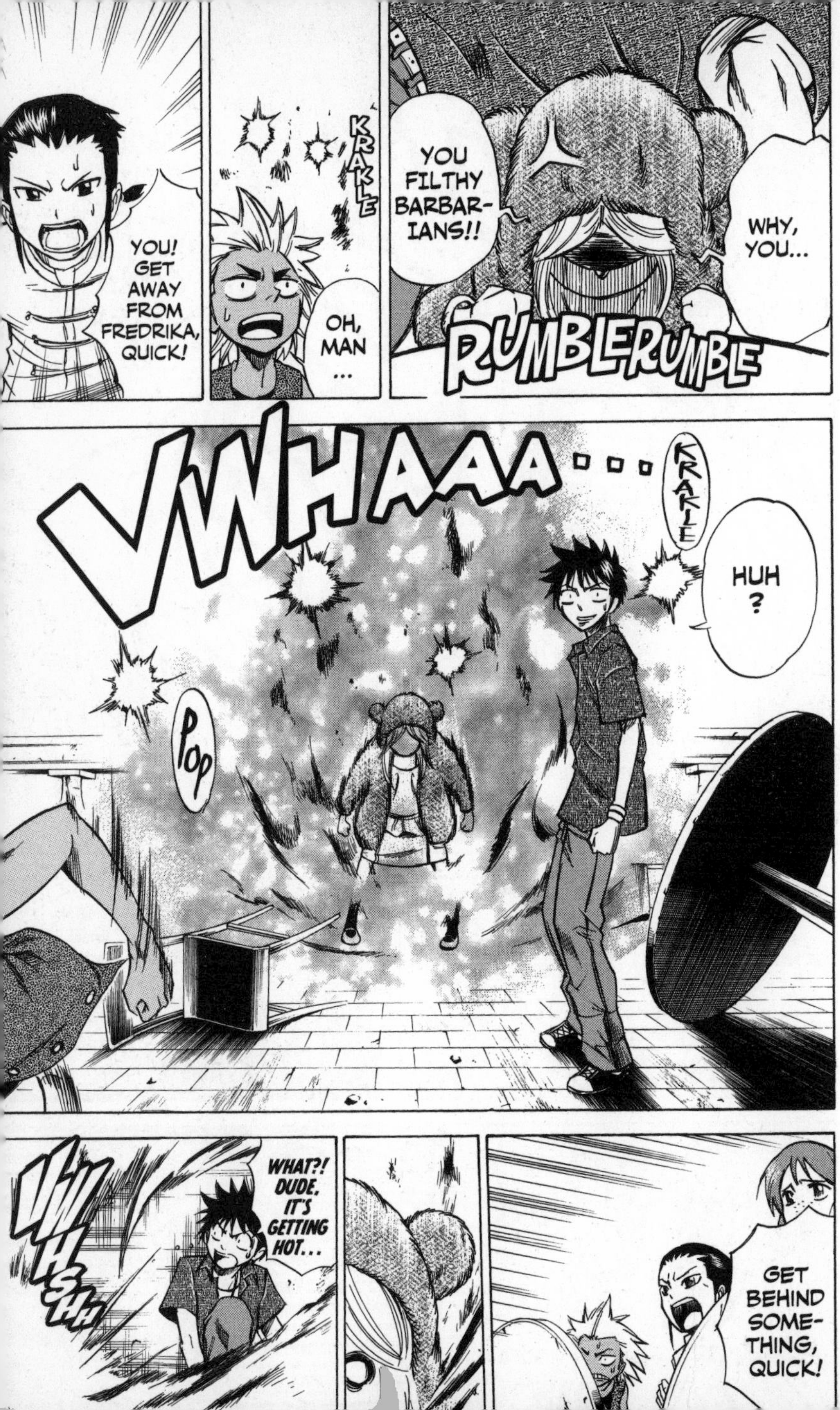
WHY, YOU...
YOU FILTHY BARBARIANS!!
RUMBLERUMBLE
KRAKLE
OH, MAN...
YOU! GET AWAY FROM FREDRIKA, QUICK!
KRAKLE
HUH?
VWHAAA...
POP
GET BEHIND SOMETHING, QUICK!
WHAT?! DUDE. IT'S GETTING HOT...
VWHSHH

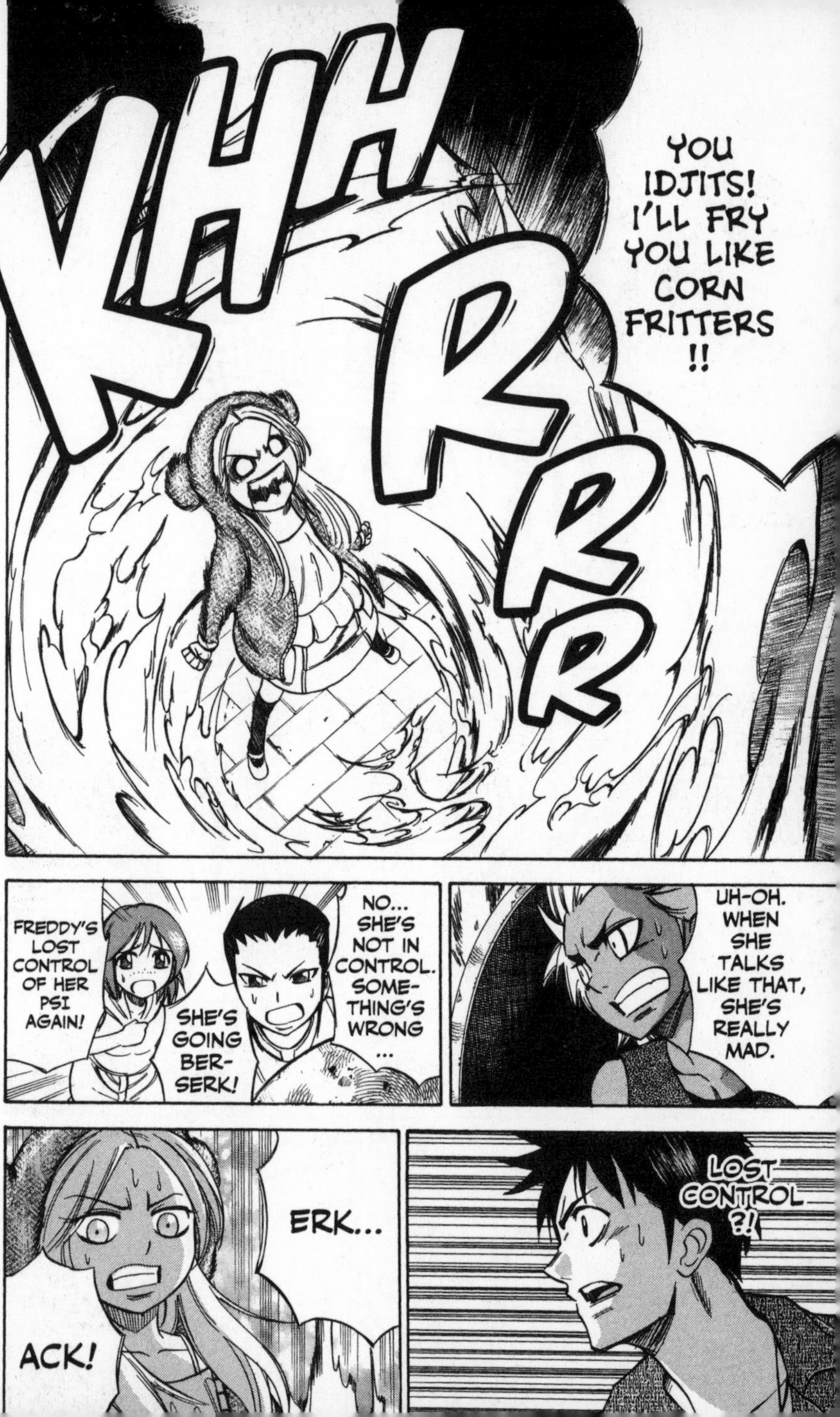
VHHRRR
YOU IDJITS! I'LL FRY YOU LIKE CORN FRITTERS!!
UH-OH. WHEN SHE TALKS LIKE THAT, SHE'S REALLY MAD.
NO... SHE'S NOT IN CONTROL. SOME-THING'S WRONG...
FREDDY'S LOST CONTROL OF HER PSI AGAIN!
SHE'S GOING BER-SERK!
LOST CONTROL?!
ERK...
ACK!

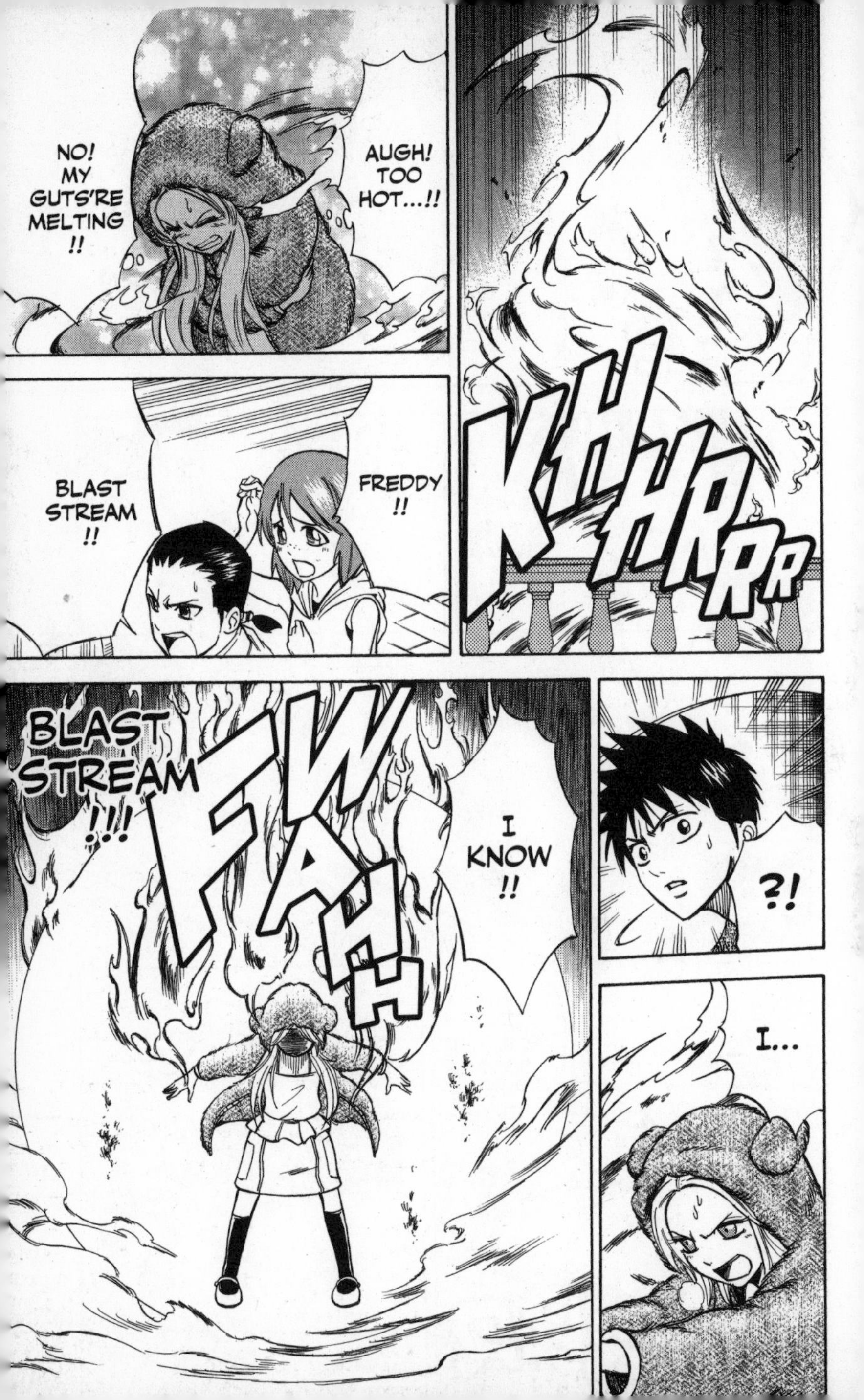
KHHRRR
AUGH! TOO HOT...!!
NO! MY GUTS'RE MELTING !!
FREDDY !!
BLAST STREAM !!
?!
I...
I KNOW !!
FWAHH
BLAST STREAM !!!

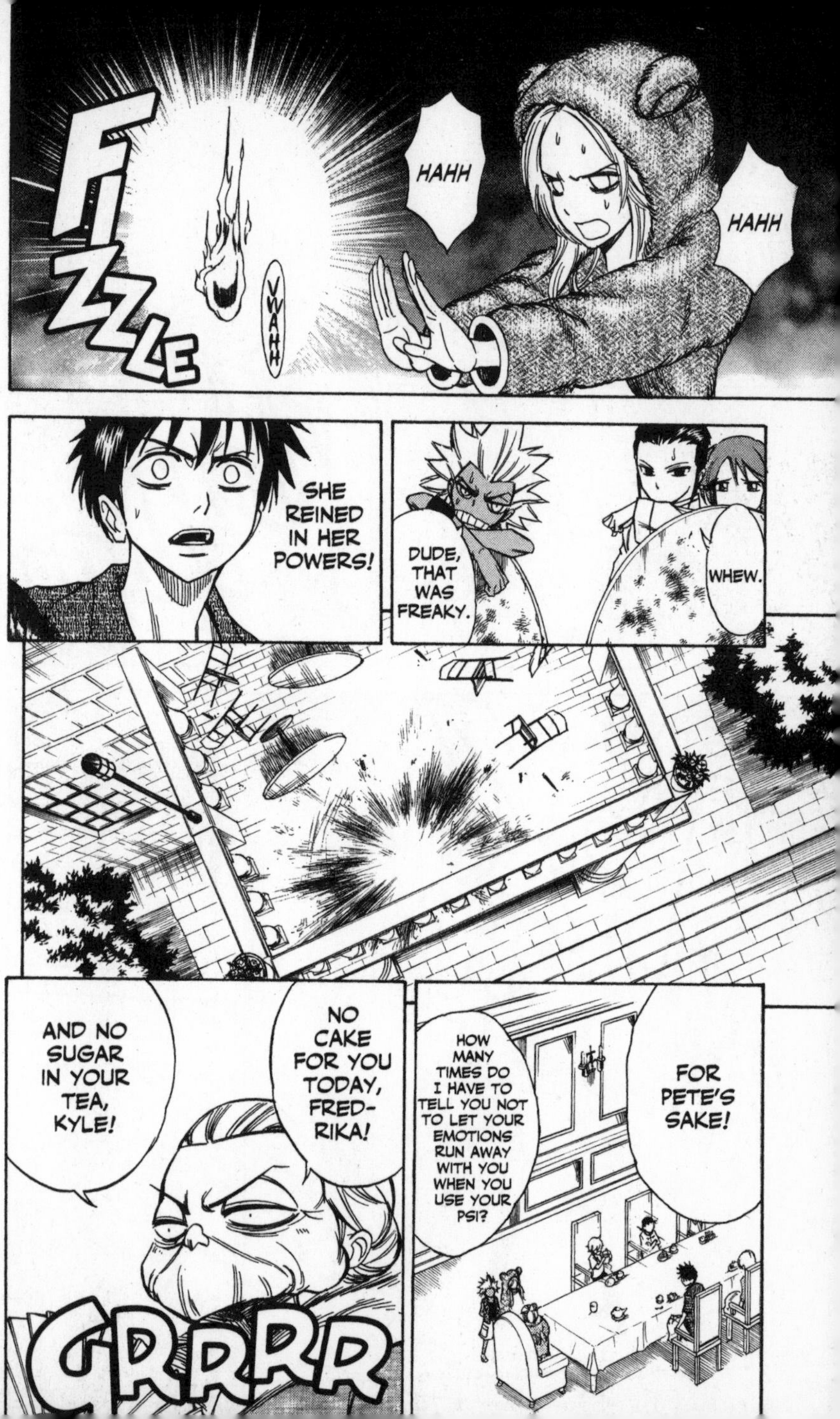
HAHH
HAHH
FIZZLE
VWAHH
WHEW.
DUDE, THAT WAS FREAKY.
SHE REINED IN HER POWERS!
FOR PETE'S SAKE!
HOW MANY TIMES DO I HAVE TO TELL YOU NOT TO LET YOUR EMOTIONS RUN AWAY WITH YOU WHEN YOU USE YOUR PSI?
NO CAKE FOR YOU TODAY, FRED-RIKA!
AND NO SUGAR IN YOUR TEA, KYLE!
GRRRR

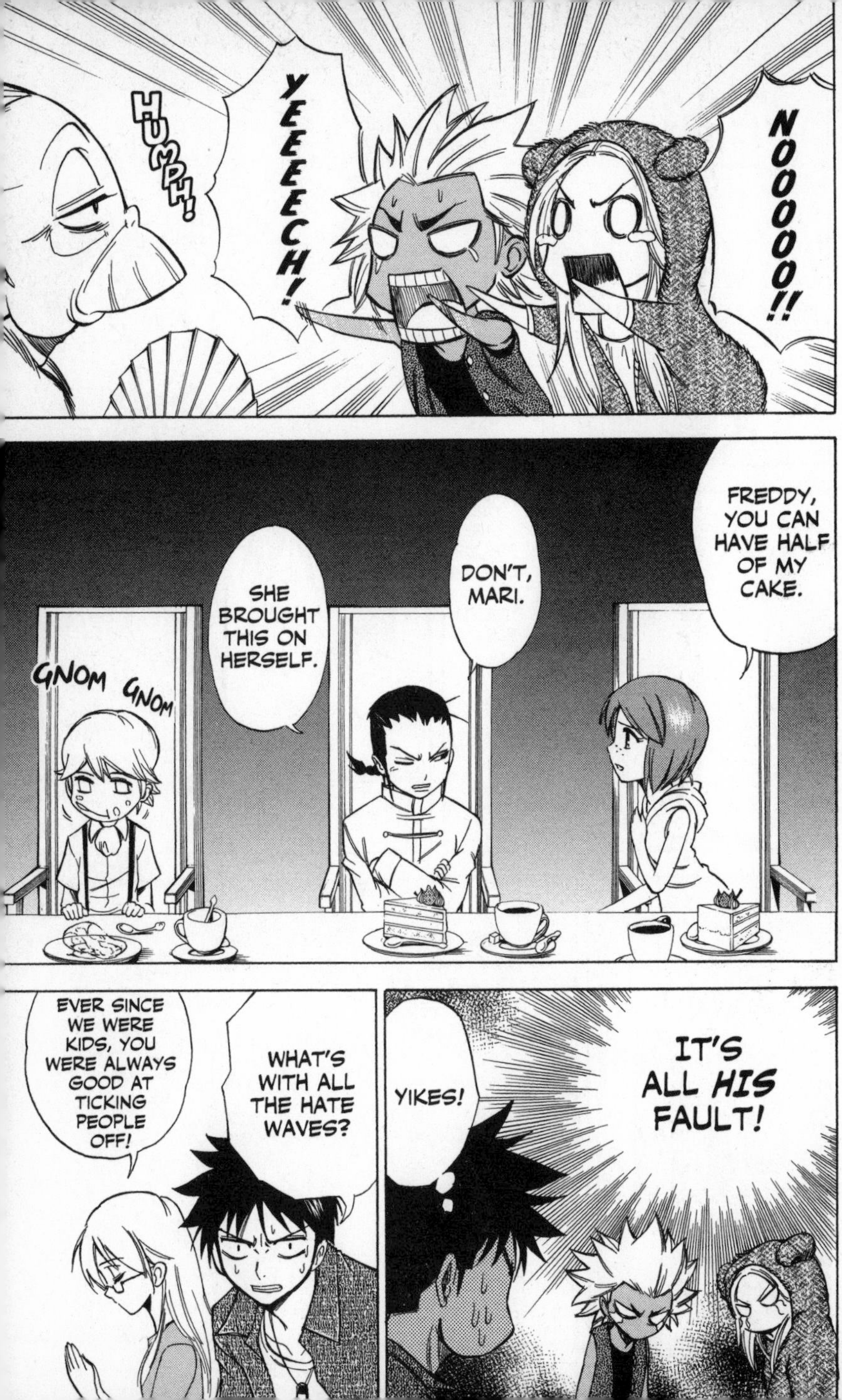
NOOOOOO!!
YEEEEECH!
HUMPH!
FREDDY, YOU CAN HAVE HALF OF MY CAKE.
DON'T, MARI.
SHE BROUGHT THIS ON HERSELF.
GNOM GNOM
IT'S ALL *HIS* FAULT!
YIKES!
WHAT'S WITH ALL THE HATE WAVES?
EVER SINCE WE WERE KIDS, YOU WERE ALWAYS GOOD AT TICKING PEOPLE OFF!

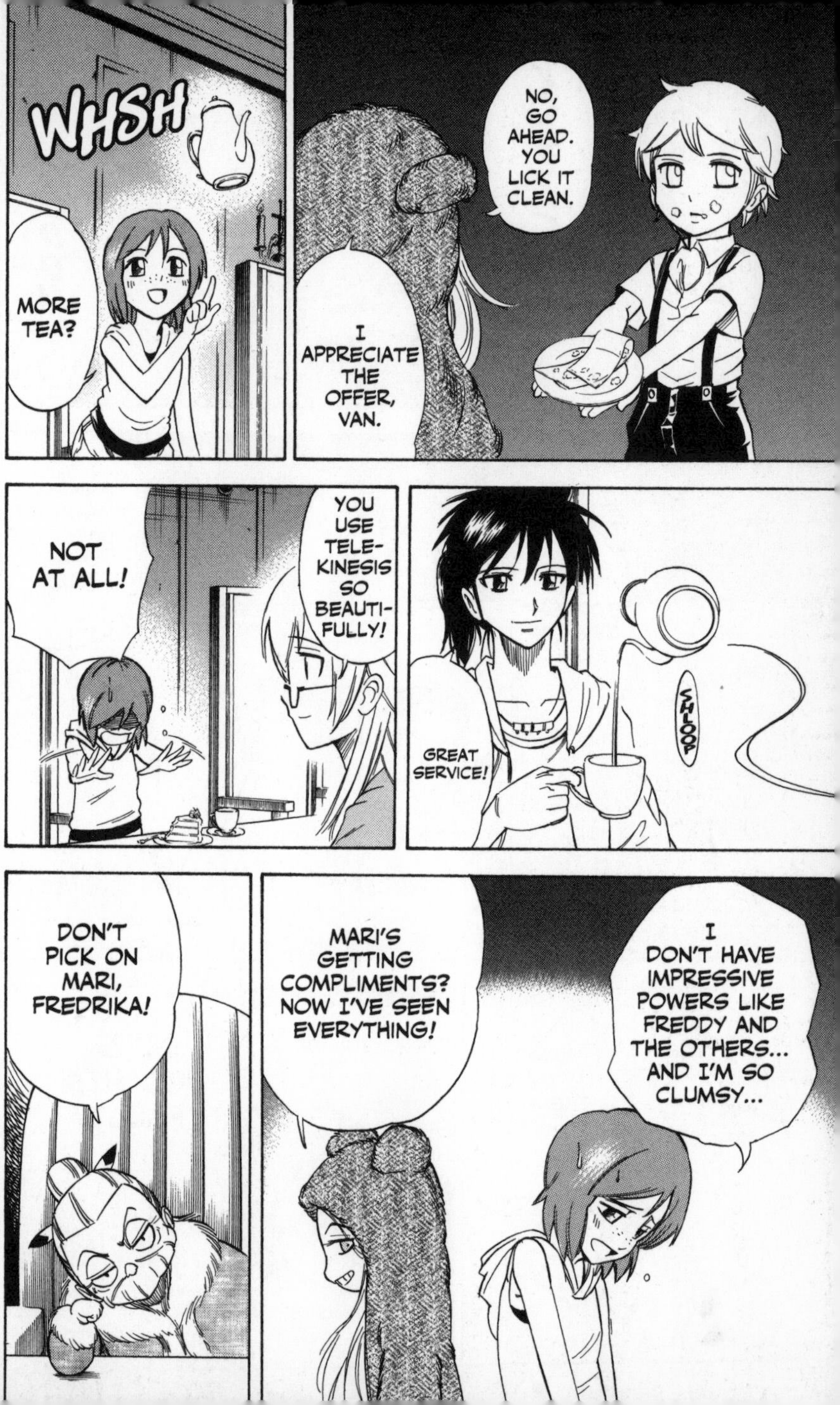
NO, GO AHEAD. YOU LICK IT CLEAN.
I APPRECIATE THE OFFER, VAN.
WHSH
MORE TEA?
SHLOOP
GREAT SERVICE!
YOU USE TELE-KINESIS SO BEAUTI-FULLY!
NOT AT ALL!
I DON'T HAVE IMPRESSIVE POWERS LIKE FREDDY AND THE OTHERS... AND I'M SO CLUMSY...
MARI'S GETTING COMPLIMENTS? NOW I'VE SEEN EVERYTHING!
DON'T PICK ON MARI, FREDRIKA!

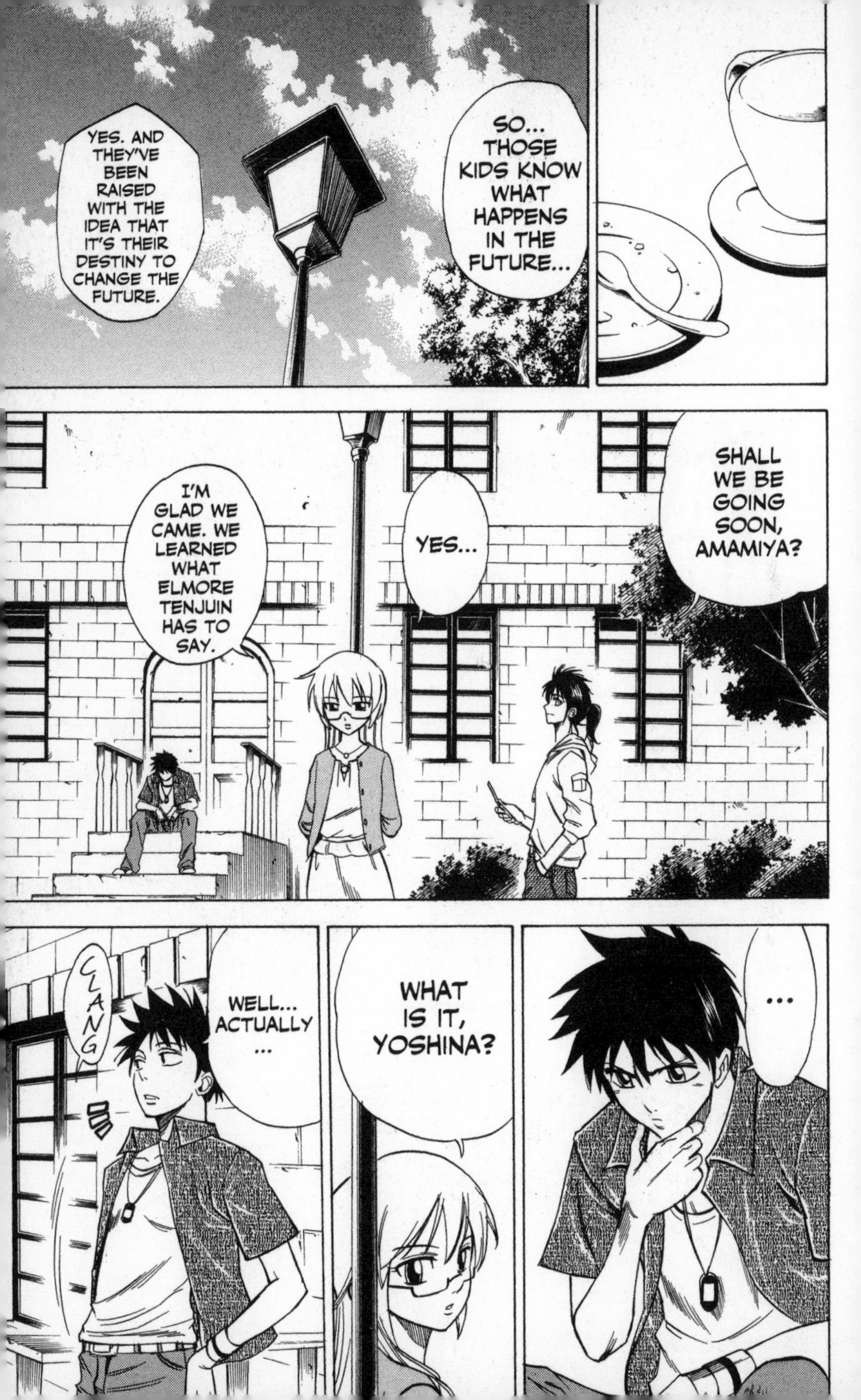
SO... THOSE KIDS KNOW WHAT HAPPENS IN THE FUTURE...
YES. AND THEY'VE BEEN RAISED WITH THE IDEA THAT IT'S THEIR DESTINY TO CHANGE THE FUTURE.
SHALL WE BE GOING SOON, AMAMIYA?
YES...
I'M GLAD WE CAME. WE LEARNED WHAT ELMORE TENJUIN HAS TO SAY.
...
WHAT IS IT, YOSHINA?
WELL... ACTUALLY ...
CLANG

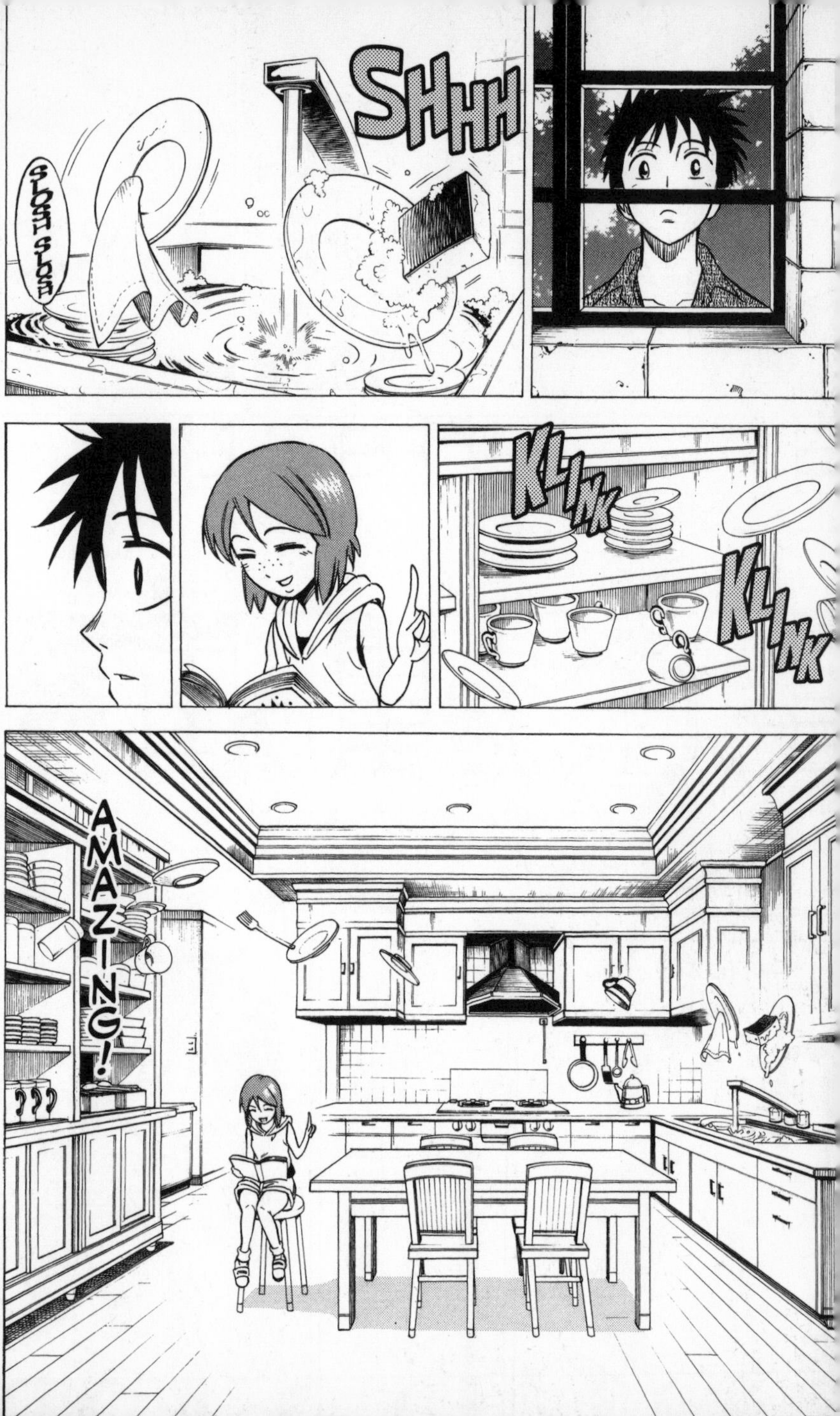
SHHH
SLOSH SLOSH
KLINK
KLINK
AMAZING!

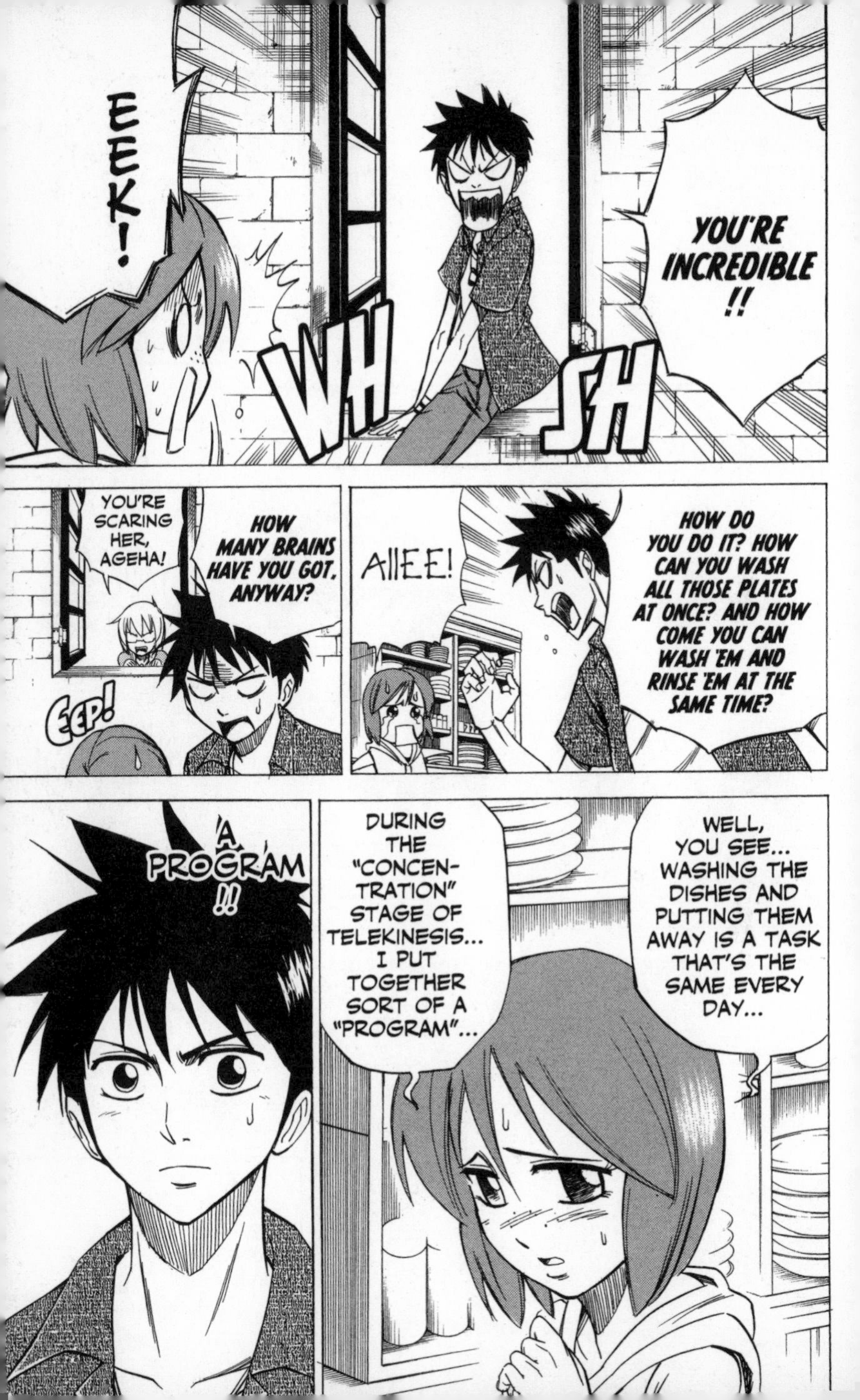

YOU'RE INCREDIBLE !!
WHSH
EEK!
HOW DO YOU DO IT? HOW CAN YOU WASH ALL THOSE PLATES AT ONCE? AND HOW COME YOU CAN WASH 'EM AND RINSE 'EM AT THE SAME TIME?
AIIEE!
HOW MANY BRAINS HAVE YOU GOT, ANYWAY?
YOU'RE SCARING HER, AGEHA!
EEP!
WELL, YOU SEE... WASHING THE DISHES AND PUTTING THEM AWAY IS A TASK THAT'S THE SAME EVERY DAY...
DURING THE "CONCENTRATION" STAGE OF TELEKINESIS... I PUT TOGETHER SORT OF A "PROGRAM"...
A PROGRAM !!

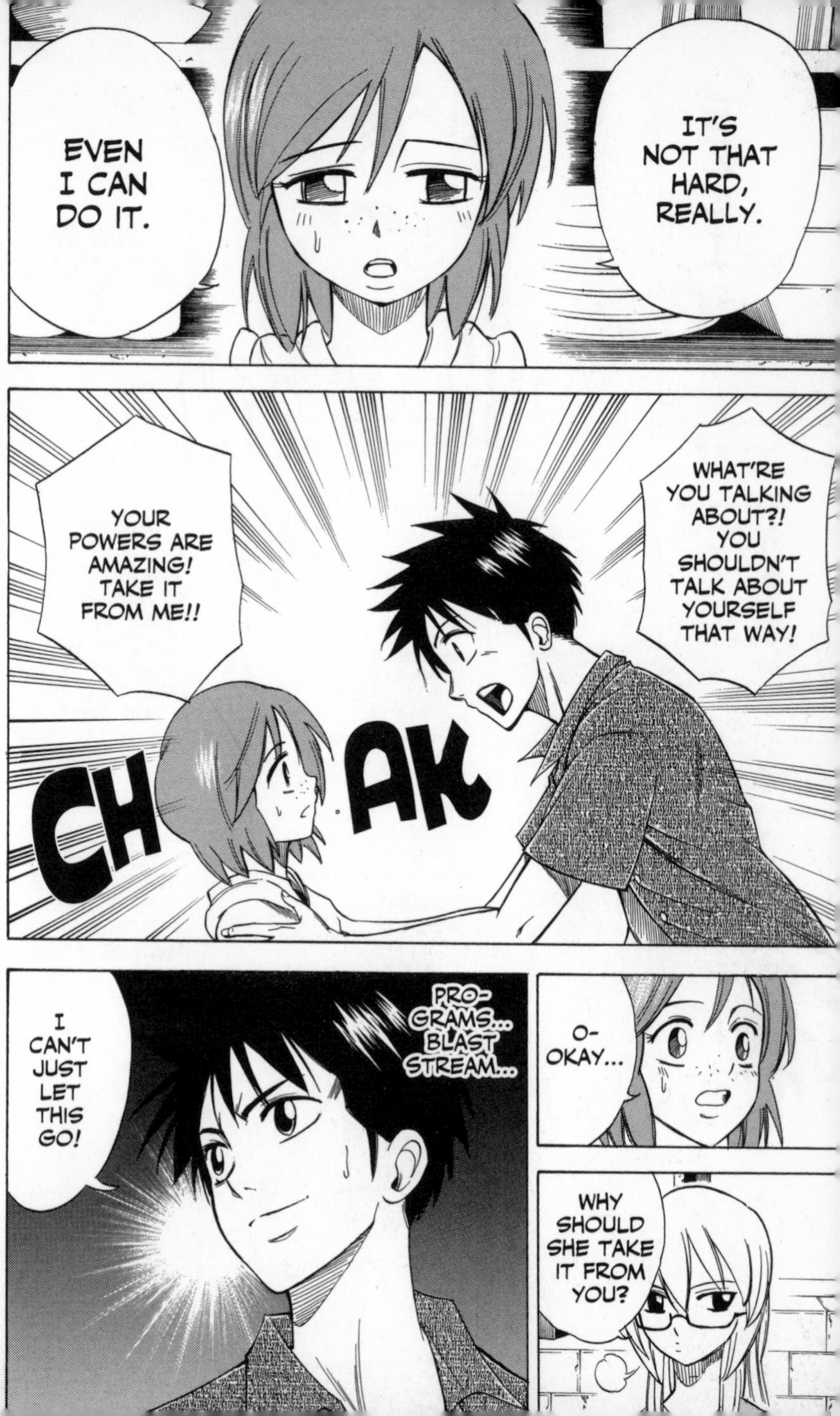
IT'S NOT THAT HARD, REALLY.
EVEN I CAN DO IT.
WHAT'RE YOU TALKING ABOUT?! YOU SHOULDN'T TALK ABOUT YOURSELF THAT WAY!
YOUR POWERS ARE AMAZING! TAKE IT FROM ME!!
CH AK
O-OKAY...
WHY SHOULD SHE TAKE IT FROM YOU?
PRO-GRAMS... BLAST STREAM...
I CAN'T JUST LET THIS GO!

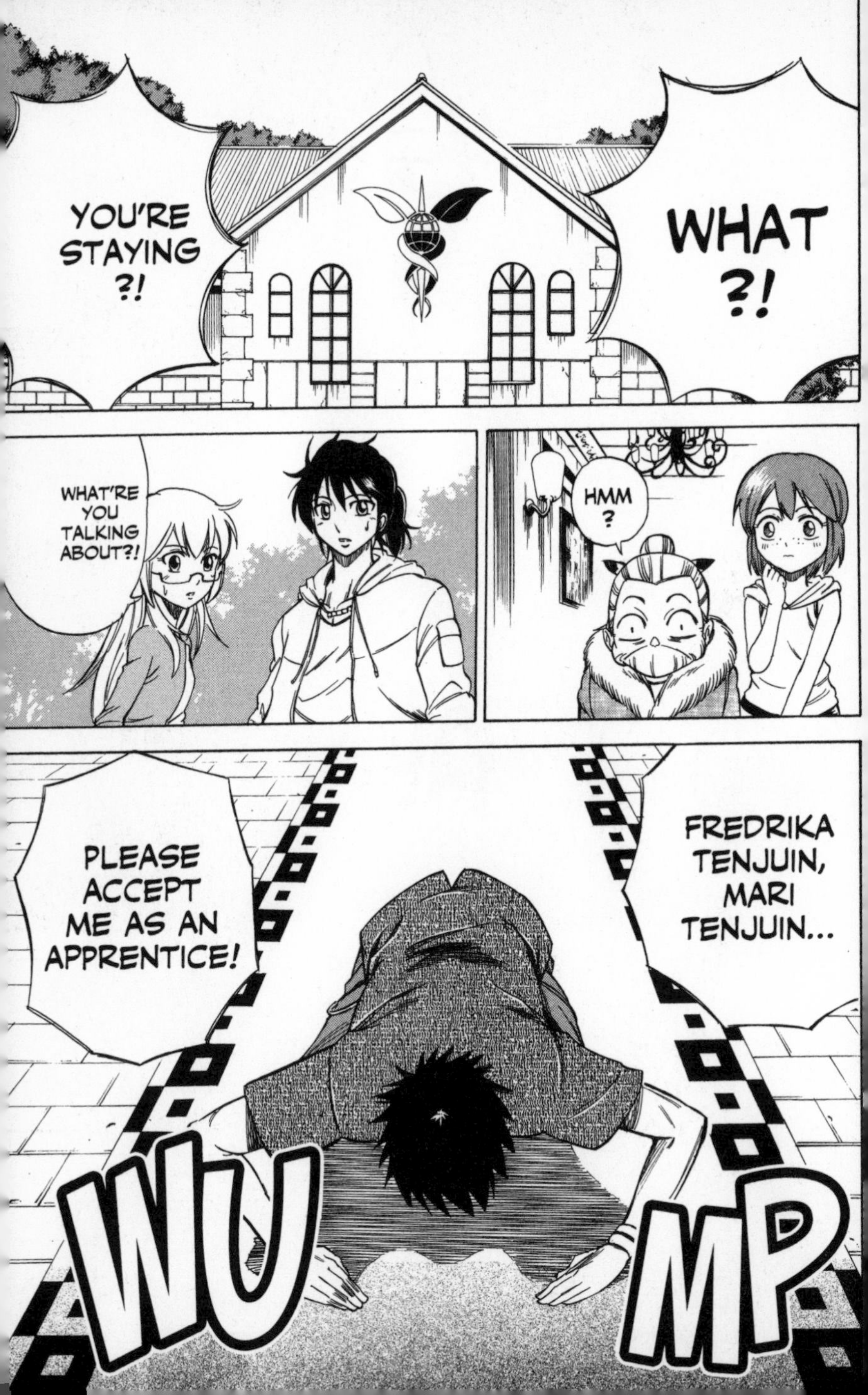
WHAT ?!
YOU'RE STAYING ?!
HMM ?
WHAT'RE YOU TALKING ABOUT?!
FREDRIKA TENJUIN, MARI TENJUIN...
PLEASE ACCEPT ME AS AN APPRENTICE!
WUMP

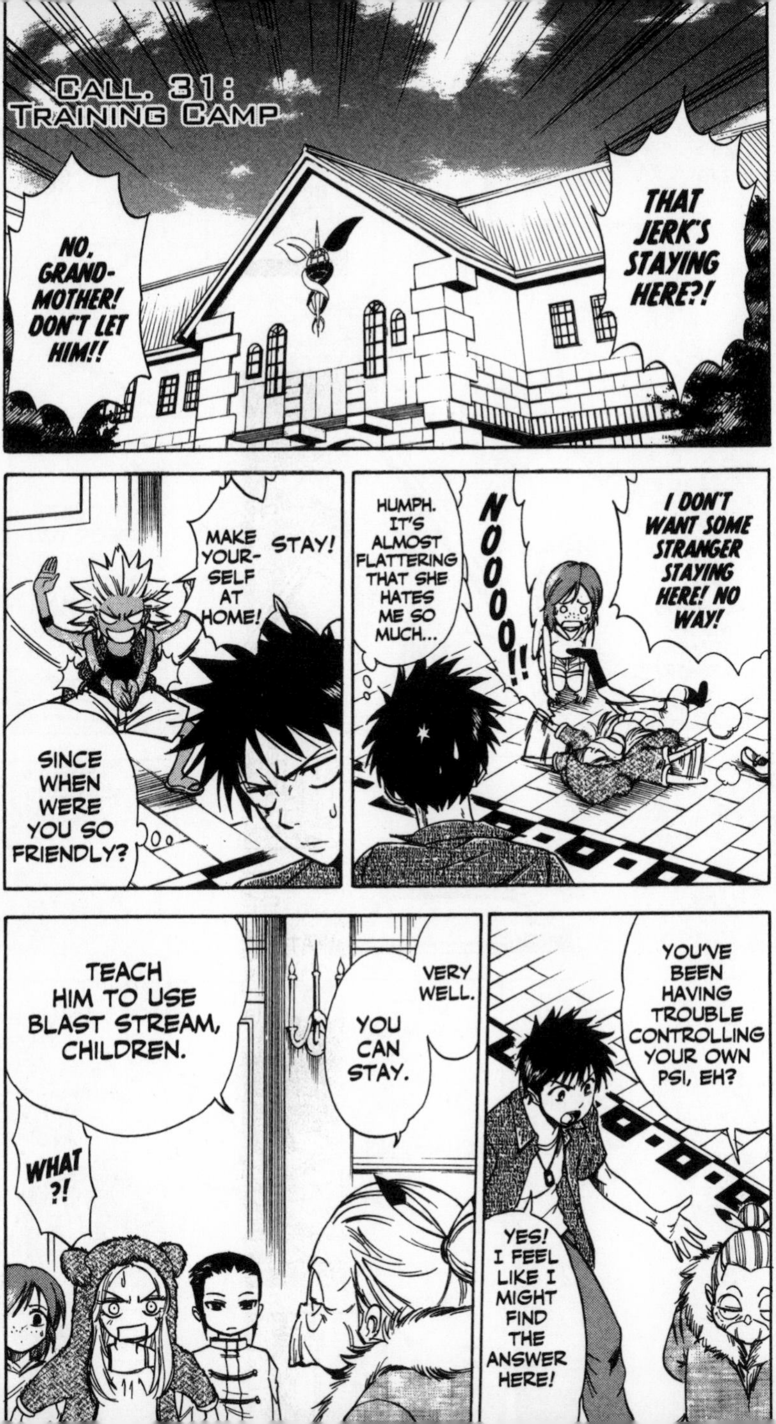
CALL. 31: TRAINING CAMP
THAT JERK'S STAYING HERE?!
NO, GRANDMOTHER! DON'T LET HIM!!
I DON'T WANT SOME STRANGER STAYING HERE! NO WAY!
NOOOOO!!
HUMPH. IT'S ALMOST FLATTERING THAT SHE HATES ME SO MUCH...
STAY!
MAKE YOURSELF AT HOME!
SINCE WHEN WERE YOU SO FRIENDLY?
YOU'VE BEEN HAVING TROUBLE CONTROLLING YOUR OWN PSI, EH?
YES! I FEEL LIKE I MIGHT FIND THE ANSWER HERE!
VERY WELL.
YOU CAN STAY.
TEACH HIM TO USE BLAST STREAM, CHILDREN.
WHAT?!

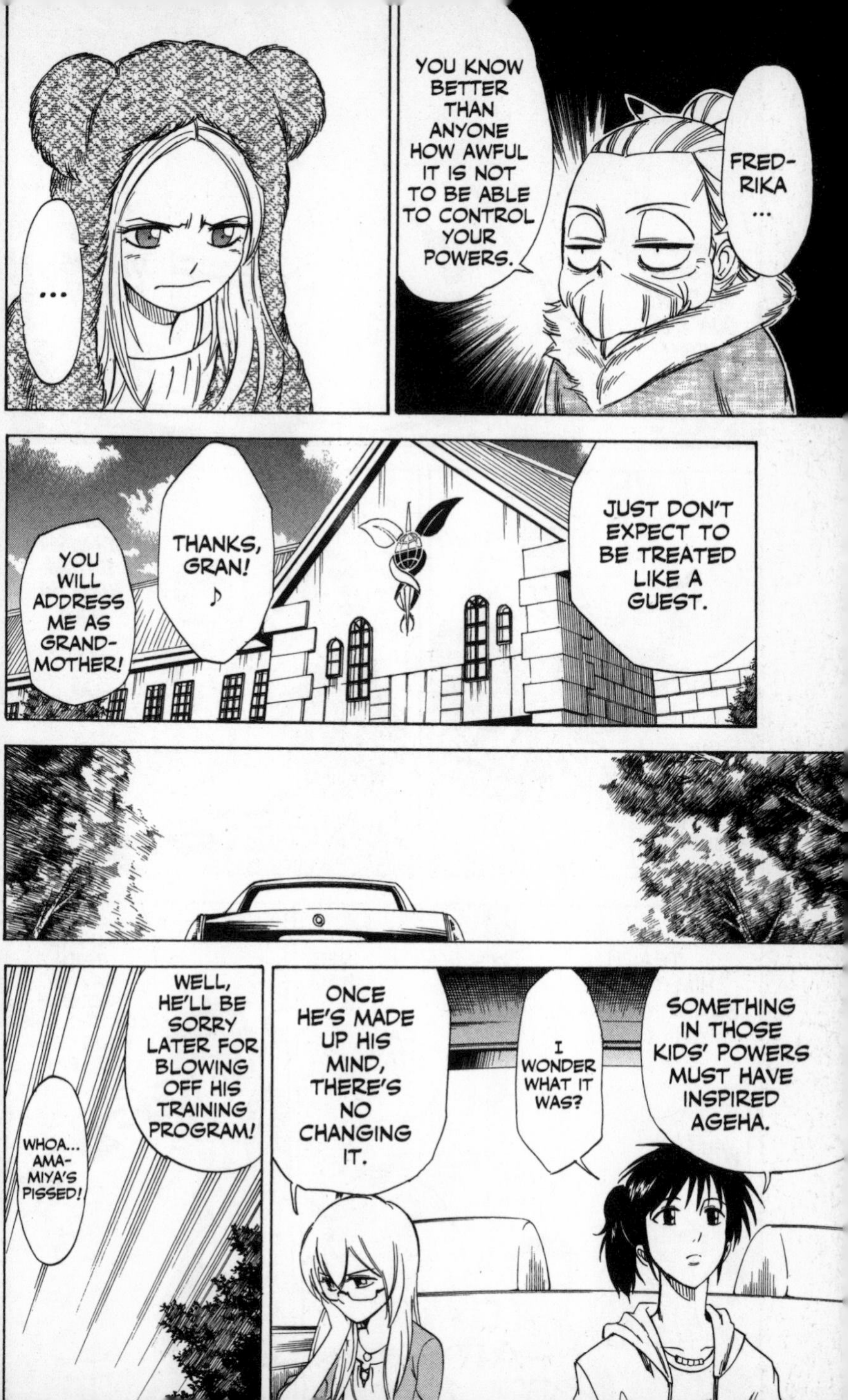
FRED-RIKA ...
YOU KNOW BETTER THAN ANYONE HOW AWFUL IT IS NOT TO BE ABLE TO CONTROL YOUR POWERS.
...
JUST DON'T EXPECT TO BE TREATED LIKE A GUEST.
THANKS, GRAN! ♪
YOU WILL ADDRESS ME AS GRAND-MOTHER!
SOMETHING IN THOSE KIDS' POWERS MUST HAVE INSPIRED AGEHA.
I WONDER WHAT IT WAS?
ONCE HE'S MADE UP HIS MIND, THERE'S NO CHANGING IT.
WELL, HE'LL BE SORRY LATER FOR BLOWING OFF HIS TRAINING PROGRAM!
WHOA... AMA-MIYA'S PISSED!

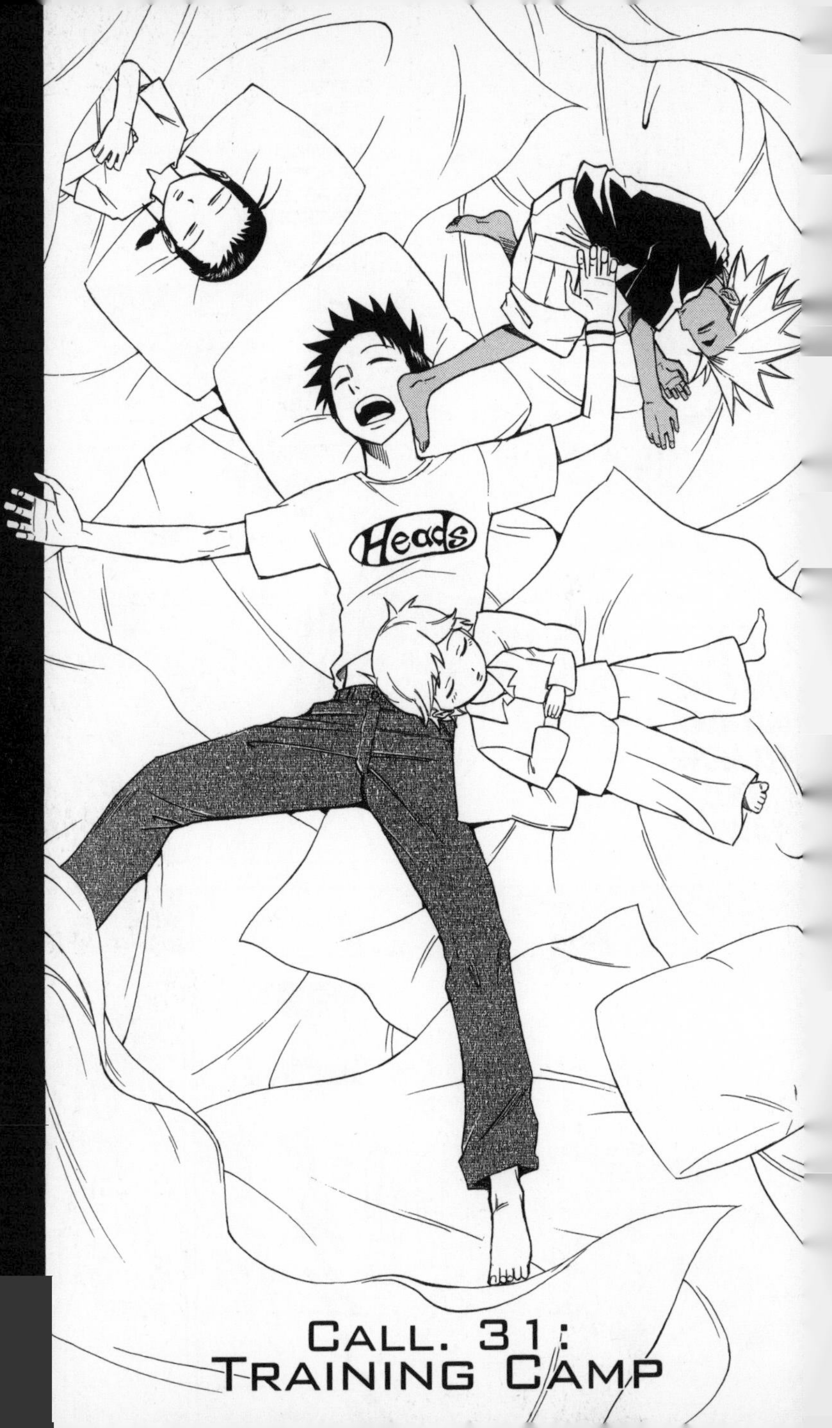
Heads

CALL. 31: TRAINING CAMP

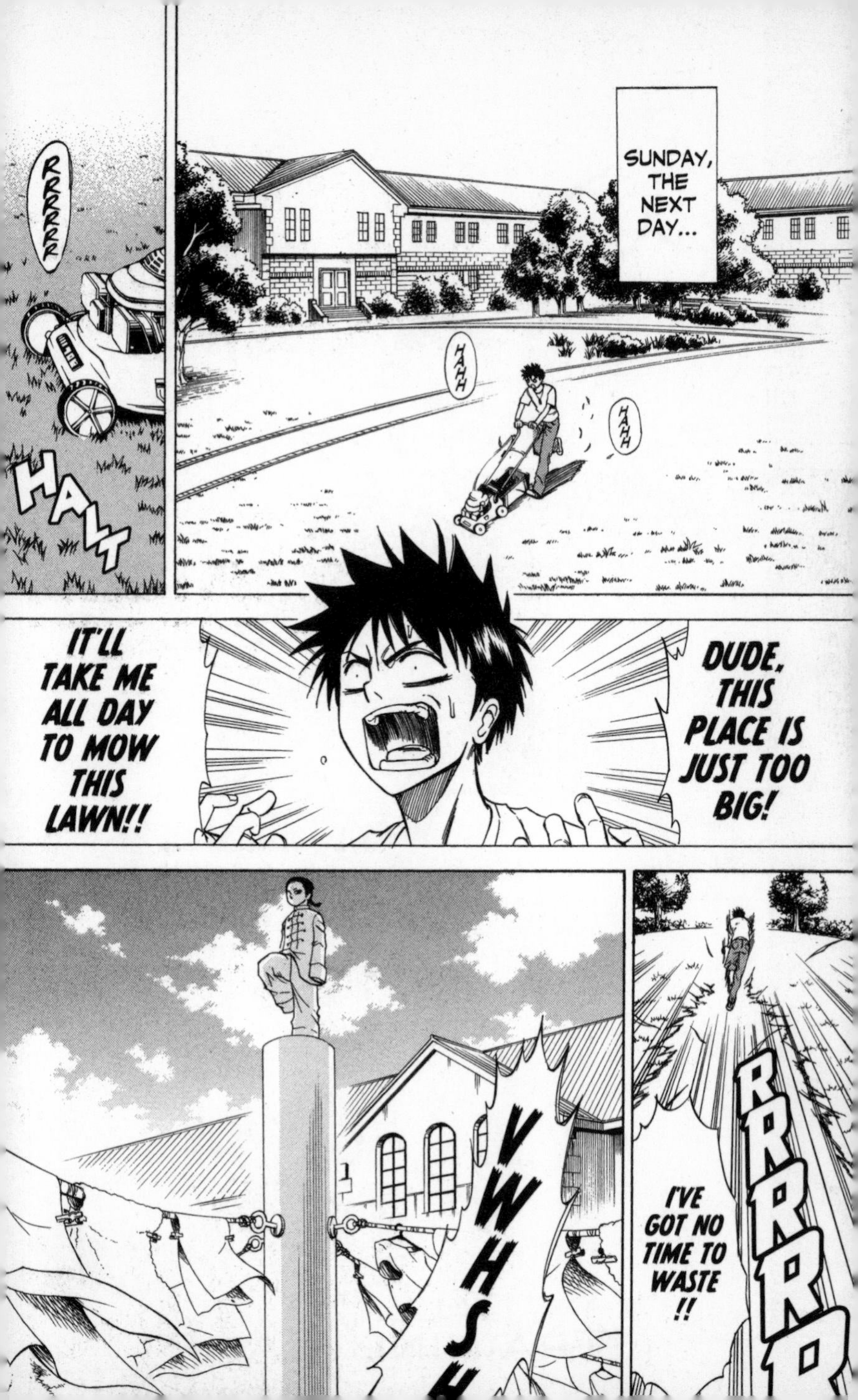

SUNDAY, THE NEXT DAY...
HAHH
HAHH
RRRRRR
HALT
DUDE, THIS PLACE IS JUST TOO BIG!
IT'LL TAKE ME ALL DAY TO MOW THIS LAWN!!
RRRRR
I'VE GOT NO TIME TO WASTE!!
VWHSH

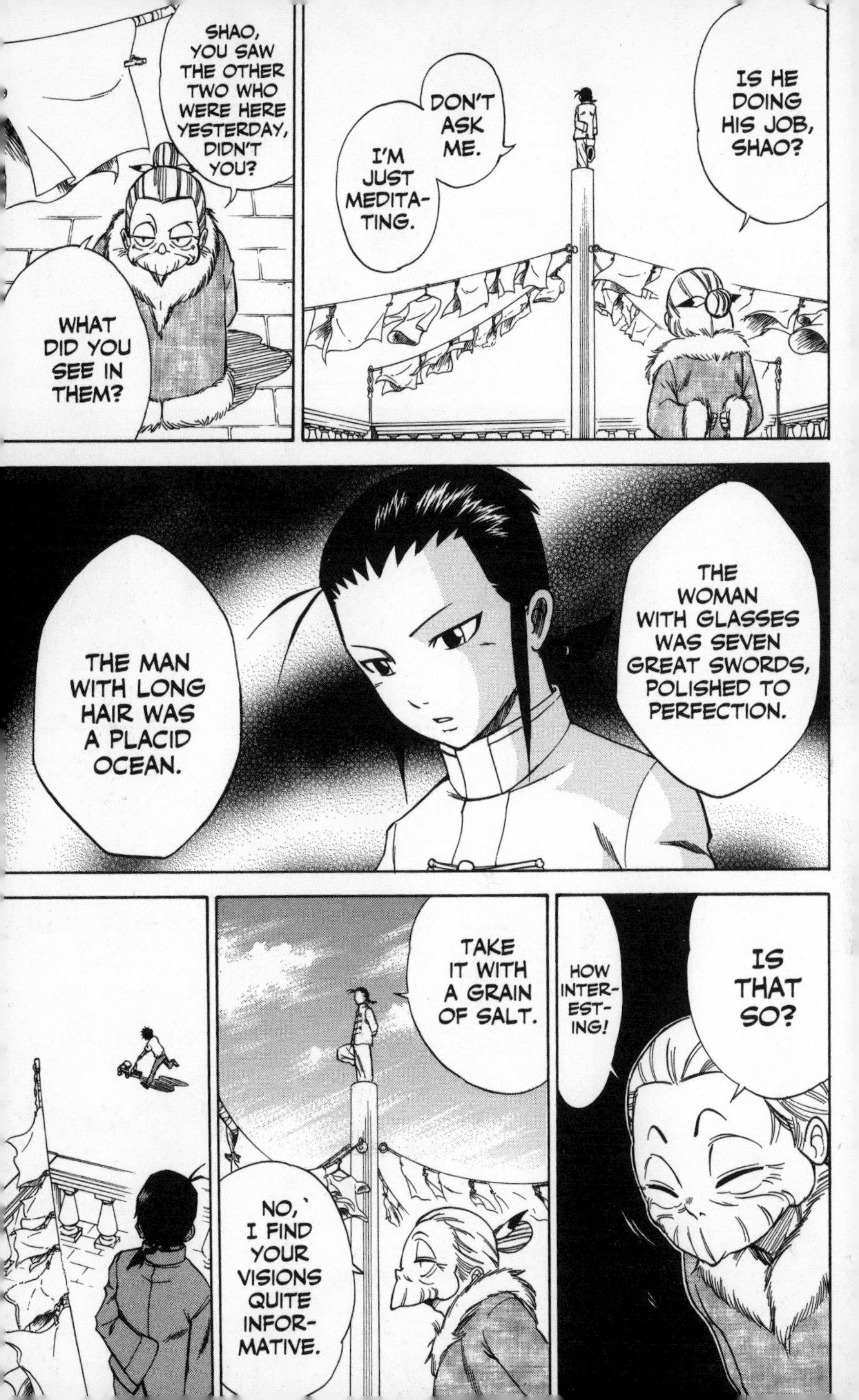
IS HE DOING HIS JOB, SHAO?
DON'T ASK ME.
I'M JUST MEDITA-TING.
SHAO, YOU SAW THE OTHER TWO WHO WERE HERE YESTERDAY, DIDN'T YOU?
WHAT DID YOU SEE IN THEM?
THE WOMAN WITH GLASSES WAS SEVEN GREAT SWORDS, POLISHED TO PERFECTION.
THE MAN WITH LONG HAIR WAS A PLACID OCEAN.
IS THAT SO?
HOW INTER-EST-ING!
TAKE IT WITH A GRAIN OF SALT.
NO, I FIND YOUR VISIONS QUITE INFOR-MATIVE.

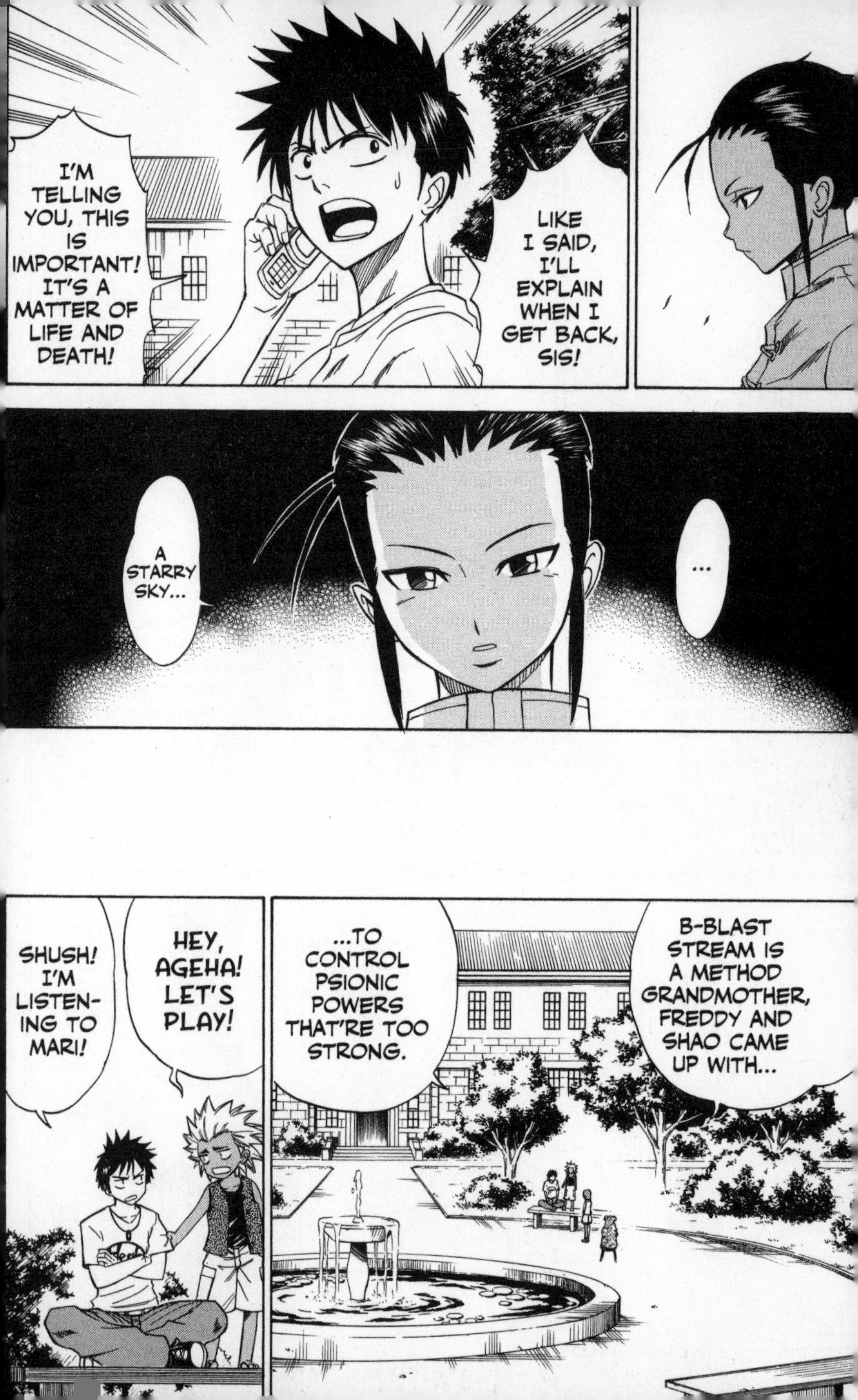
LIKE I SAID, I'LL EXPLAIN WHEN I GET BACK, SIS!
I'M TELLING YOU, THIS IS IMPORTANT! IT'S A MATTER OF LIFE AND DEATH!
...
A STARRY SKY...
B-BLAST STREAM IS A METHOD GRANDMOTHER, FREDDY AND SHAO CAME UP WITH...
...TO CONTROL PSIONIC POWERS THAT'RE TOO STRONG.
HEY, AGEHA! LET'S PLAY!
SHUSH! I'M LISTENING TO MARI!

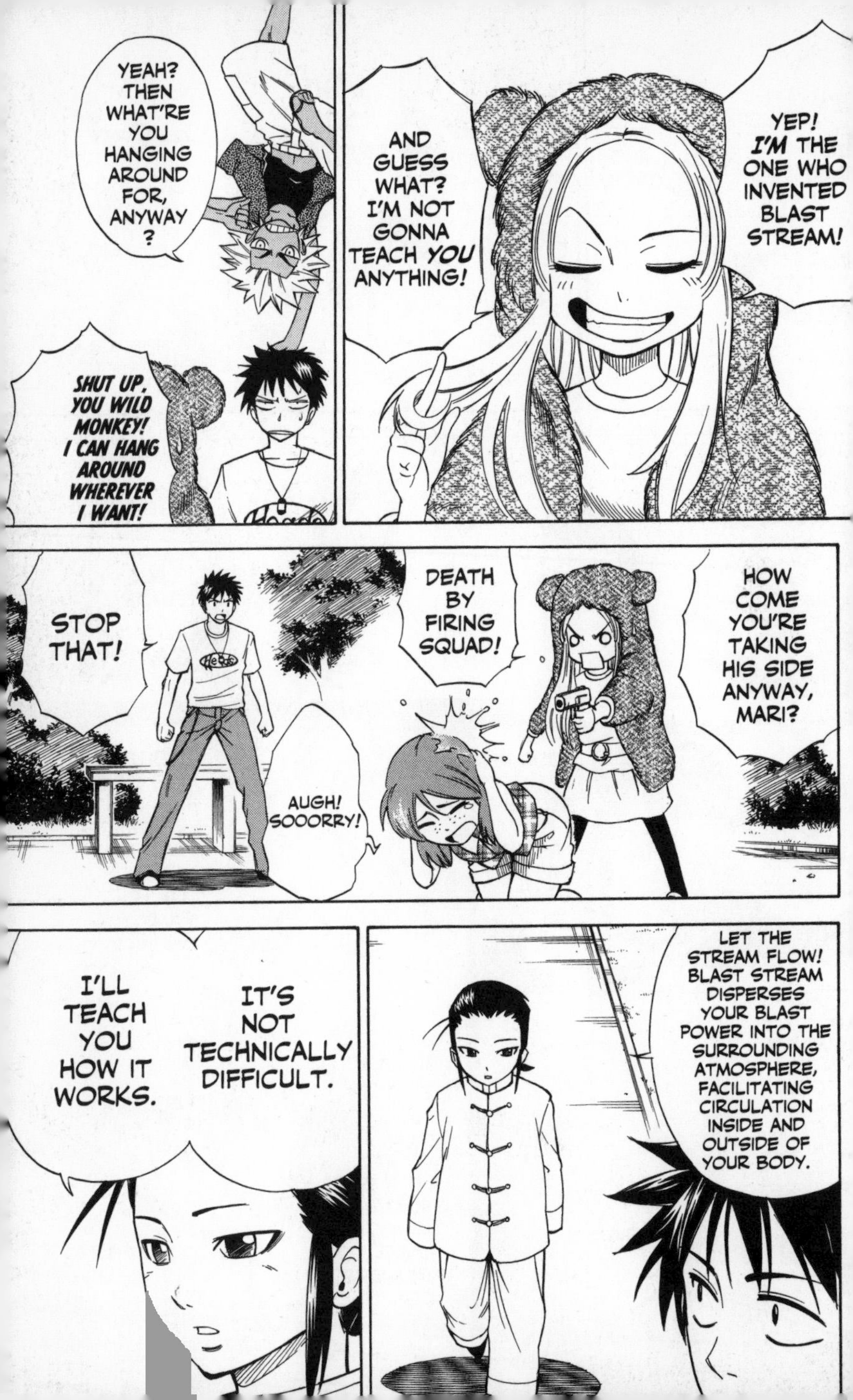
YEP! *I'M* THE ONE WHO INVENTED BLAST STREAM!
AND GUESS WHAT? I'M NOT GONNA TEACH *YOU* ANYTHING!
YEAH? THEN WHAT'RE YOU HANGING AROUND FOR, ANYWAY?
SHUT UP, YOU WILD MONKEY! I CAN HANG AROUND WHEREVER I WANT!
HOW COME YOU'RE TAKING HIS SIDE ANYWAY, MARI?
DEATH BY FIRING SQUAD!
AUGH! SOOORRY!
STOP THAT!
LET THE STREAM FLOW! BLAST STREAM DISPERSES YOUR BLAST POWER INTO THE SURROUNDING ATMOSPHERE, FACILITATING CIRCULATION INSIDE AND OUTSIDE OF YOUR BODY.
IT'S NOT TECHNICALLY DIFFICULT.
I'LL TEACH YOU HOW IT WORKS.

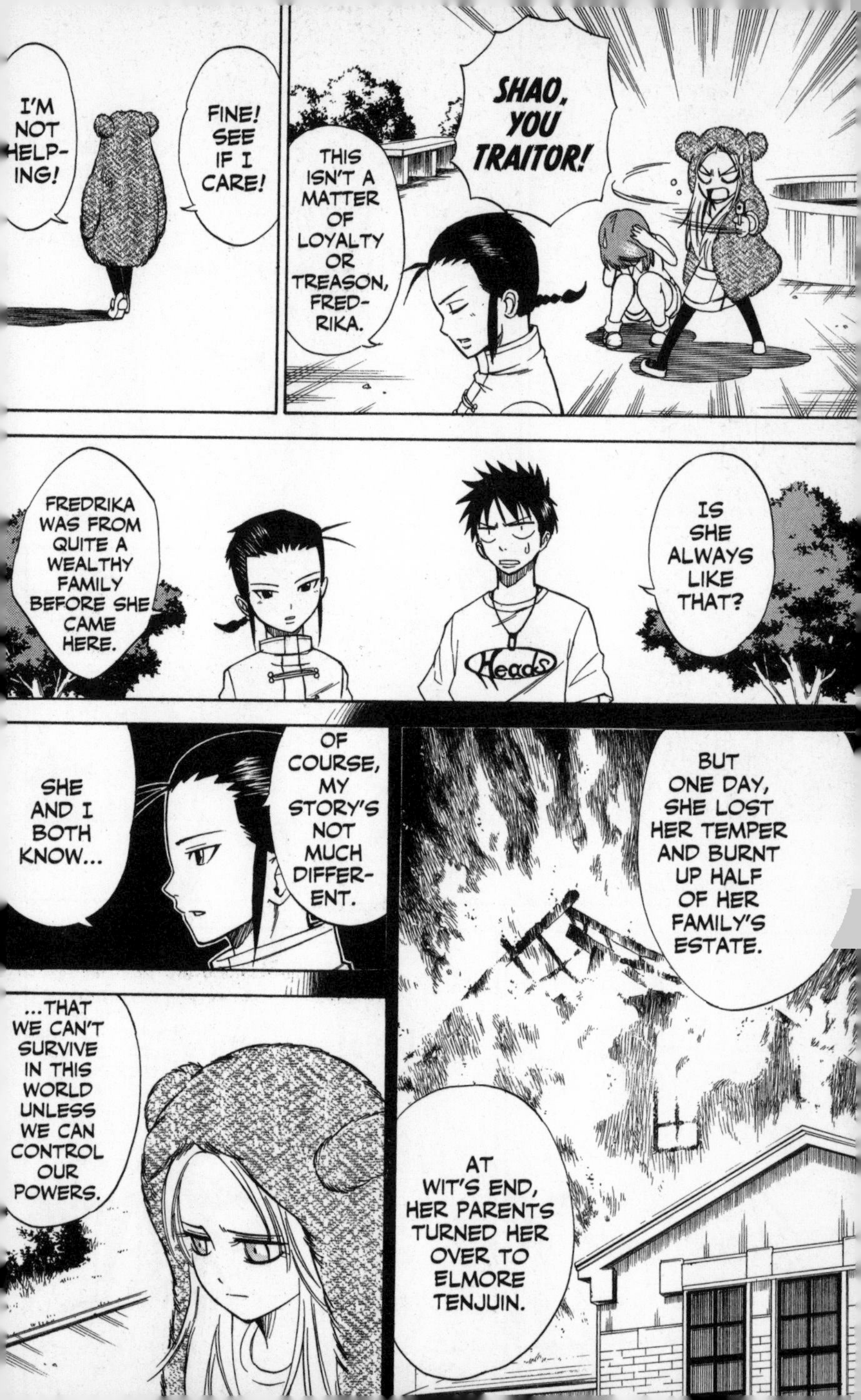
SHAO, YOU TRAITOR!
THIS ISN'T A MATTER OF LOYALTY OR TREASON, FREDRIKA.
FINE! SEE IF I CARE!
I'M NOT HELPING!
IS SHE ALWAYS LIKE THAT?
FREDRIKA WAS FROM QUITE A WEALTHY FAMILY BEFORE SHE CAME HERE.
Heads
BUT ONE DAY, SHE LOST HER TEMPER AND BURNT UP HALF OF HER FAMILY'S ESTATE.
AT WIT'S END, HER PARENTS TURNED HER OVER TO ELMORE TENJUIN.
OF COURSE, MY STORY'S NOT MUCH DIFFERENT.
SHE AND I BOTH KNOW...
...THAT WE CAN'T SURVIVE IN THIS WORLD UNLESS WE CAN CONTROL OUR POWERS.

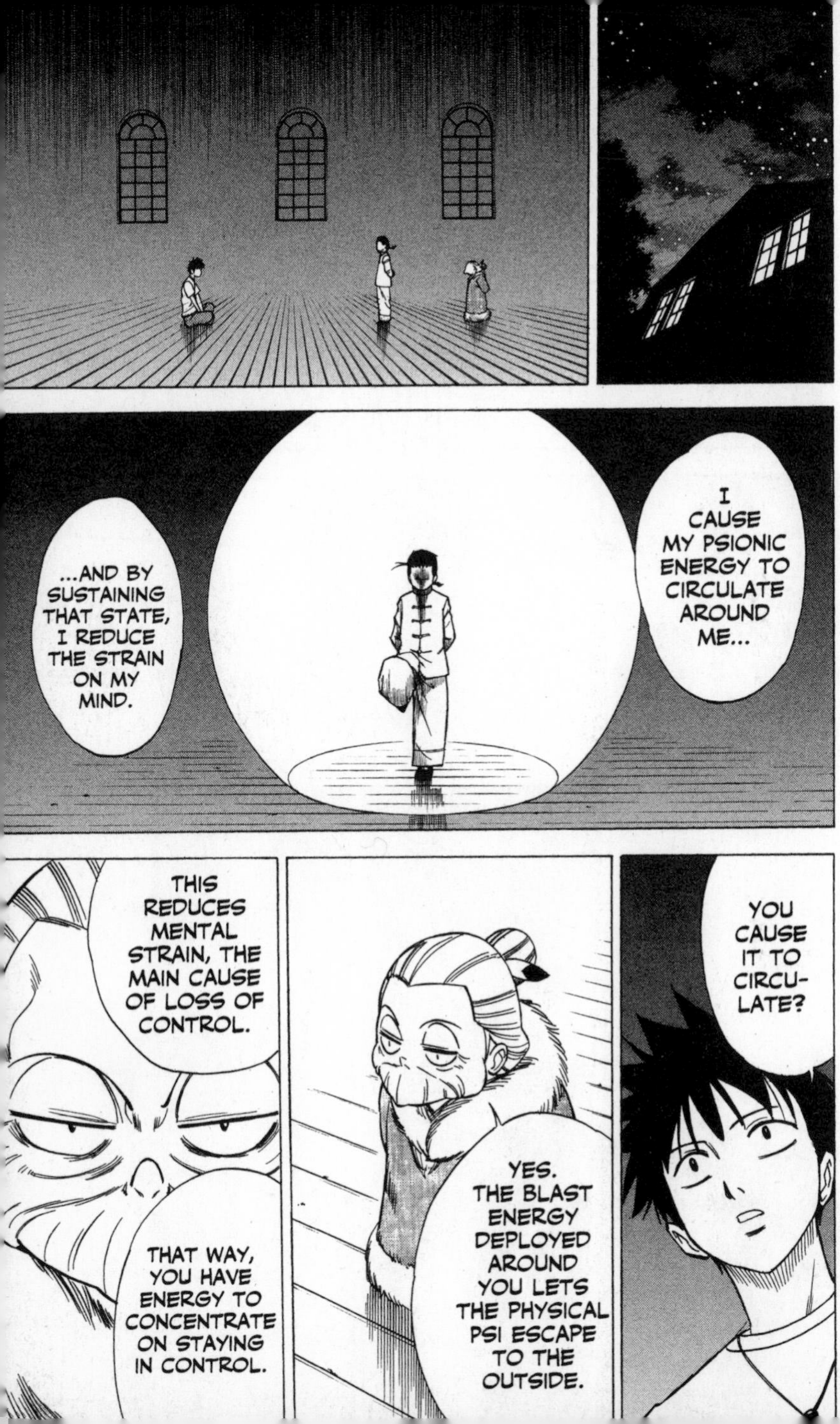
I CAUSE MY PSIONIC ENERGY TO CIRCULATE AROUND ME...
...AND BY SUSTAINING THAT STATE, I REDUCE THE STRAIN ON MY MIND.
YOU CAUSE IT TO CIRCU-LATE?
YES. THE BLAST ENERGY DEPLOYED AROUND YOU LETS THE PHYSICAL PSI ESCAPE TO THE OUTSIDE.
THIS REDUCES MENTAL STRAIN, THE MAIN CAUSE OF LOSS OF CONTROL.
THAT WAY, YOU HAVE ENERGY TO CONCENTRATE ON STAYING IN CONTROL.

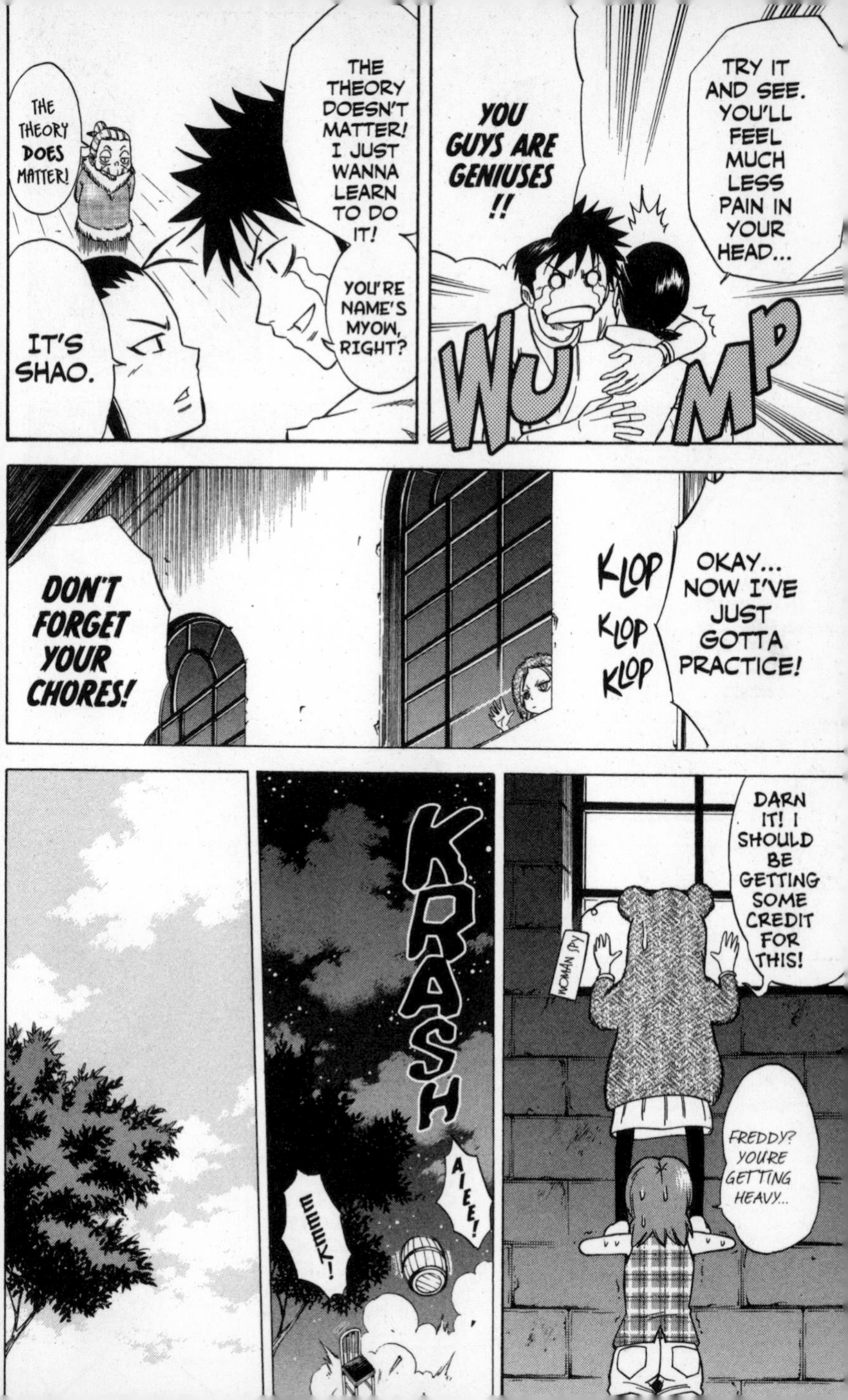
TRY IT AND SEE. YOU'LL FEEL MUCH LESS PAIN IN YOUR HEAD...
YOU GUYS ARE GENIUSES!!
WUMP
THE THEORY DOESN'T MATTER! I JUST WANNA LEARN TO DO IT!
THE THEORY DOES MATTER!
YOU'RE NAME'S MYOW, RIGHT?
IT'S SHAO.
OKAY... NOW I'VE JUST GOTTA PRACTICE!
KLOP KLOP KLOP
DON'T FORGET YOUR CHORES!
DARN IT! I SHOULD BE GETTING SOME CREDIT FOR THIS!
WOMAN SPY
FREDDY? YOU'RE GETTING HEAVY...
KRASH
AIEEE!
EEEEK!

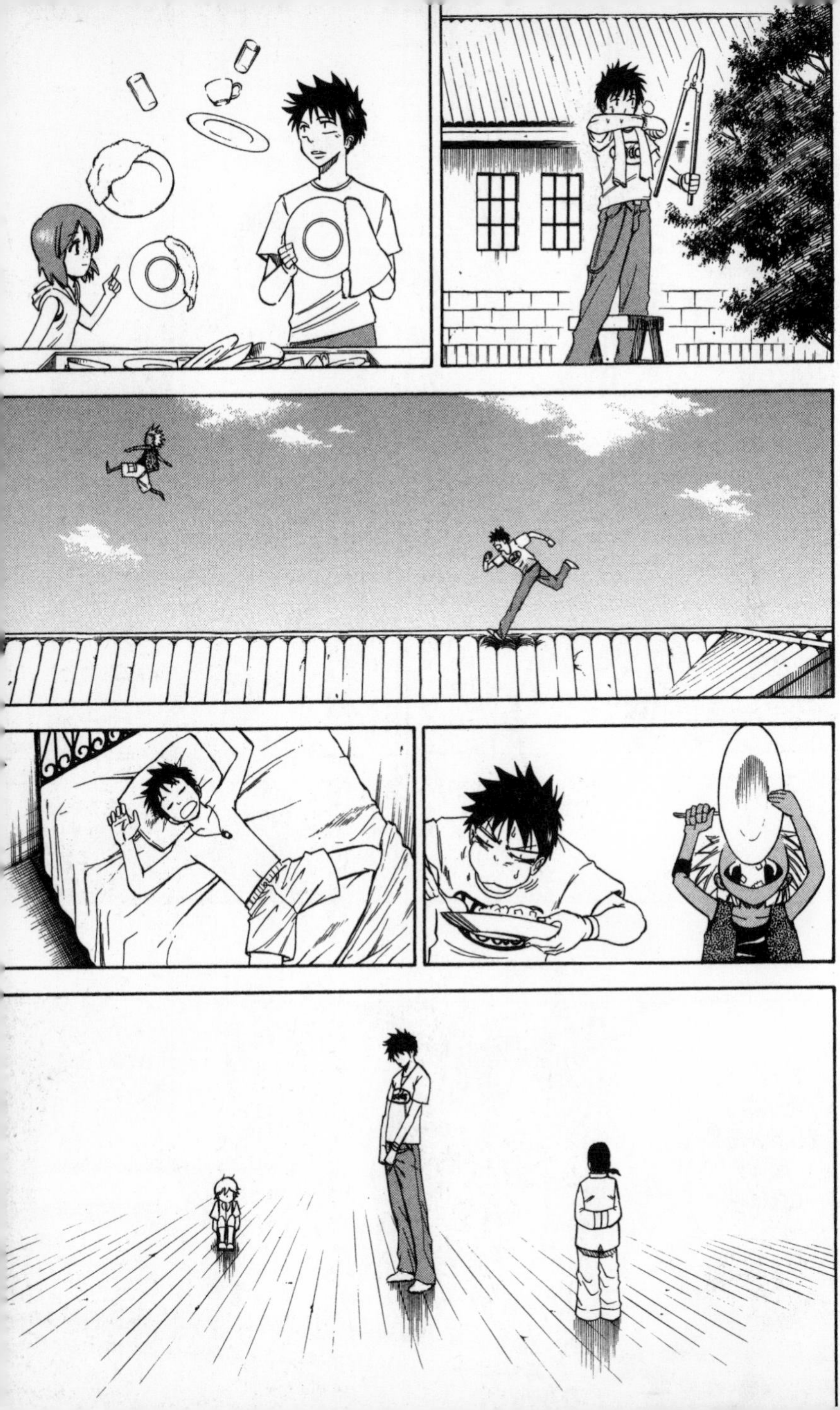

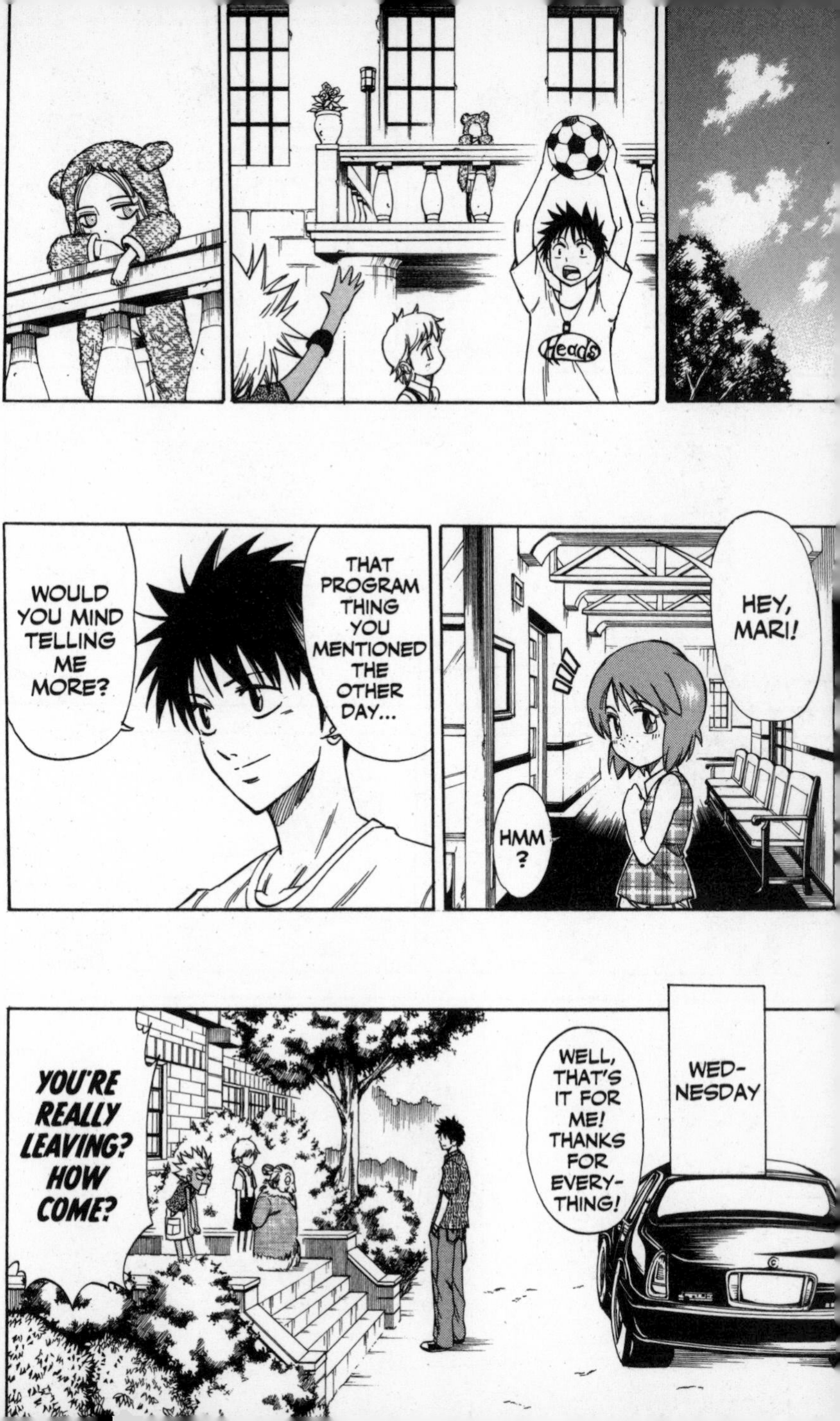
HEY, MARI!
HMM?
THAT PROGRAM THING YOU MENTIONED THE OTHER DAY...
WOULD YOU MIND TELLING ME MORE?
WED-NESDAY
WELL, THAT'S IT FOR ME! THANKS FOR EVERY-THING!
YOU'RE REALLY LEAVING? HOW COME?

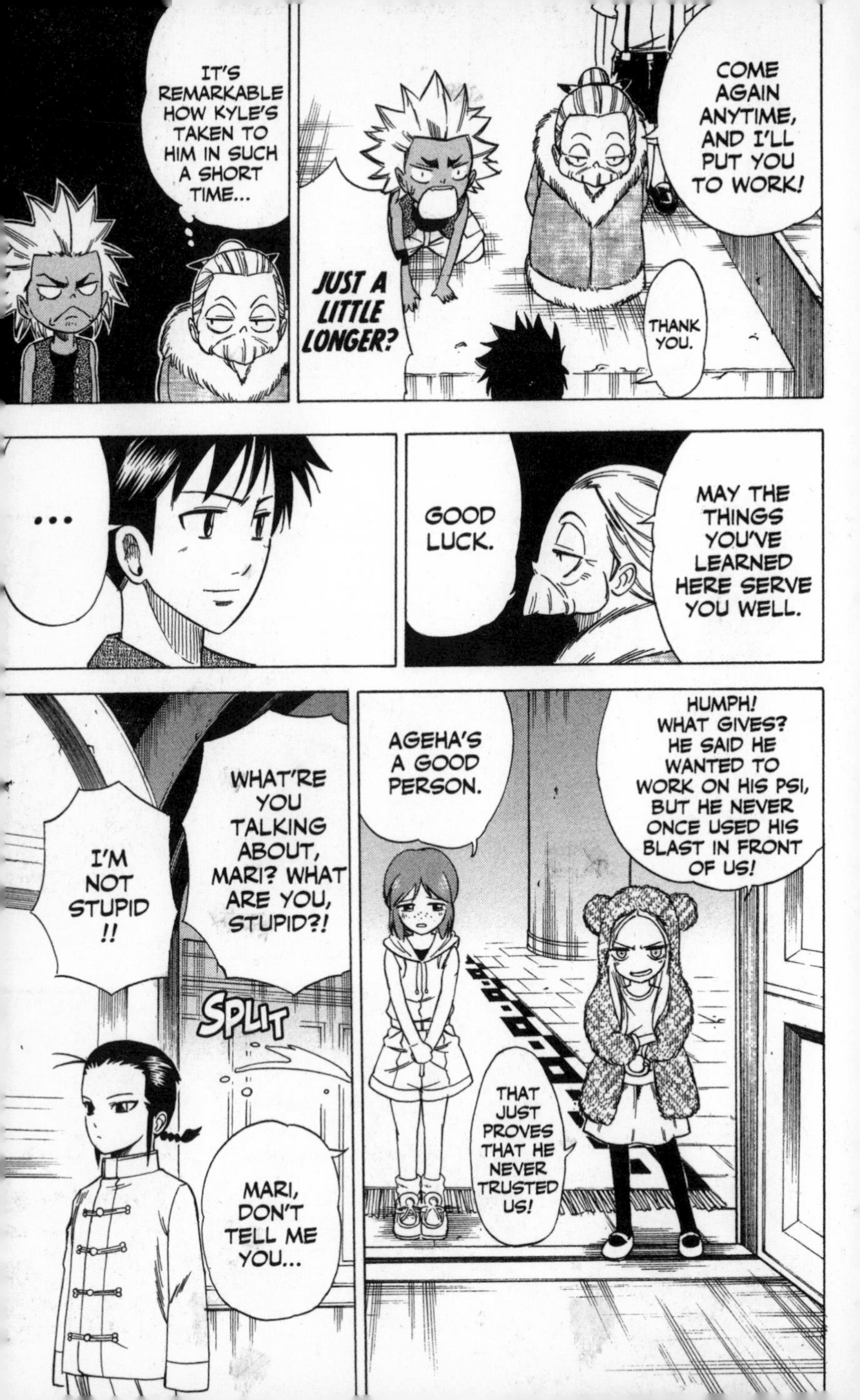
COME AGAIN ANYTIME, AND I'LL PUT YOU TO WORK!
JUST A LITTLE LONGER?
THANK YOU.
IT'S REMARKABLE HOW KYLE'S TAKEN TO HIM IN SUCH A SHORT TIME...
MAY THE THINGS YOU'VE LEARNED HERE SERVE YOU WELL.
GOOD LUCK.
...
HUMPH! WHAT GIVES? HE SAID HE WANTED TO WORK ON HIS PSI, BUT HE NEVER ONCE USED HIS BLAST IN FRONT OF US!
AGEHA'S A GOOD PERSON.
THAT JUST PROVES THAT HE NEVER TRUSTED US!
WHAT'RE YOU TALKING ABOUT, MARI? WHAT ARE YOU, STUPID?!
I'M NOT STUPID !!
SPLIT
MARI, DON'T TELL ME YOU...

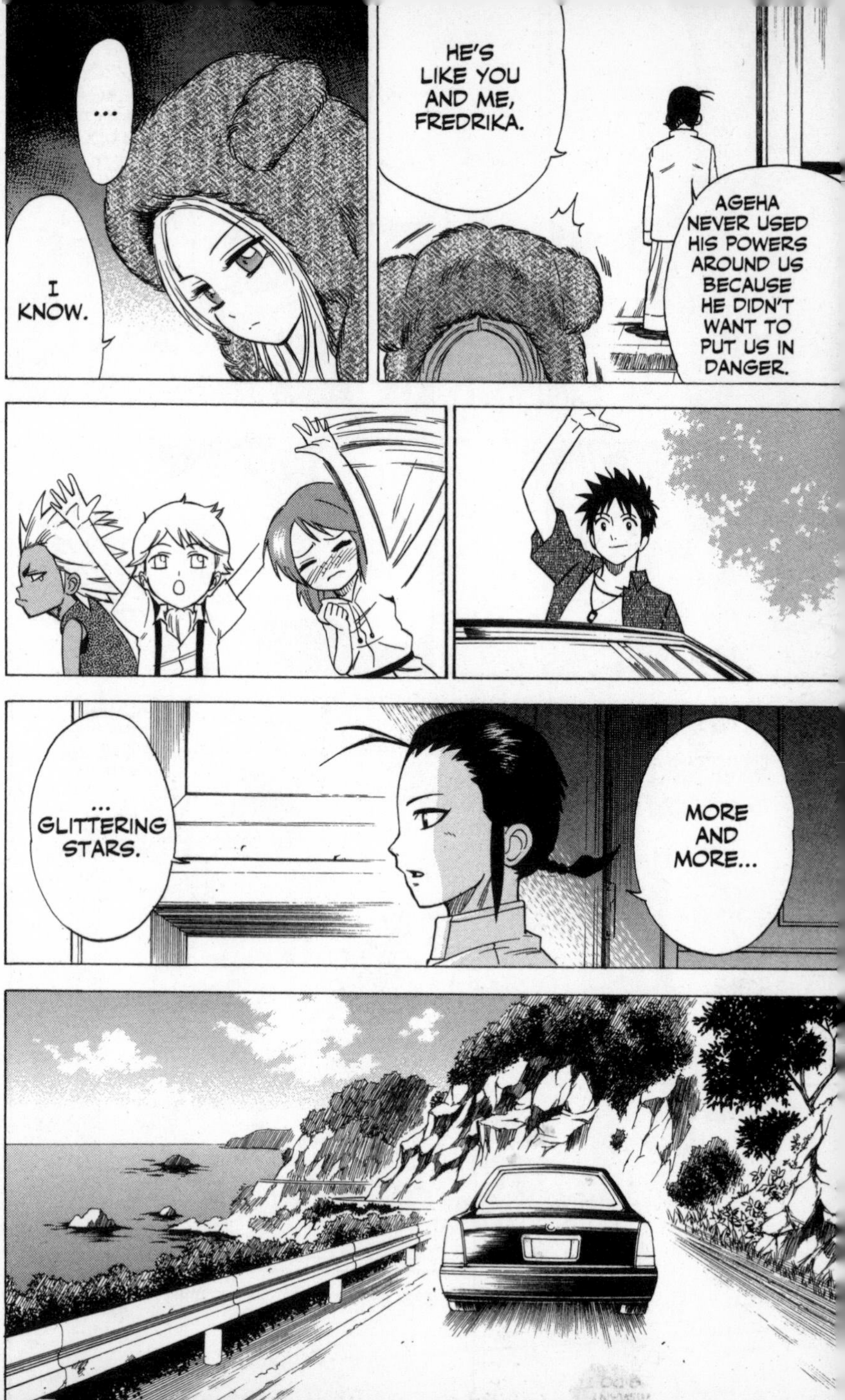
HE'S LIKE YOU AND ME, FREDRIKA.
AGEHA NEVER USED HIS POWERS AROUND US BECAUSE HE DIDN'T WANT TO PUT US IN DANGER.
...
I KNOW.
MORE AND MORE...
... GLITTERING STARS.

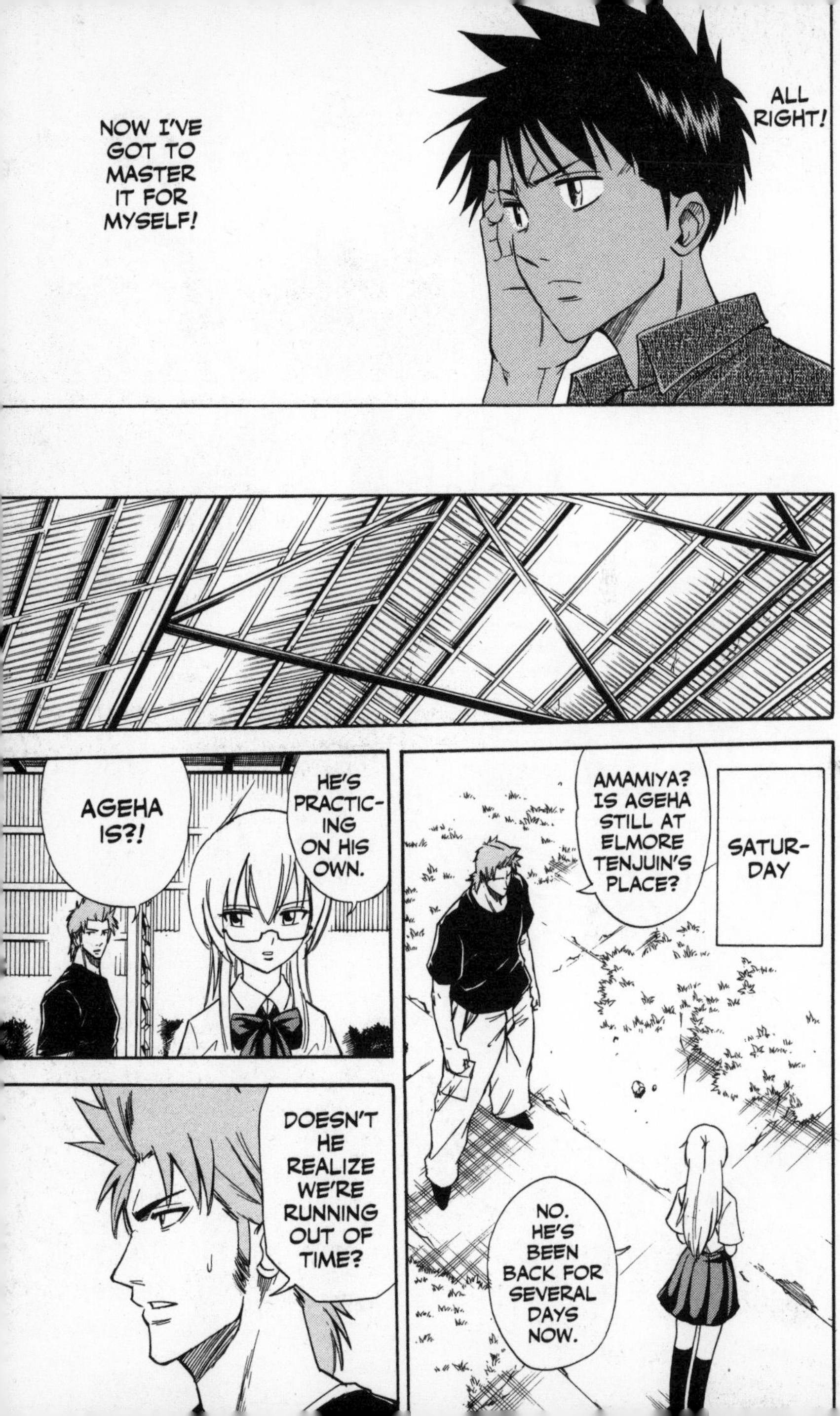
ALL RIGHT!
NOW I'VE GOT TO MASTER IT FOR MYSELF!
SATURDAY
AMAMIYA? IS AGEHA STILL AT ELMORE TENJUIN'S PLACE?
NO. HE'S BEEN BACK FOR SEVERAL DAYS NOW.
HE'S PRACTICING ON HIS OWN.
AGEHA IS?!
DOESN'T HE REALIZE WE'RE RUNNING OUT OF TIME?

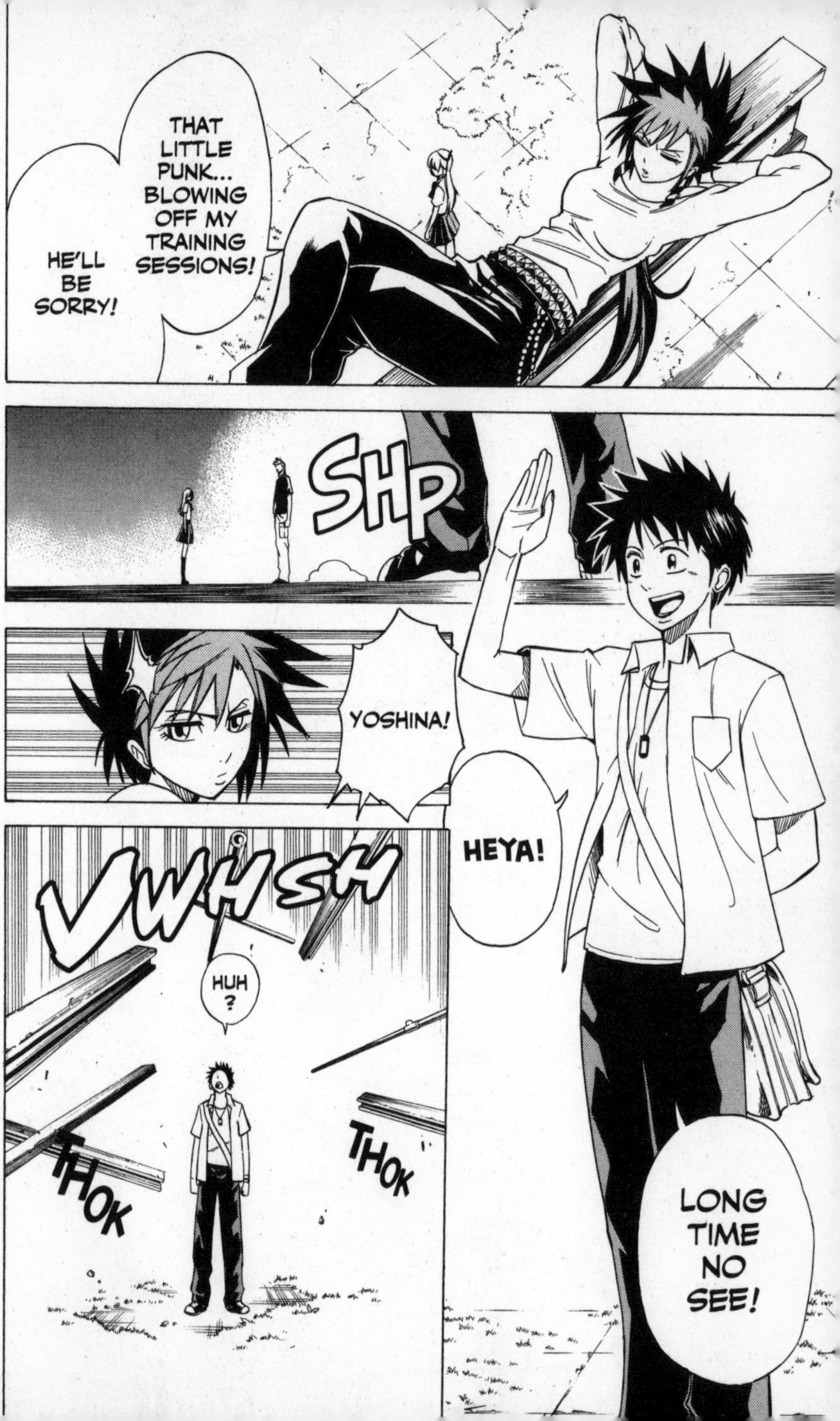
THAT LITTLE PUNK... BLOWING OFF MY TRAINING SESSIONS!
HE'LL BE SORRY!
SHP
HEYA!
LONG TIME NO SEE!
YOSHINA!
VWHSH
HUH?
THOK
THOK

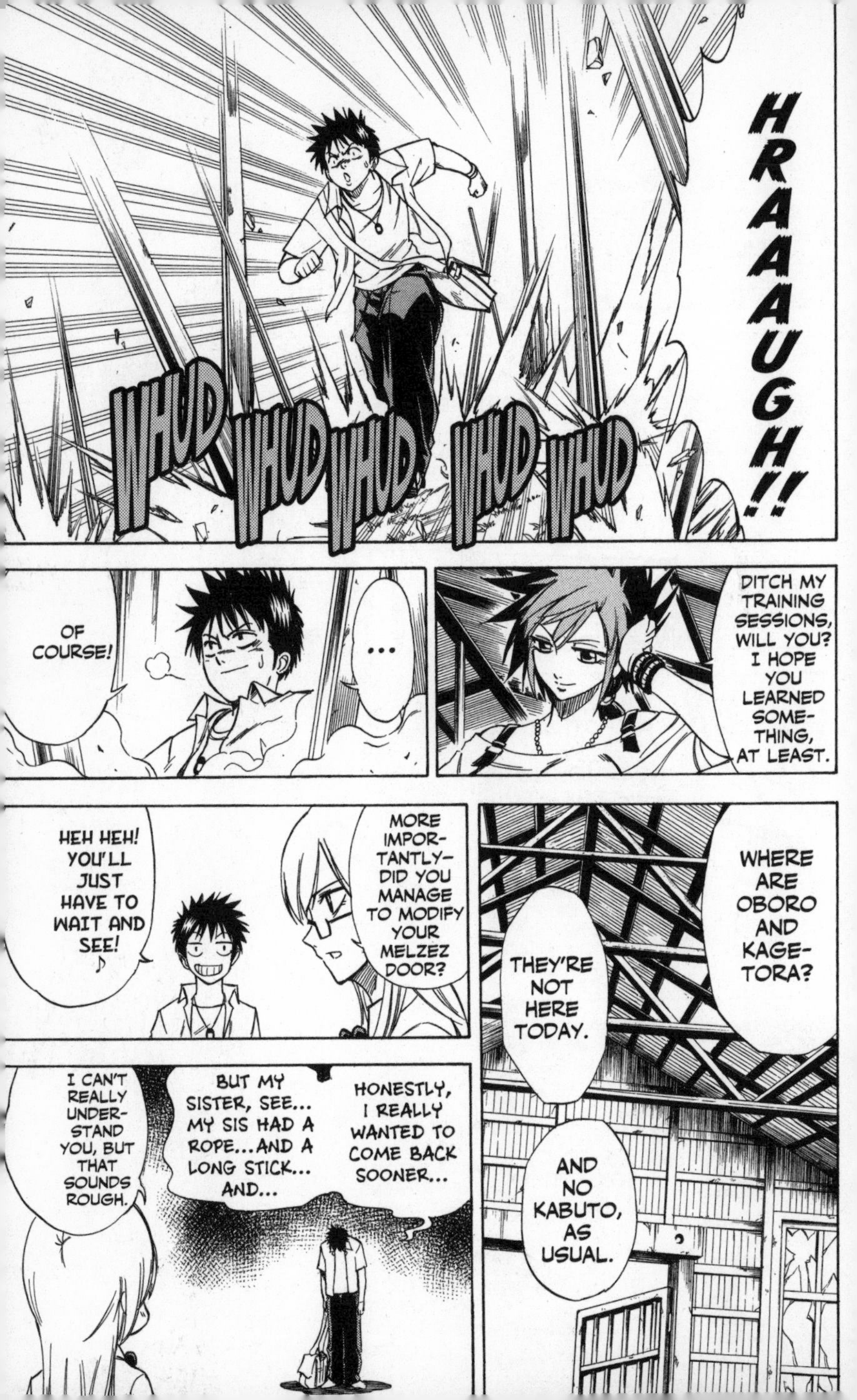
HRAAAAUGH!!
WHUD WHUD WHUD WHUD WHUD
DITCH MY TRAINING SESSIONS, WILL YOU? I HOPE YOU LEARNED SOMETHING, AT LEAST.
...
OF COURSE!
WHERE ARE OBORO AND KAGETORA?
THEY'RE NOT HERE TODAY.
AND NO KABUTO, AS USUAL.
MORE IMPORTANTLY—DID YOU MANAGE TO MODIFY YOUR MELZEZ DOOR?
HEH HEH! YOU'LL JUST HAVE TO WAIT AND SEE! ♪
HONESTLY, I REALLY WANTED TO COME BACK SOONER...
BUT MY SISTER, SEE... MY SIS HAD A ROPE...AND A LONG STICK... AND...
I CAN'T REALLY UNDERSTAND YOU, BUT THAT SOUNDS ROUGH.

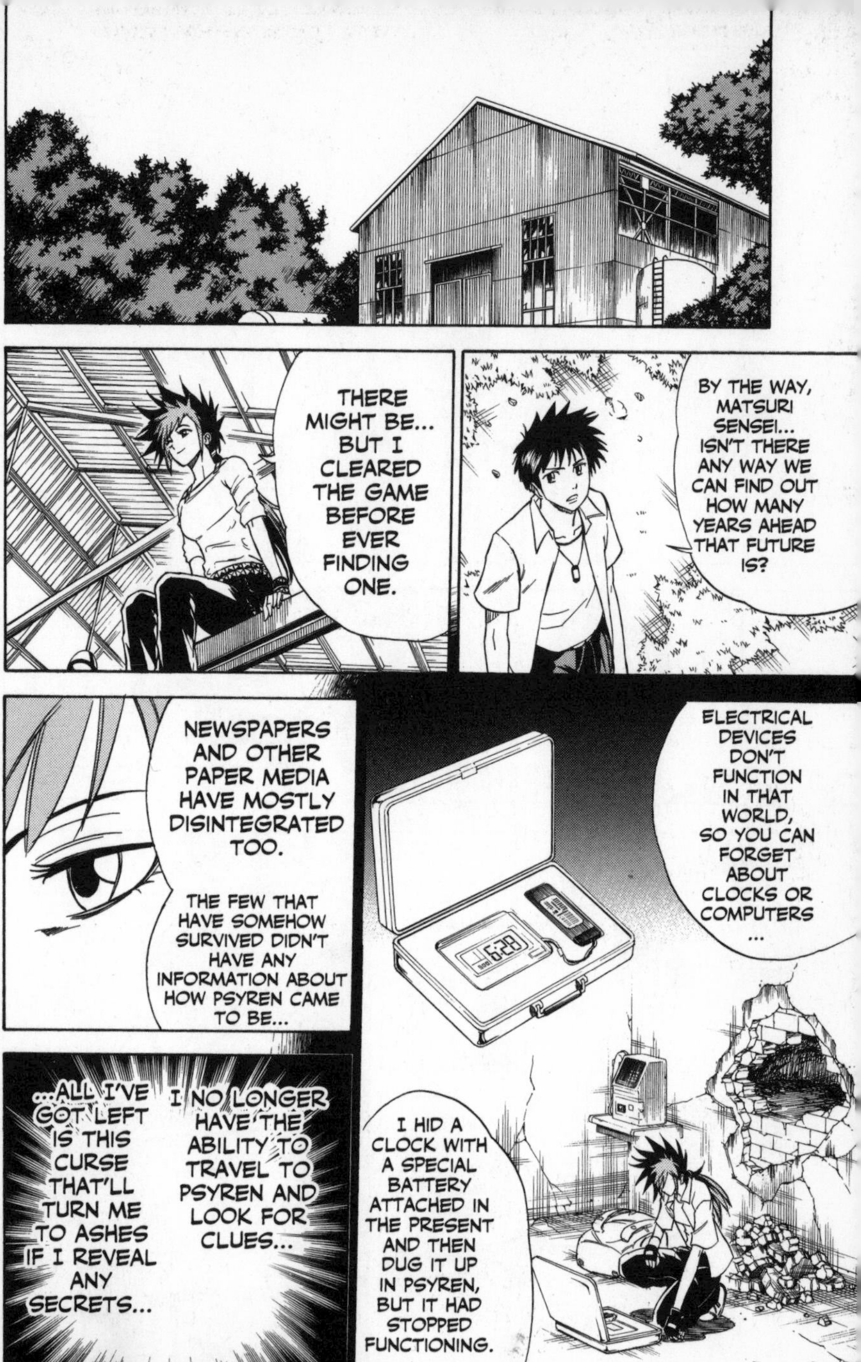
BY THE WAY, MATSURI SENSEI... ISN'T THERE ANY WAY WE CAN FIND OUT HOW MANY YEARS AHEAD THAT FUTURE IS?
THERE MIGHT BE... BUT I CLEARED THE GAME BEFORE EVER FINDING ONE.
ELECTRICAL DEVICES DON'T FUNCTION IN THAT WORLD, SO YOU CAN FORGET ABOUT CLOCKS OR COMPUTERS...
I HID A CLOCK WITH A SPECIAL BATTERY ATTACHED IN THE PRESENT AND THEN DUG IT UP IN PSYREN, BUT IT HAD STOPPED FUNCTIONING.
NEWSPAPERS AND OTHER PAPER MEDIA HAVE MOSTLY DISINTEGRATED TOO.
THE FEW THAT HAVE SOMEHOW SURVIVED DIDN'T HAVE ANY INFORMATION ABOUT HOW PSYREN CAME TO BE...
I NO LONGER HAVE THE ABILITY TO TRAVEL TO PSYREN AND LOOK FOR CLUES...
...ALL I'VE GOT LEFT IS THIS CURSE THAT'LL TURN ME TO ASHES IF I REVEAL ANY SECRETS...

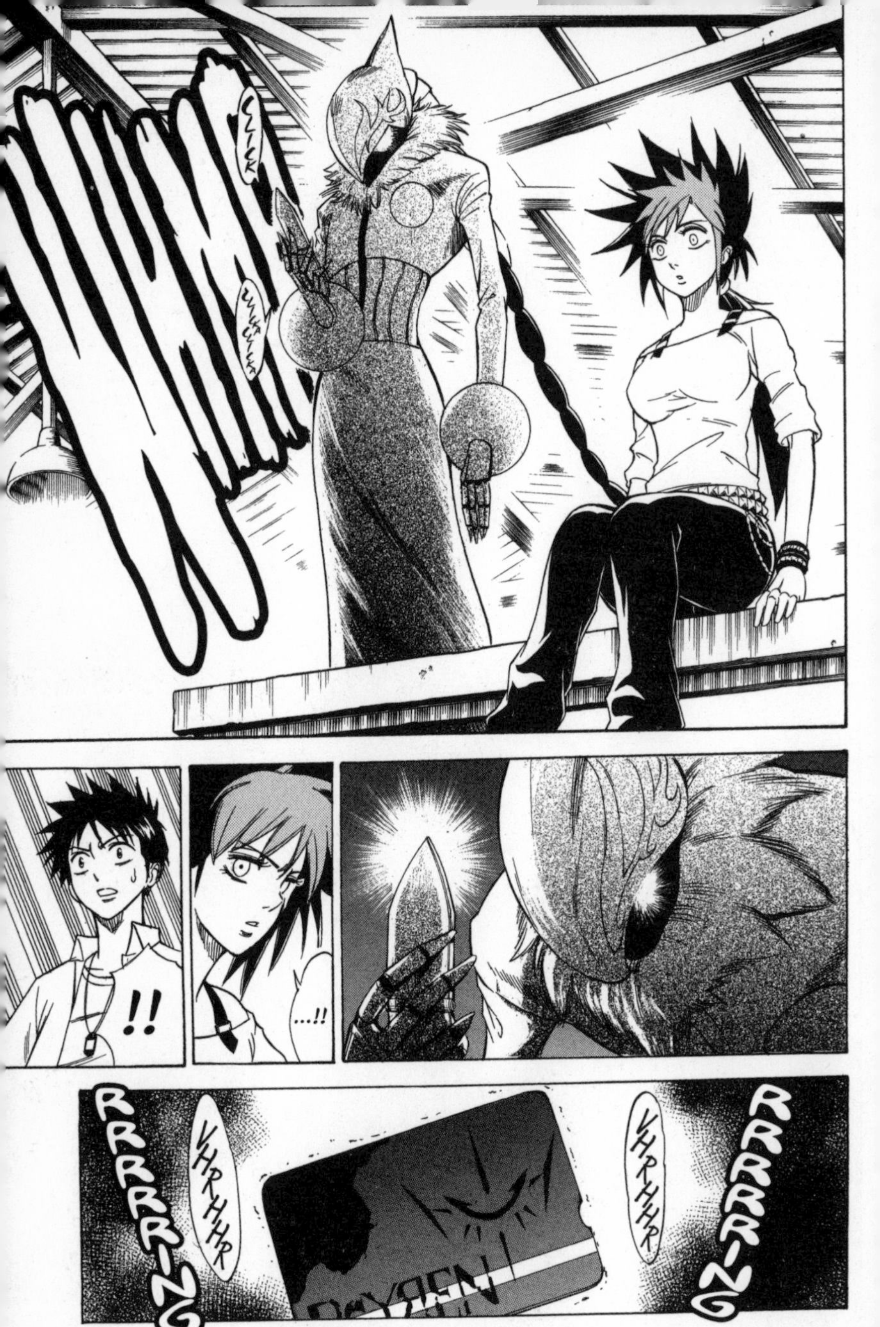
CLICK
CLICK CLICK
...!!
!!
RRRRRING
VHRHHR
VHRHHR
RRRRRING

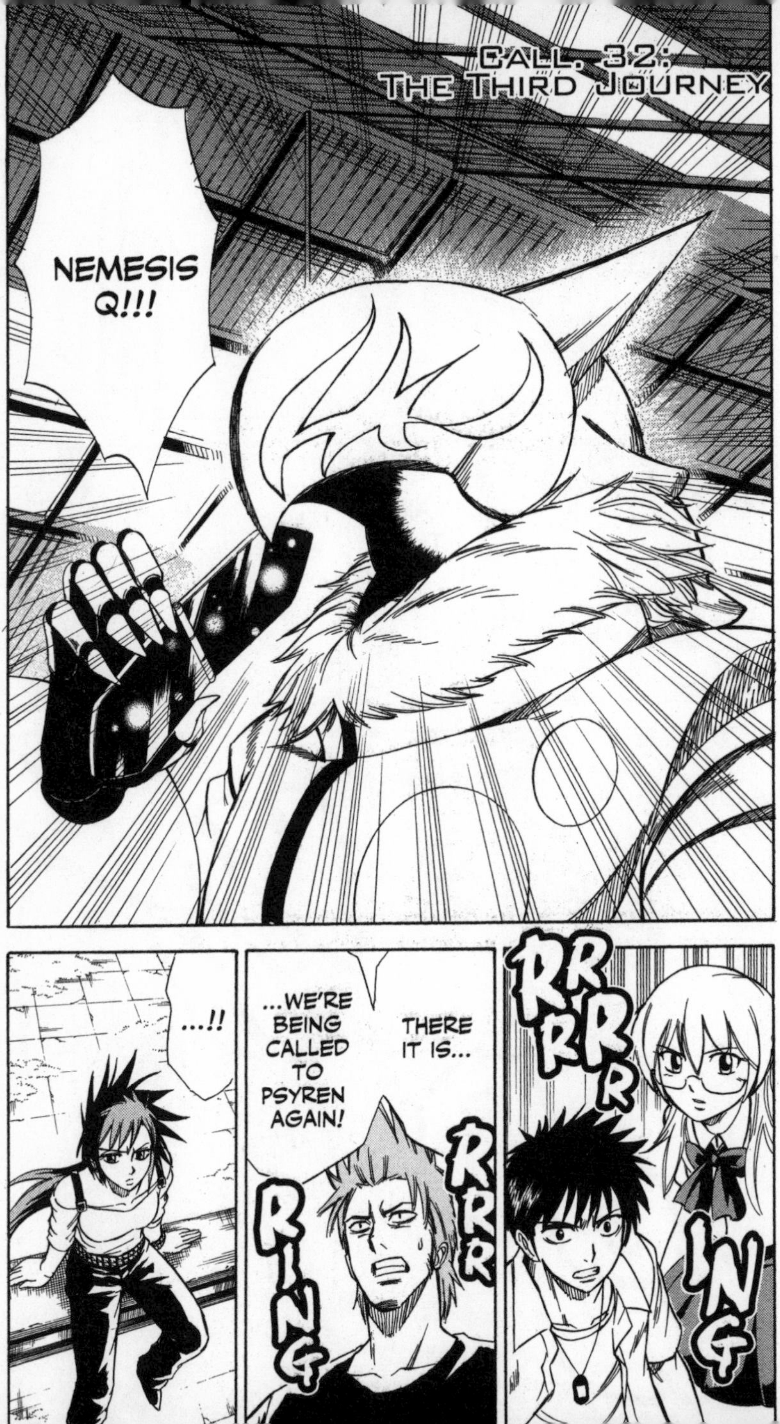
CALL. 32:
THE THIRD JOURNEY
NEMESIS Q!!!
RRRRR
ING
RRR
RING
THERE IT IS...
...WE'RE BEING CALLED TO PSYREN AGAIN!
...!!

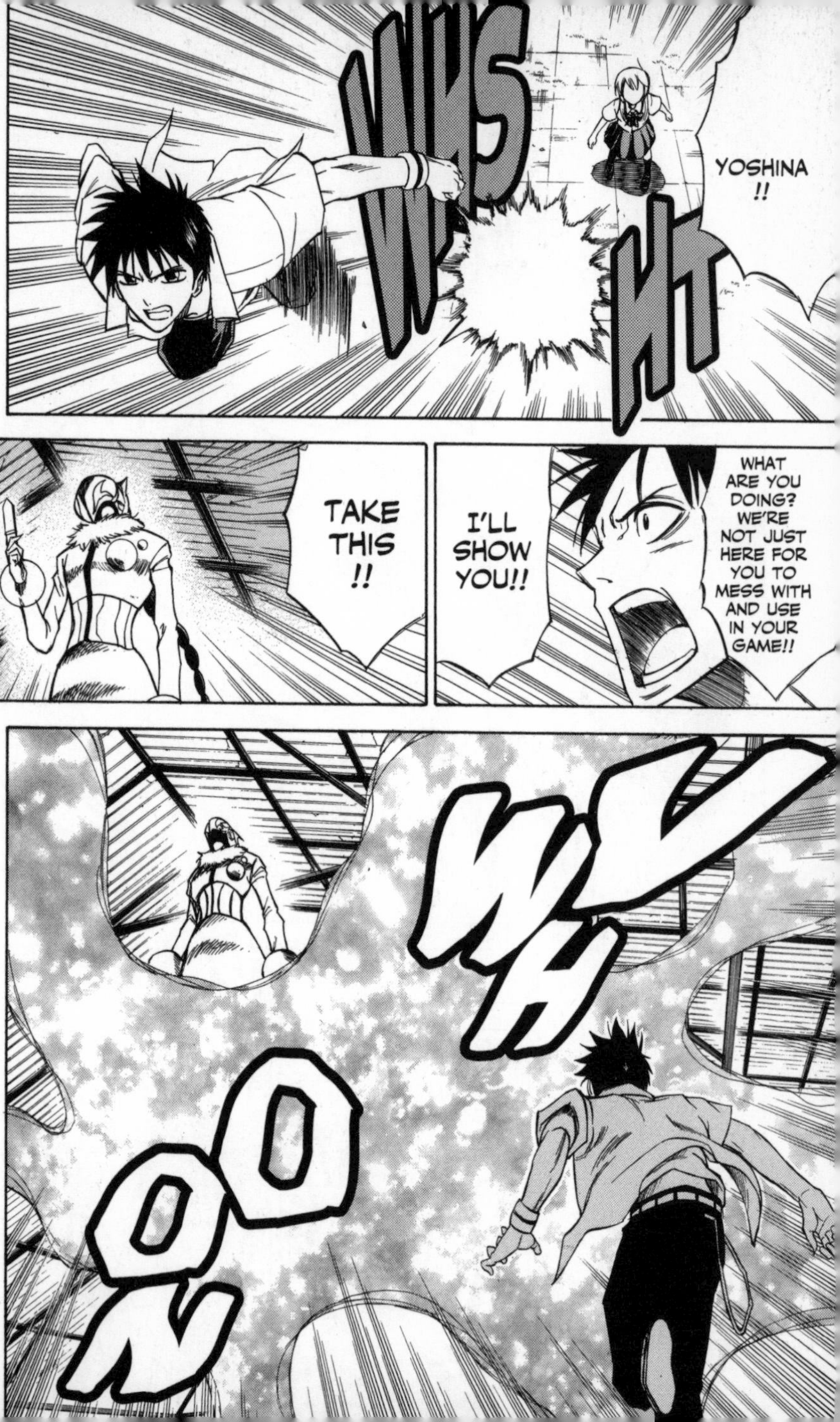
YOSHINA!!
WHAT ARE YOU DOING? WE'RE NOT JUST HERE FOR YOU TO MESS WITH AND USE IN YOUR GAME!!
I'LL SHOW YOU!!
TAKE THIS!!

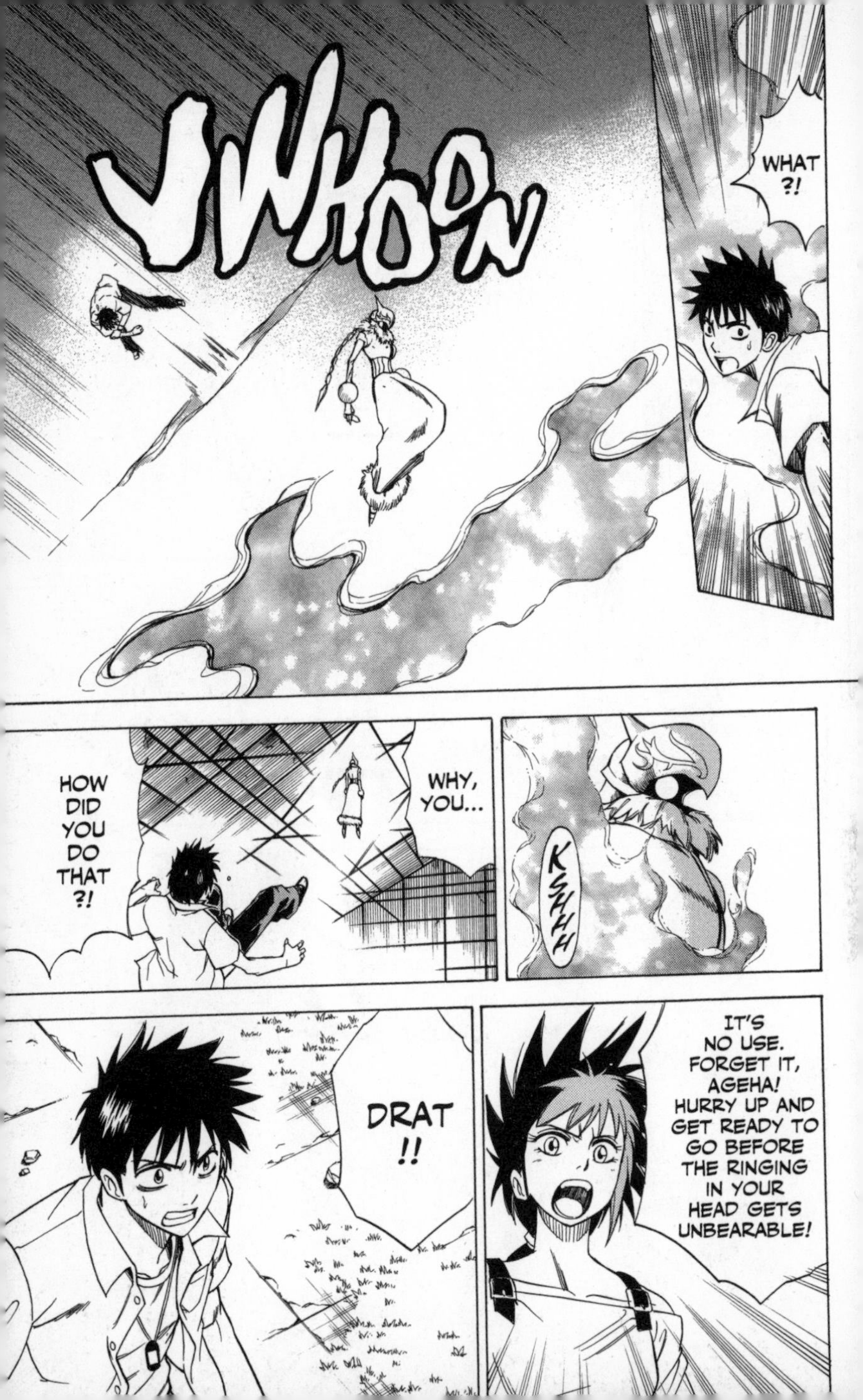
WHAT ?!
VWHOOON
KSHHH
WHY, YOU...
HOW DID YOU DO THAT ?!
IT'S NO USE. FORGET IT, AGEHA! HURRY UP AND GET READY TO GO BEFORE THE RINGING IN YOUR HEAD GETS UNBEARABLE!
DRAT !!

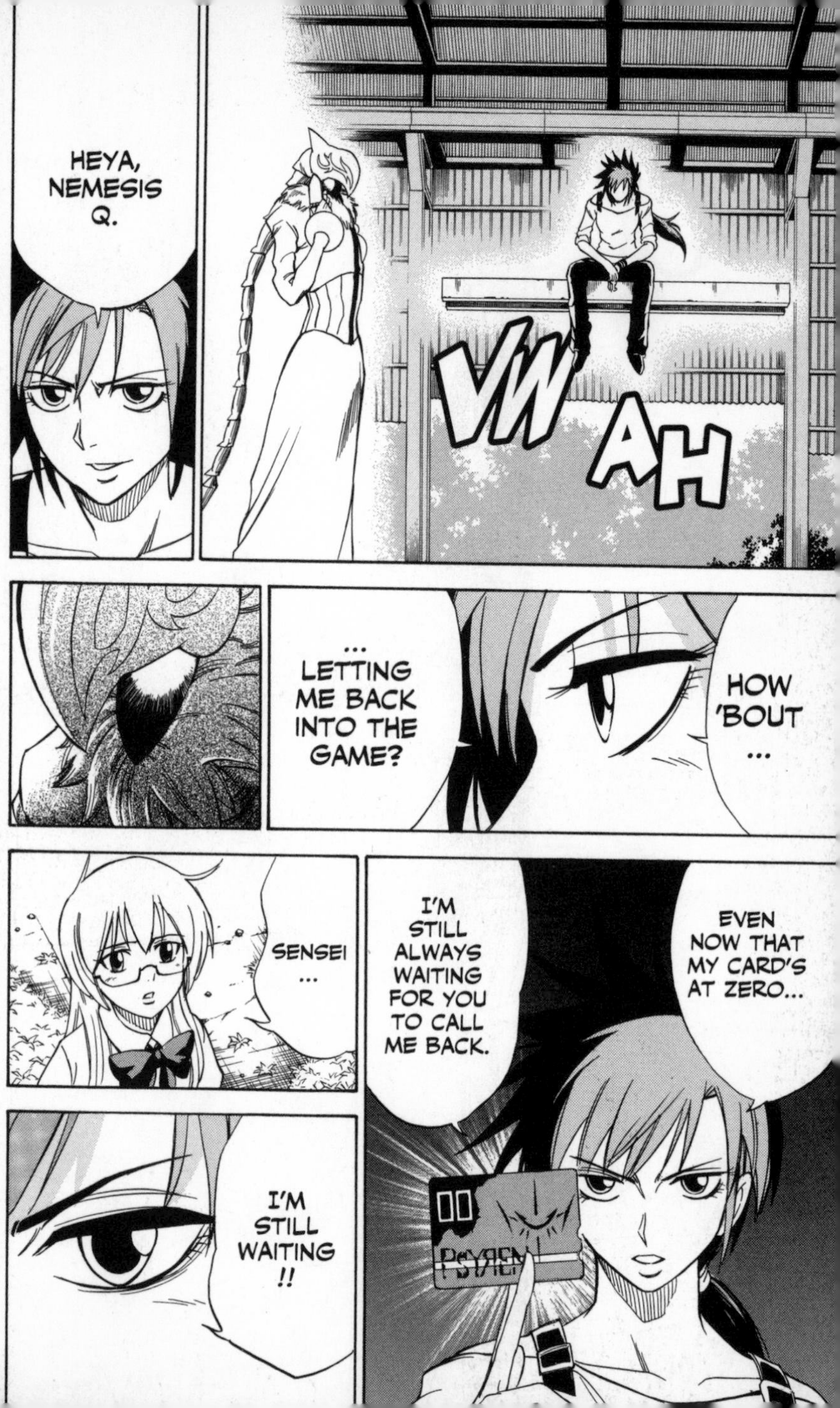
VWAH
HEYA, NEMESIS Q.
HOW 'BOUT ...
... LETTING ME BACK INTO THE GAME?
EVEN NOW THAT MY CARD'S AT ZERO...
I'M STILL ALWAYS WAITING FOR YOU TO CALL ME BACK.
00
PSYREN
SENSEI ...
I'M STILL WAITING !!

Call. 32: The Third Journey

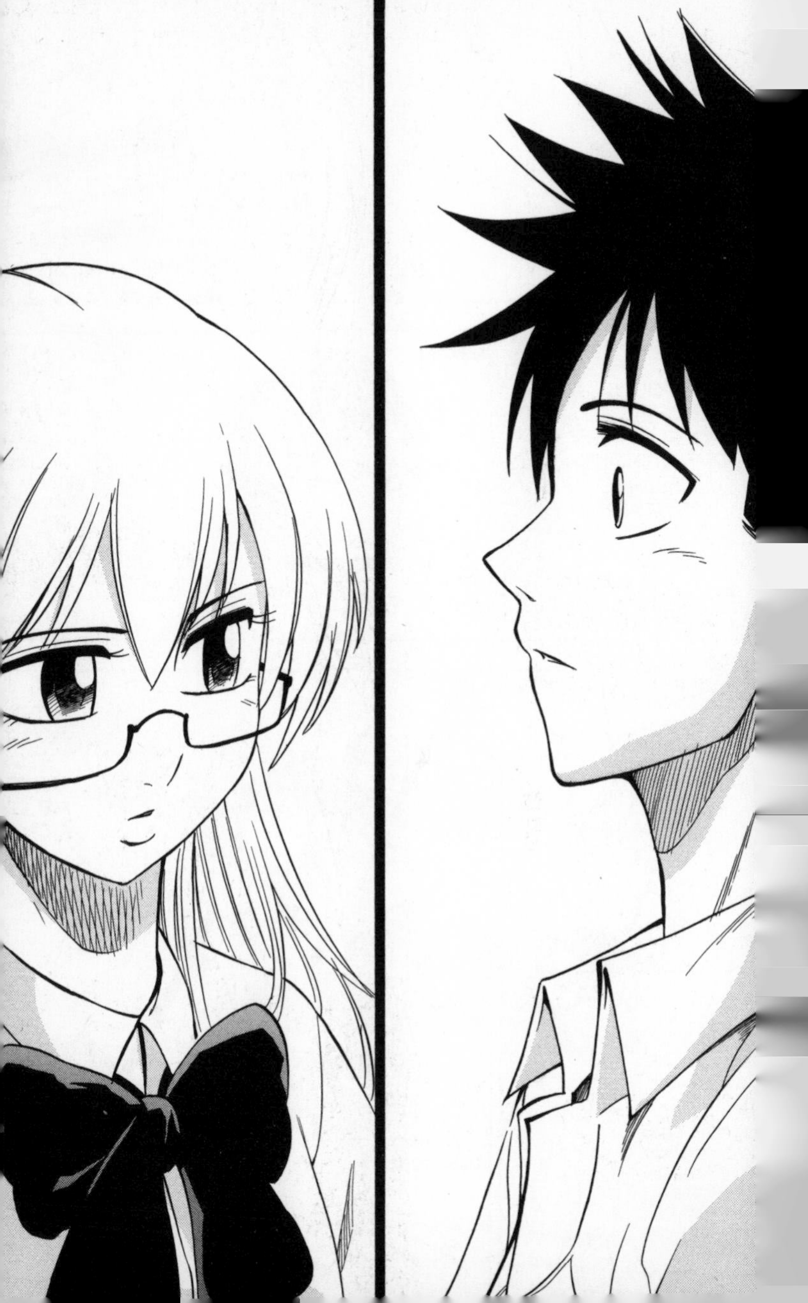

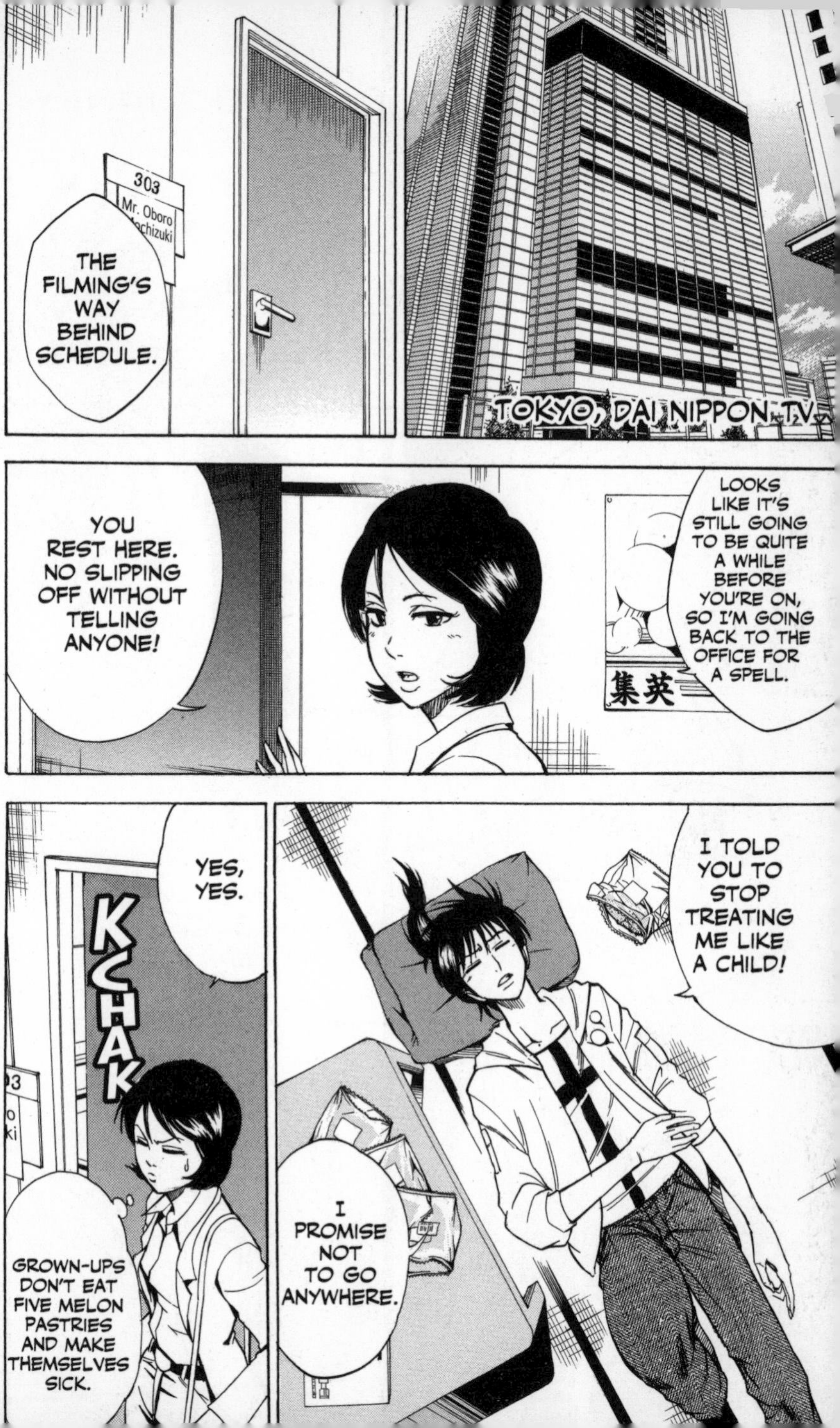
TOKYO, DAI NIPPON TV
303
Mr. Oboro
THE FILMING'S WAY BEHIND SCHEDULE.
LOOKS LIKE IT'S STILL GOING TO BE QUITE A WHILE BEFORE YOU'RE ON, SO I'M GOING BACK TO THE OFFICE FOR A SPELL.
集英
YOU REST HERE. NO SLIPPING OFF WITHOUT TELLING ANYONE!
I TOLD YOU TO STOP TREATING ME LIKE A CHILD!
I PROMISE NOT TO GO ANYWHERE.
YES, YES.
KCHAK
GROWN-UPS DON'T EAT FIVE MELON PASTRIES AND MAKE THEMSELVES SICK.

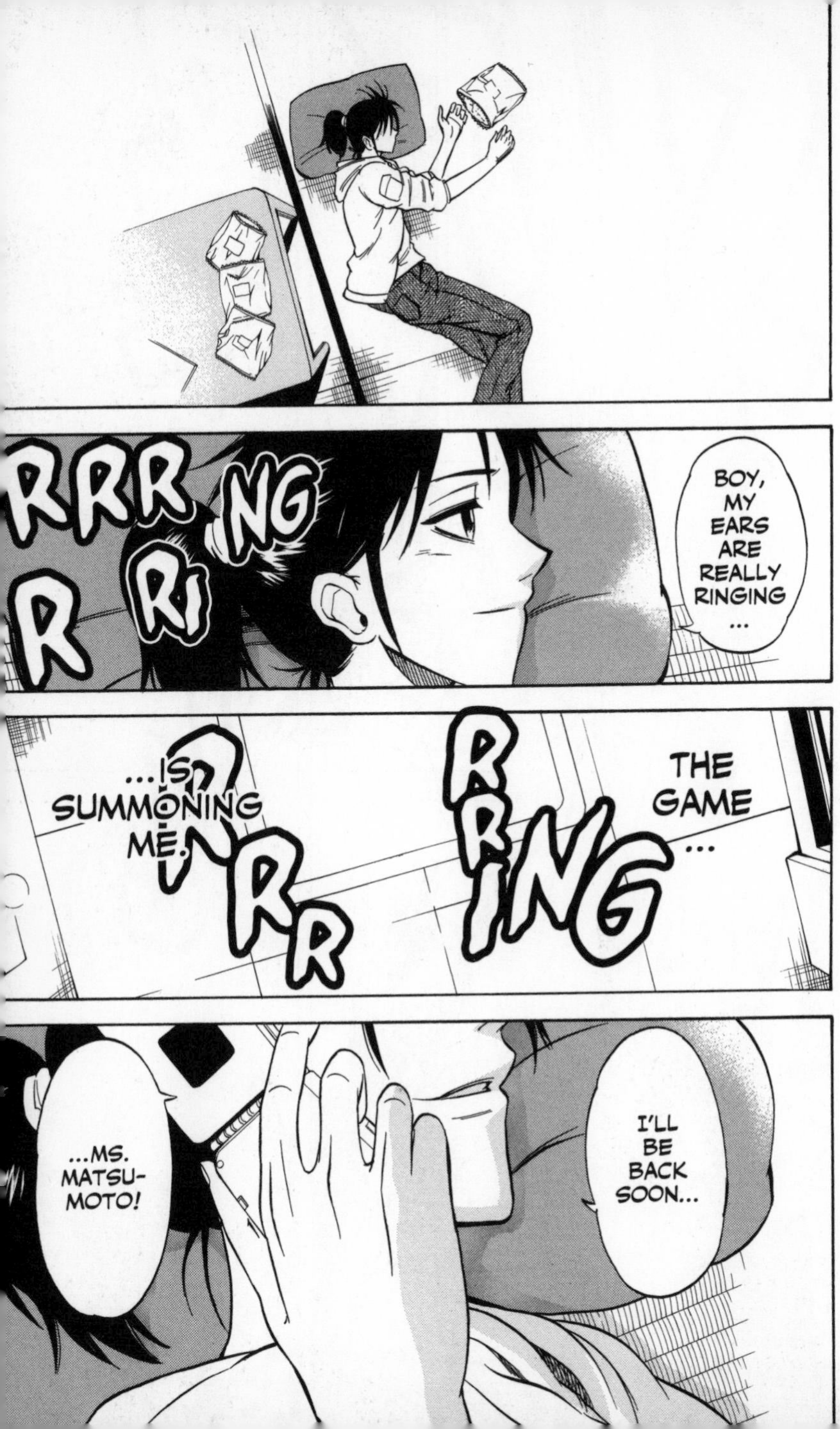
BOY, MY EARS ARE REALLY RINGING ...
RRRRRING
THE GAME ...
RRRRING
...IS SUMMONING ME.
I'LL BE BACK SOON...
...MS. MATSU-MOTO!

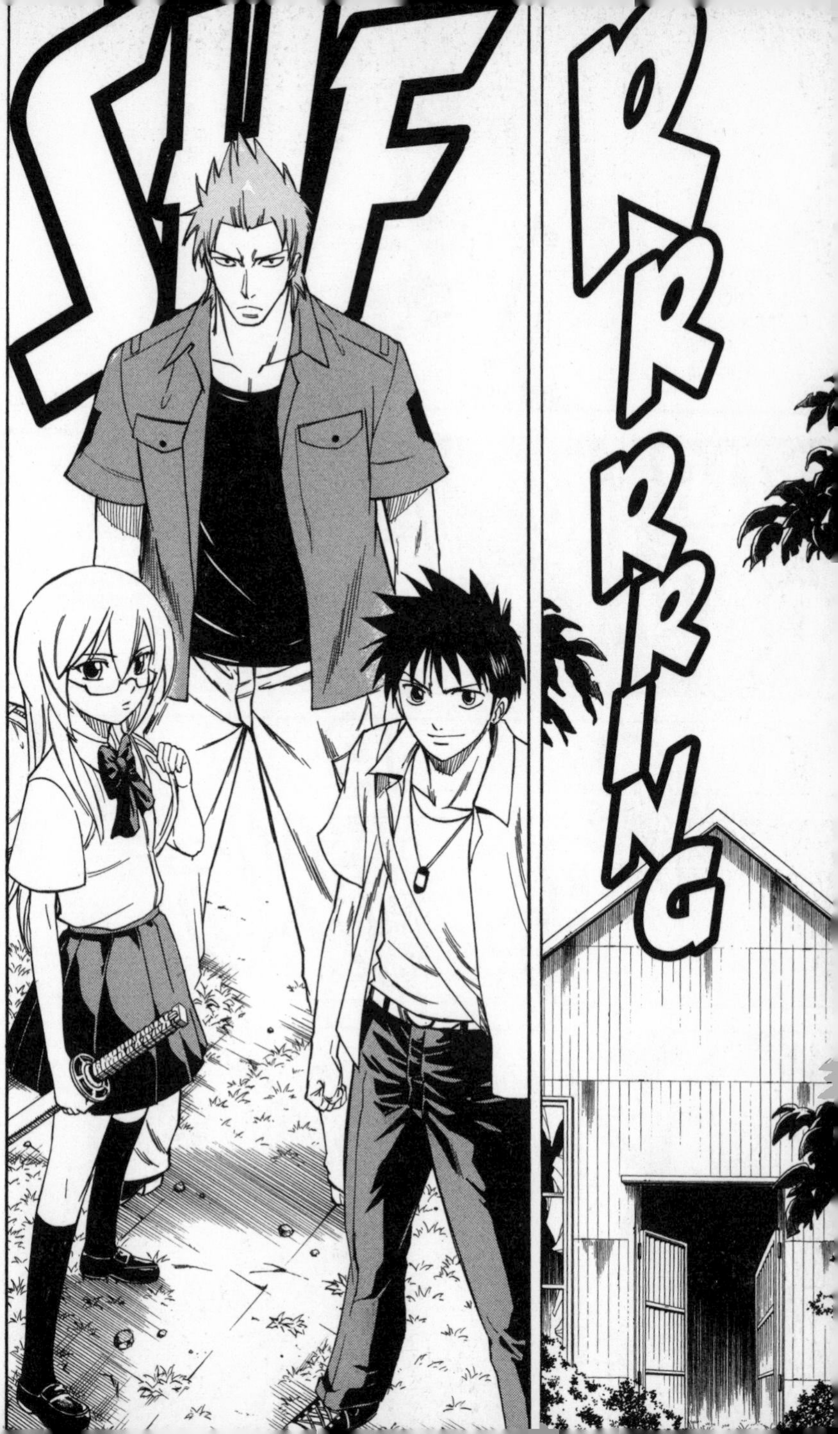
RRRRING
SUF

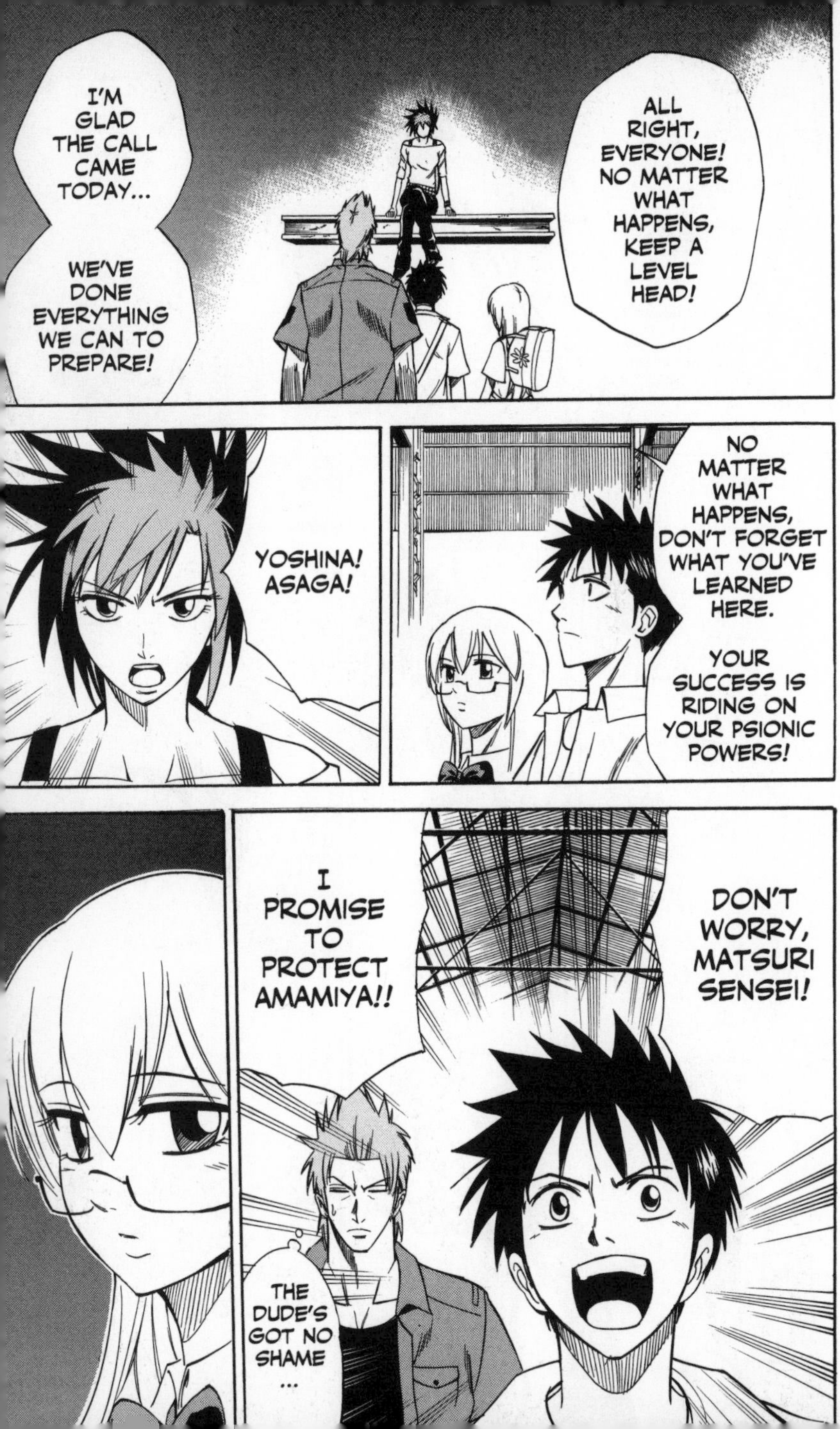
ALL RIGHT, EVERYONE! NO MATTER WHAT HAPPENS, KEEP A LEVEL HEAD!
I'M GLAD THE CALL CAME TODAY...
WE'VE DONE EVERYTHING WE CAN TO PREPARE!
NO MATTER WHAT HAPPENS, DON'T FORGET WHAT YOU'VE LEARNED HERE.
YOUR SUCCESS IS RIDING ON YOUR PSIONIC POWERS!
YOSHINA! ASAGA!
DON'T WORRY, MATSURI SENSEI!
I PROMISE TO PROTECT AMAMIYA!!
THE DUDE'S GOT NO SHAME ...

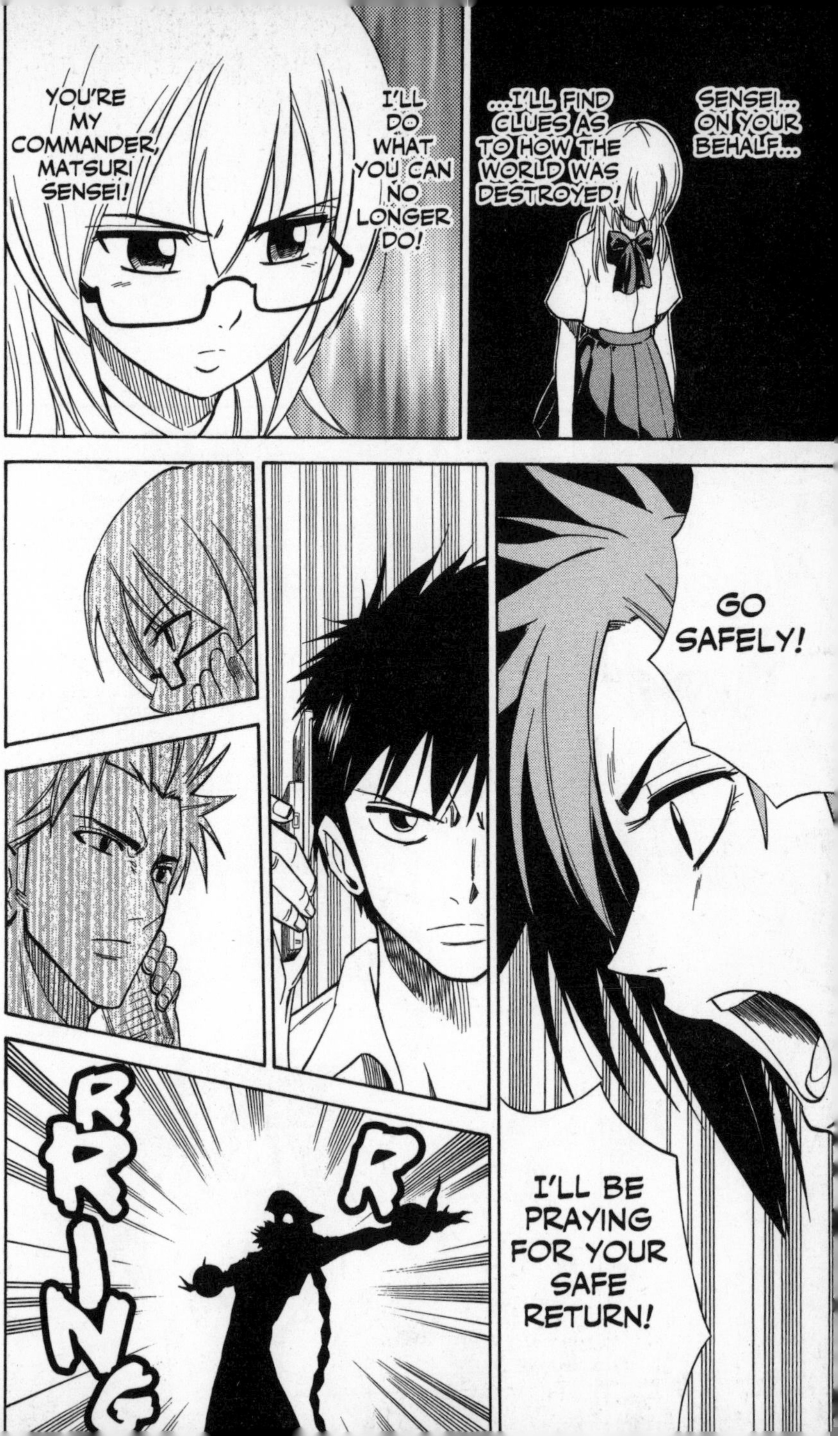
SENSEI... ON YOUR BEHALF...
...I'LL FIND CLUES AS TO HOW THE WORLD WAS DESTROYED!
I'LL DO WHAT YOU CAN NO LONGER DO!
YOU'RE MY COMMANDER, MATSURI SENSEI!
GO SAFELY!
I'LL BE PRAYING FOR YOUR SAFE RETURN!
RRING
R

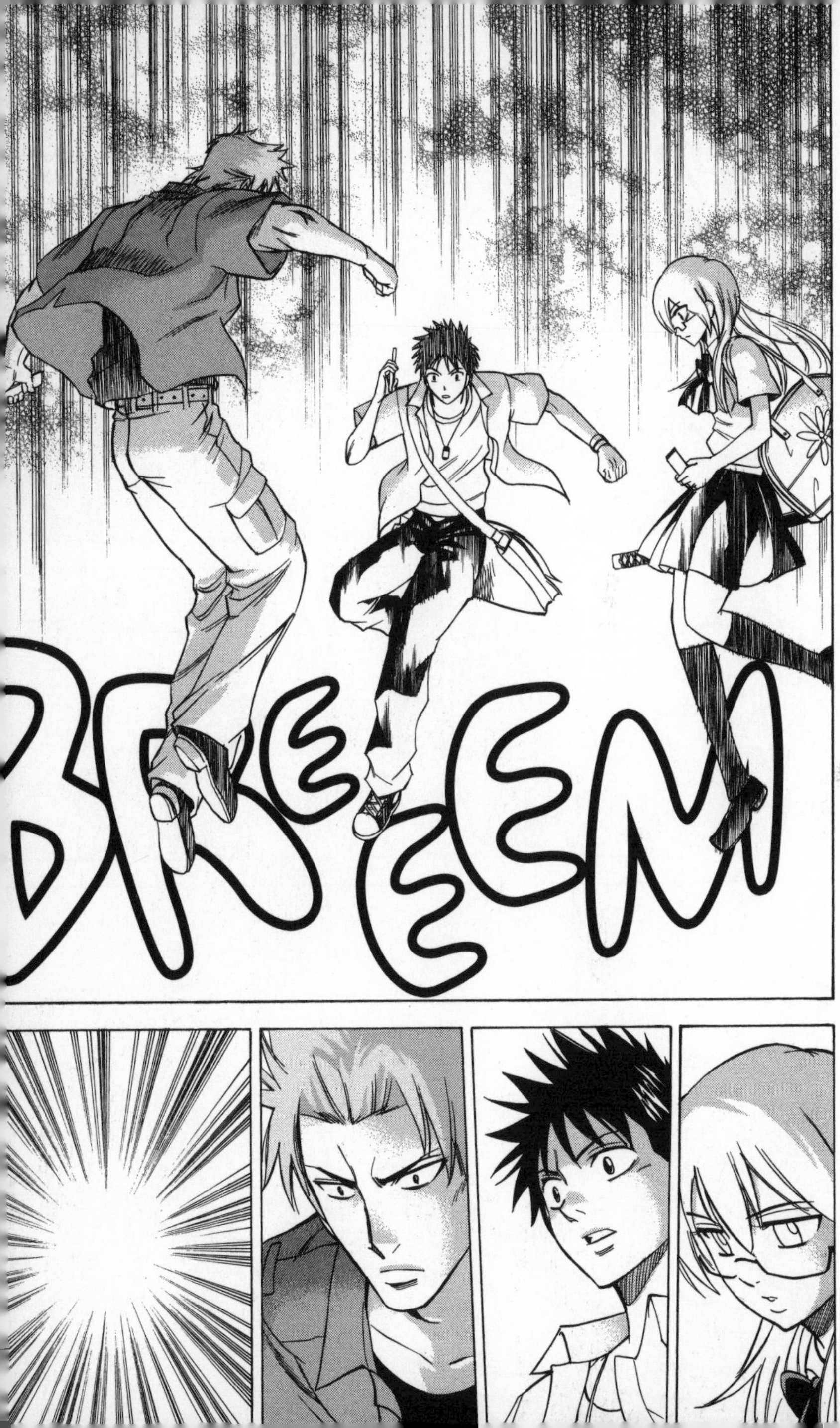
BREEEM

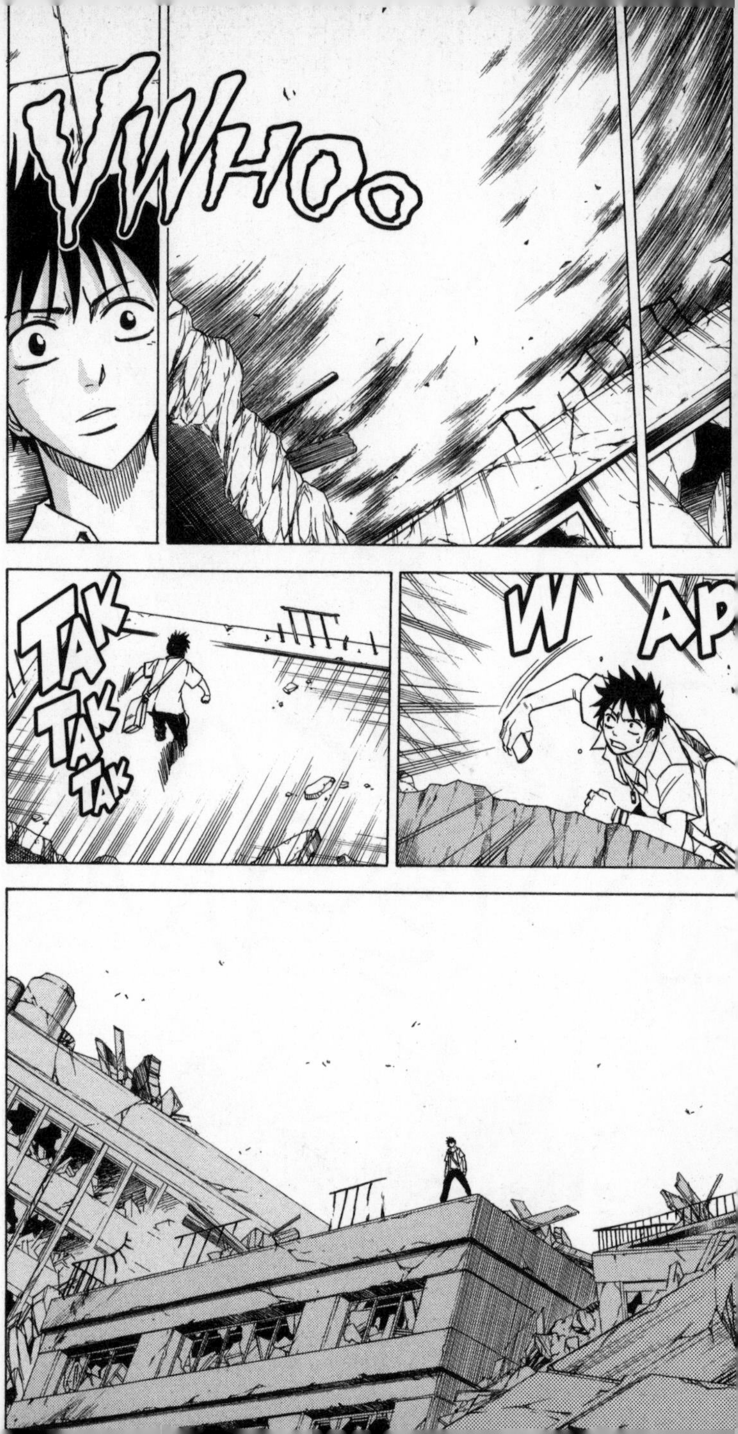
VWHOO
W AP
TAK
TAK
TAK

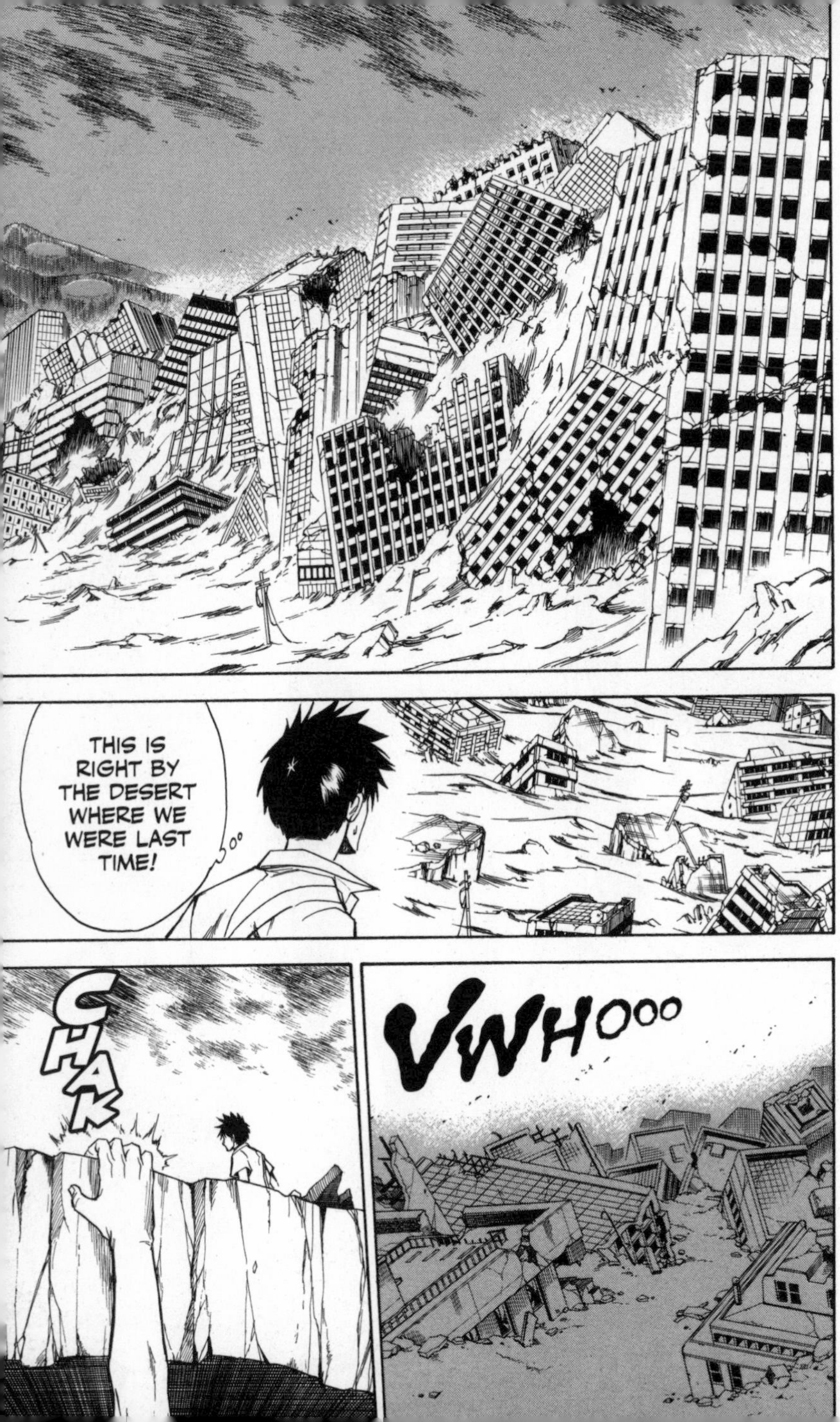
THIS IS RIGHT BY THE DESERT WHERE WE WERE LAST TIME!
VWHOOO
CHAK

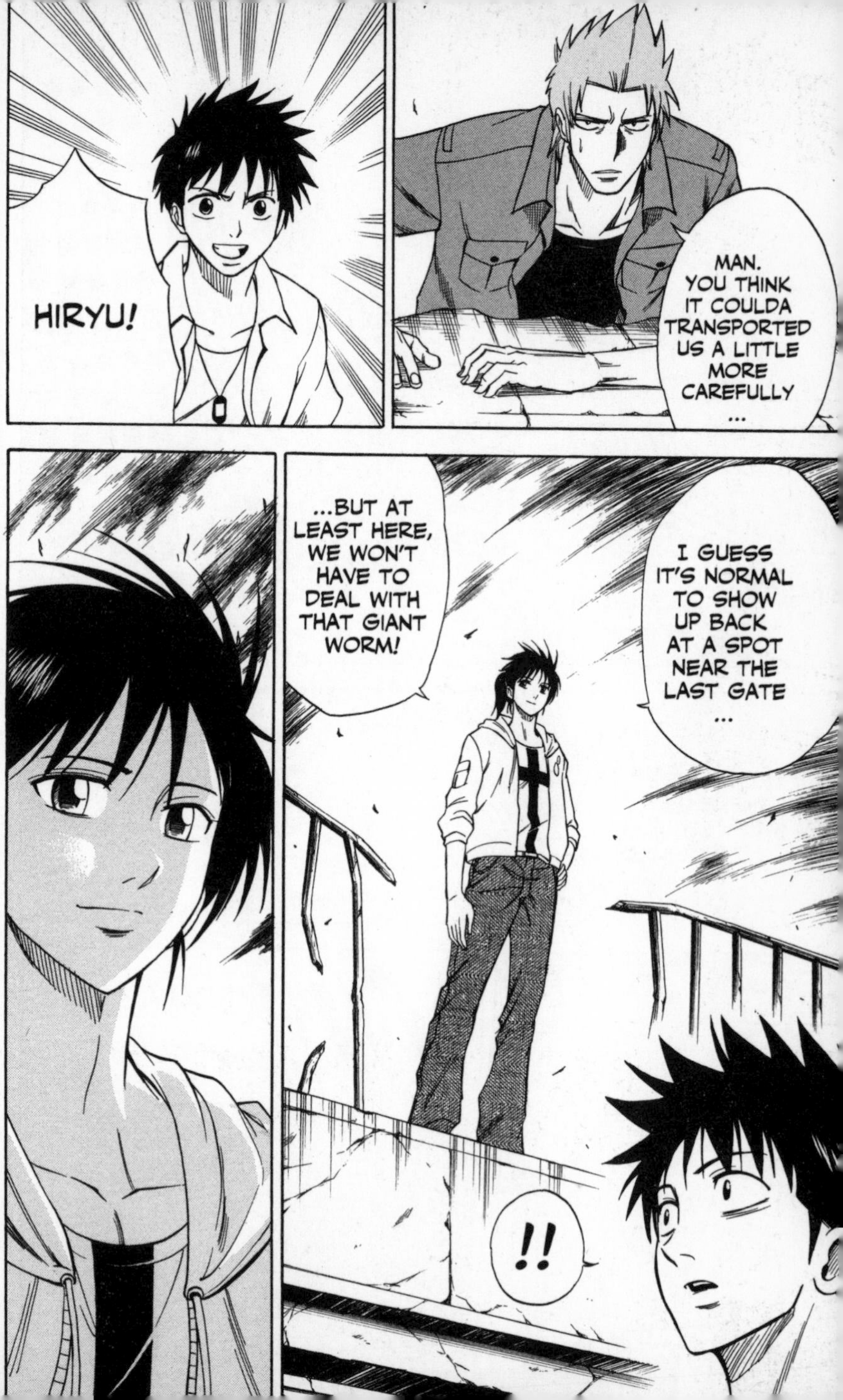
MAN. YOU THINK IT COULDA TRANSPORTED US A LITTLE MORE CAREFULLY ...
HIRYU!
I GUESS IT'S NORMAL TO SHOW UP BACK AT A SPOT NEAR THE LAST GATE ...
...BUT AT LEAST HERE, WE WON'T HAVE TO DEAL WITH THAT GIANT WORM!
!!

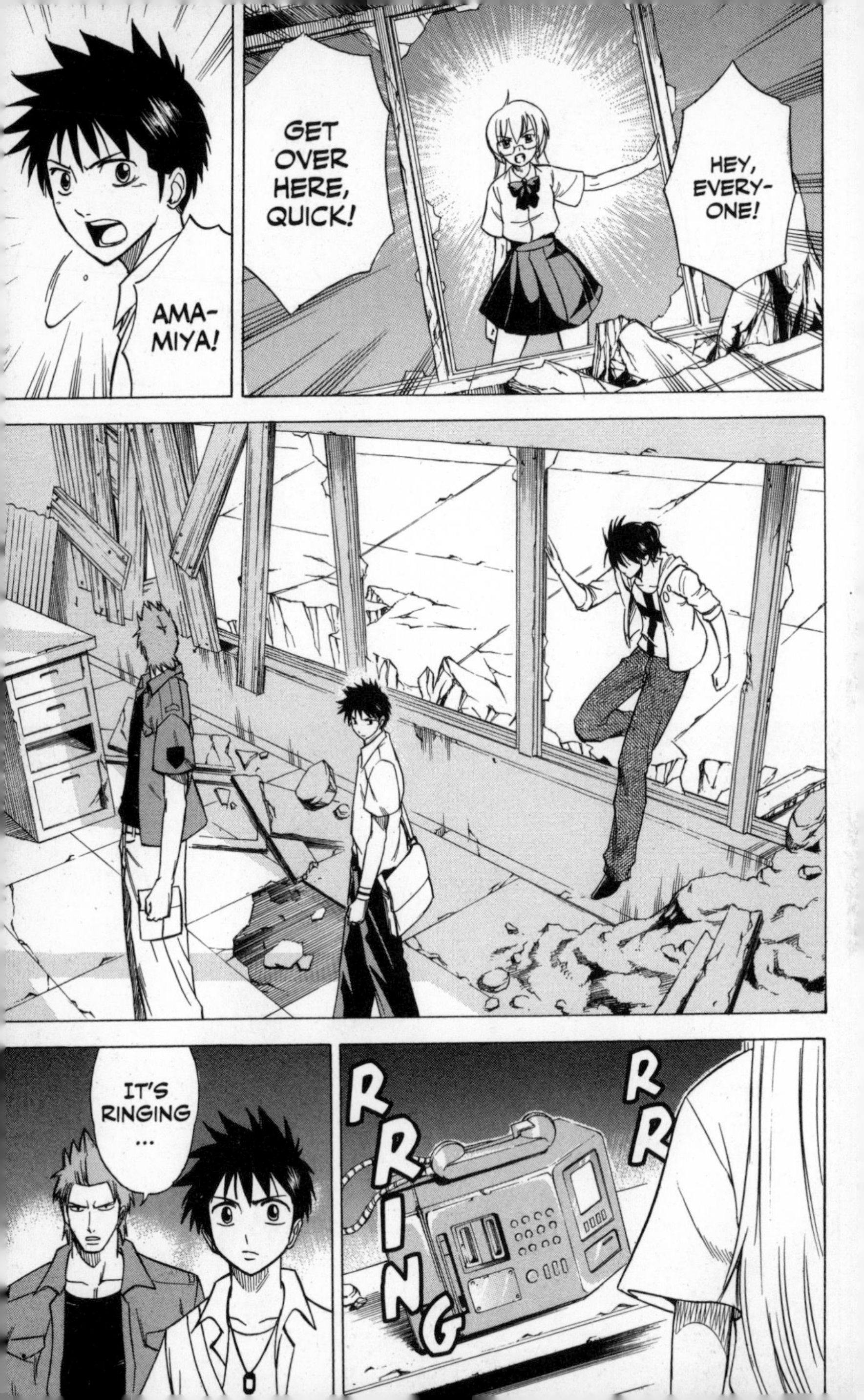
HEY, EVERY-ONE!
GET OVER HERE, QUICK!
AMA-MIYA!
RR
RRING
IT'S RINGING ...

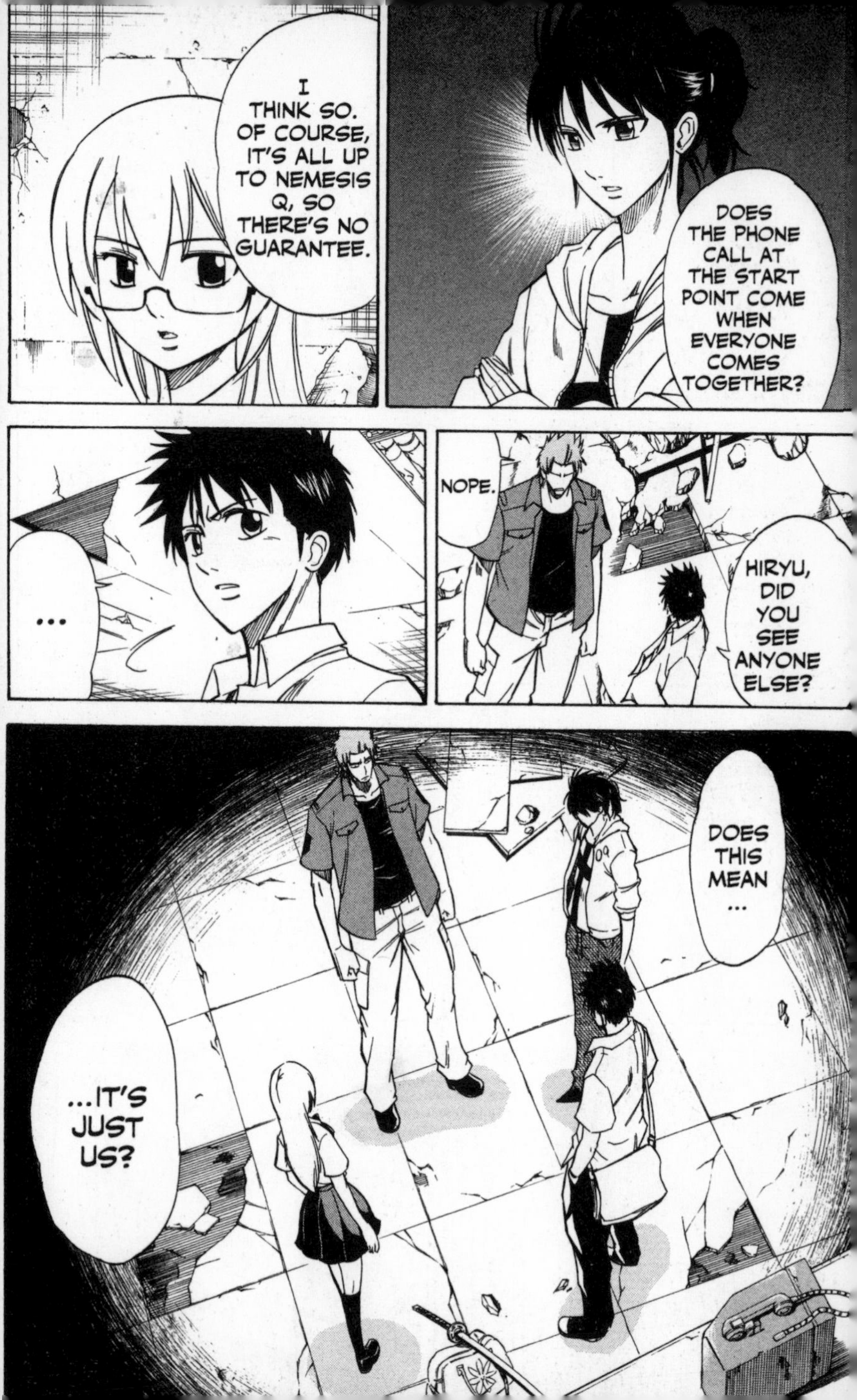
DOES THE PHONE CALL AT THE START POINT COME WHEN EVERYONE COMES TOGETHER?
I THINK SO. OF COURSE, IT'S ALL UP TO NEMESIS Q, SO THERE'S NO GUARANTEE.
HIRYU, DID YOU SEE ANYONE ELSE?
NOPE.
...
DOES THIS MEAN ...
...IT'S JUST US?

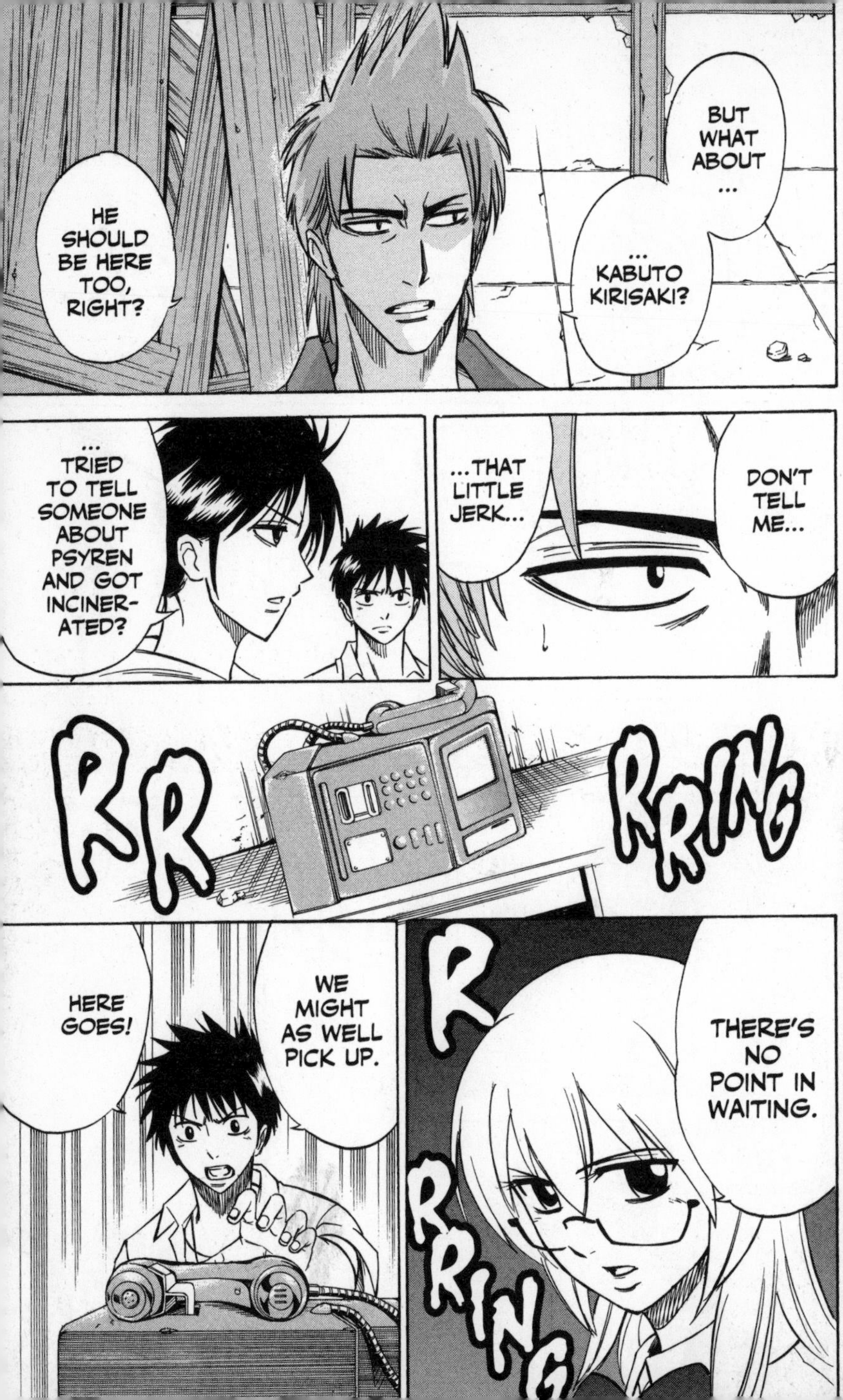
BUT WHAT ABOUT ...
... KABUTO KIRISAKI?
HE SHOULD BE HERE TOO, RIGHT?
DON'T TELL ME...
...THAT LITTLE JERK...
... TRIED TO TELL SOMEONE ABOUT PSYREN AND GOT INCINERATED?
RR
RRING
THERE'S NO POINT IN WAITING.
R
RRING
WE MIGHT AS WELL PICK UP.
HERE GOES!

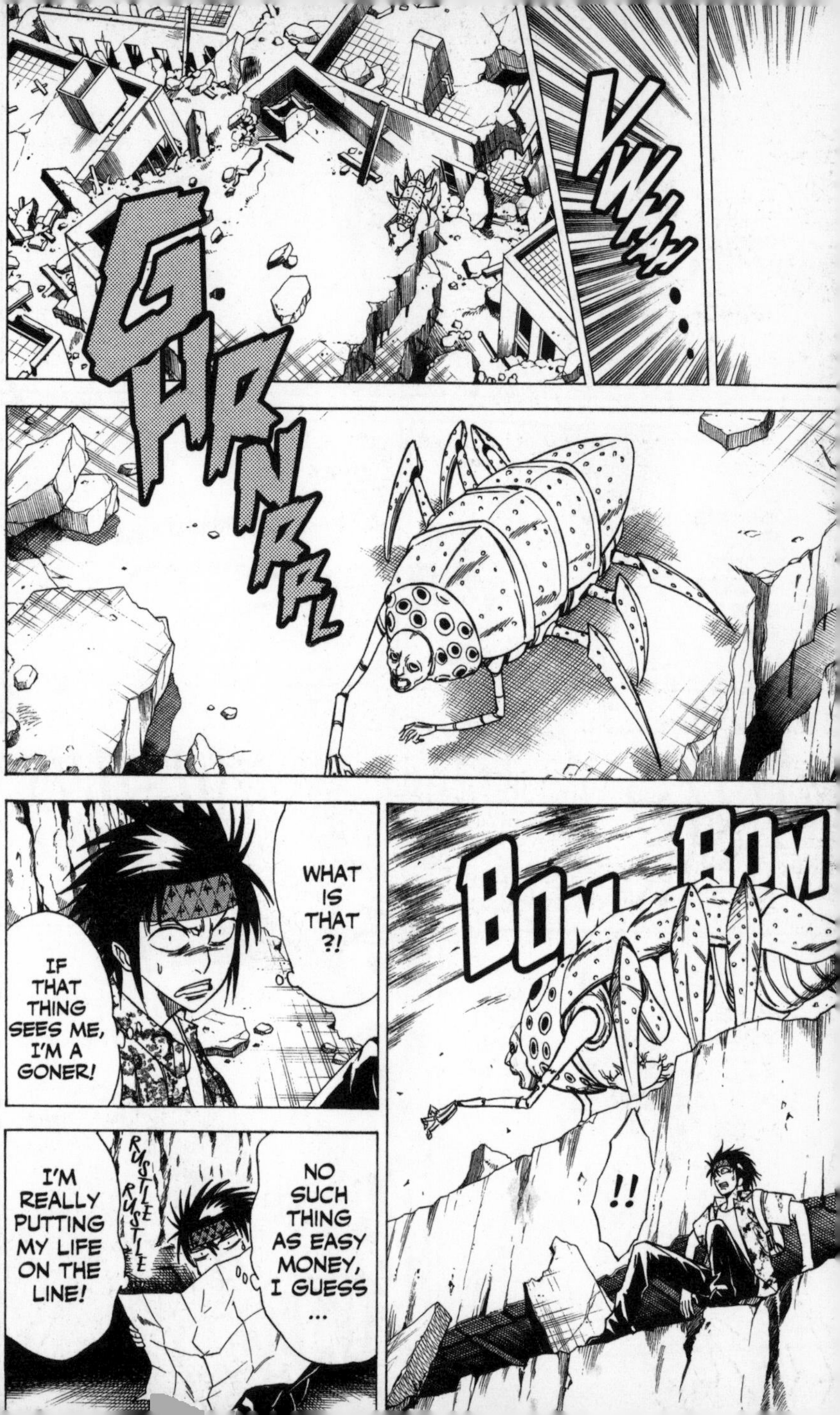
VWHAM...
GURNRRL
BOM BOM
!!
WHAT IS THAT?!
IF THAT THING SEES ME, I'M A GONER!
NO SUCH THING AS EASY MONEY, I GUESS...
RUSTLE RUSTLE
I'M REALLY PUTTING MY LIFE ON THE LINE!

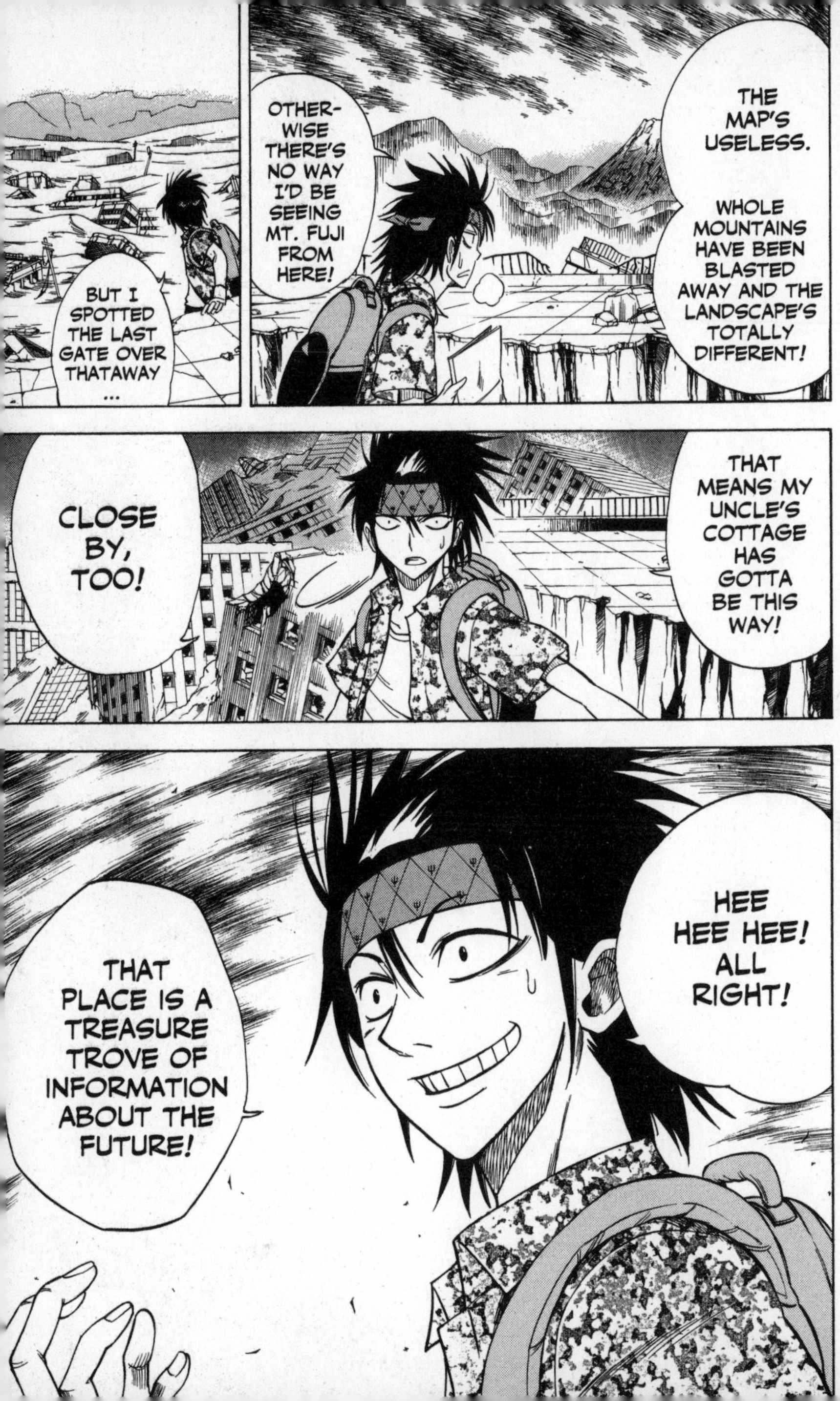
THE MAP'S USELESS.
WHOLE MOUNTAINS HAVE BEEN BLASTED AWAY AND THE LANDSCAPE'S TOTALLY DIFFERENT!
OTHER-WISE THERE'S NO WAY I'D BE SEEING MT. FUJI FROM HERE!
BUT I SPOTTED THE LAST GATE OVER THATAWAY...
THAT MEANS MY UNCLE'S COTTAGE HAS GOTTA BE THIS WAY!
CLOSE BY, TOO!
HEE HEE HEE! ALL RIGHT!
THAT PLACE IS A TREASURE TROVE OF INFORMATION ABOUT THE FUTURE!

Mutters and mumblings...

IN THE *PSYREN* COLLECTIONS, I'M NEVER SURE
WHAT TO DO WITH THE EXTRA PAGES—WHETHER
THEY SHOULD BE CHARACTER PROFILES, OR
WHAT. I'M ALWAYS AFRAID OF GIVING SOMETHING
AWAY TOO SOON... I WISH I COULD WRITE THEM
WITHOUT WORRYING SO MUCH...

Call.33: Treasure Shelter

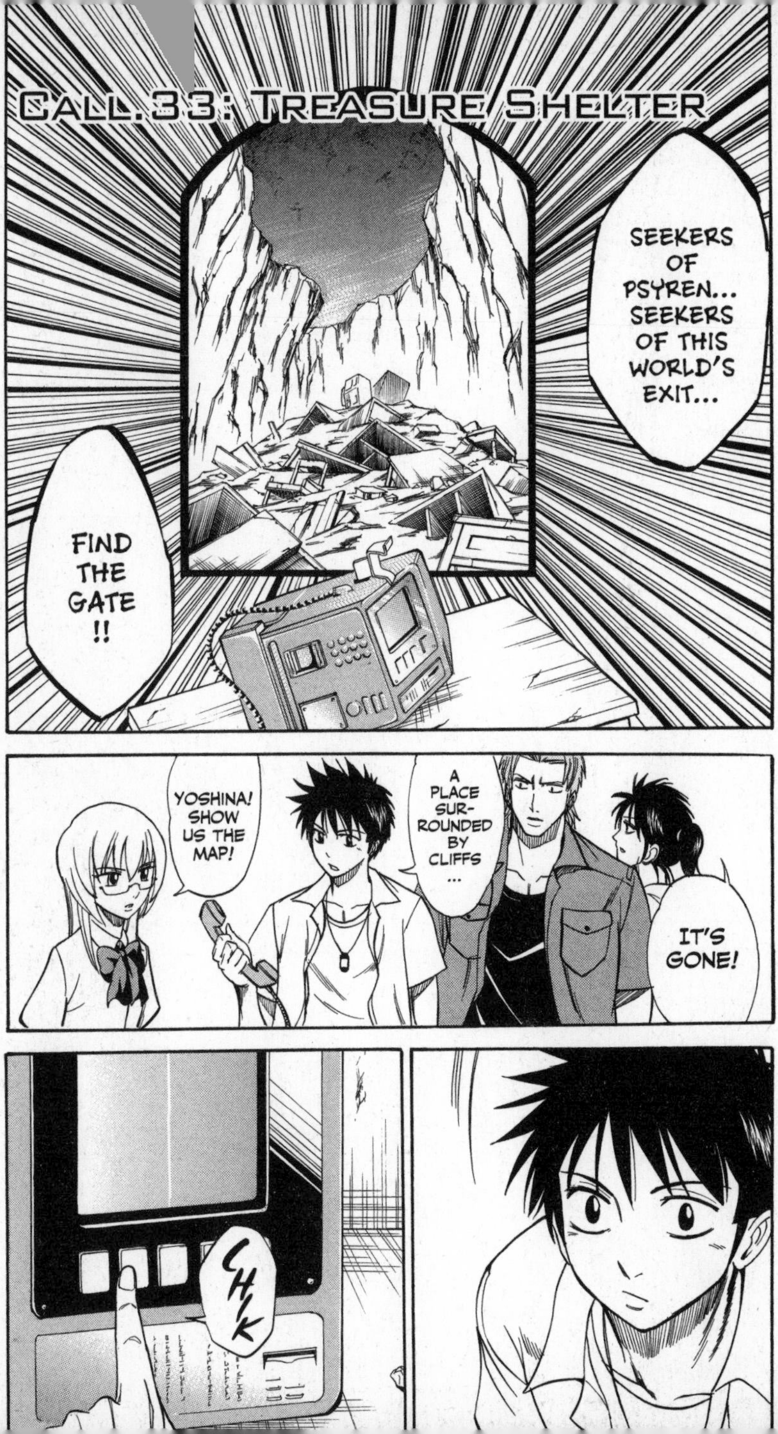

SEEKERS OF PSYREN... SEEKERS OF THIS WORLD'S EXIT...
FIND THE GATE!!
IT'S GONE!
A PLACE SUR-ROUNDED BY CLIFFS...
YOSHINA! SHOW US THE MAP!
CHIK

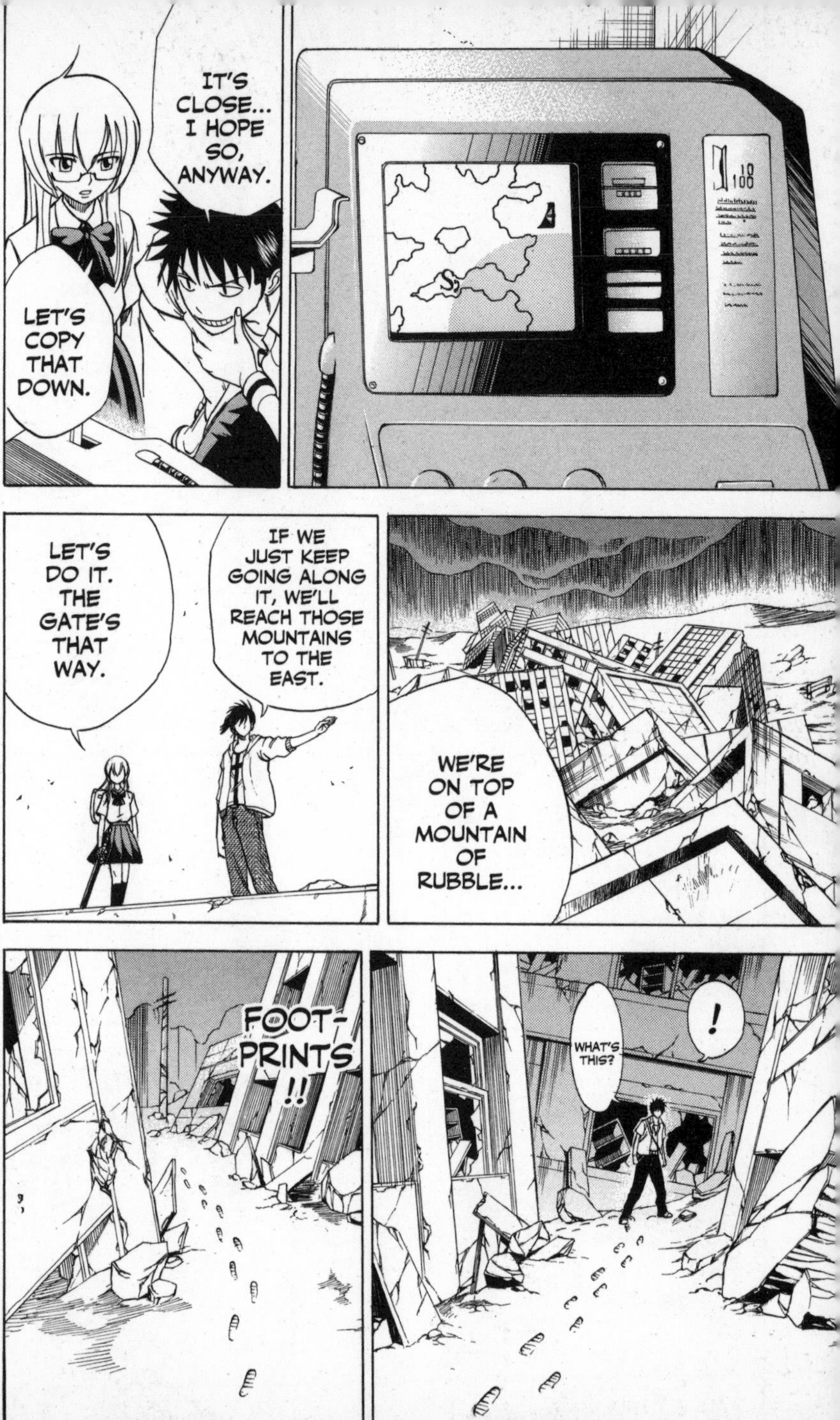
IT'S CLOSE... I HOPE SO, ANYWAY.
LET'S COPY THAT DOWN.
WE'RE ON TOP OF A MOUNTAIN OF RUBBLE...
IF WE JUST KEEP GOING ALONG IT, WE'LL REACH THOSE MOUNTAINS TO THE EAST.
LET'S DO IT. THE GATE'S THAT WAY.
!
WHAT'S THIS?
FOOT-PRINTS!!

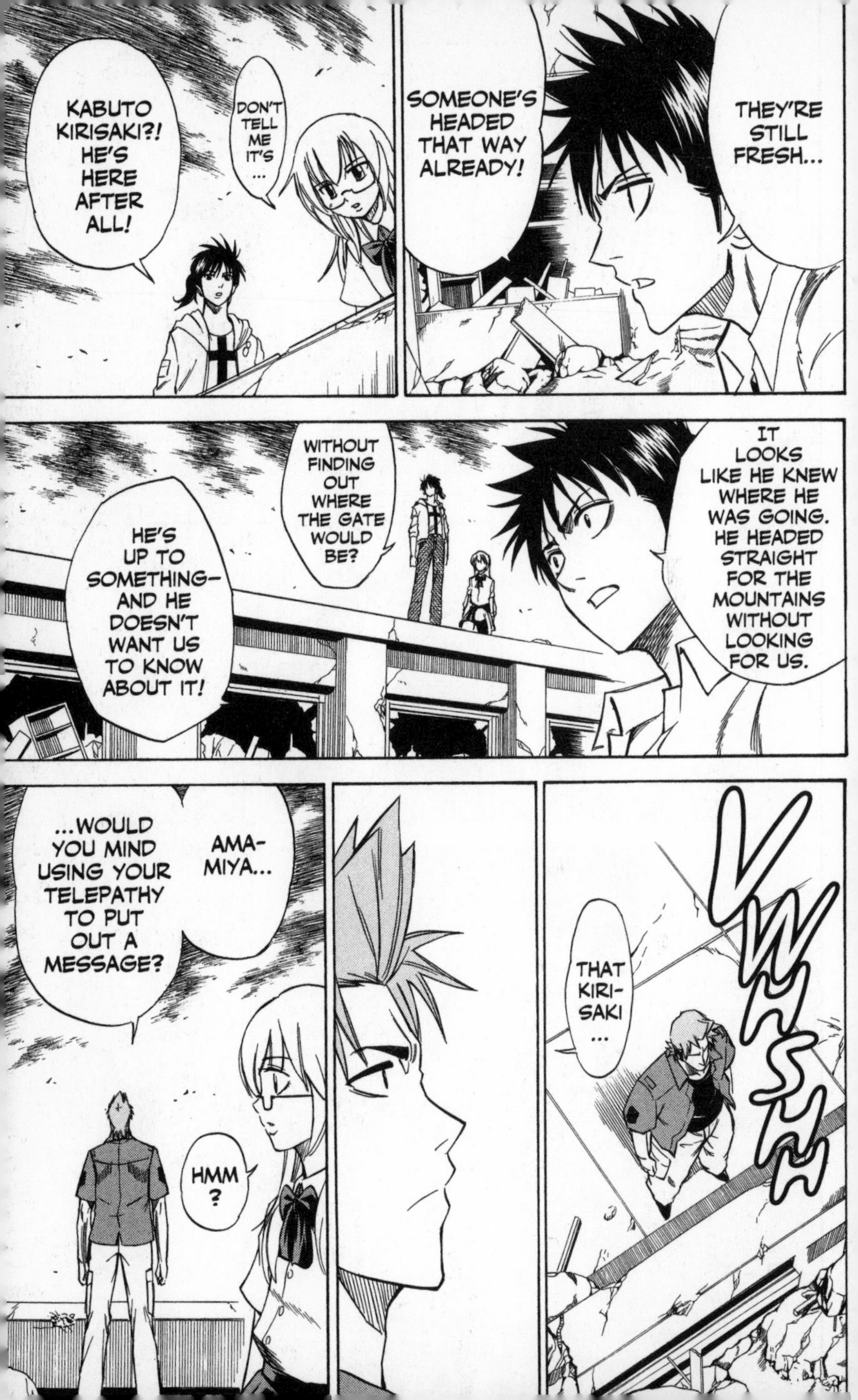
THEY'RE STILL FRESH...
SOMEONE'S HEADED THAT WAY ALREADY!
DON'T TELL ME IT'S...
KABUTO KIRISAKI?! HE'S HERE AFTER ALL!
IT LOOKS LIKE HE KNEW WHERE HE WAS GOING. HE HEADED STRAIGHT FOR THE MOUNTAINS WITHOUT LOOKING FOR US.
WITHOUT FINDING OUT WHERE THE GATE WOULD BE?
HE'S UP TO SOMETHING—AND HE DOESN'T WANT US TO KNOW ABOUT IT!
THAT KIRI-SAKI...
AMA-MIYA...
...WOULD YOU MIND USING YOUR TELEPATHY TO PUT OUT A MESSAGE?
HMM?

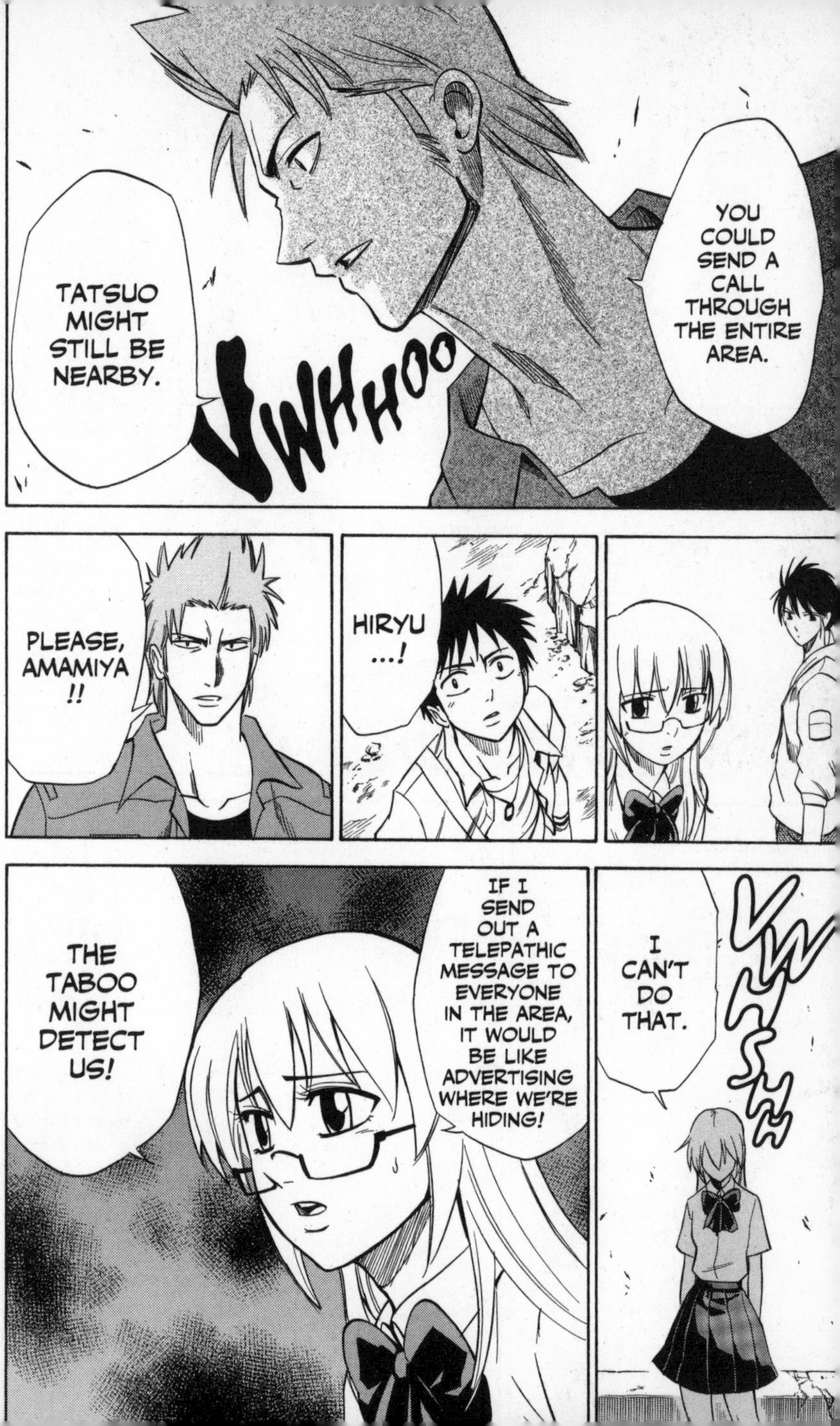
YOU COULD SEND A CALL THROUGH THE ENTIRE AREA.
TATSUO MIGHT STILL BE NEARBY.
HIRYU ...!
PLEASE, AMAMIYA !!
I CAN'T DO THAT.
IF I SEND OUT A TELEPATHIC MESSAGE TO EVERYONE IN THE AREA, IT WOULD BE LIKE ADVERTISING WHERE WE'RE HIDING!
THE TABOO MIGHT DETECT US!

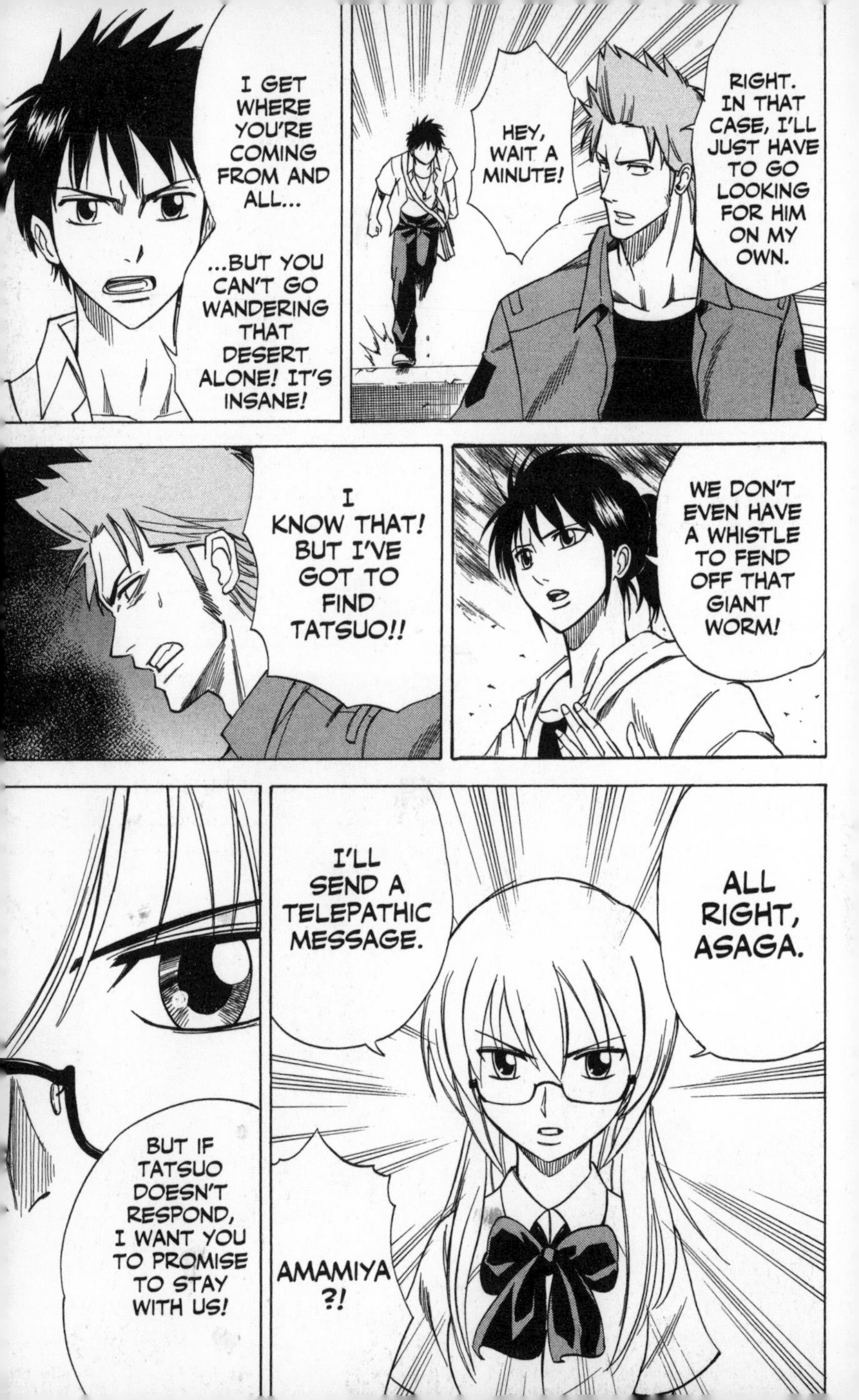
RIGHT. IN THAT CASE, I'LL JUST HAVE TO GO LOOKING FOR HIM ON MY OWN.
HEY, WAIT A MINUTE!
I GET WHERE YOU'RE COMING FROM AND ALL...
...BUT YOU CAN'T GO WANDERING THAT DESERT ALONE! IT'S INSANE!
WE DON'T EVEN HAVE A WHISTLE TO FEND OFF THAT GIANT WORM!
I KNOW THAT! BUT I'VE GOT TO FIND TATSUO!!
ALL RIGHT, ASAGA.
I'LL SEND A TELEPATHIC MESSAGE.
AMAMIYA ?!
BUT IF TATSUO DOESN'T RESPOND, I WANT YOU TO PROMISE TO STAY WITH US!

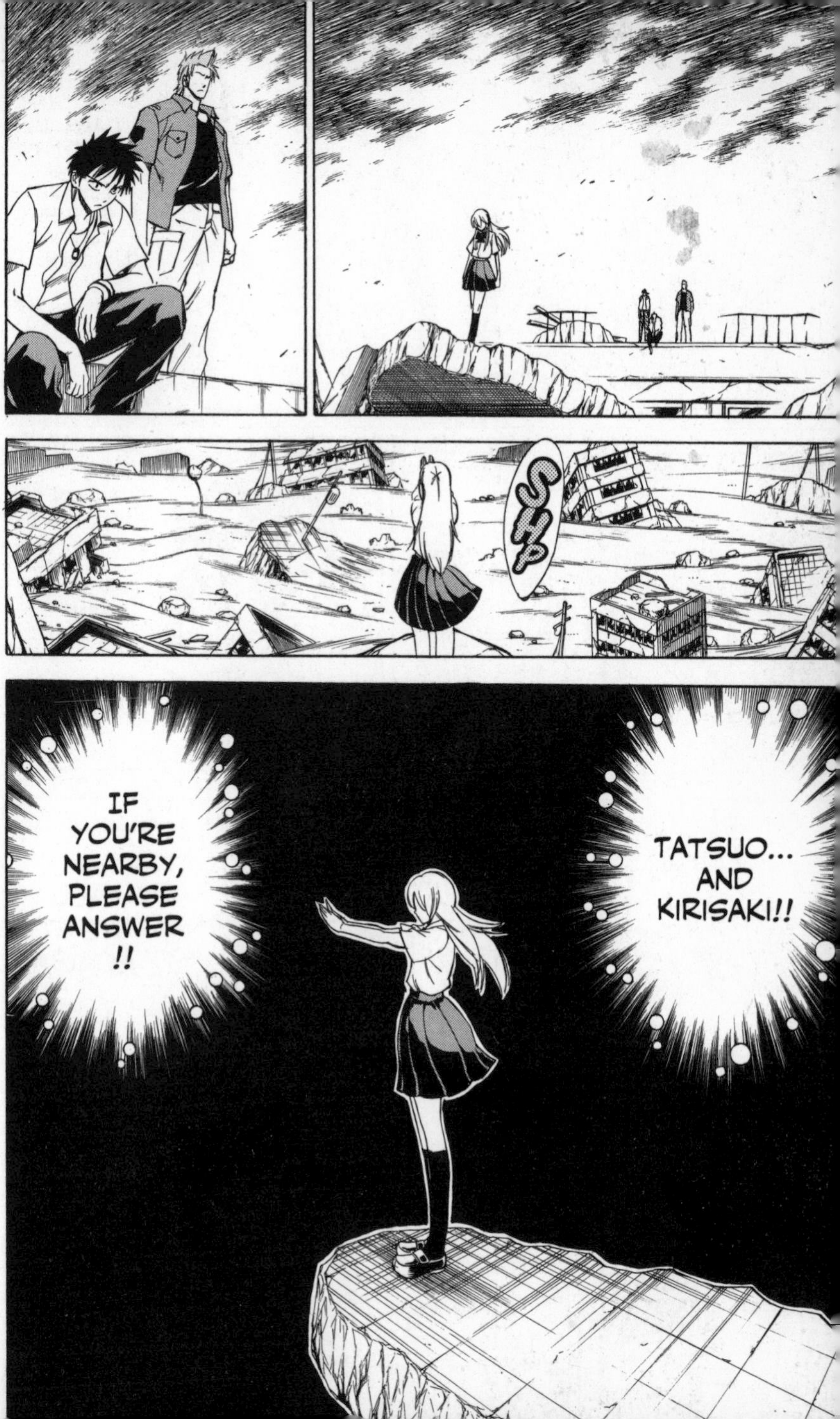
SHP
TATSUO... AND KIRISAKI!!
IF YOU'RE NEARBY, PLEASE ANSWER!!

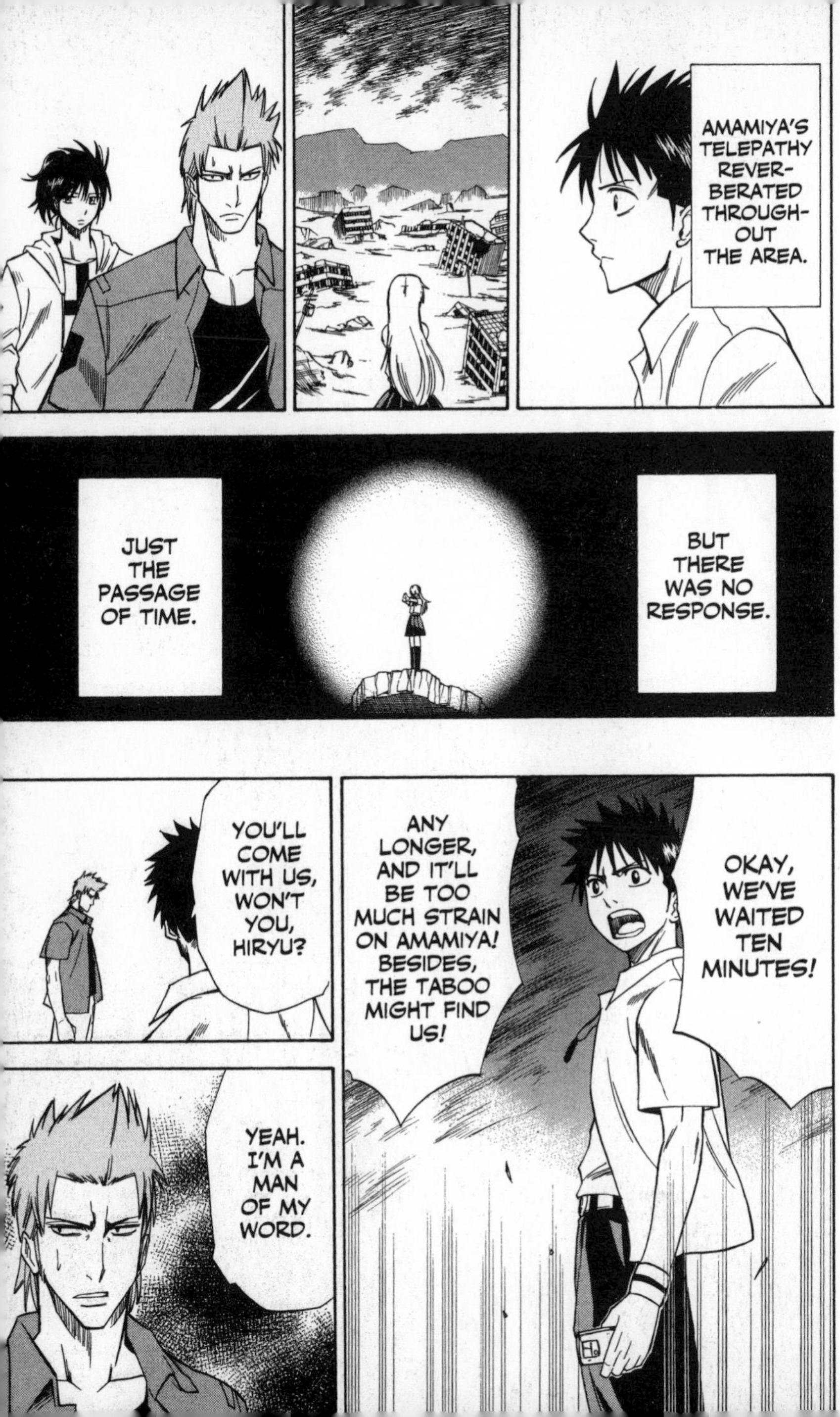
AMAMIYA'S TELEPATHY REVER-BERATED THROUGH-OUT THE AREA.
BUT THERE WAS NO RESPONSE.
JUST THE PASSAGE OF TIME.
OKAY, WE'VE WAITED TEN MINUTES!
ANY LONGER, AND IT'LL BE TOO MUCH STRAIN ON AMAMIYA! BESIDES, THE TABOO MIGHT FIND US!
YOU'LL COME WITH US, WON'T YOU, HIRYU?
YEAH. I'M A MAN OF MY WORD.

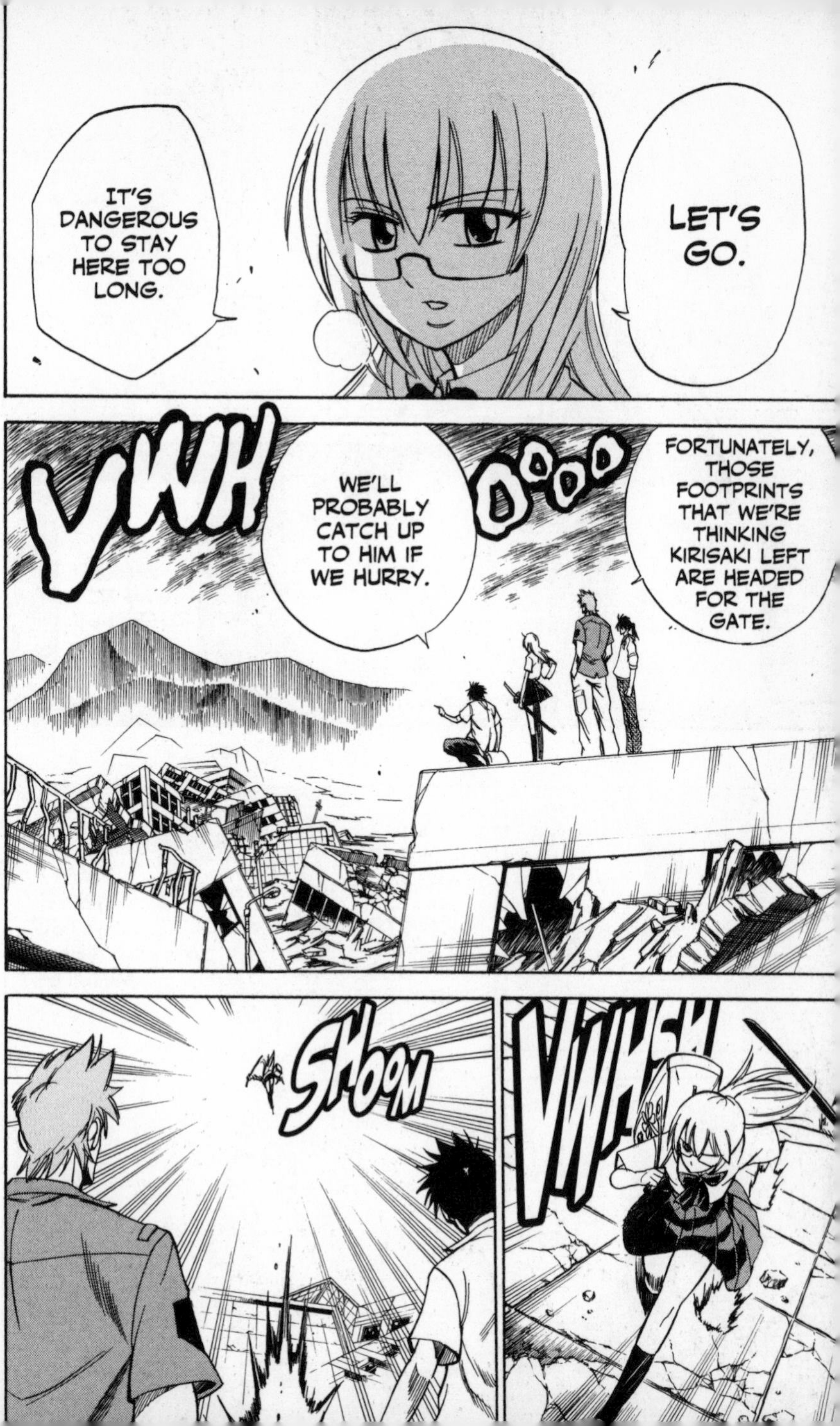

LET'S GO.
IT'S DANGEROUS TO STAY HERE TOO LONG.
FORTUNATELY, THOSE FOOTPRINTS THAT WE'RE THINKING KIRISAKI LEFT ARE HEADED FOR THE GATE.
OOOO
WE'LL PROBABLY CATCH UP TO HIM IF WE HURRY.
VWH
VWHSH
SHOOM

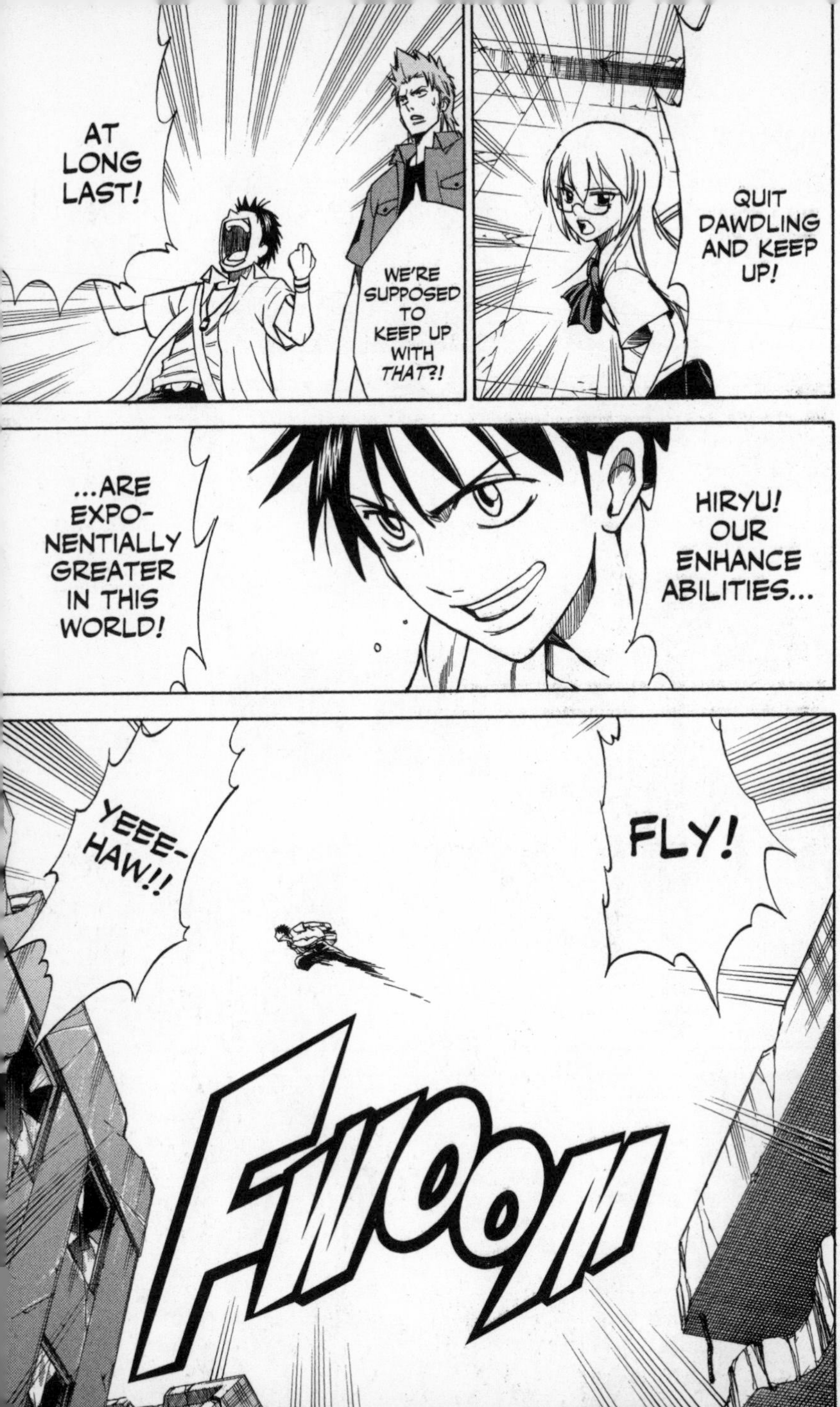
QUIT DAWDLING AND KEEP UP!
WE'RE SUPPOSED TO KEEP UP WITH *THAT?!*
AT LONG LAST!
HIRYU! OUR ENHANCE ABILITIES...
...ARE EXPO-NENTIALLY GREATER IN THIS WORLD!
FLY!
YEEEE-HAW!!
FWOOM

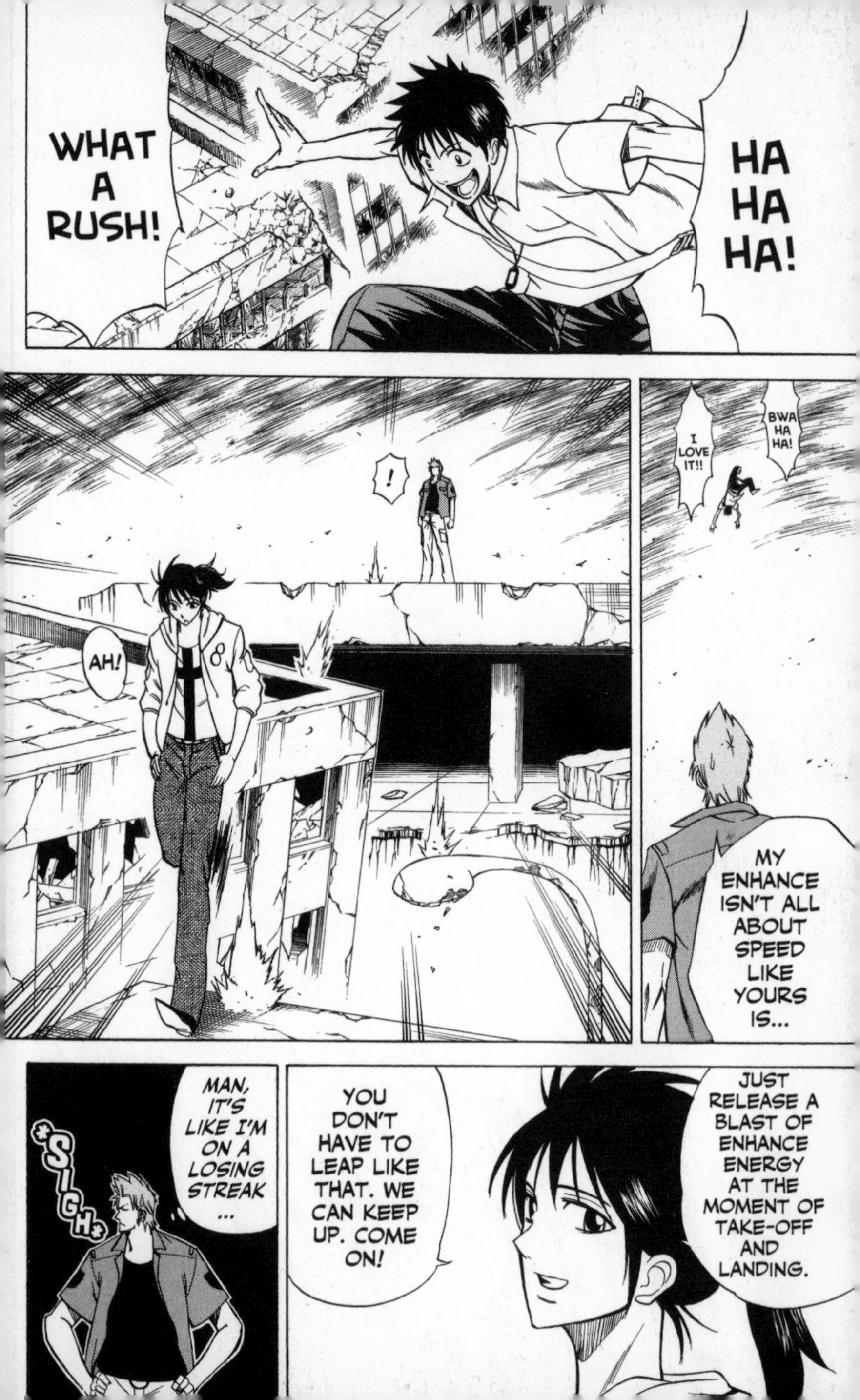
HA HA HA!
WHAT A RUSH!
BWA HA HA!
I LOVE IT!!
MY ENHANCE ISN'T ALL ABOUT SPEED LIKE YOURS IS...
!
AH!
JUST RELEASE A BLAST OF ENHANCE ENERGY AT THE MOMENT OF TAKE-OFF AND LANDING.
YOU DON'T HAVE TO LEAP LIKE THAT. WE CAN KEEP UP. COME ON!
SIGH
MAN, IT'S LIKE I'M ON A LOSING STREAK...

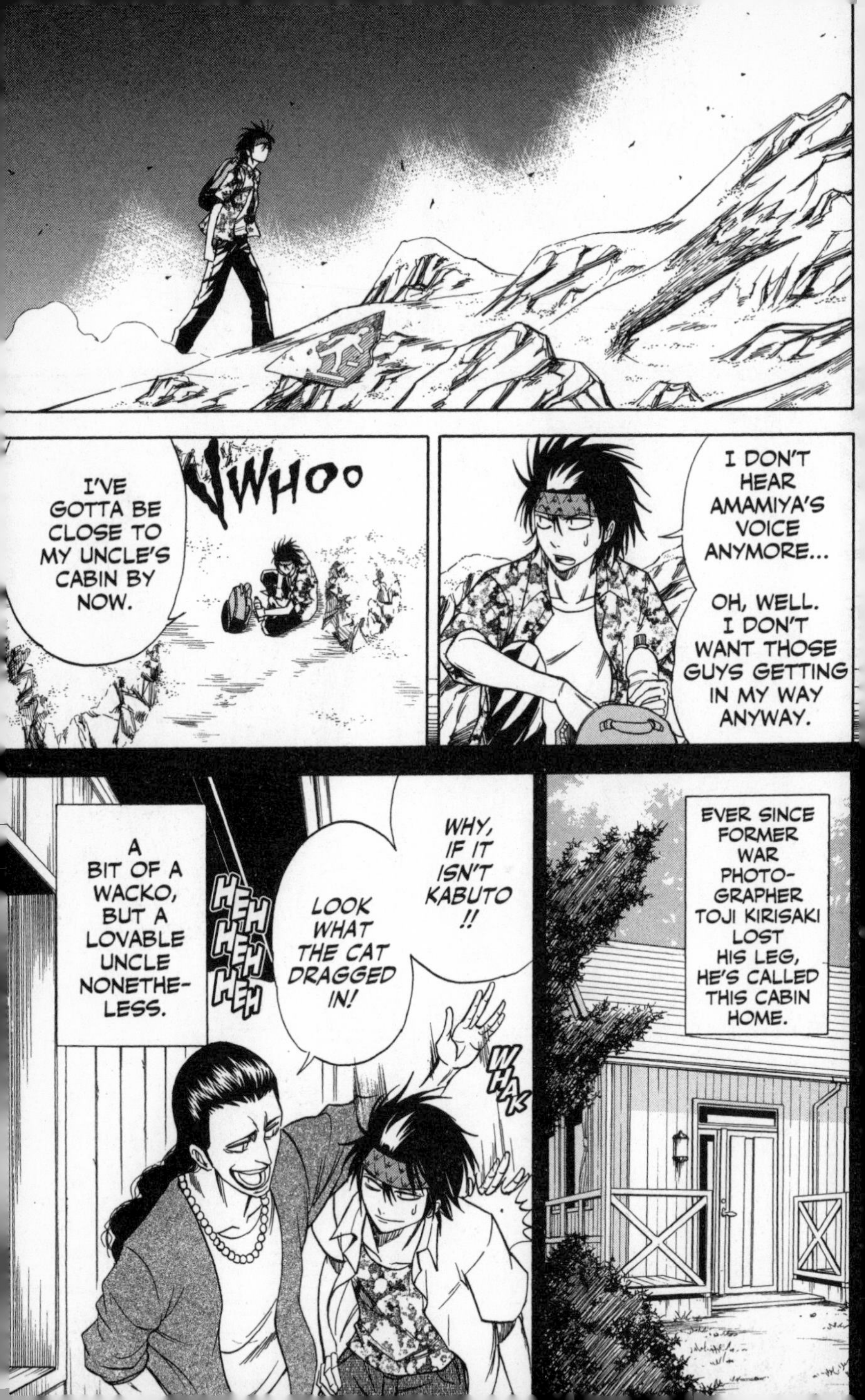
I DON'T HEAR AMAMIYA'S VOICE ANYMORE...
OH, WELL. I DON'T WANT THOSE GUYS GETTING IN MY WAY ANYWAY.
VWHOO
I'VE GOTTA BE CLOSE TO MY UNCLE'S CABIN BY NOW.
EVER SINCE FORMER WAR PHOTO-GRAPHER TOJI KIRISAKI LOST HIS LEG, HE'S CALLED THIS CABIN HOME.
WHY, IF IT ISN'T KABUTO !!
LOOK WHAT THE CAT DRAGGED IN!
WHAK
HEH HEH HEH
A BIT OF A WACKO, BUT A LOVABLE UNCLE NONETHE-LESS.

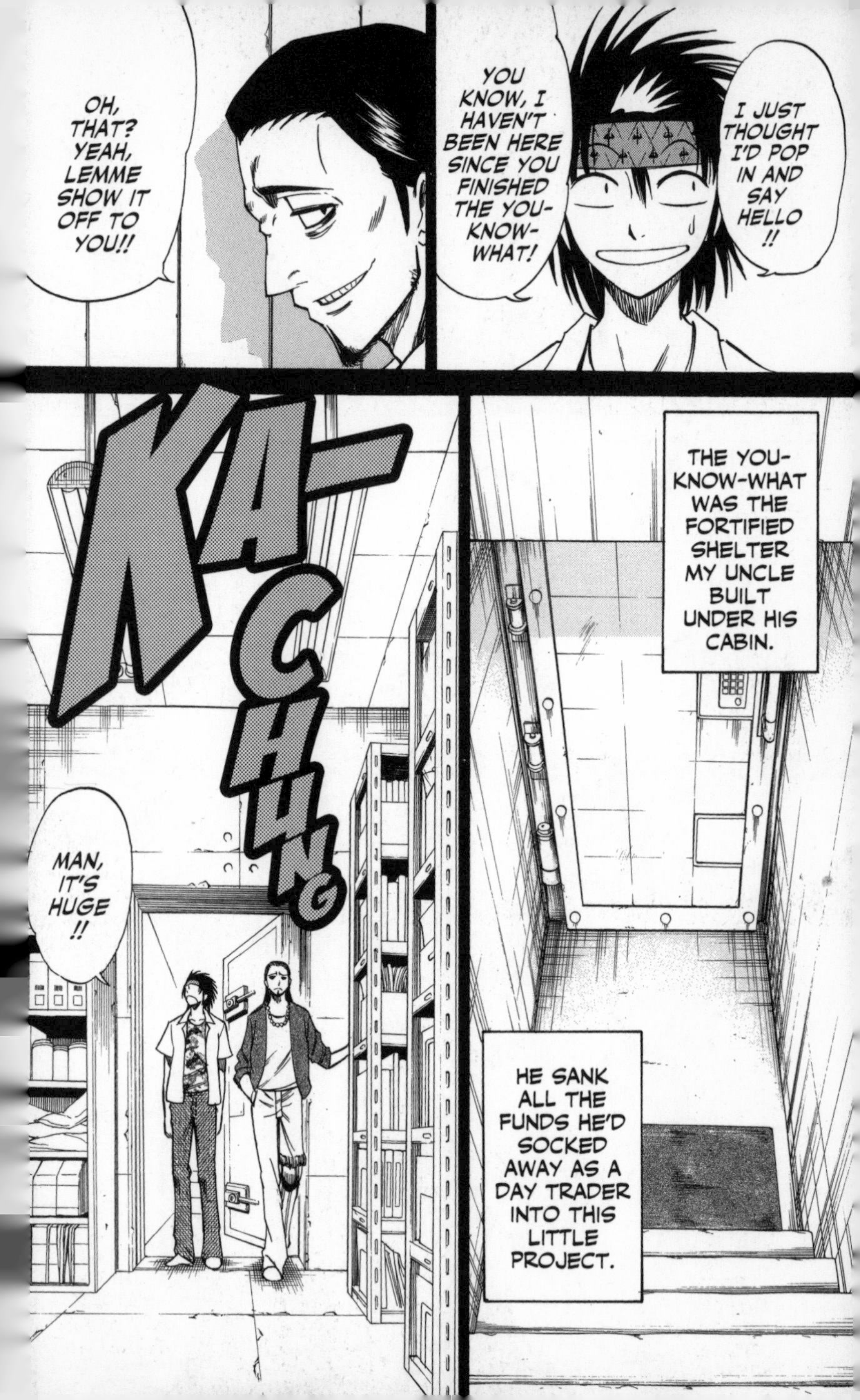
I JUST THOUGHT I'D POP IN AND SAY HELLO!!
YOU KNOW, I HAVEN'T BEEN HERE SINCE YOU FINISHED THE YOU-KNOW-WHAT!
OH, THAT? YEAH, LEMME SHOW IT OFF TO YOU!!
THE YOU-KNOW-WHAT WAS THE FORTIFIED SHELTER MY UNCLE BUILT UNDER HIS CABIN.
HE SANK ALL THE FUNDS HE'D SOCKED AWAY AS A DAY TRADER INTO THIS LITTLE PROJECT.
KA-CHUNG
MAN, IT'S HUGE!!

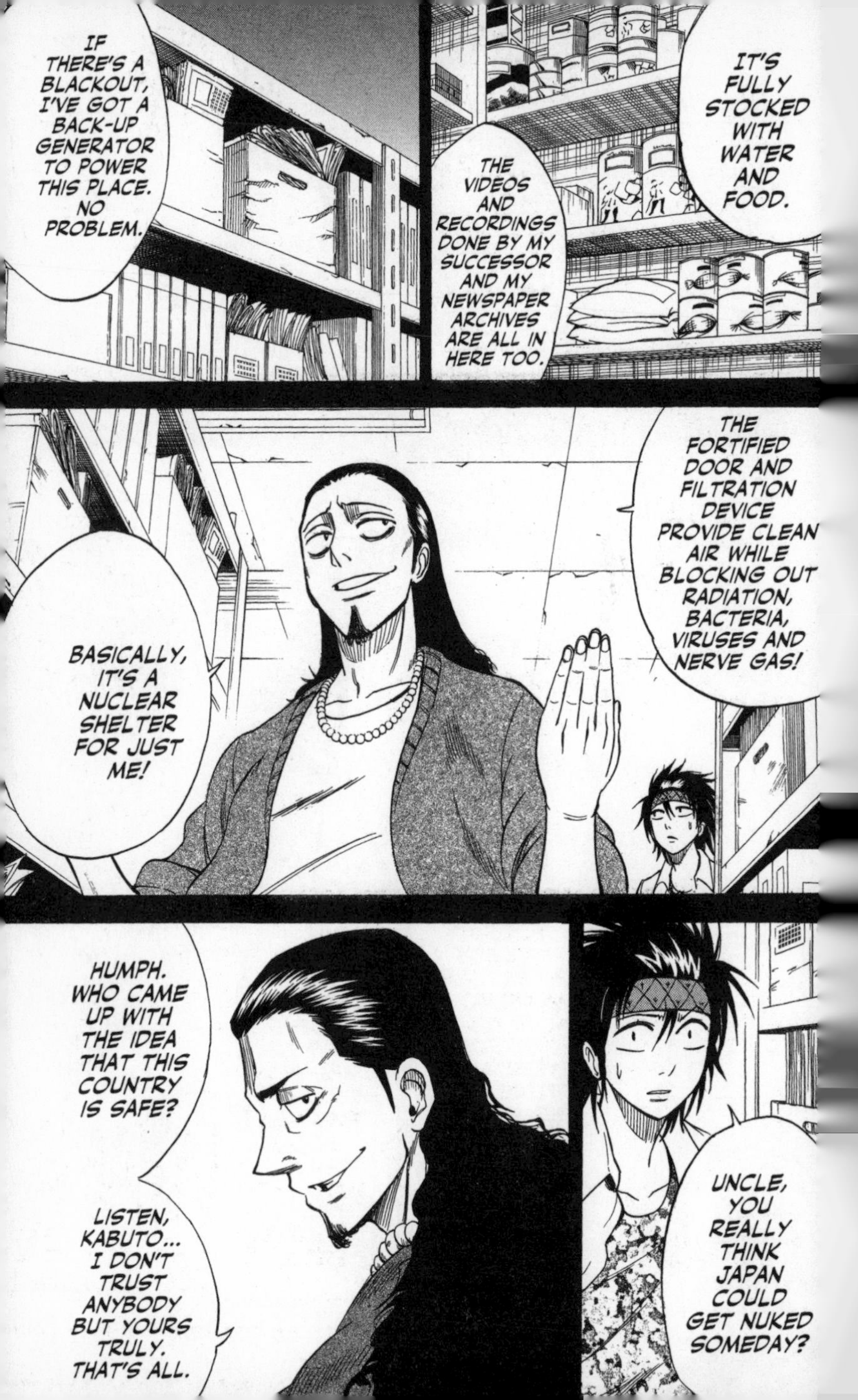
IT'S FULLY STOCKED WITH WATER AND FOOD.
THE VIDEOS AND RECORDINGS DONE BY MY SUCCESSOR AND MY NEWSPAPER ARCHIVES ARE ALL IN HERE TOO.
IF THERE'S A BLACKOUT, I'VE GOT A BACK-UP GENERATOR TO POWER THIS PLACE. NO PROBLEM.
THE FORTIFIED DOOR AND FILTRATION DEVICE PROVIDE CLEAN AIR WHILE BLOCKING OUT RADIATION, BACTERIA, VIRUSES AND NERVE GAS!
BASICALLY, IT'S A NUCLEAR SHELTER FOR JUST ME!
UNCLE, YOU REALLY THINK JAPAN COULD GET NUKED SOMEDAY?
HUMPH. WHO CAME UP WITH THE IDEA THAT THIS COUNTRY IS SAFE?
LISTEN, KABUTO... I DON'T TRUST ANYBODY BUT YOURS TRULY. THAT'S ALL.

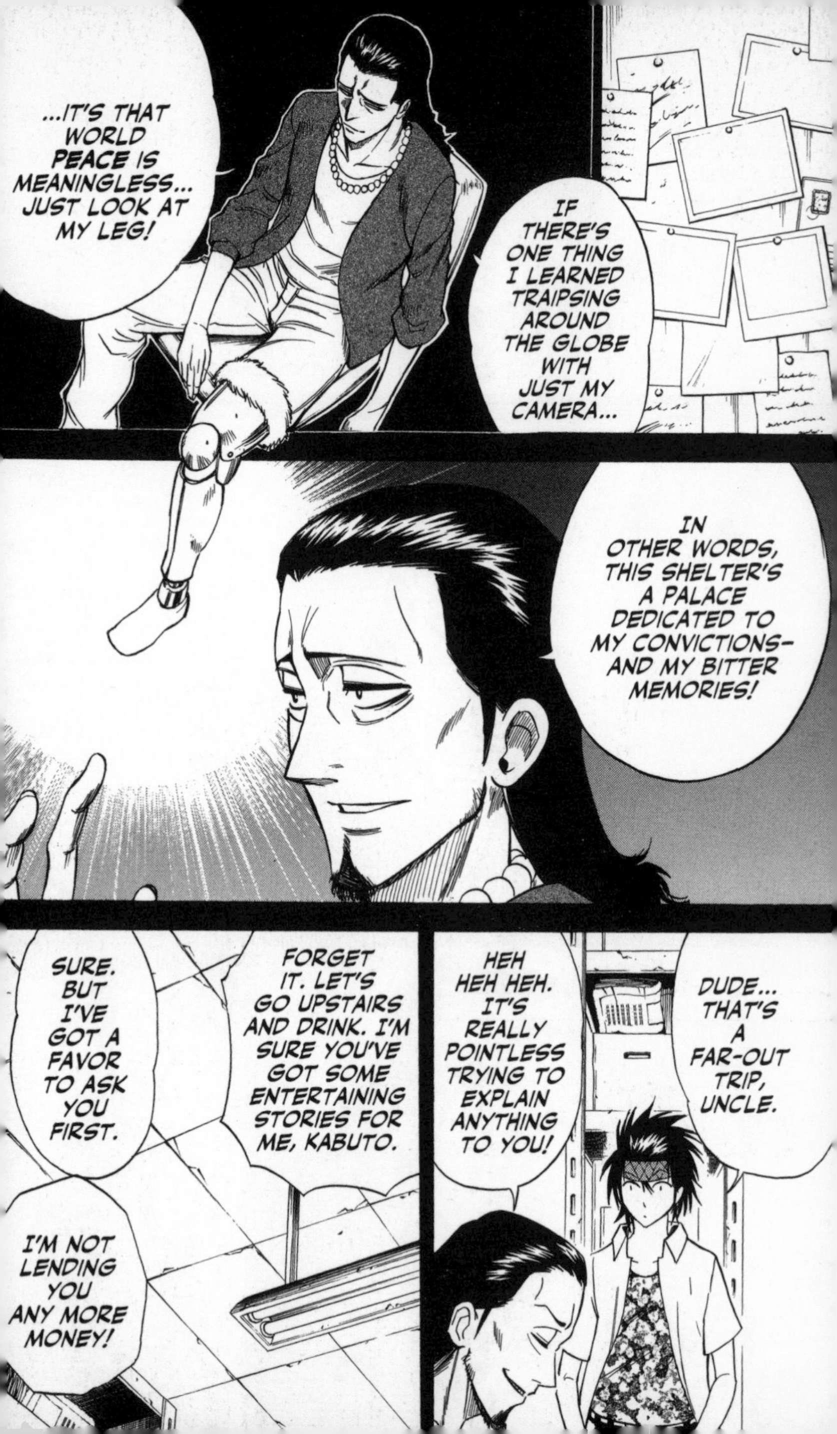
IF THERE'S ONE THING I LEARNED TRAIPSING AROUND THE GLOBE WITH JUST MY CAMERA...
...IT'S THAT WORLD PEACE IS MEANINGLESS... JUST LOOK AT MY LEG!
IN OTHER WORDS, THIS SHELTER'S A PALACE DEDICATED TO MY CONVICTIONS- AND MY BITTER MEMORIES!
DUDE... THAT'S A FAR-OUT TRIP, UNCLE.
HEH HEH HEH. IT'S REALLY POINTLESS TRYING TO EXPLAIN ANYTHING TO YOU!
FORGET IT. LET'S GO UPSTAIRS AND DRINK. I'M SURE YOU'VE GOT SOME ENTERTAINING STORIES FOR ME, KABUTO.
SURE. BUT I'VE GOT A FAVOR TO ASK YOU FIRST.
I'M NOT LENDING YOU ANY MORE MONEY!

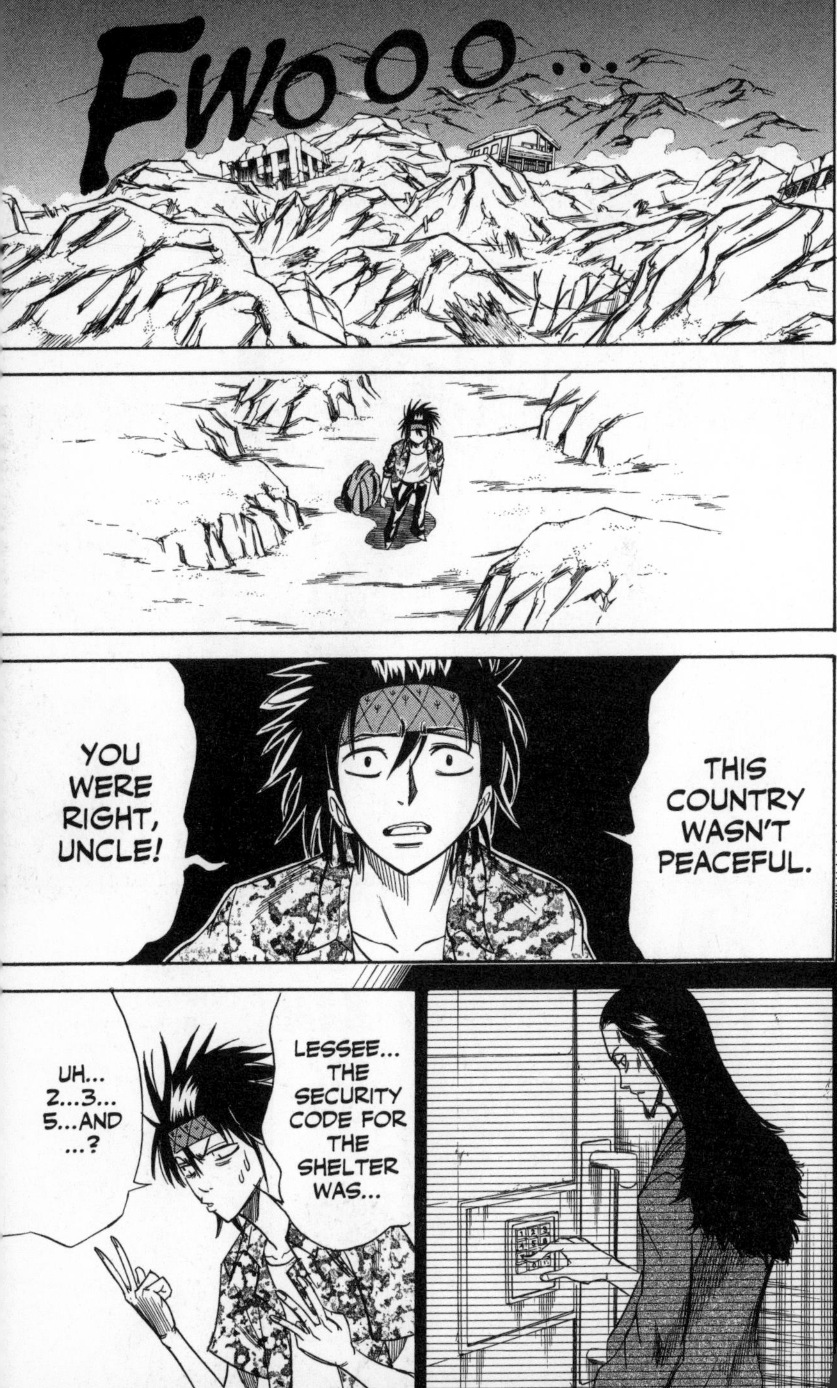
FWOOO...
THIS COUNTRY WASN'T PEACEFUL.
YOU WERE RIGHT, UNCLE!
LESSEE... THE SECURITY CODE FOR THE SHELTER WAS...
UH... 2...3... 5...AND ...?

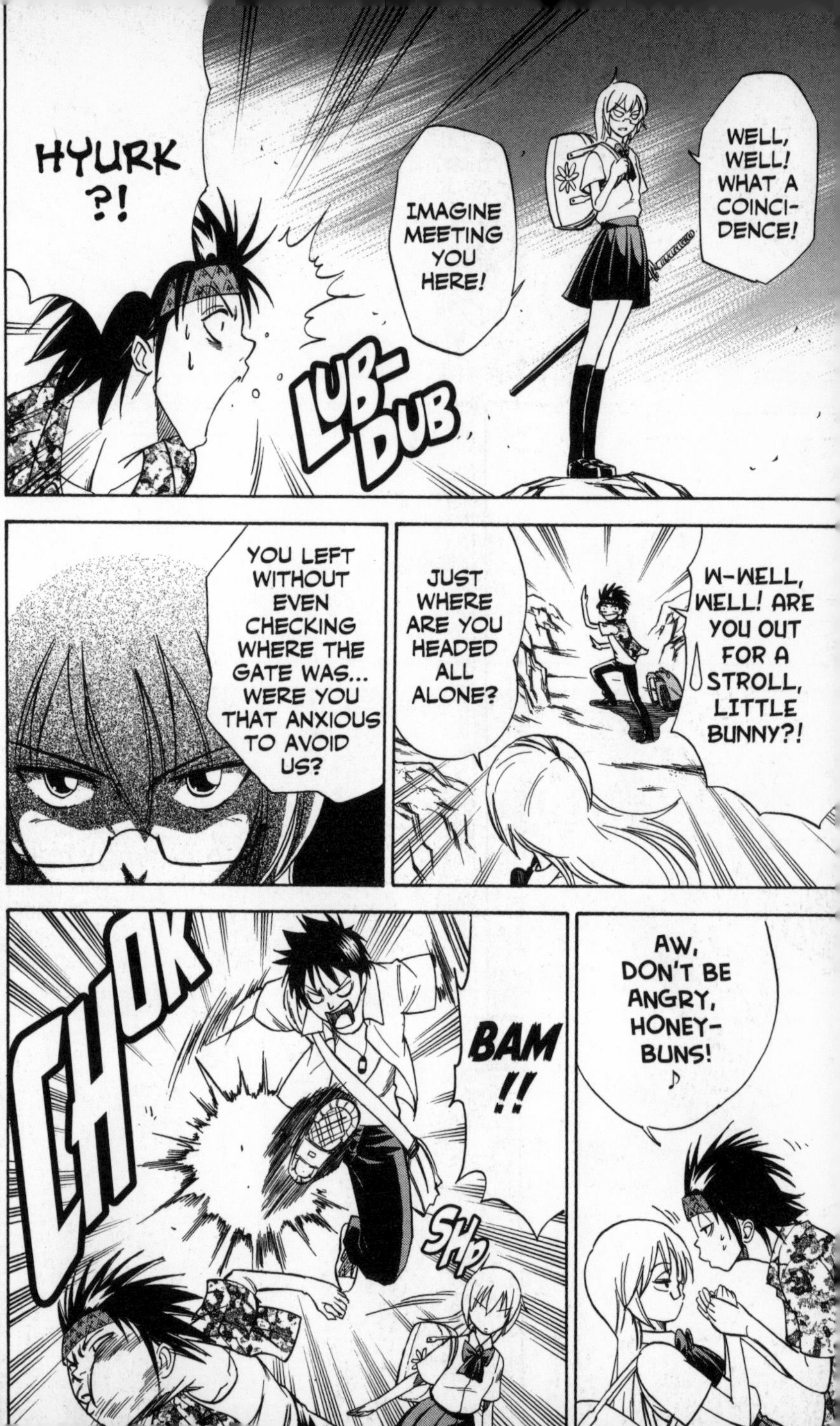
WELL, WELL! WHAT A COINCIDENCE!
IMAGINE MEETING YOU HERE!
LUB-DUB
HYURK ?!
W-WELL, WELL! ARE YOU OUT FOR A STROLL, LITTLE BUNNY?!
JUST WHERE ARE YOU HEADED ALL ALONE?
YOU LEFT WITHOUT EVEN CHECKING WHERE THE GATE WAS... WERE YOU THAT ANXIOUS TO AVOID US?
AW, DON'T BE ANGRY, HONEY-BUNS! ♪
CHOK
BAM !!
SHP

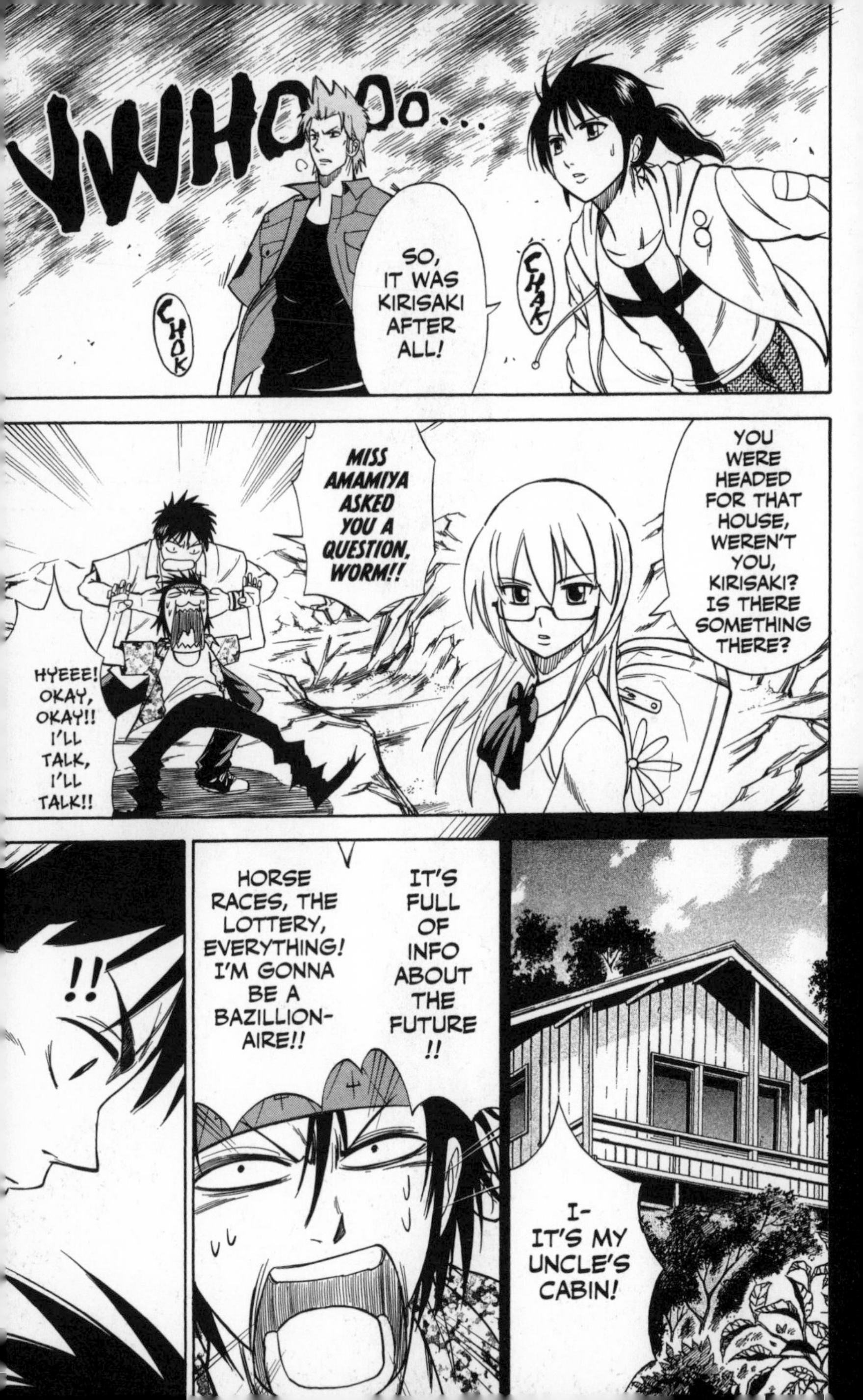
VWHOOOO...
CHAK
SO, IT WAS KIRISAKI AFTER ALL!
CHOK
YOU WERE HEADED FOR THAT HOUSE, WEREN'T YOU, KIRISAKI? IS THERE SOMETHING THERE?
MISS AMAMIYA ASKED YOU A QUESTION, WORM!!
HYEEE! OKAY, OKAY!! I'LL TALK, I'LL TALK!!
I- IT'S MY UNCLE'S CABIN!
IT'S FULL OF INFO ABOUT THE FUTURE!!
HORSE RACES, THE LOTTERY, EVERYTHING! I'M GONNA BE A BAZILLION-AIRE!!
!!

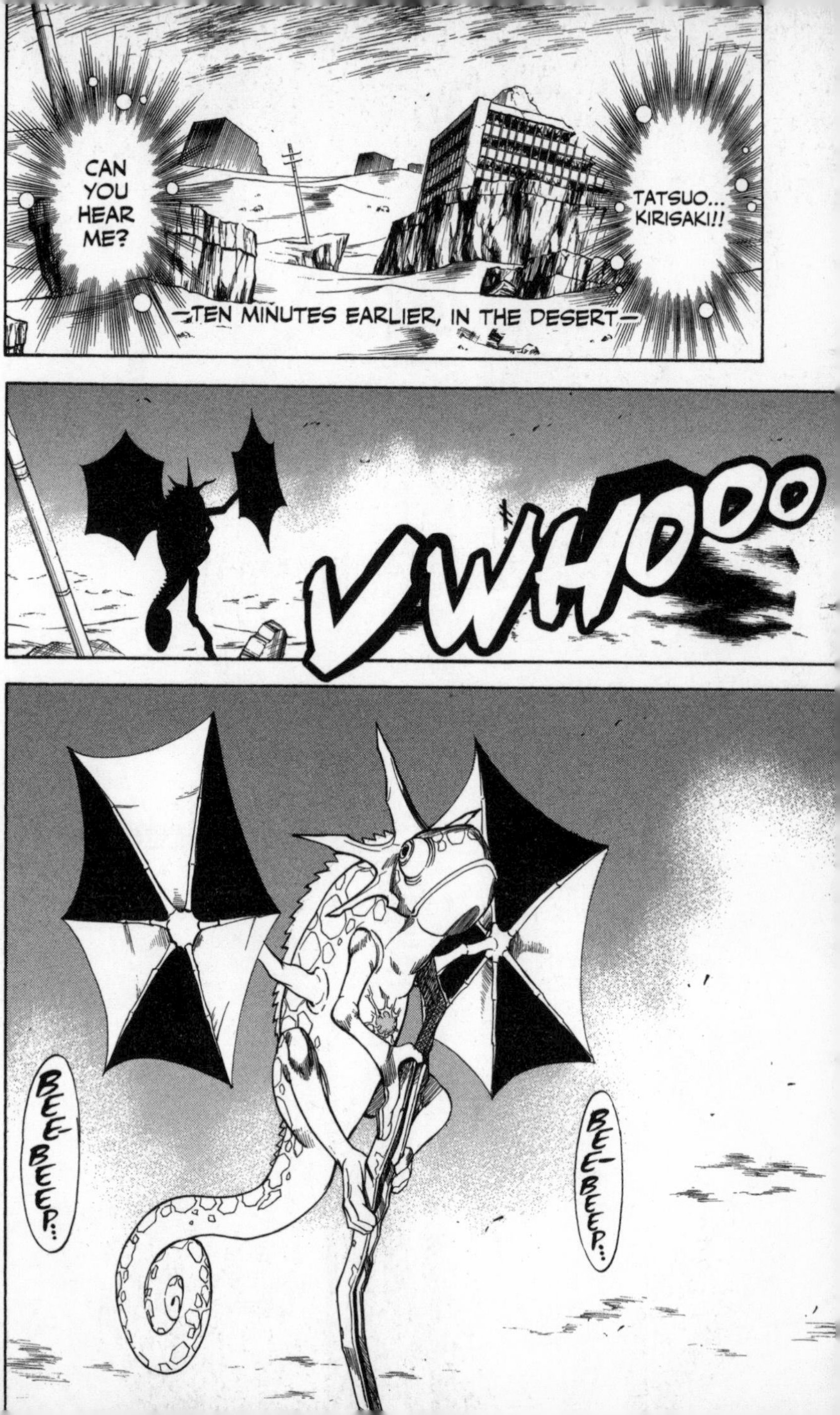
TATSUO... KIRISAKI!!
CAN YOU HEAR ME?
—TEN MINUTES EARLIER, IN THE DESERT—
VWHOOO
BEE BEEP...
BEE BEEP...

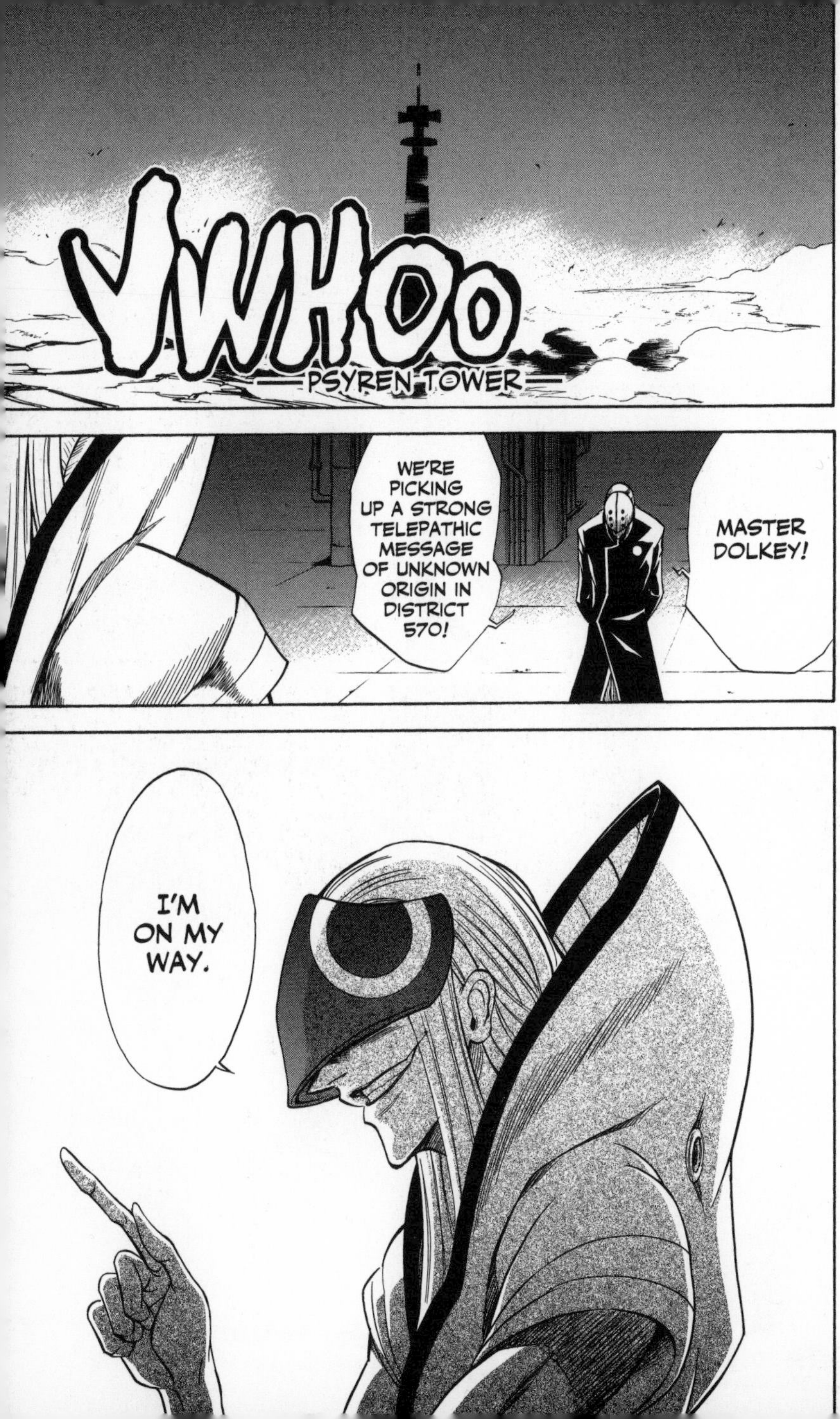
VWHOO
PSYREN TOWER
MASTER DOLKEY!
WE'RE PICKING UP A STRONG TELEPATHIC MESSAGE OF UNKNOWN ORIGIN IN DISTRICT 570!
I'M ON MY WAY.

DISCARDED SKETCH
FOR VOLUME 4 COVER

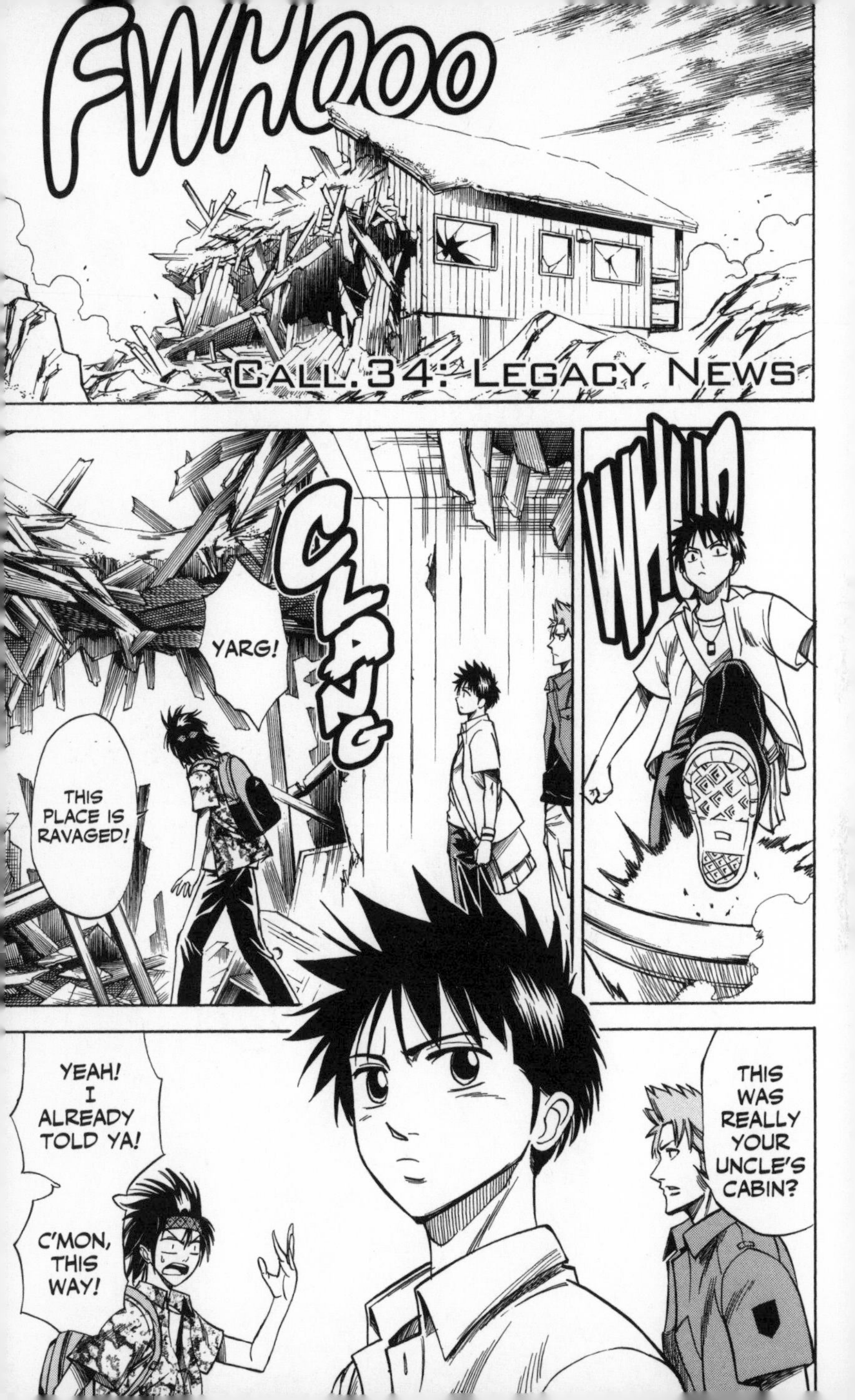
FWHOOO
CALL.34: LEGACY NEWS
WHUD
CLANG
YARG!
THIS PLACE IS RAVAGED!
THIS WAS REALLY YOUR UNCLE'S CABIN?
YEAH! I ALREADY TOLD YA!
C'MON, THIS WAY!

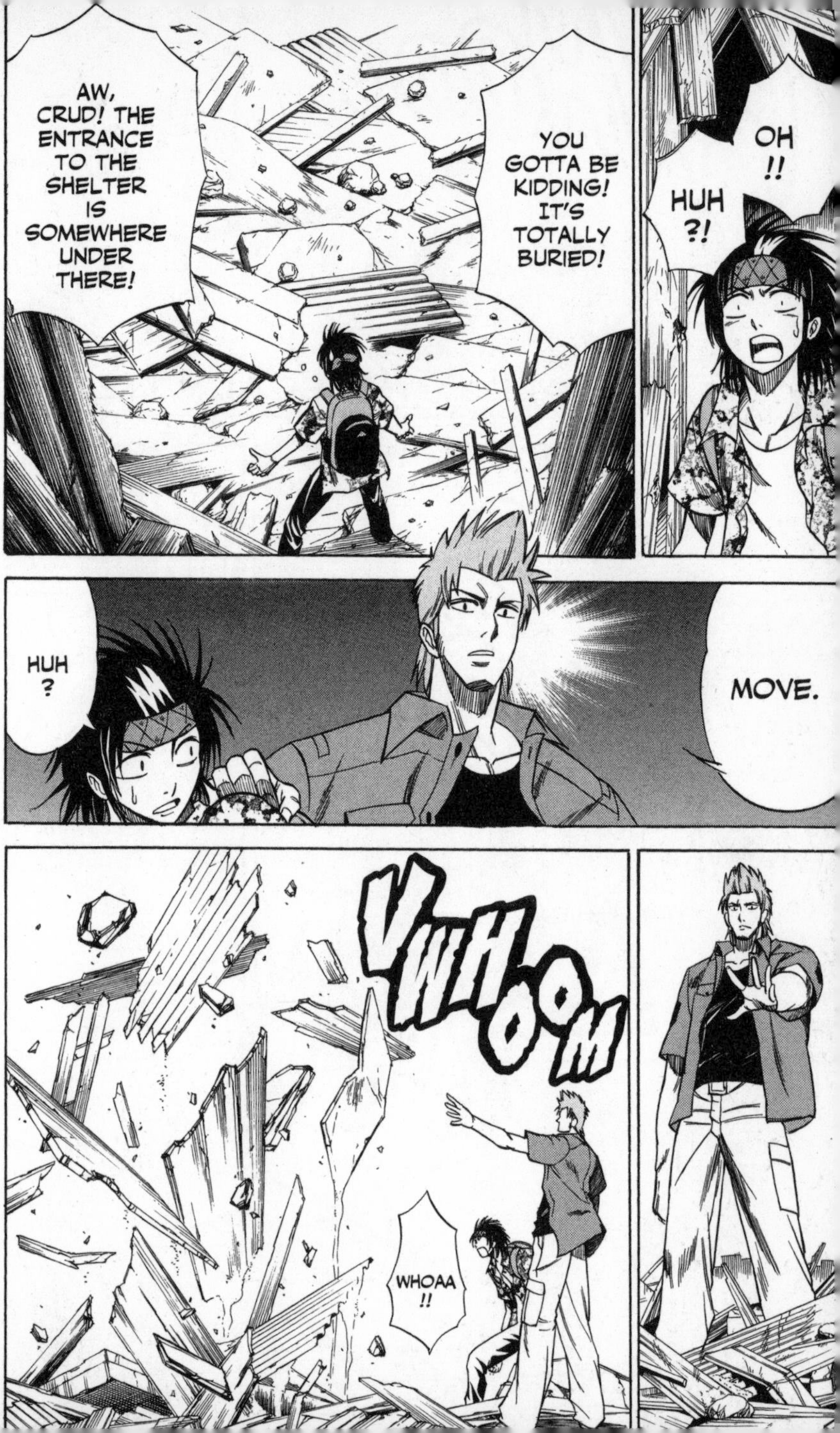
OH !!
HUH ?!
YOU GOTTA BE KIDDING! IT'S TOTALLY BURIED!
AW, CRUD! THE ENTRANCE TO THE SHELTER IS SOMEWHERE UNDER THERE!
MOVE.
HUH ?
VWHOOM
WHOAA !!

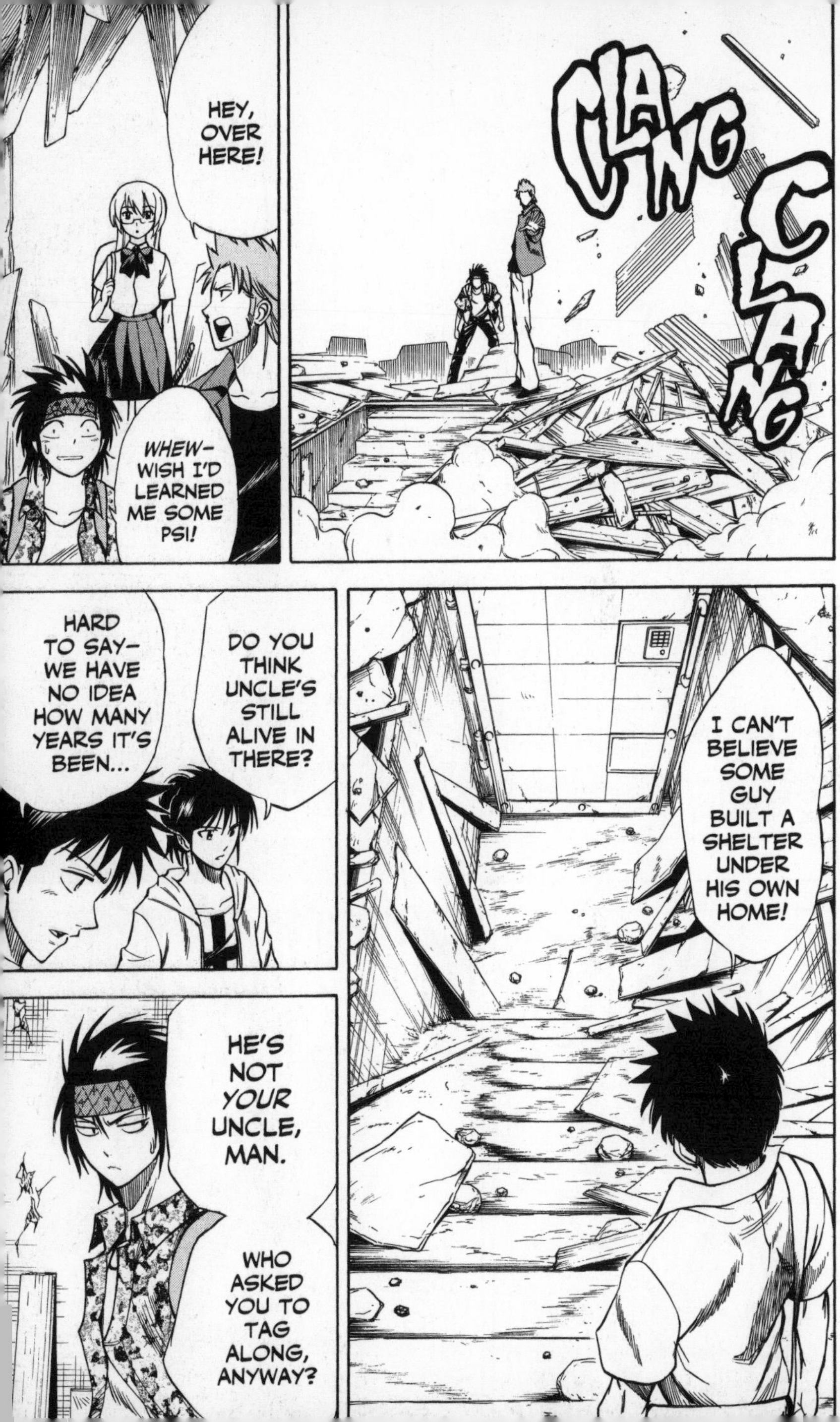
CLANG
CLANG
HEY, OVER HERE!
WHEW- WISH I'D LEARNED ME SOME PSI!
I CAN'T BELIEVE SOME GUY BUILT A SHELTER UNDER HIS OWN HOME!
DO YOU THINK UNCLE'S STILL ALIVE IN THERE?
HARD TO SAY- WE HAVE NO IDEA HOW MANY YEARS IT'S BEEN...
HE'S NOT *YOUR* UNCLE, MAN.
WHO ASKED YOU TO TAG ALONG, ANYWAY?

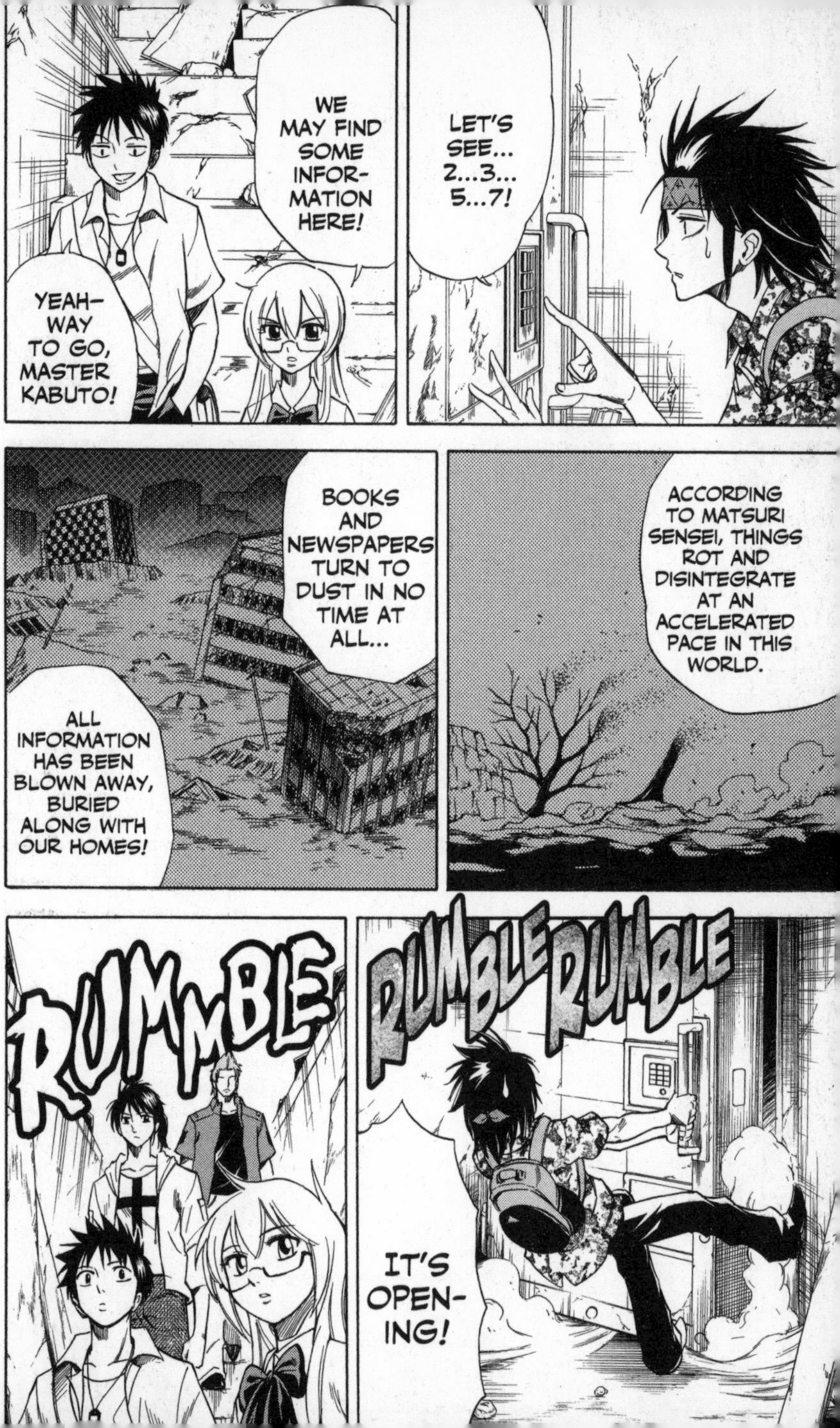
LET'S SEE... 2...3... 5...7!
WE MAY FIND SOME INFOR-MATION HERE!
YEAH— WAY TO GO, MASTER KABUTO!
ACCORDING TO MATSURI SENSEI, THINGS ROT AND DISINTEGRATE AT AN ACCELERATED PACE IN THIS WORLD.
BOOKS AND NEWSPAPERS TURN TO DUST IN NO TIME AT ALL...
ALL INFORMATION HAS BEEN BLOWN AWAY, BURIED ALONG WITH OUR HOMES!
RUMBLE RUMBLE
IT'S OPEN-ING!
RUMMBLE

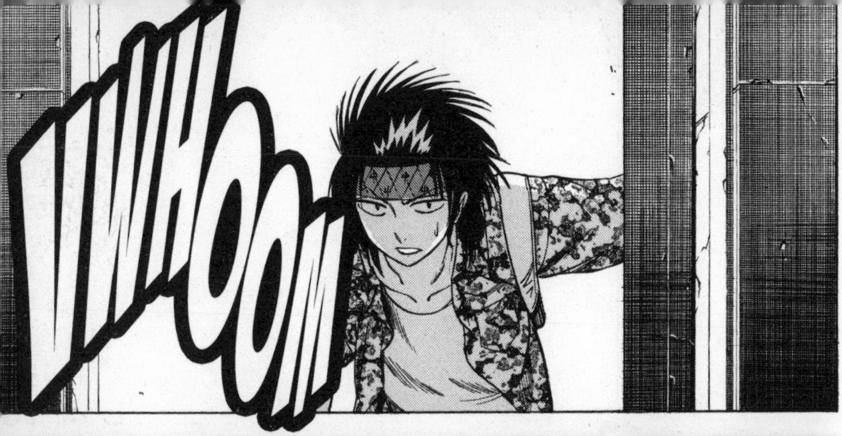
WHOOM
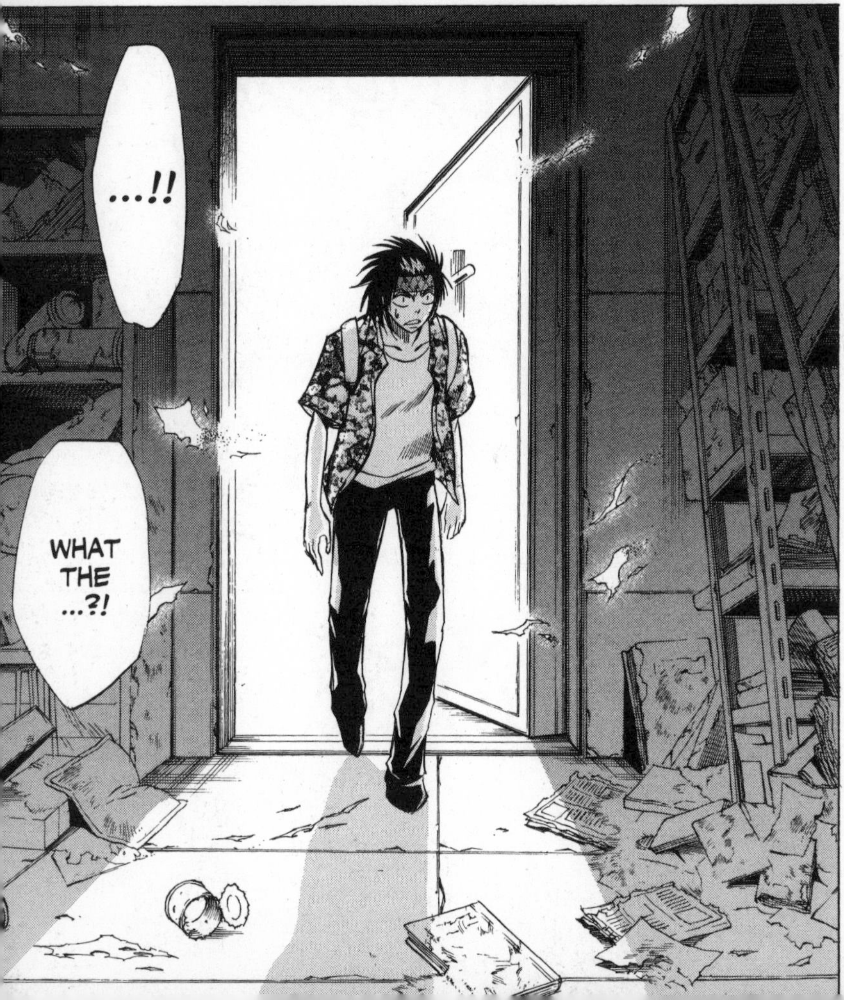
...!!
WHAT THE ...?!

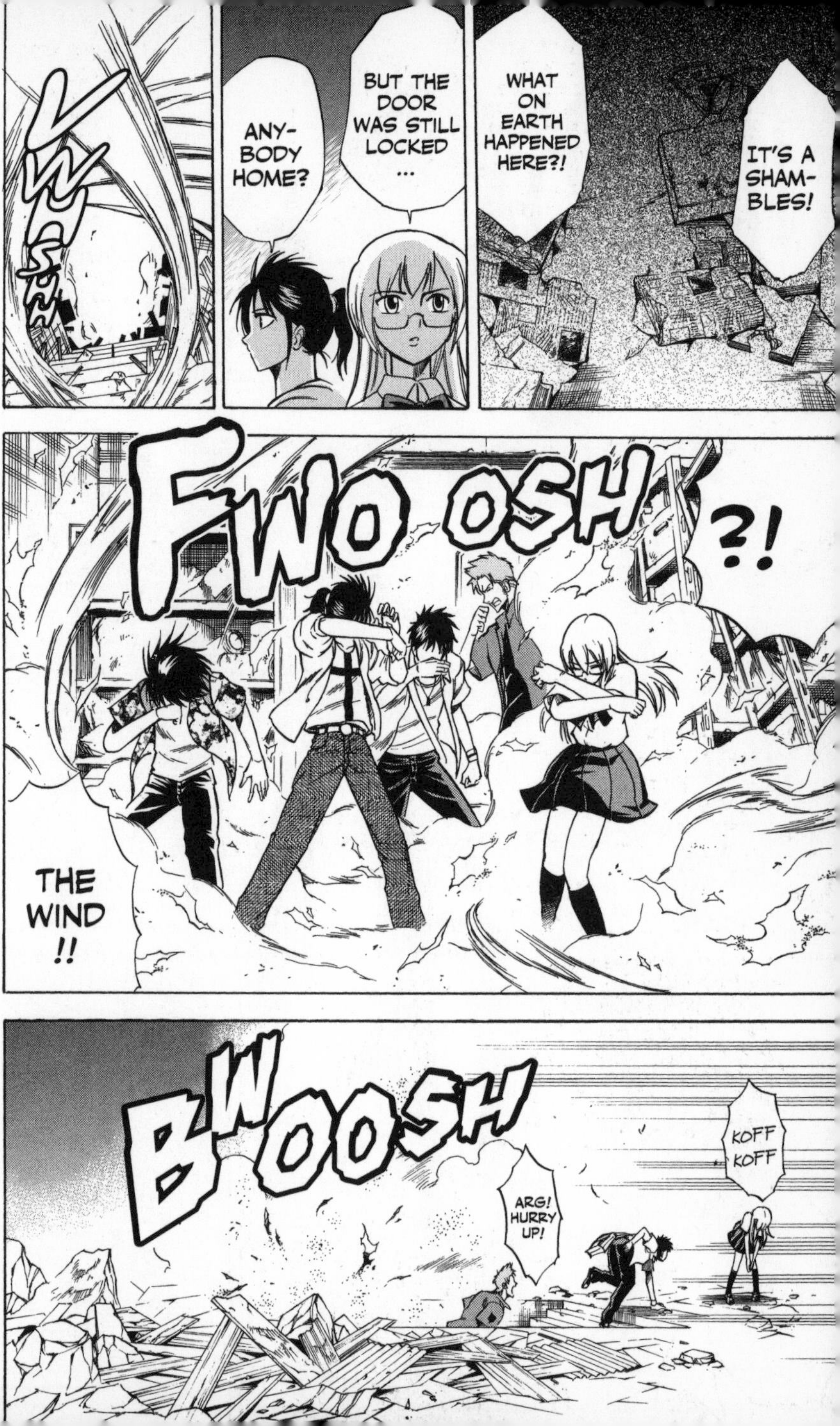
IT'S A SHAMBLES!
WHAT ON EARTH HAPPENED HERE?!
BUT THE DOOR WAS STILL LOCKED ...
ANYBODY HOME?
FWOOSH
?!
THE WIND !!
KOFF KOFF
ARG! HURRY UP!
BWOOSH

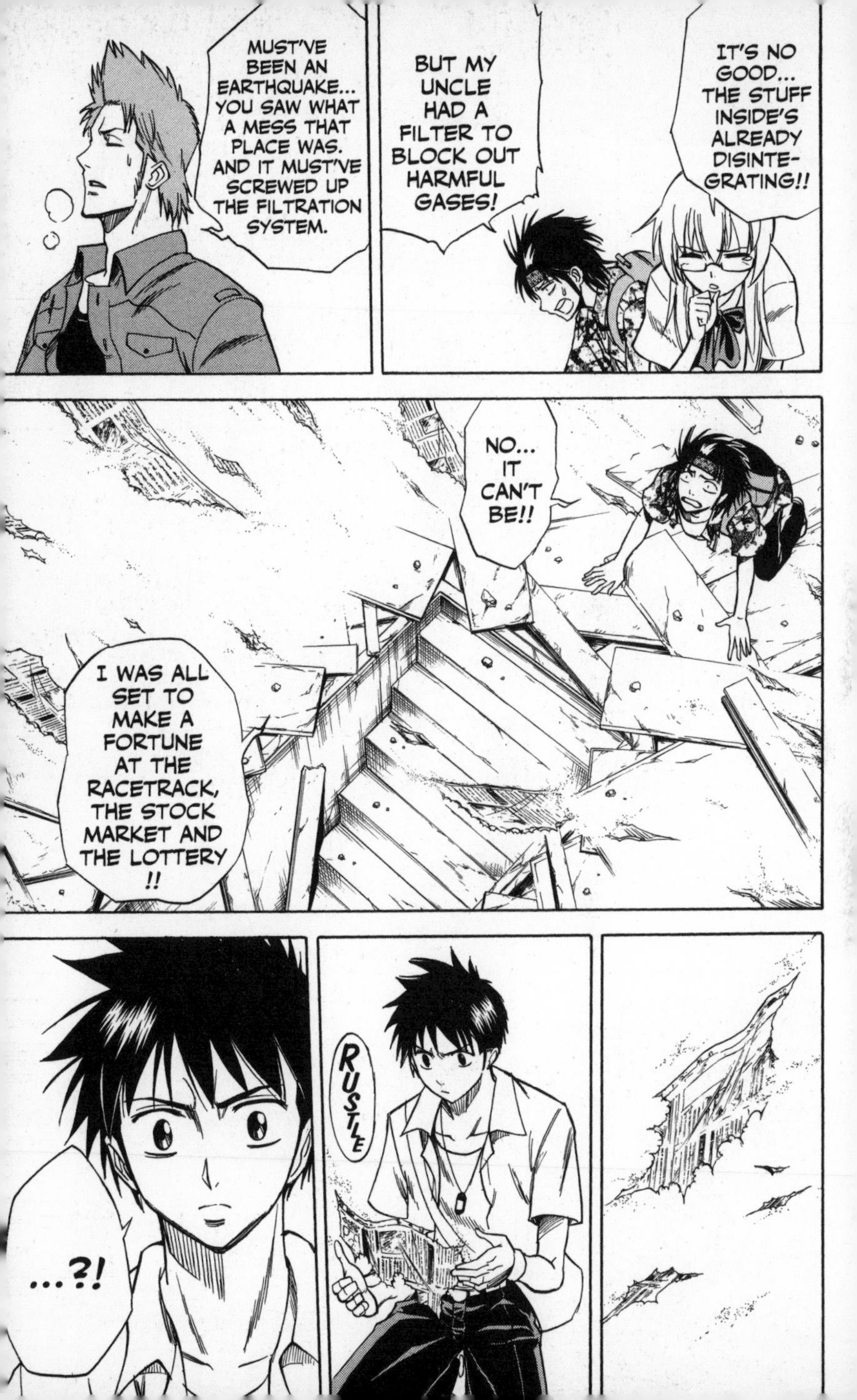
IT'S NO GOOD... THE STUFF INSIDE'S ALREADY DISINTEGRATING!!
BUT MY UNCLE HAD A FILTER TO BLOCK OUT HARMFUL GASES!
MUST'VE BEEN AN EARTHQUAKE... YOU SAW WHAT A MESS THAT PLACE WAS. AND IT MUST'VE SCREWED UP THE FILTRATION SYSTEM.
NO... IT CAN'T BE!!
I WAS ALL SET TO MAKE A FORTUNE AT THE RACETRACK, THE STOCK MARKET AND THE LOTTERY!!
RUSTLE
...?!

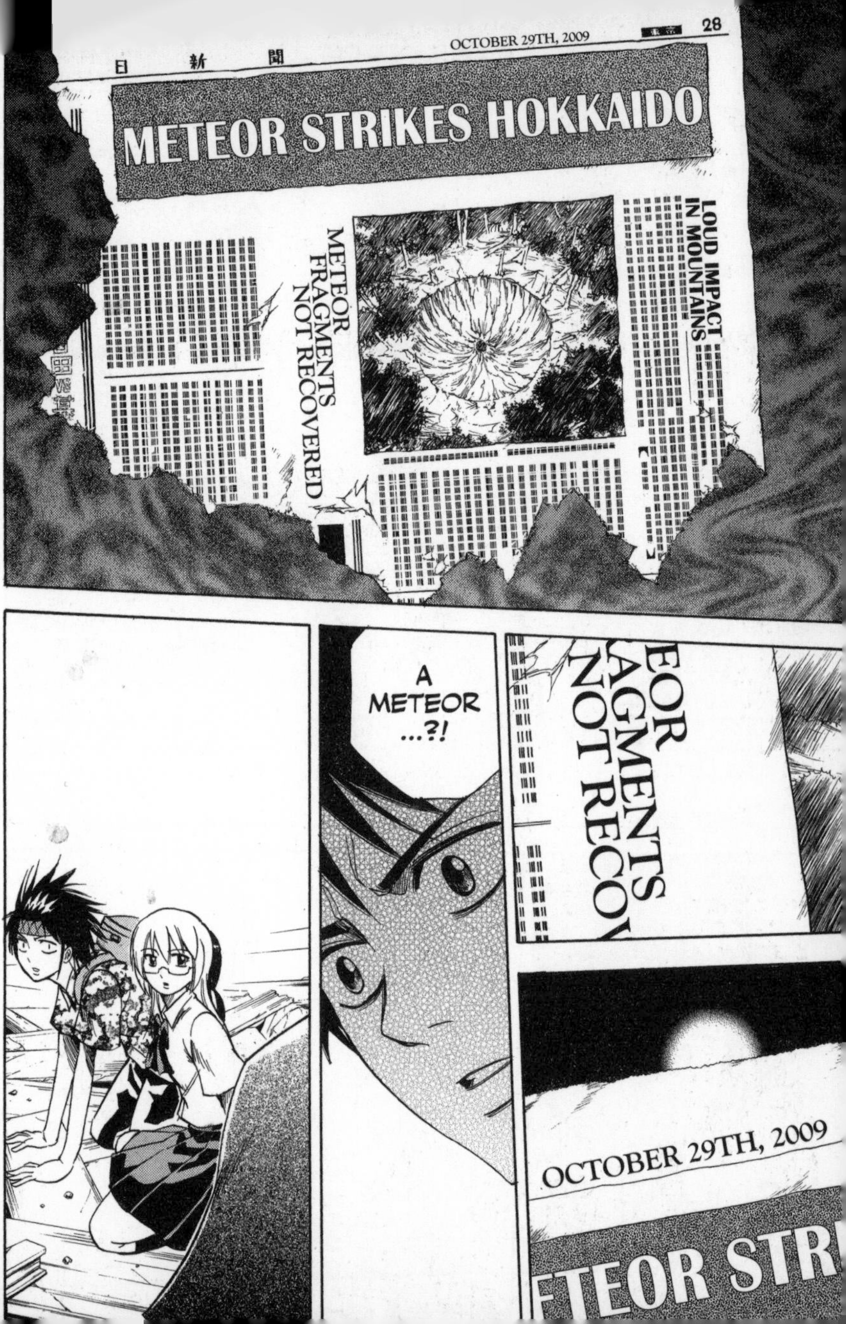
28
OCTOBER 29TH, 2009
日 新 聞
METEOR STRIKES HOKKAIDO
LOUD IMPACT IN MOUNTAINS
METEOR FRAGMENTS NOT RECOVERED
EOR AGMENTS NOT RECO
OCTOBER 29TH, 2009
FTEOR STR
A METEOR ...?!

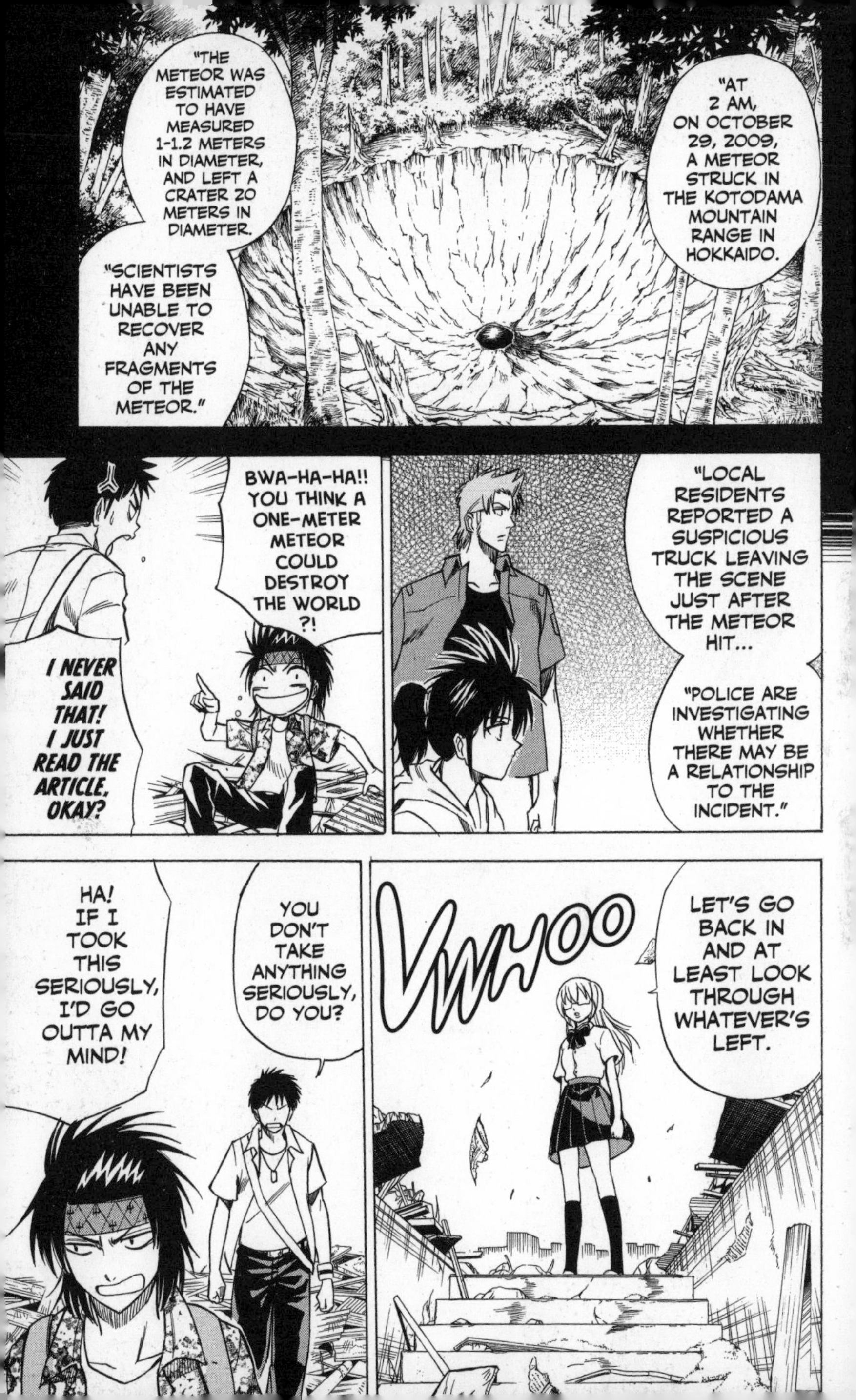
"AT 2 AM, ON OCTOBER 29, 2009, A METEOR STRUCK IN THE KOTODAMA MOUNTAIN RANGE IN HOKKAIDO.
"THE METEOR WAS ESTIMATED TO HAVE MEASURED 1-1.2 METERS IN DIAMETER, AND LEFT A CRATER 20 METERS IN DIAMETER.
"SCIENTISTS HAVE BEEN UNABLE TO RECOVER ANY FRAGMENTS OF THE METEOR."
"LOCAL RESIDENTS REPORTED A SUSPICIOUS TRUCK LEAVING THE SCENE JUST AFTER THE METEOR HIT...
"POLICE ARE INVESTIGATING WHETHER THERE MAY BE A RELATIONSHIP TO THE INCIDENT."
BWA-HA-HA!! YOU THINK A ONE-METER METEOR COULD DESTROY THE WORLD?!
I NEVER SAID THAT! I JUST READ THE ARTICLE, OKAY?
LET'S GO BACK IN AND AT LEAST LOOK THROUGH WHATEVER'S LEFT.
VWOO
YOU DON'T TAKE ANYTHING SERIOUSLY, DO YOU?
HA! IF I TOOK THIS SERIOUSLY, I'D GO OUTTA MY MIND!

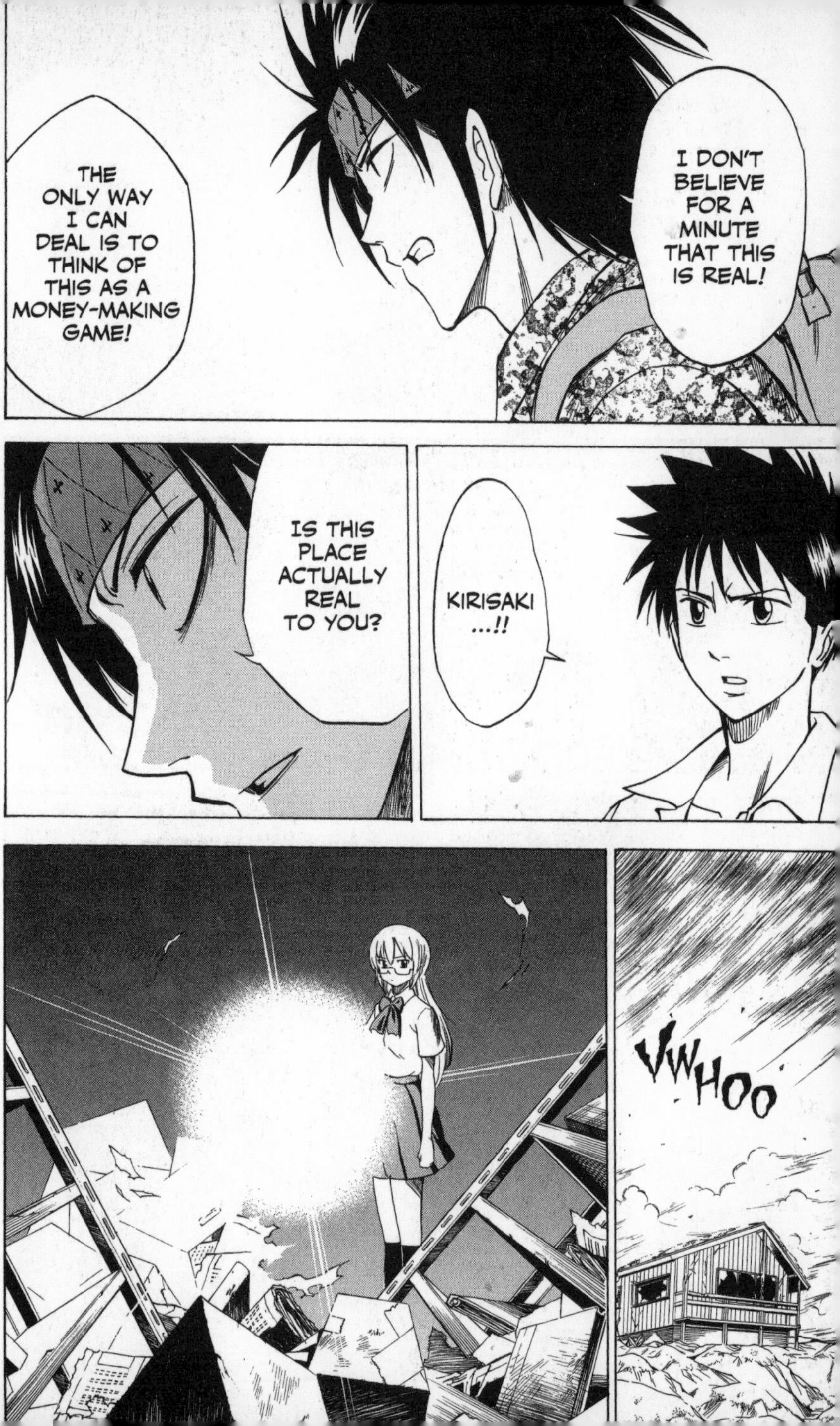
I DON'T BELIEVE FOR A MINUTE THAT THIS IS REAL!
THE ONLY WAY I CAN DEAL IS TO THINK OF THIS AS A MONEY-MAKING GAME!
KIRISAKI ...!!
IS THIS PLACE ACTUALLY REAL TO YOU?
VWHOO

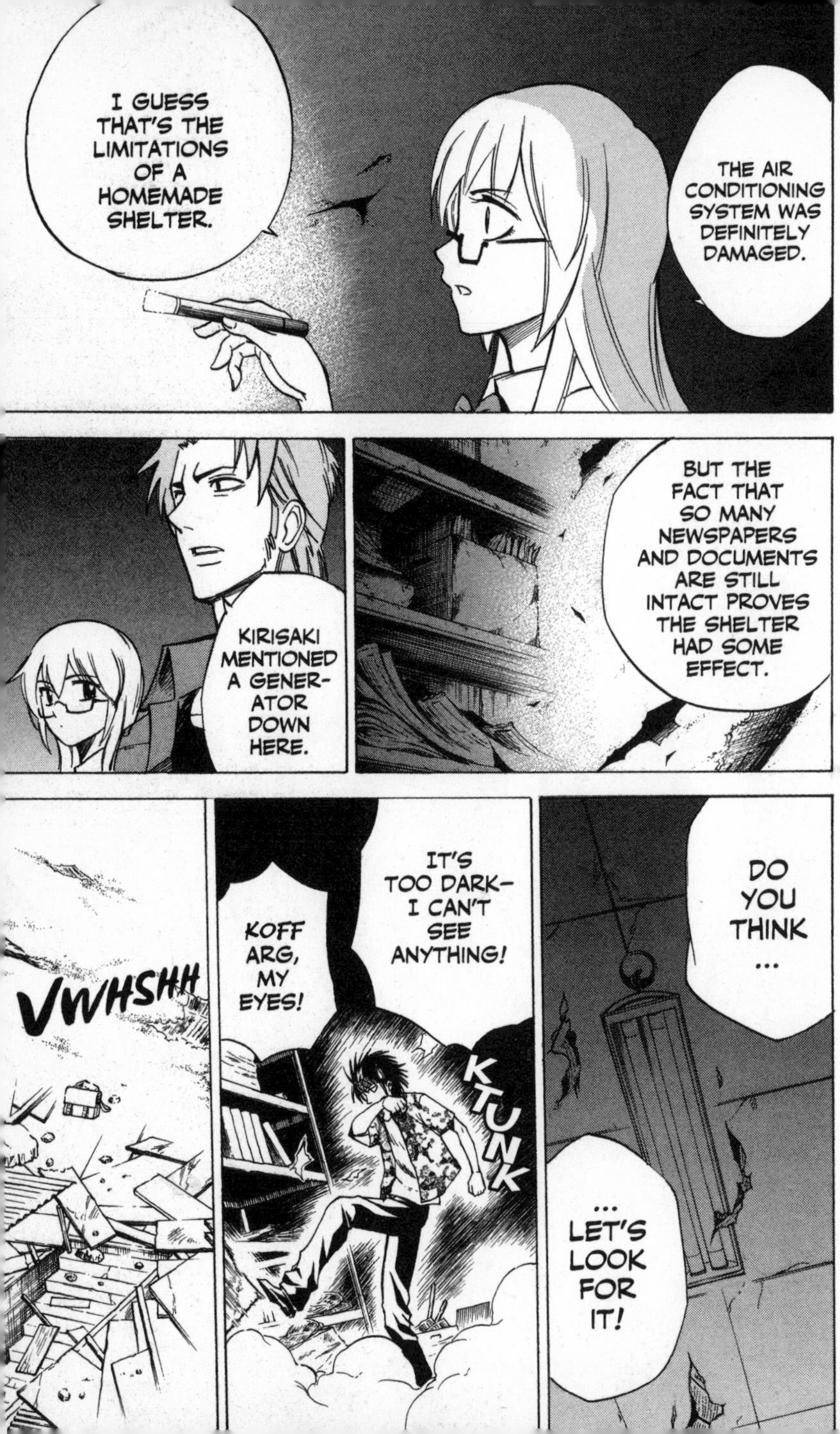
THE AIR CONDITIONING SYSTEM WAS DEFINITELY DAMAGED.
I GUESS THAT'S THE LIMITATIONS OF A HOMEMADE SHELTER.
BUT THE FACT THAT SO MANY NEWSPAPERS AND DOCUMENTS ARE STILL INTACT PROVES THE SHELTER HAD SOME EFFECT.
KIRISAKI MENTIONED A GENER-ATOR DOWN HERE.
DO YOU THINK ...
... LET'S LOOK FOR IT!
IT'S TOO DARK— I CAN'T SEE ANYTHING!
KOFF ARG, MY EYES!
KTUNK
VWHSHH

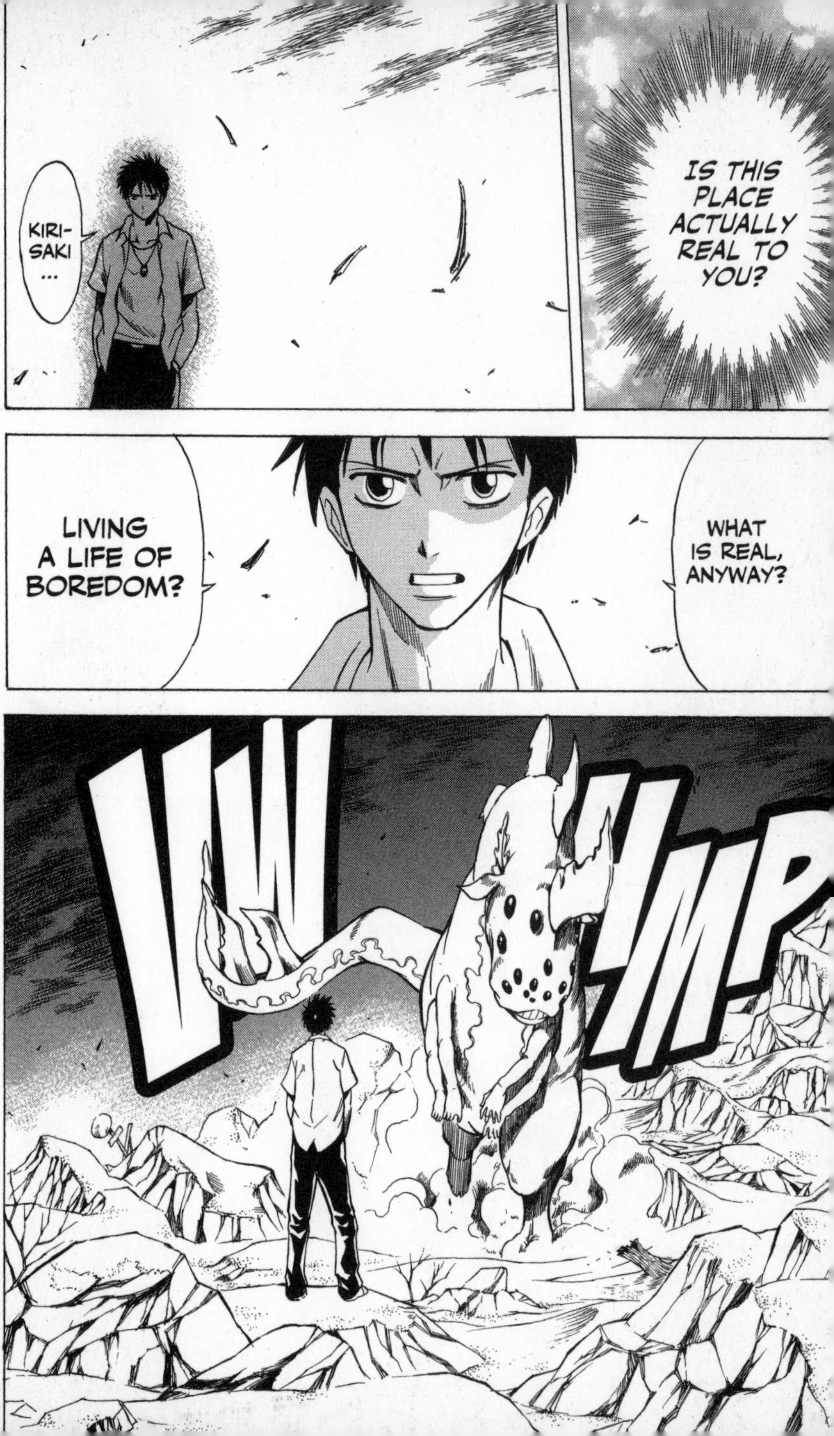
IS THIS PLACE ACTUALLY REAL TO YOU?
KIRI-SAKI ...
WHAT IS REAL, ANYWAY?
LIVING A LIFE OF BOREDOM?

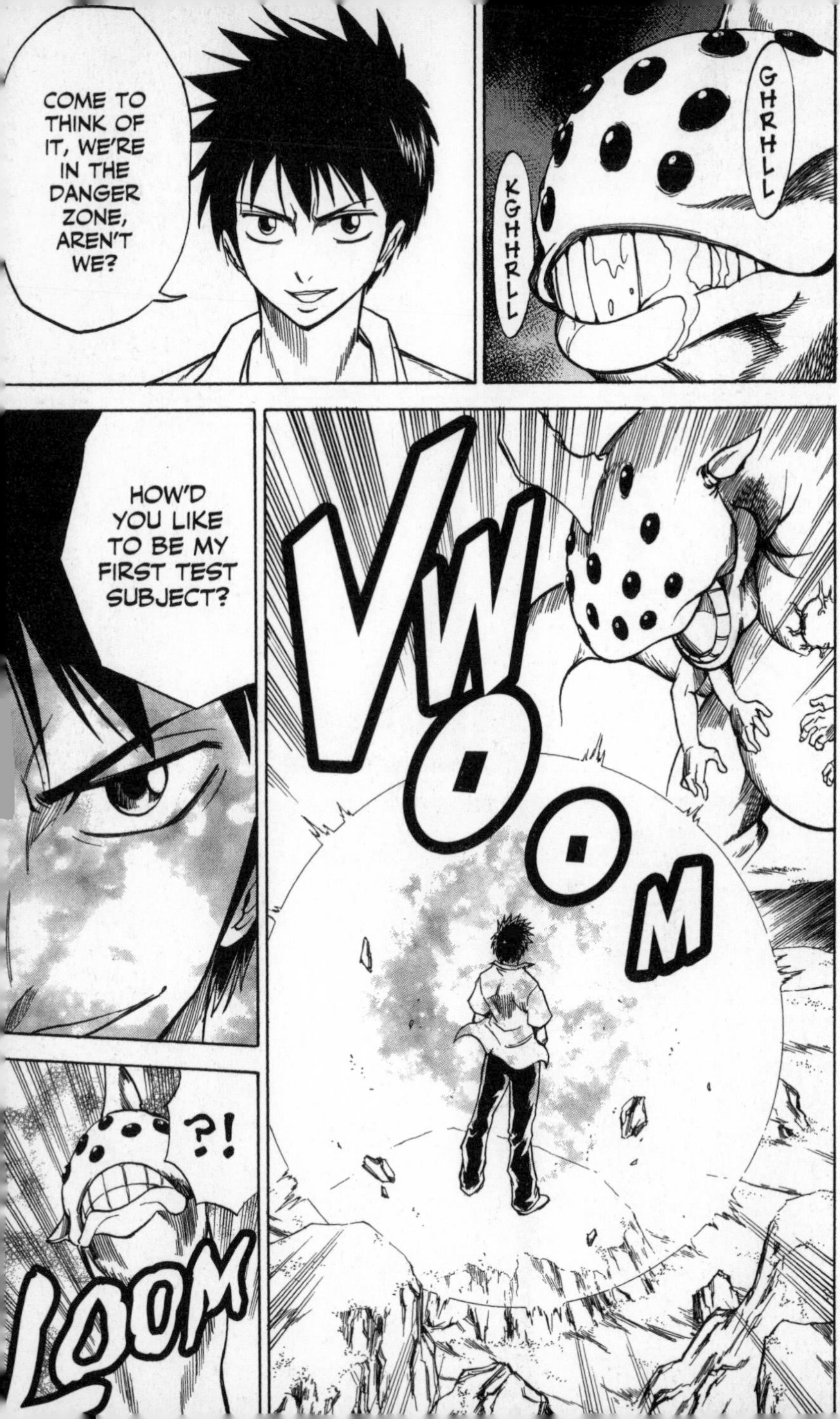
GHRHLL
KGHHRLL
COME TO THINK OF IT, WE'RE IN THE DANGER ZONE, AREN'T WE?
VWOOOM
HOW'D YOU LIKE TO BE MY FIRST TEST SUBJECT?
?!
LOOM

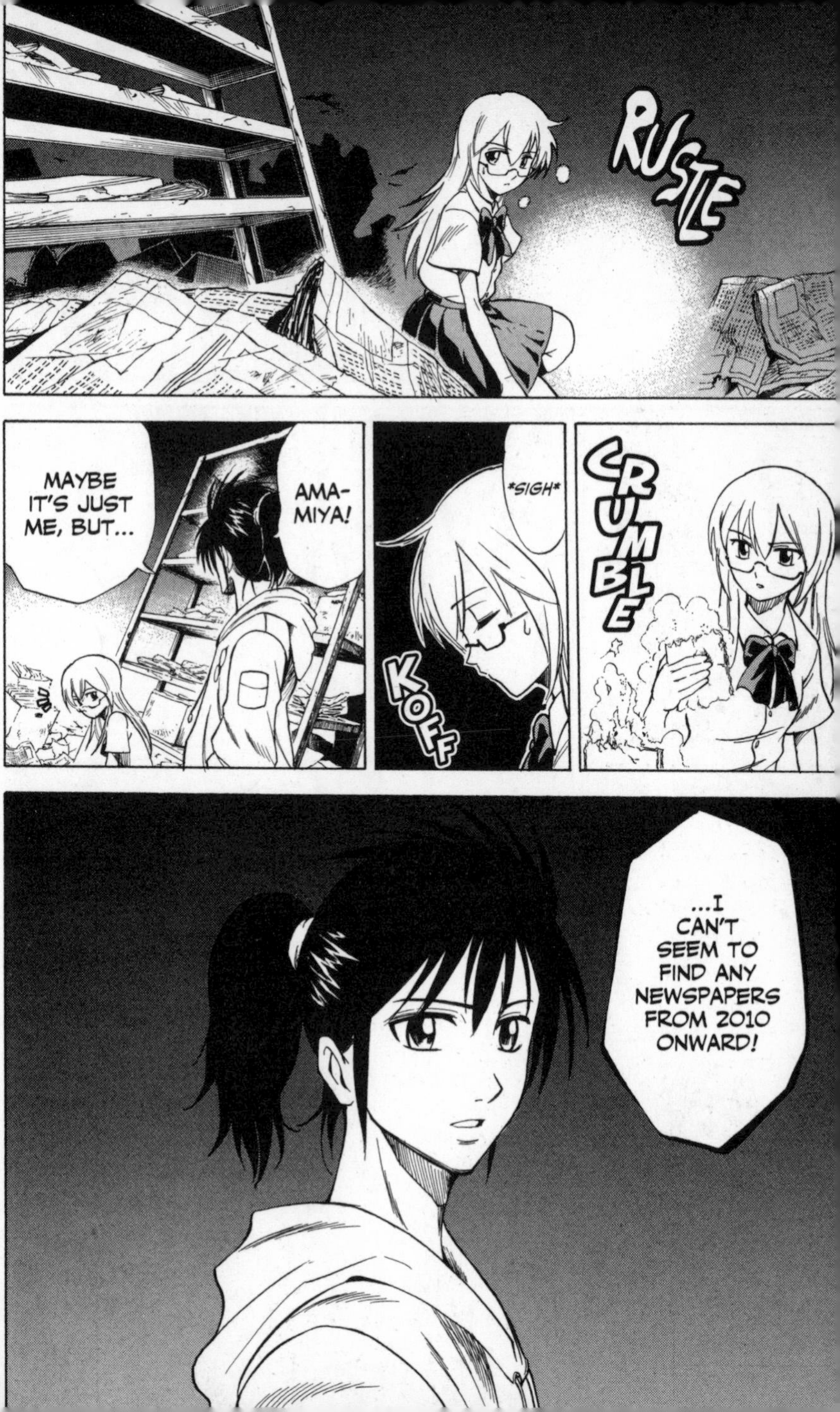
RUSTLE
CRUMBLE
SIGH
KOFF
AMA-MIYA!
MAYBE IT'S JUST ME, BUT...
...I CAN'T SEEM TO FIND ANY NEWSPAPERS FROM 2010 ONWARD!

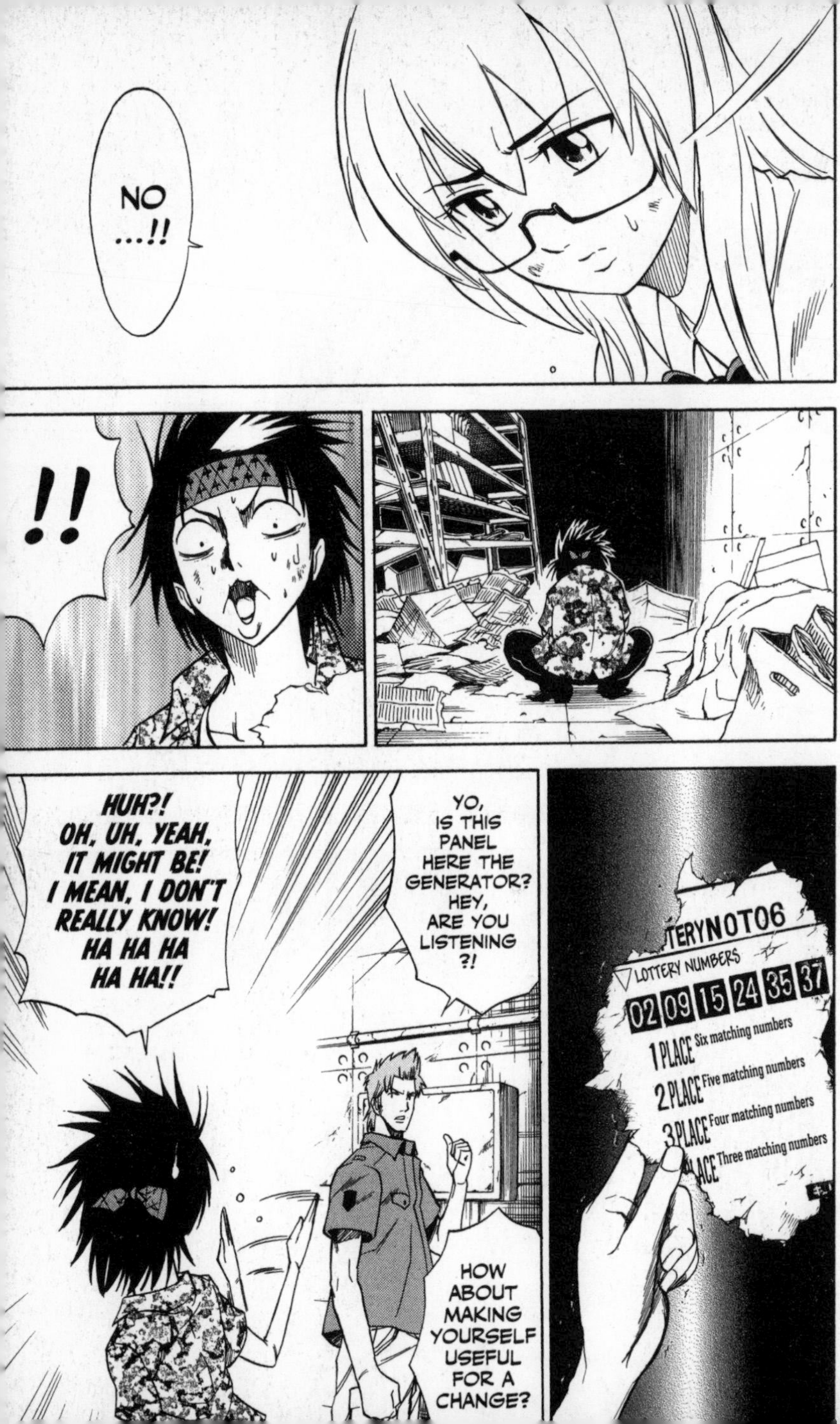
NO ...!!
!!
TERYNOTO6
LOTTERY NUMBERS
02 09 15 24 35 37
1 PLACE Six matching numbers
2 PLACE Five matching numbers
3 PLACE Four matching numbers
ACE Three matching numbers
YO, IS THIS PANEL HERE THE GENERATOR? HEY, ARE YOU LISTENING ?!
HUH?! OH, UH, YEAH, IT MIGHT BE! I MEAN, I DON'T REALLY KNOW! HA HA HA HA HA!!
HOW ABOUT MAKING YOURSELF USEFUL FOR A CHANGE?

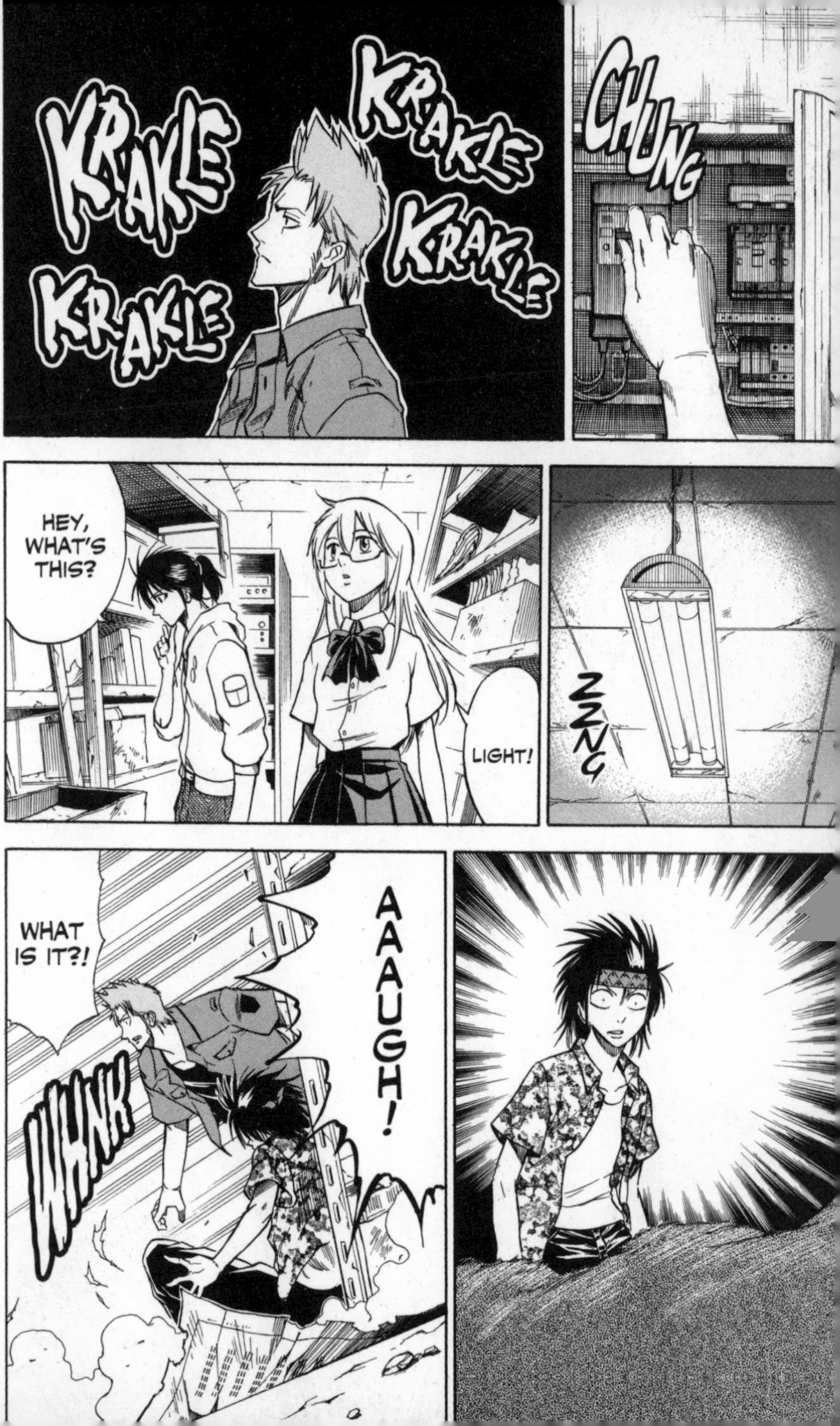
CHUNG
KRAKLE
KRAKLE
KRAKLE
KRAKLE
ZZNG
LIGHT!
HEY, WHAT'S THIS?
AAAAUGH!
WHAT IS IT?!
WHUNK

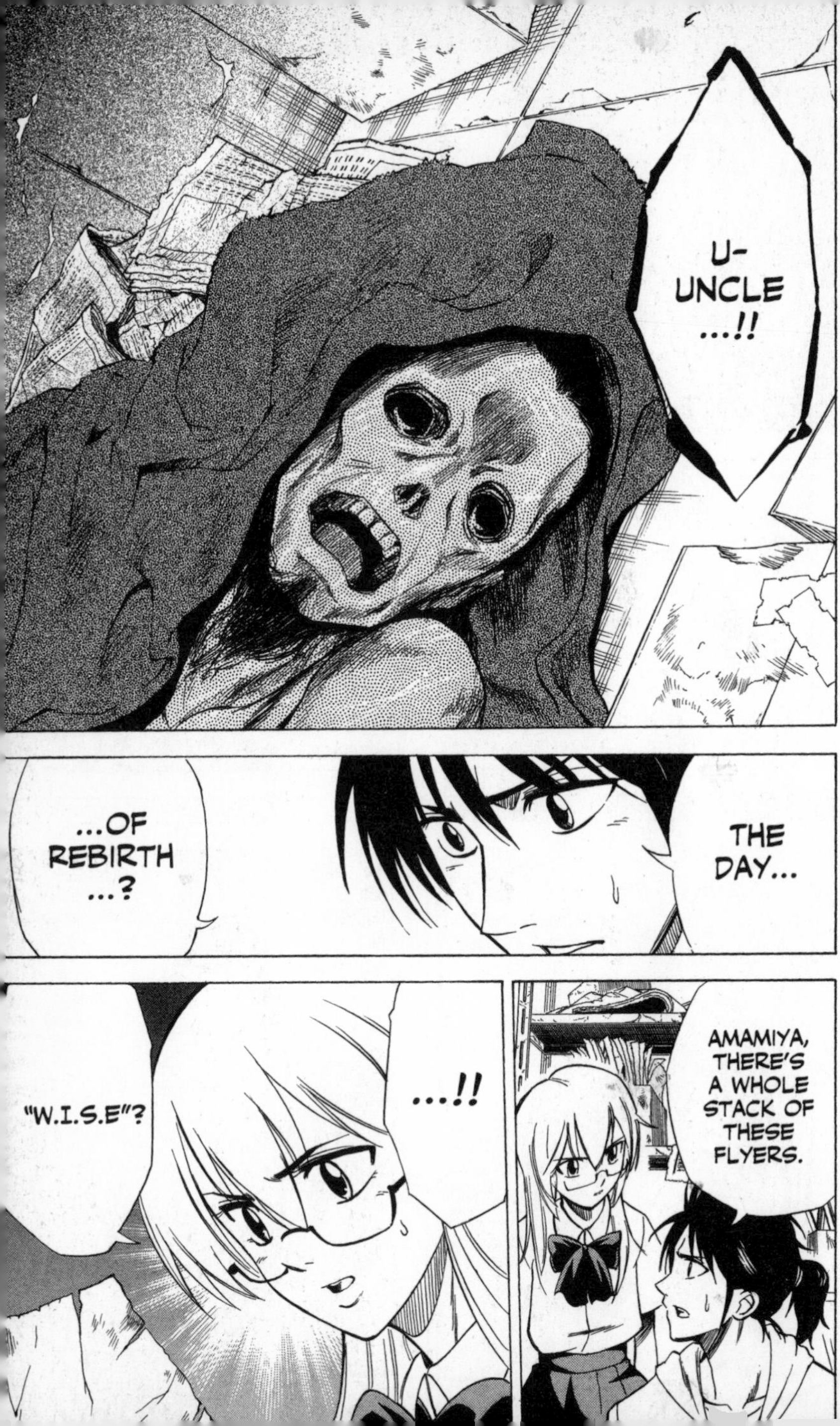
U-UNCLE ...!!
THE DAY...
...OF REBIRTH ...?
AMAMIYA, THERE'S A WHOLE STACK OF THESE FLYERS.
...!!
"W.I.S.E"?

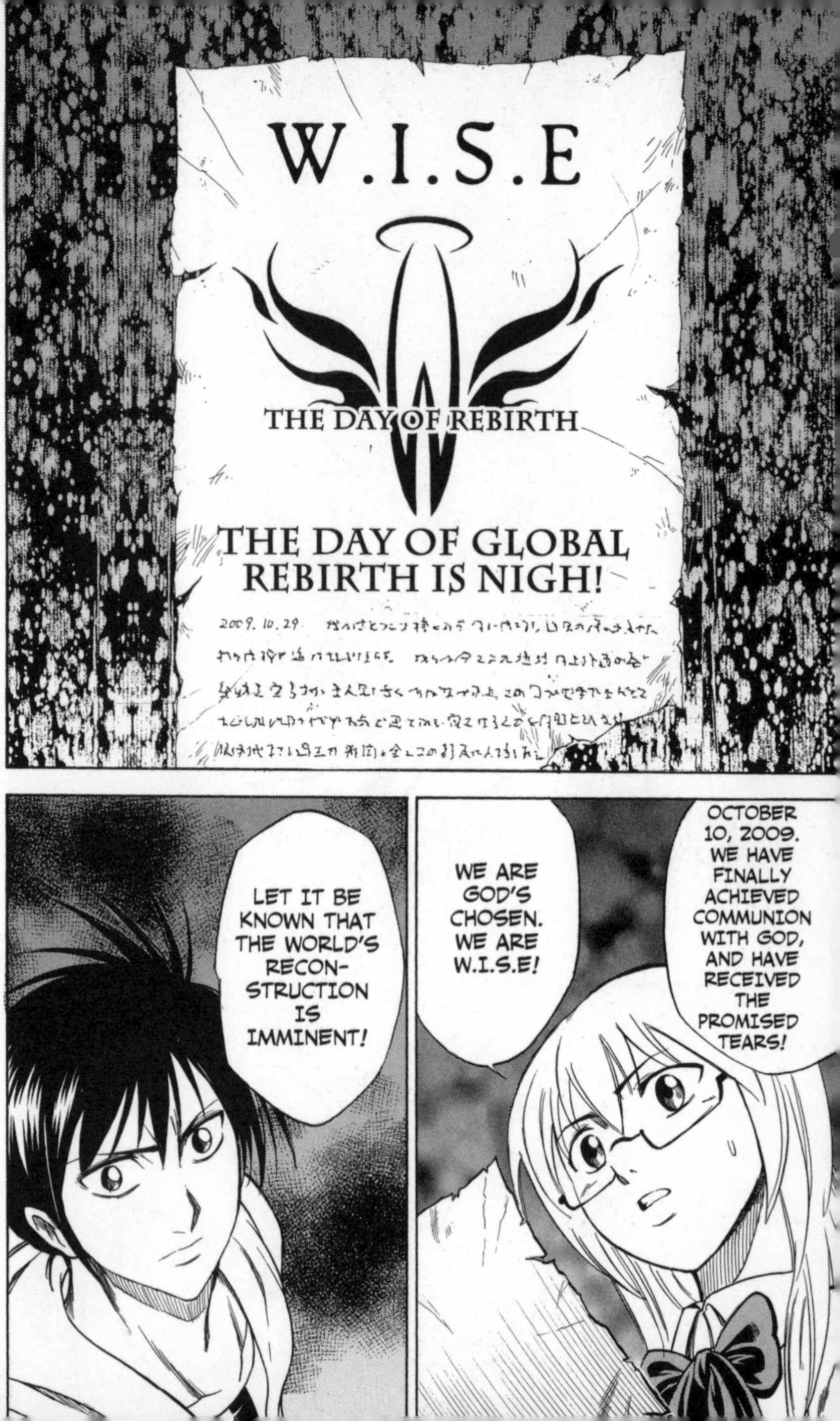
W.I.S.E
THE DAY OF REBIRTH
THE DAY OF GLOBAL REBIRTH IS NIGH!
2009. 10. 29
OCTOBER 10, 2009. WE HAVE FINALLY ACHIEVED COMMUNION WITH GOD, AND HAVE RECEIVED THE PROMISED TEARS!
WE ARE GOD'S CHOSEN. WE ARE W.I.S.E!
LET IT BE KNOWN THAT THE WORLD'S RECON-STRUCTION IS IMMINENT!

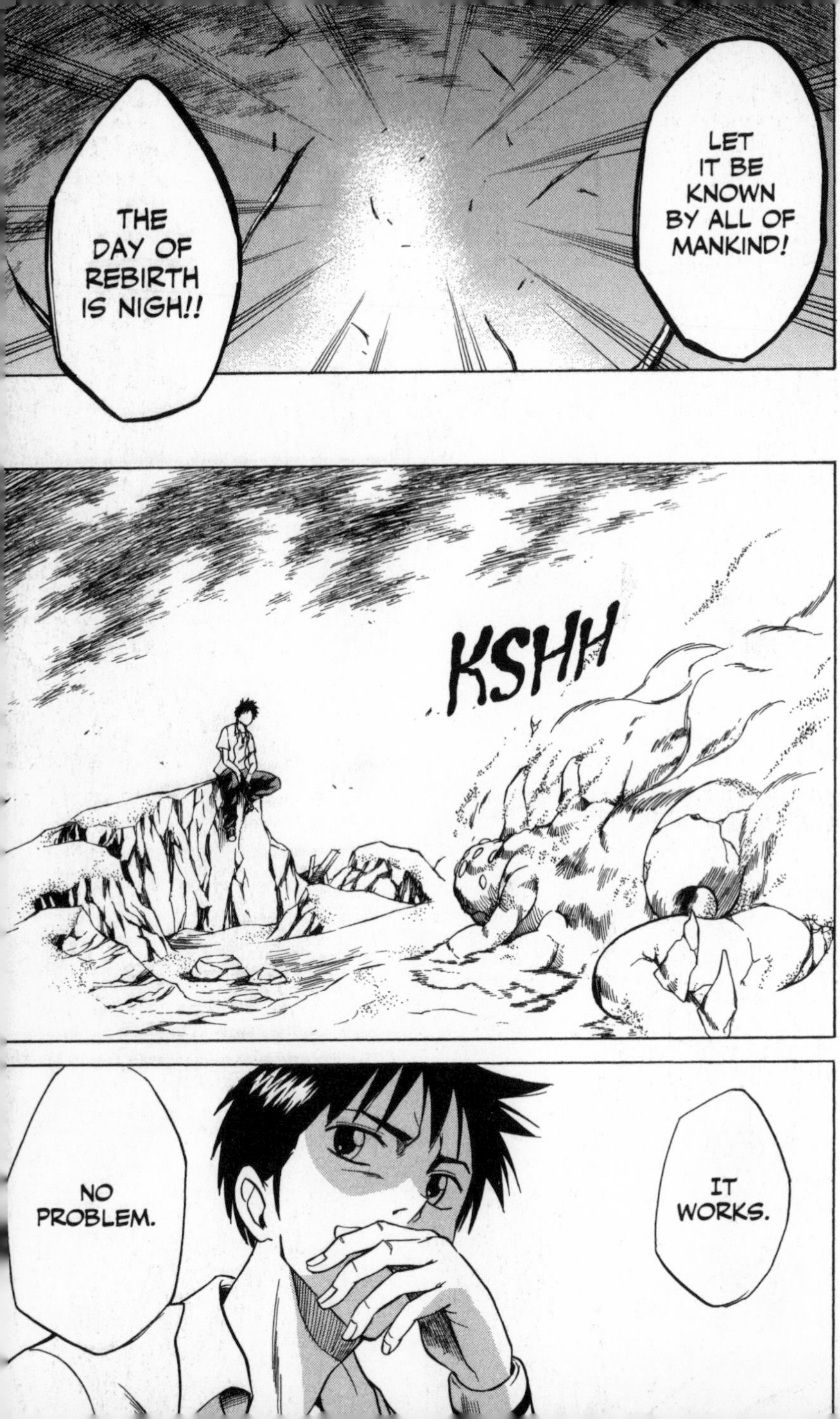

LET IT BE KNOWN BY ALL OF MANKIND!
THE DAY OF REBIRTH IS NIGH!!
KSHH
IT WORKS.
NO PROBLEM.

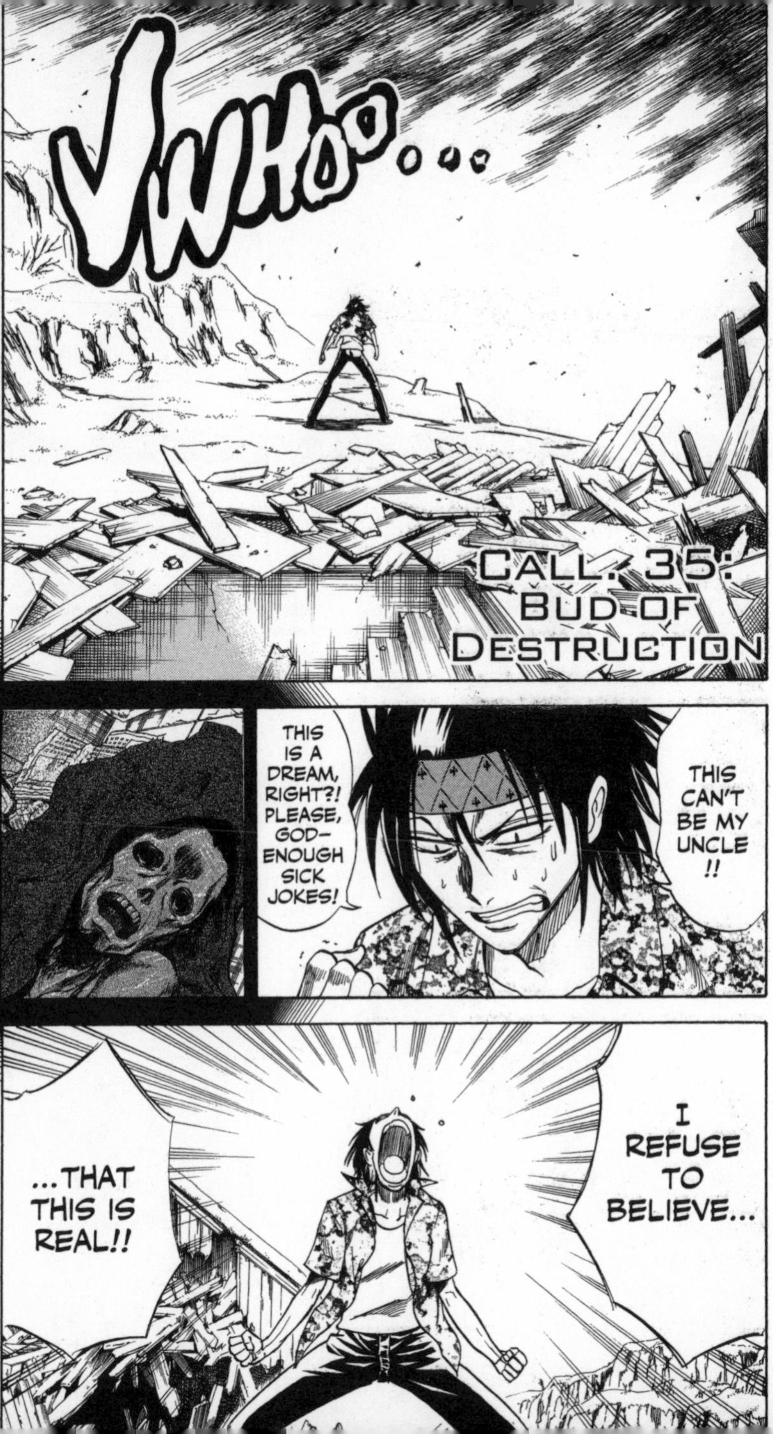
VWHOO...
CALL. 35: BUD OF DESTRUCTION
THIS CAN'T BE MY UNCLE!!
THIS IS A DREAM, RIGHT?! PLEASE, GOD— ENOUGH SICK JOKES!
I REFUSE TO BELIEVE...
...THAT THIS IS REAL!!

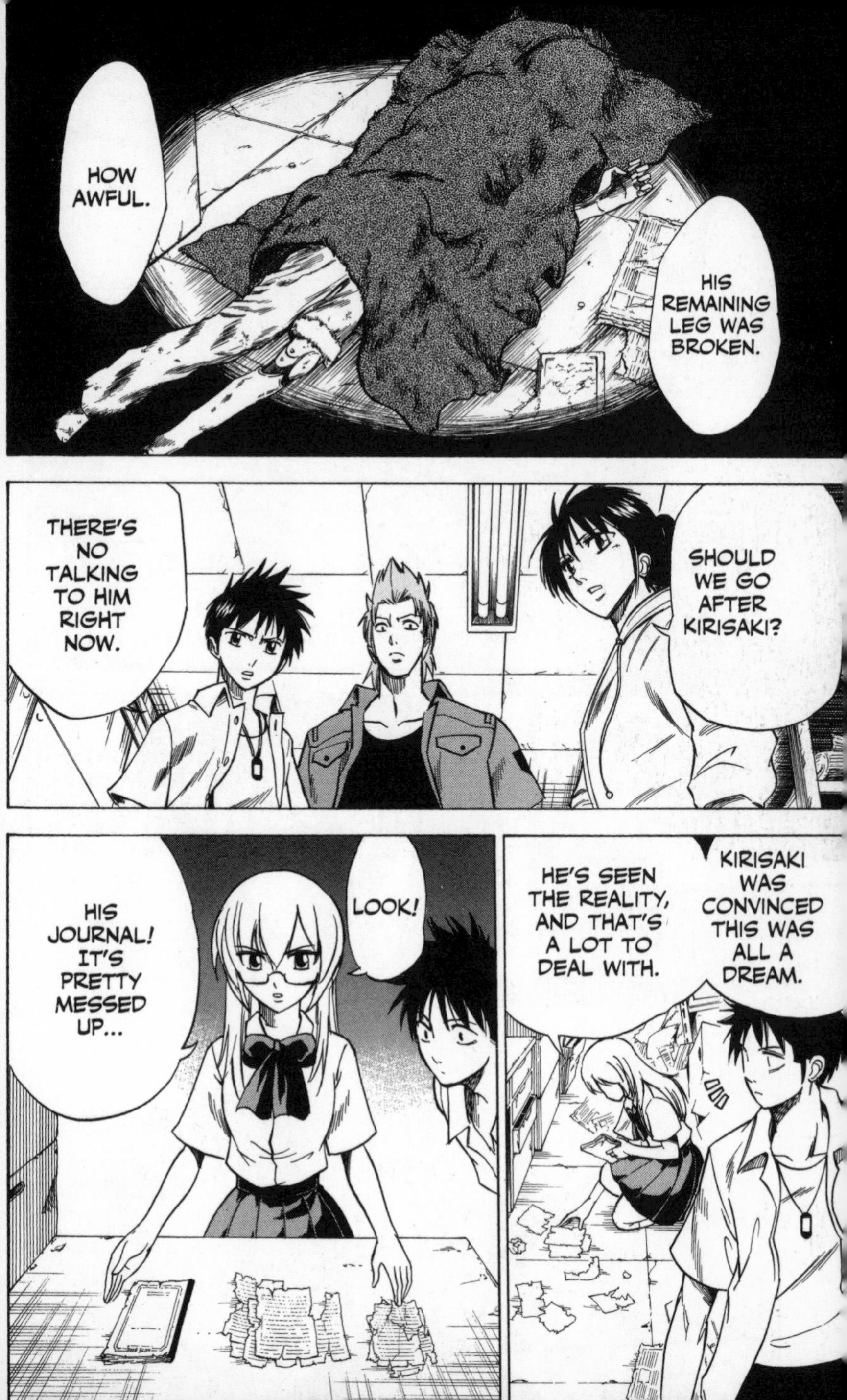
HIS REMAINING LEG WAS BROKEN.
HOW AWFUL.
SHOULD WE GO AFTER KIRISAKI?
THERE'S NO TALKING TO HIM RIGHT NOW.
KIRISAKI WAS CONVINCED THIS WAS ALL A DREAM.
HE'S SEEN THE REALITY, AND THAT'S A LOT TO DEAL WITH.
LOOK!
HIS JOURNAL! IT'S PRETTY MESSED UP...

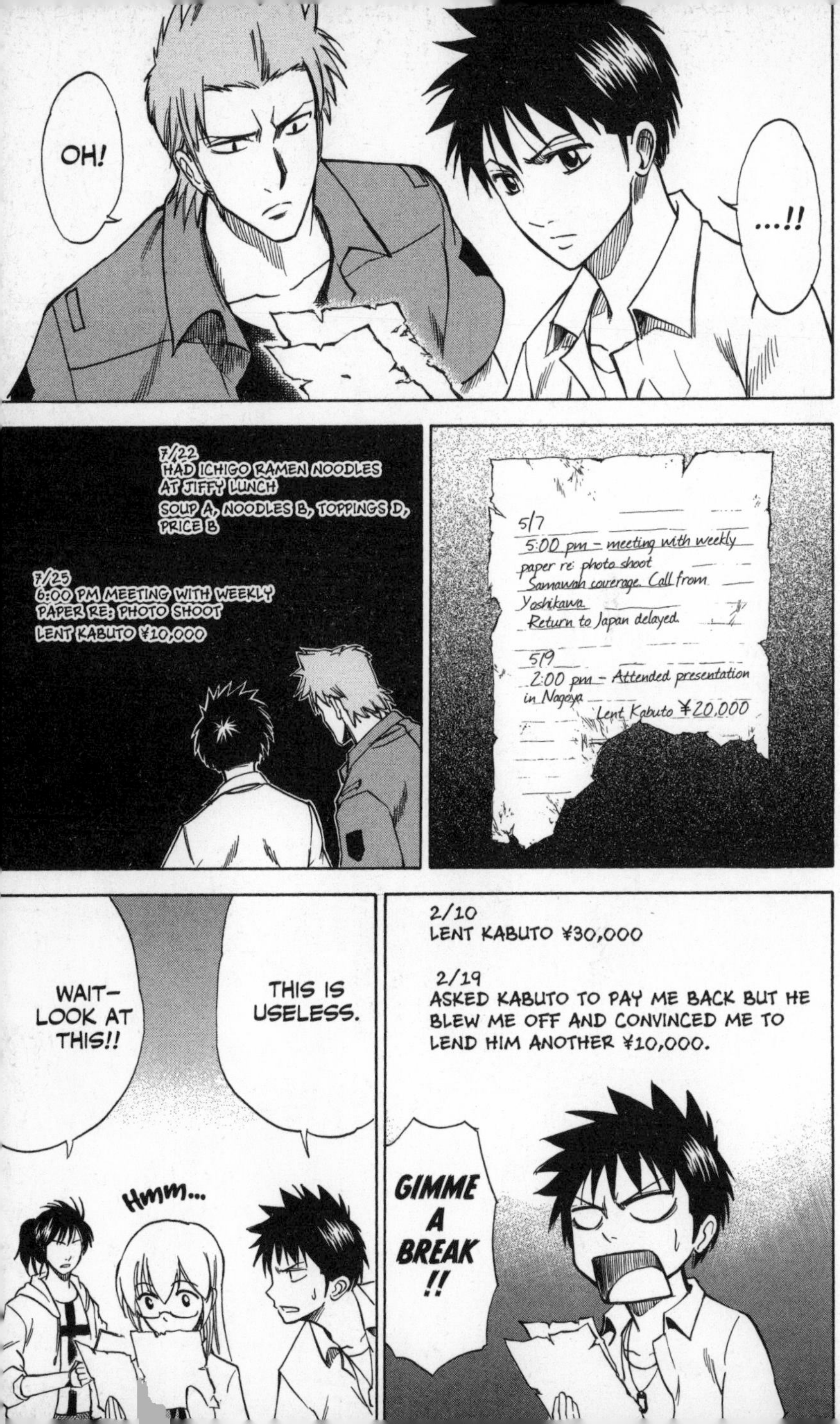

...!!
OH!
5/7
5:00 pm – meeting with weekly paper re: photo shoot
Samawah coverage. Call from Yoshikawa
Return to Japan delayed.
5/9
2:00 pm – Attended presentation in Nagoya
Lent Kabuto ¥20,000
7/22
HAD ICHIGO RAMEN NOODLES AT JIFFY LUNCH
SOUP A, NOODLES B, TOPPINGS D, PRICE B
7/25
6:00 PM MEETING WITH WEEKLY PAPER RE: PHOTO SHOOT
LENT KABUTO ¥10,000
2/10
LENT KABUTO ¥30,000
2/19
ASKED KABUTO TO PAY ME BACK BUT HE BLEW ME OFF AND CONVINCED ME TO LEND HIM ANOTHER ¥10,000.
GIMME A BREAK!!
THIS IS USELESS.
WAIT— LOOK AT THIS!!
Hmm...

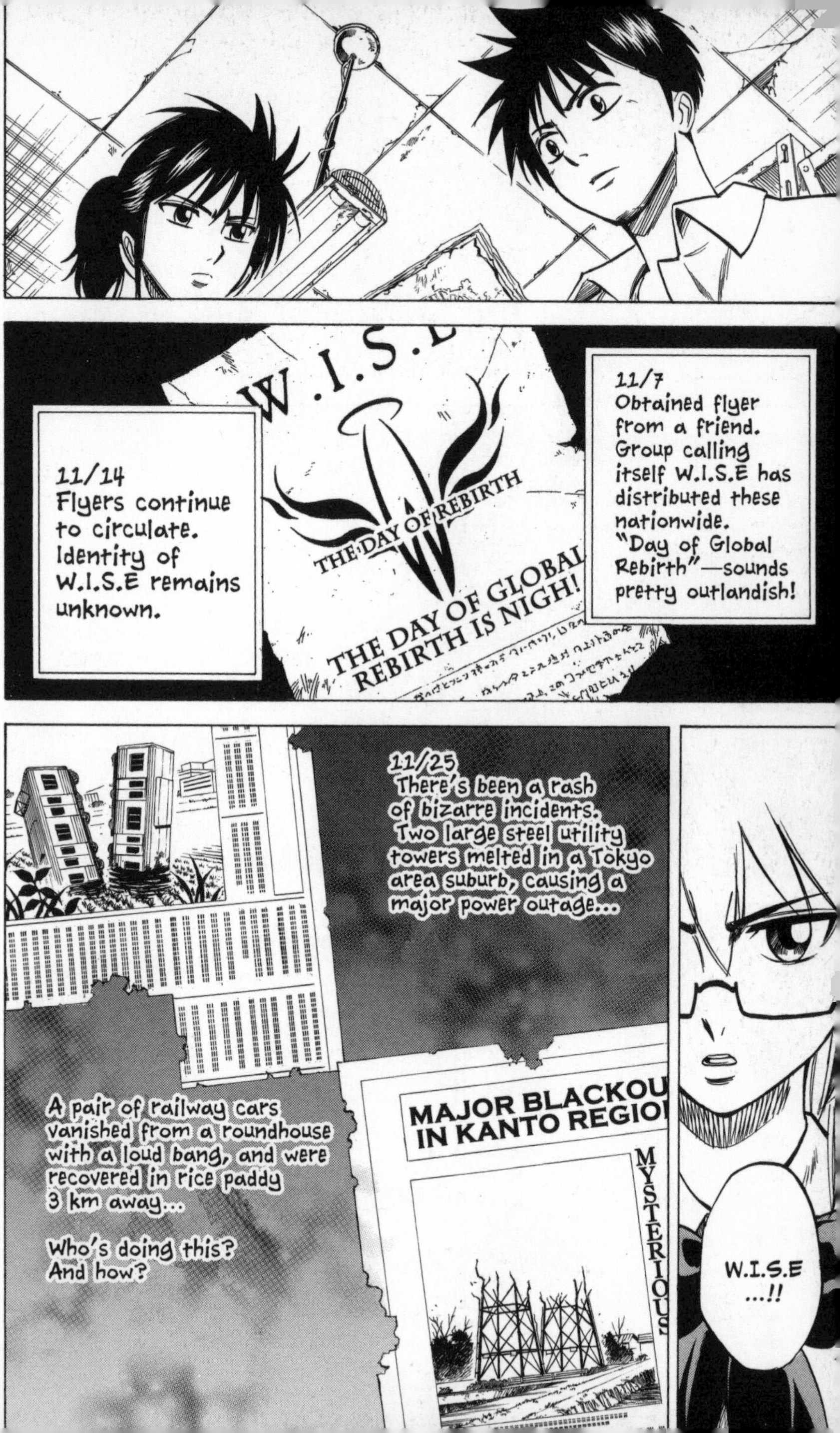
11/7
Obtained flyer from a friend. Group calling itself W.I.S.E has distributed these nationwide. "Day of Global Rebirth"—sounds pretty outlandish!
W.I.S.E
THE DAY OF REBIRTH
THE DAY OF GLOBAL REBIRTH IS NIGH!
11/14
Flyers continue to circulate. Identity of W.I.S.E remains unknown.
W.I.S.E ...!!
11/25
There's been a rash of bizarre incidents. Two large steel utility towers melted in a Tokyo area suburb, causing a major power outage...
MAJOR BLACKOU
IN KANTO REGIO
MYSTERIOUS
A pair of railway cars vanished from a roundhouse with a loud bang, and were recovered in rice paddy 3 km away...
Who's doing this? And how?

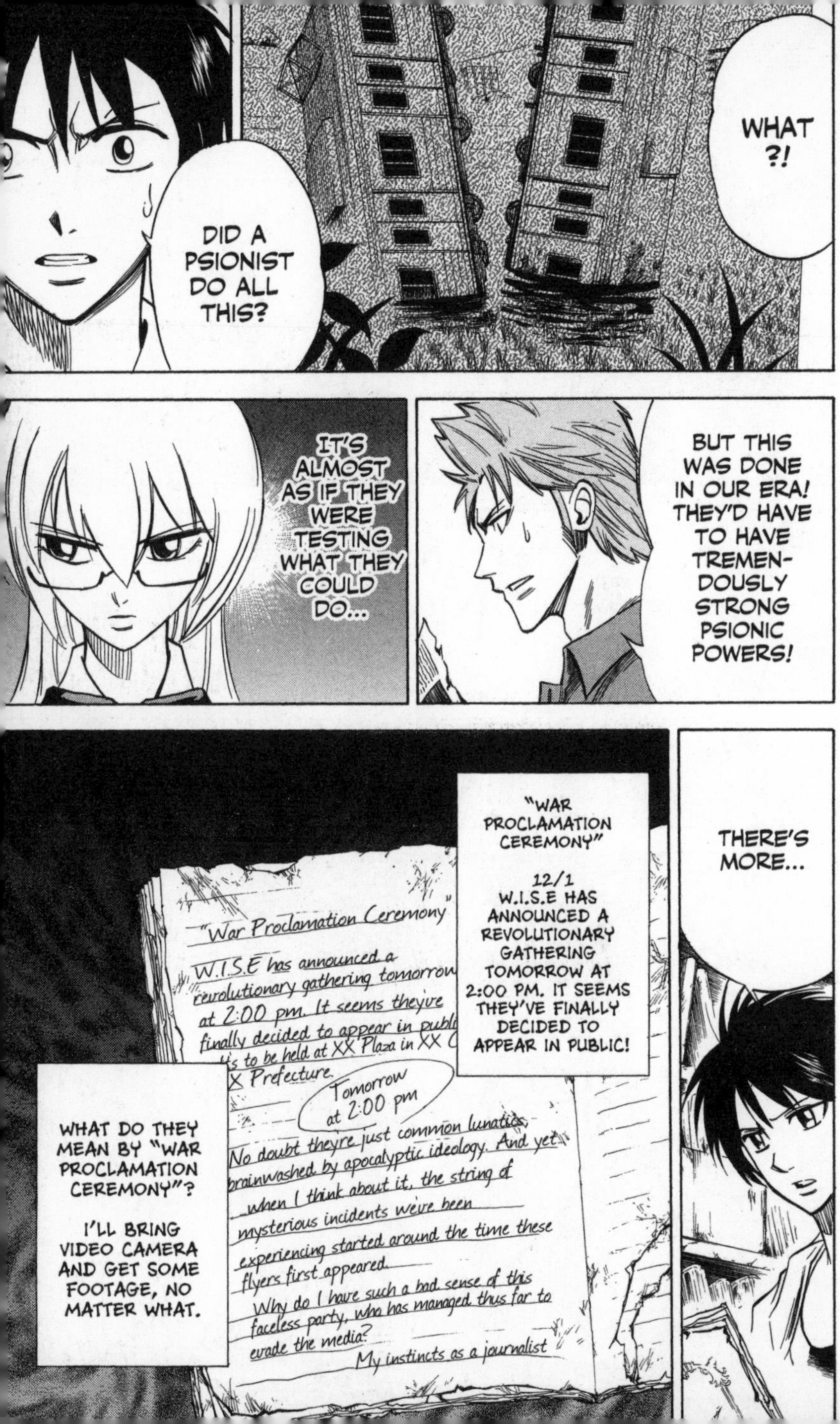

WHAT ?!
DID A PSIONIST DO ALL THIS?
BUT THIS WAS DONE IN OUR ERA! THEY'D HAVE TO HAVE TREMEN-DOUSLY STRONG PSIONIC POWERS!
IT'S ALMOST AS IF THEY WERE TESTING WHAT THEY COULD DO...
THERE'S MORE...
"WAR PROCLAMATION CEREMONY" 12/1 W.I.S.E HAS ANNOUNCED A REVOLUTIONARY GATHERING TOMORROW AT 2:00 PM. IT SEEMS THEY'VE FINALLY DECIDED TO APPEAR IN PUBLIC!
"War Proclamation Ceremony"
W.I.S.E has announced a
revolutionary gathering tomorrow
at 2:00 pm. It seems theyre
finally decided to appear in publi
is to be held at XX Plaza in XX C
X Prefecture.
Tomorrow at 2:00 pm
No doubt theyre just common lunatics
brainwashed by apocalyptic ideology. And yet
when I think about it, the string of
mysterious incidents we're been
experiencing started around the time these
flyers first appeared.
Why do I have such a bad sense of this
faceless party, who has managed thus far to
evade the media?
My instincts as a journalist
WHAT DO THEY MEAN BY "WAR PROCLAMATION CEREMONY"? I'LL BRING VIDEO CAMERA AND GET SOME FOOTAGE, NO MATTER WHAT.

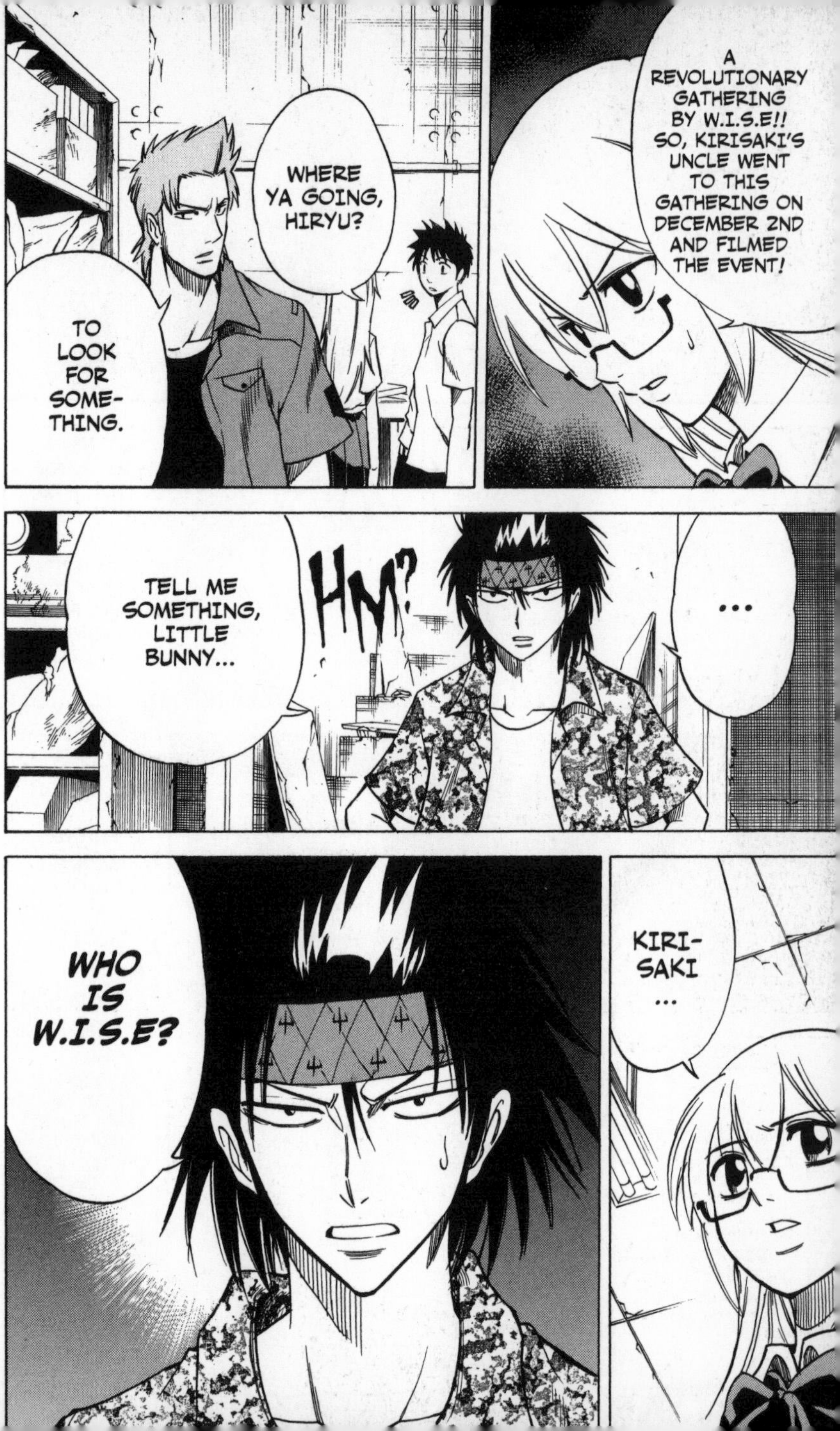
A REVOLUTIONARY GATHERING BY W.I.S.E!! SO, KIRISAKI'S UNCLE WENT TO THIS GATHERING ON DECEMBER 2ND AND FILMED THE EVENT!
WHERE YA GOING, HIRYU?
TO LOOK FOR SOME-THING.
...
HM?
TELL ME SOMETHING, LITTLE BUNNY...
KIRI-SAKI ...
WHO IS W.I.S.E?

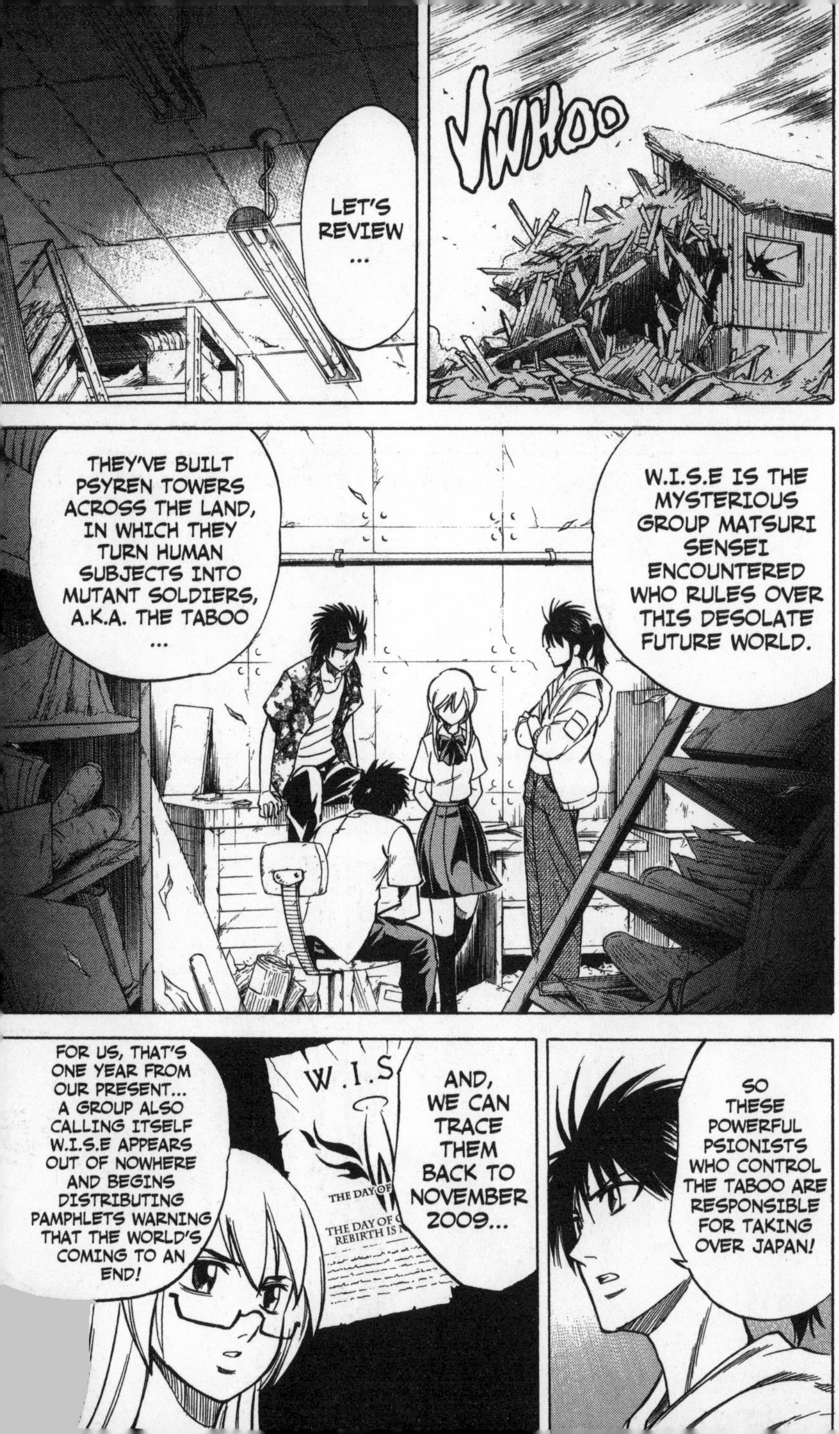
VWHOO
LET'S REVIEW ...
W.I.S.E IS THE MYSTERIOUS GROUP MATSURI SENSEI ENCOUNTERED WHO RULES OVER THIS DESOLATE FUTURE WORLD.
THEY'VE BUILT PSYREN TOWERS ACROSS THE LAND, IN WHICH THEY TURN HUMAN SUBJECTS INTO MUTANT SOLDIERS, A.K.A. THE TABOO ...
SO THESE POWERFUL PSIONISTS WHO CONTROL THE TABOO ARE RESPONSIBLE FOR TAKING OVER JAPAN!
AND, WE CAN TRACE THEM BACK TO NOVEMBER 2009...
FOR US, THAT'S ONE YEAR FROM OUR PRESENT... A GROUP ALSO CALLING ITSELF W.I.S.E APPEARS OUT OF NOWHERE AND BEGINS DISTRIBUTING PAMPHLETS WARNING THAT THE WORLD'S COMING TO AN END!

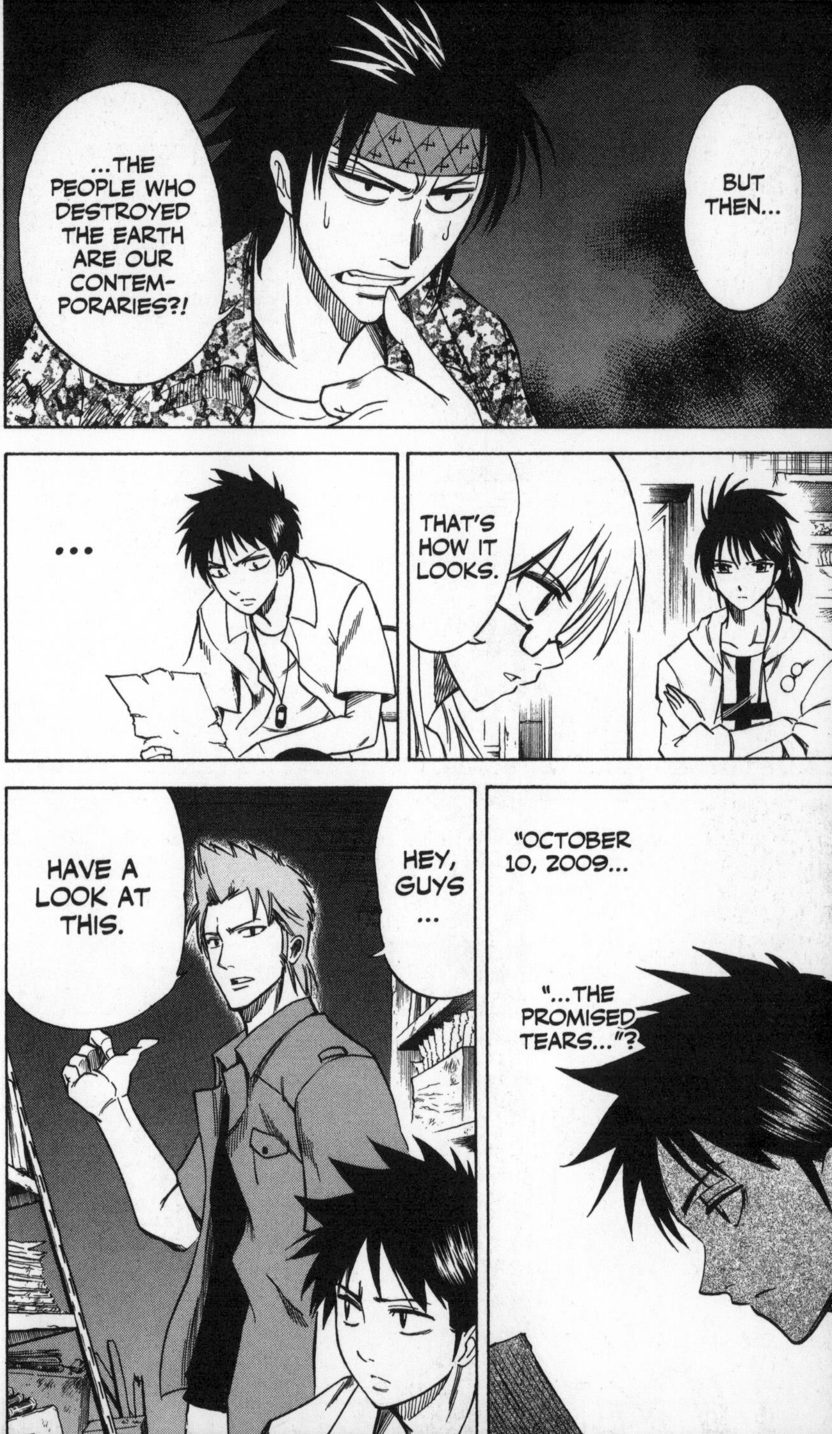
BUT THEN...
...THE PEOPLE WHO DESTROYED THE EARTH ARE OUR CONTEM-PORARIES?!
THAT'S HOW IT LOOKS.
...
"OCTOBER 10, 2009...
"...THE PROMISED TEARS..."?
HEY, GUYS ...
HAVE A LOOK AT THIS.

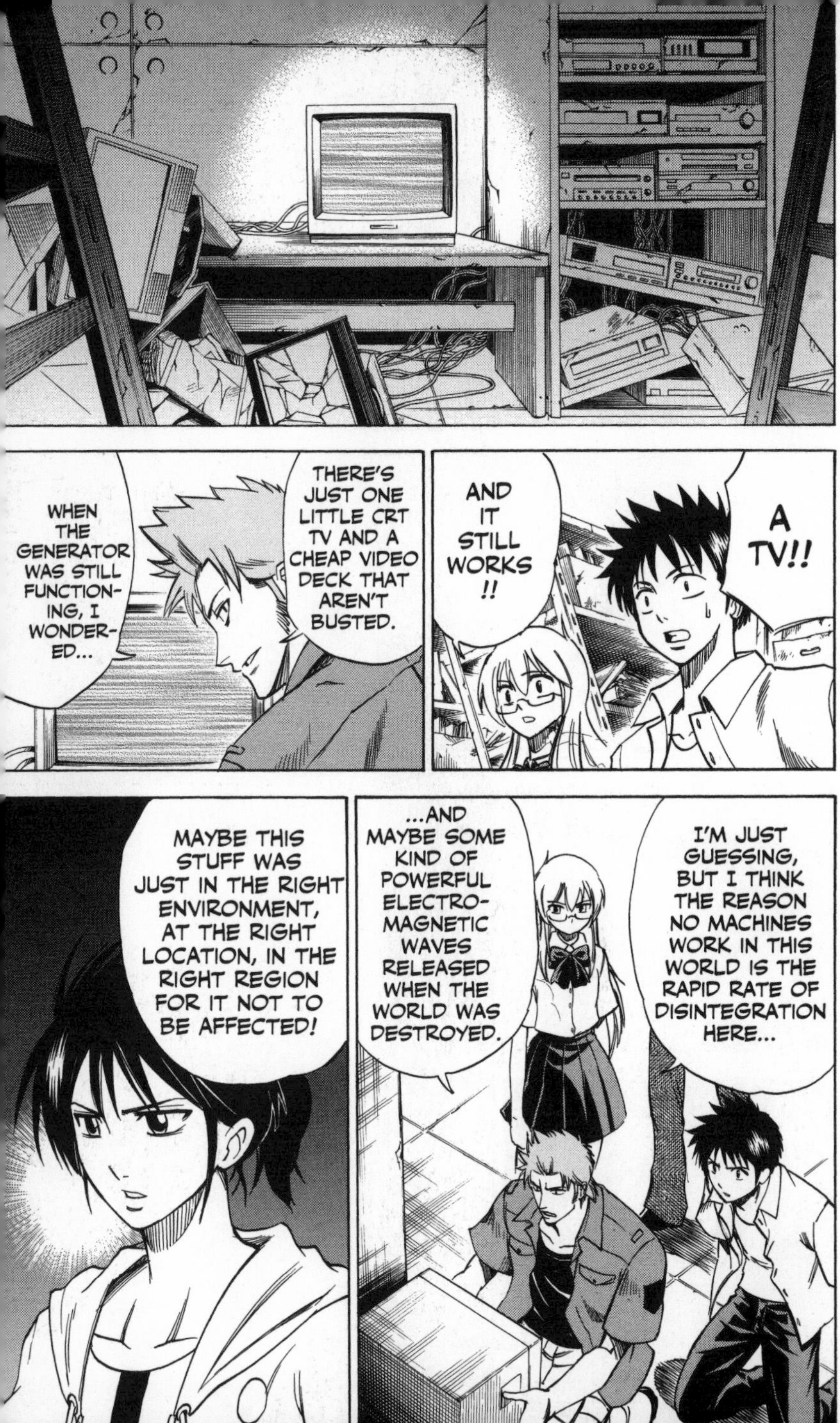
A TV!!
AND IT STILL WORKS!!
THERE'S JUST ONE LITTLE CRT TV AND A CHEAP VIDEO DECK THAT AREN'T BUSTED.
WHEN THE GENERATOR WAS STILL FUNCTIONING, I WONDERED...
I'M JUST GUESSING, BUT I THINK THE REASON NO MACHINES WORK IN THIS WORLD IS THE RAPID RATE OF DISINTEGRATION HERE...
...AND MAYBE SOME KIND OF POWERFUL ELECTROMAGNETIC WAVES RELEASED WHEN THE WORLD WAS DESTROYED.
MAYBE THIS STUFF WAS JUST IN THE RIGHT ENVIRONMENT, AT THE RIGHT LOCATION, IN THE RIGHT REGION FOR IT NOT TO BE AFFECTED!

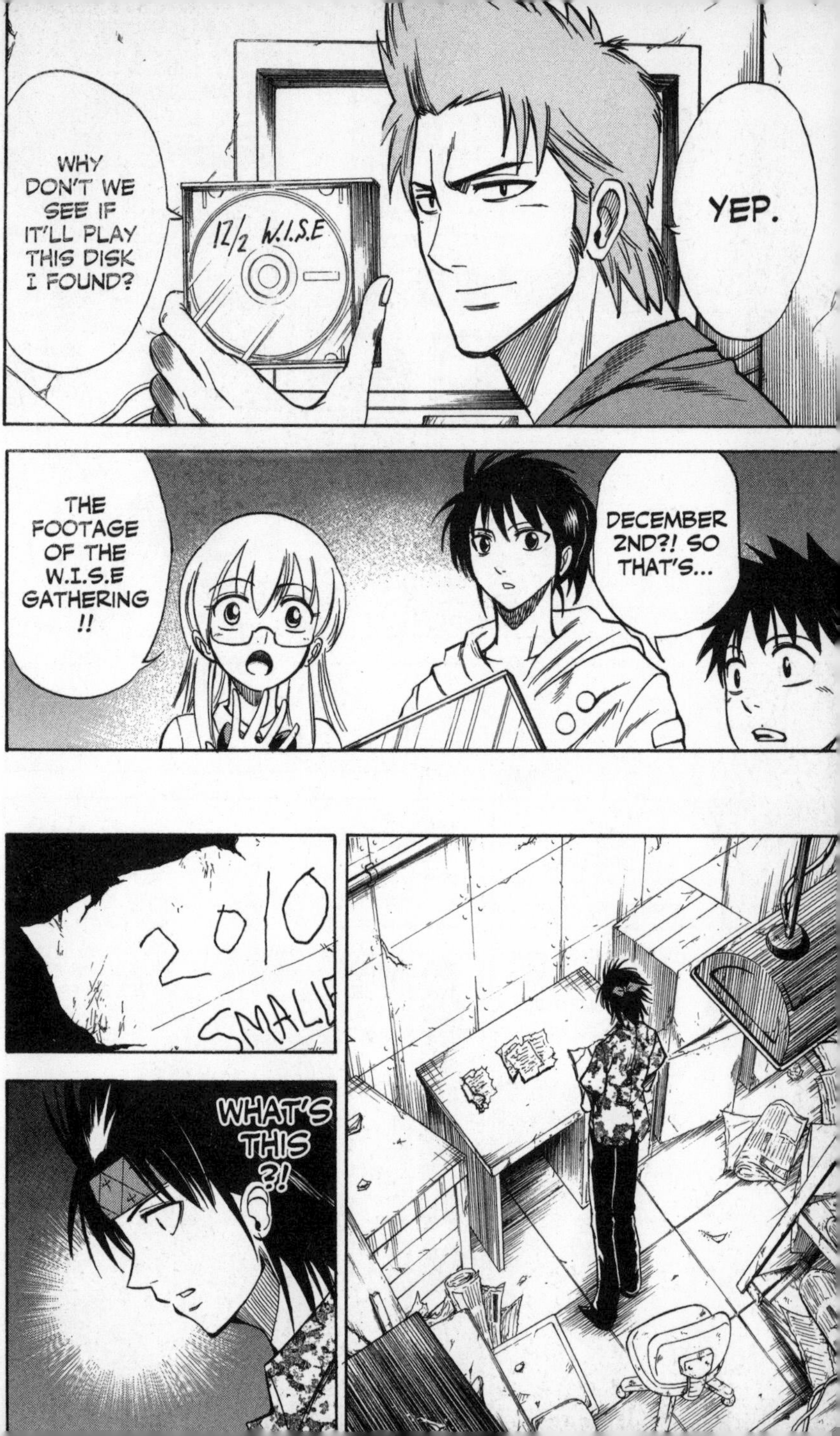
YEP.
WHY DON'T WE SEE IF IT'LL PLAY THIS DISK I FOUND?
12/2 W.I.S.E
DECEMBER 2ND?! SO THAT'S...
THE FOOTAGE OF THE W.I.S.E GATHERING !!
2010
WHAT'S THIS ?!

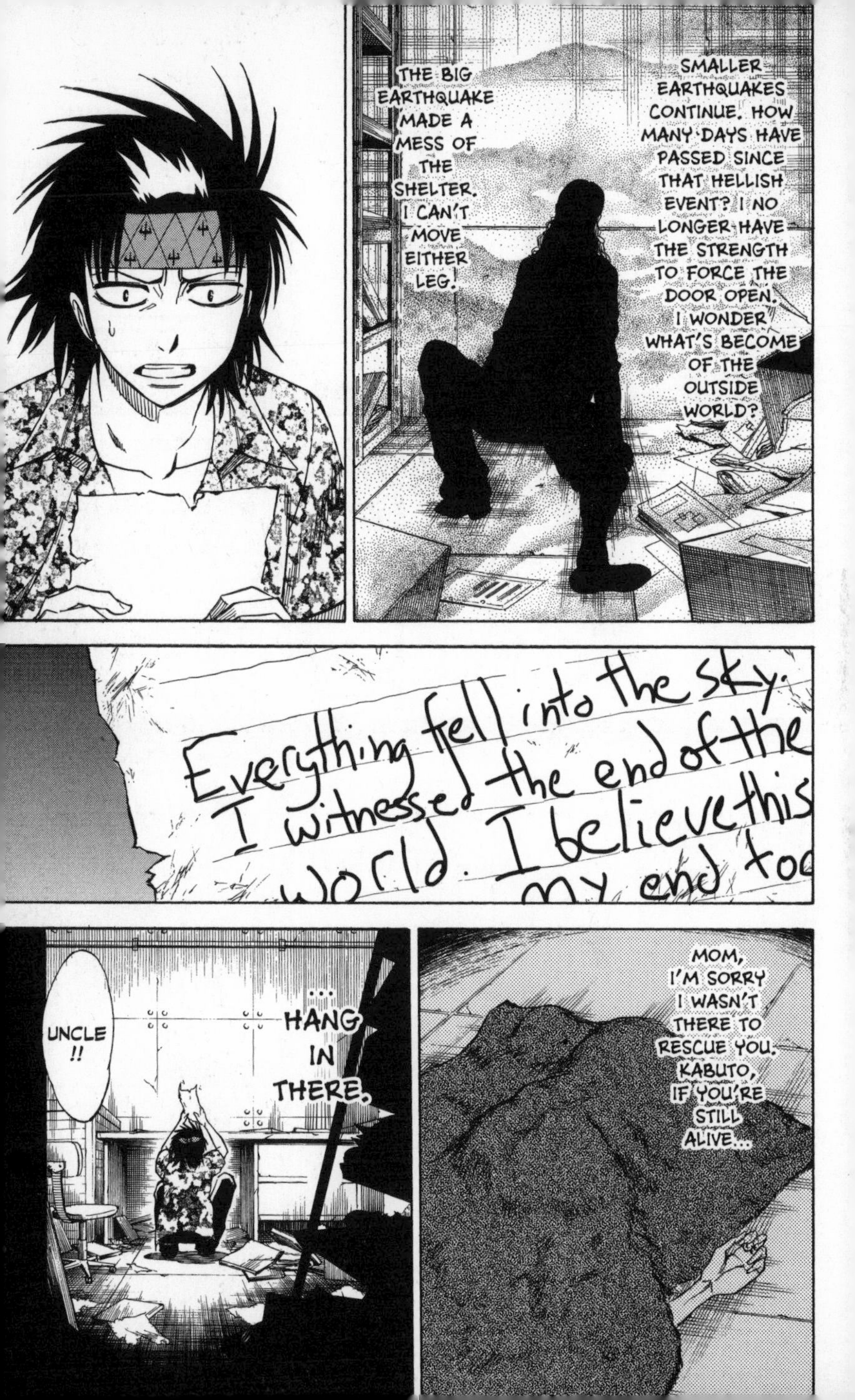
SMALLER EARTHQUAKES CONTINUE. HOW MANY DAYS HAVE PASSED SINCE THAT HELLISH EVENT? I NO LONGER HAVE THE STRENGTH TO FORCE THE DOOR OPEN. I WONDER WHAT'S BECOME OF THE OUTSIDE WORLD?
THE BIG EARTHQUAKE MADE A MESS OF THE SHELTER. I CAN'T MOVE EITHER LEG!
Everything fell into the sky. I witnessed the end of the world. I believe this my end too
MOM, I'M SORRY I WASN'T THERE TO RESCUE YOU. KABUTO, IF YOU'RE STILL ALIVE...
...HANG IN THERE.
UNCLE !!

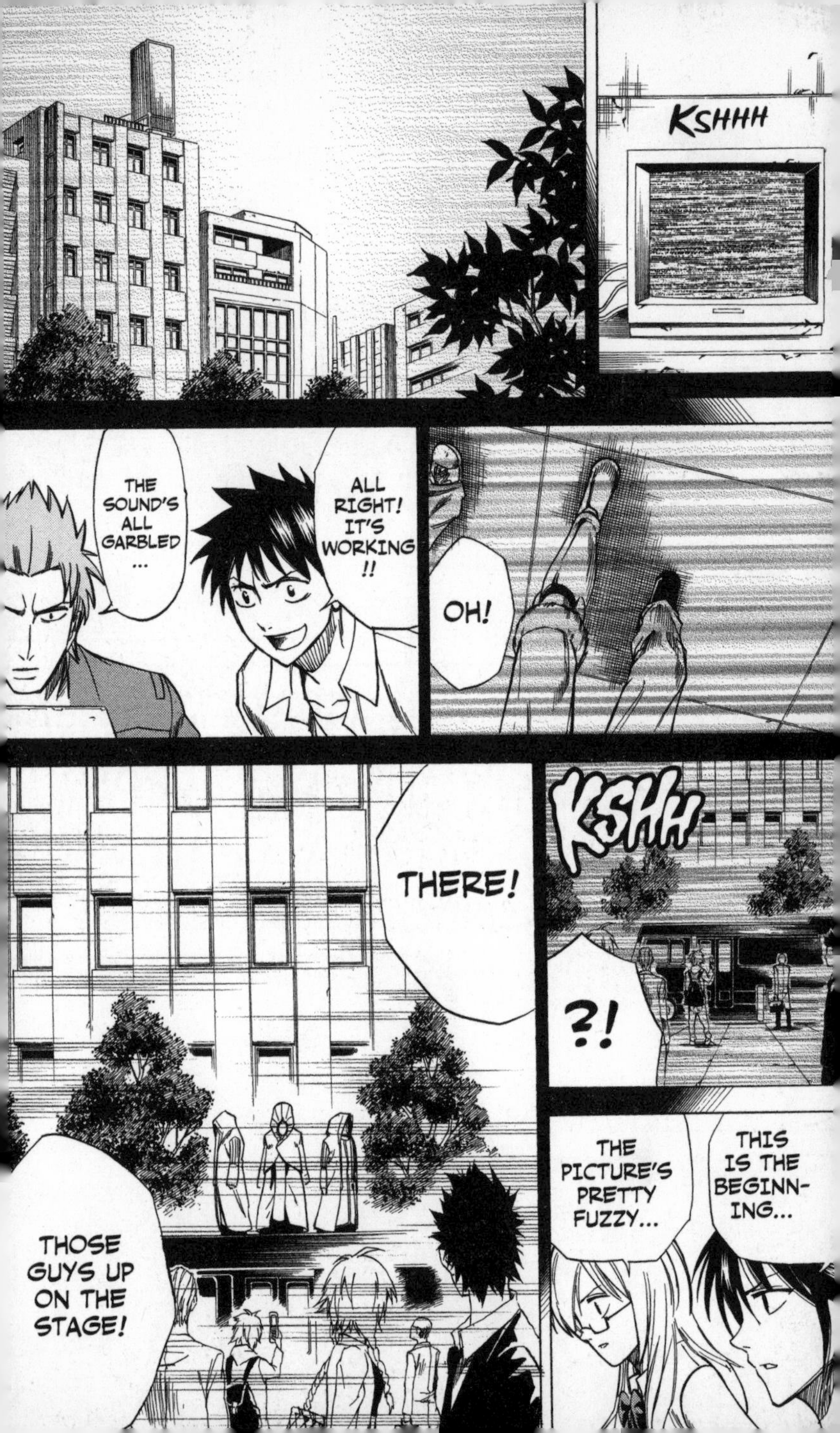
KSHHH
OH!
ALL RIGHT! IT'S WORKING !!
THE SOUND'S ALL GARBLED ...
KSHH
?!
THIS IS THE BEGINNING...
THE PICTURE'S PRETTY FUZZY...
THERE!
THOSE GUYS UP ON THE STAGE!

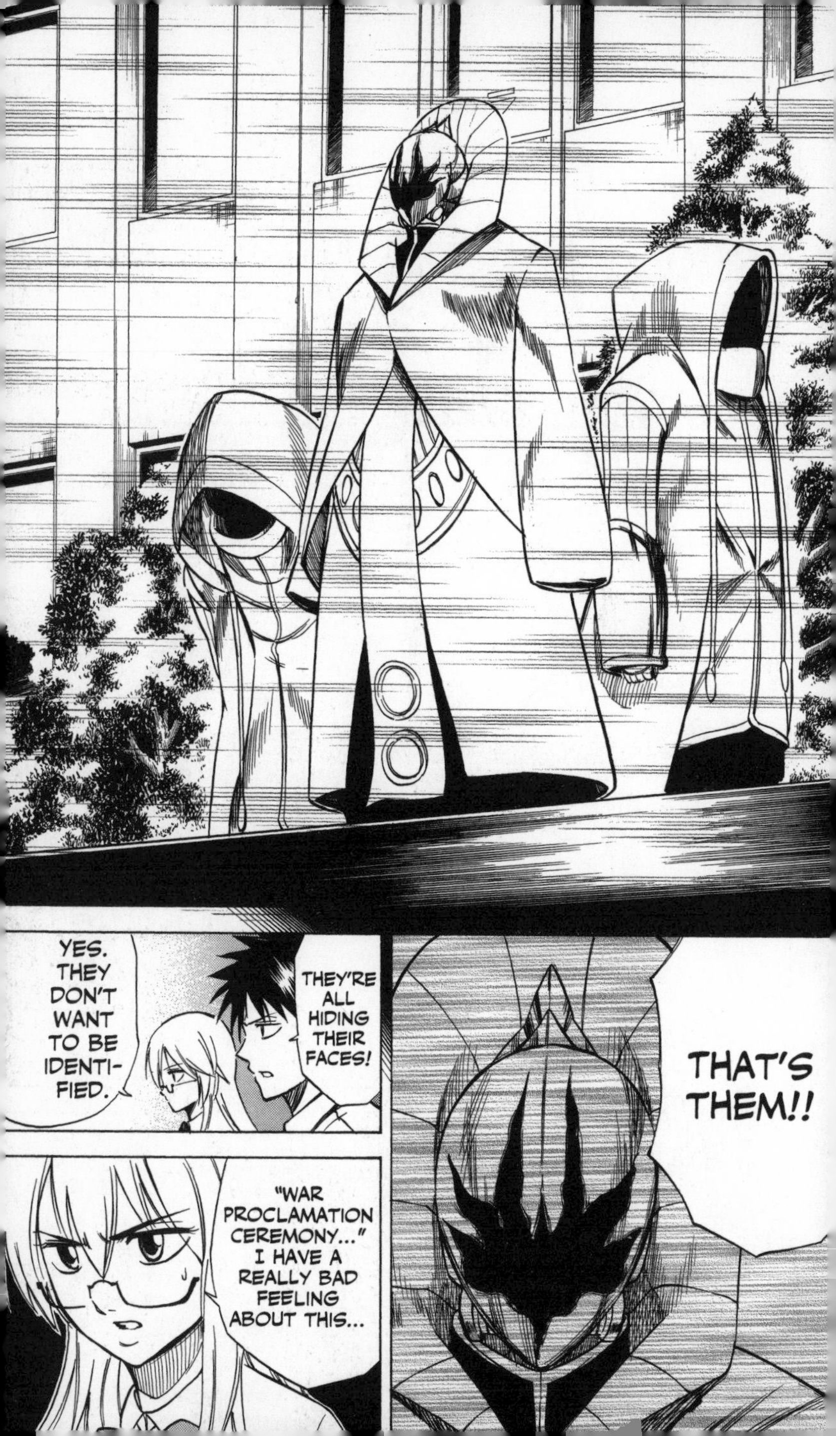
THAT'S THEM!!
THEY'RE ALL HIDING THEIR FACES!
YES. THEY DON'T WANT TO BE IDENTI-FIED.
"WAR PROCLAMATION CEREMONY..." I HAVE A REALLY BAD FEELING ABOUT THIS...

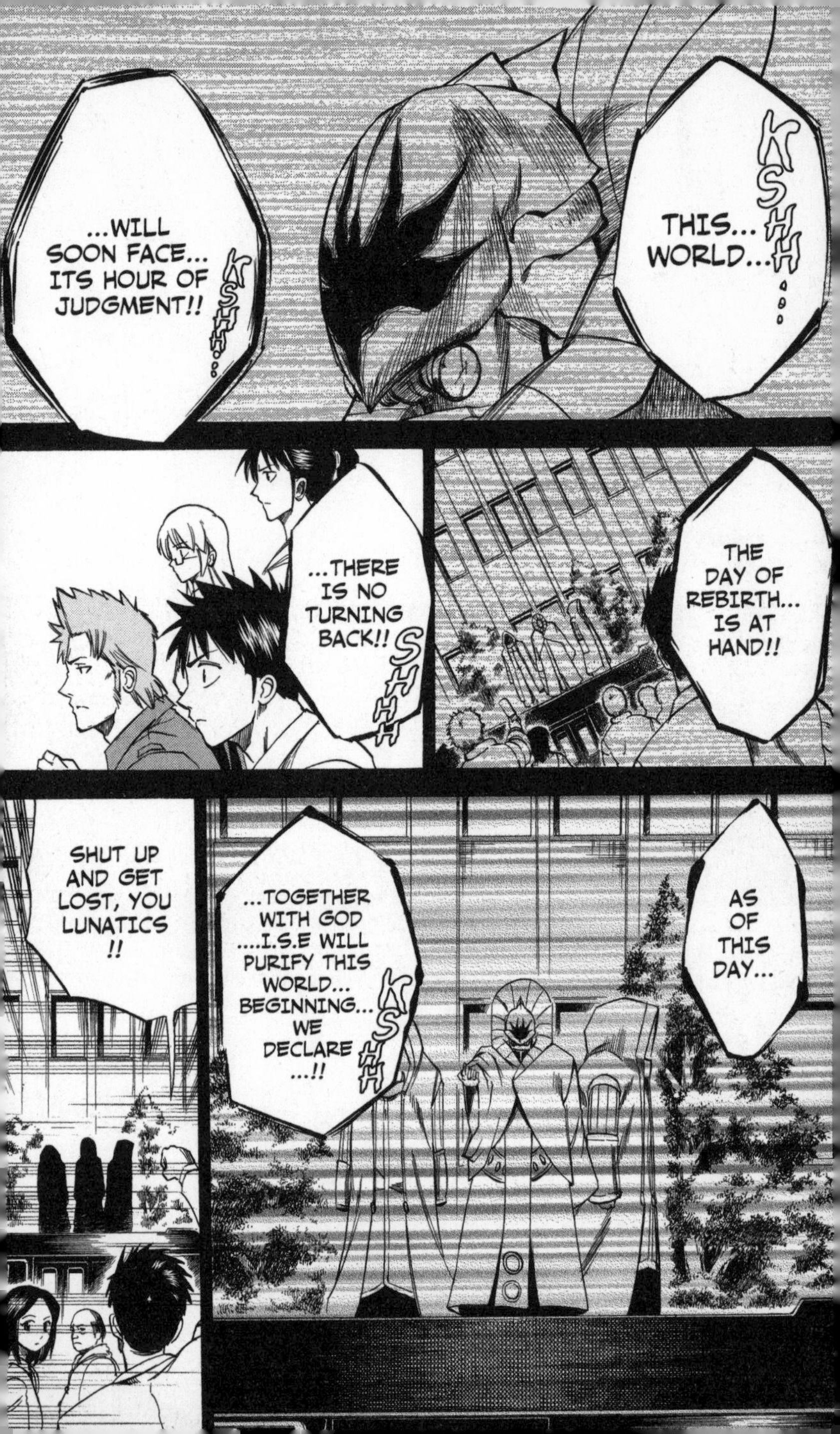
THIS... WORLD...
KSHH...
...WILL SOON FACE... ITS HOUR OF JUDGMENT!!
KSHH...
THE DAY OF REBIRTH... IS AT HAND!!
...THERE IS NO TURNING BACK!!
SHHH
AS OF THIS DAY...
...TOGETHER WITH GOD ....I.S.E WILL PURIFY THIS WORLD... BEGINNING... WE DECLARE ...!!
KSHH
SHUT UP AND GET LOST, YOU LUNATICS !!

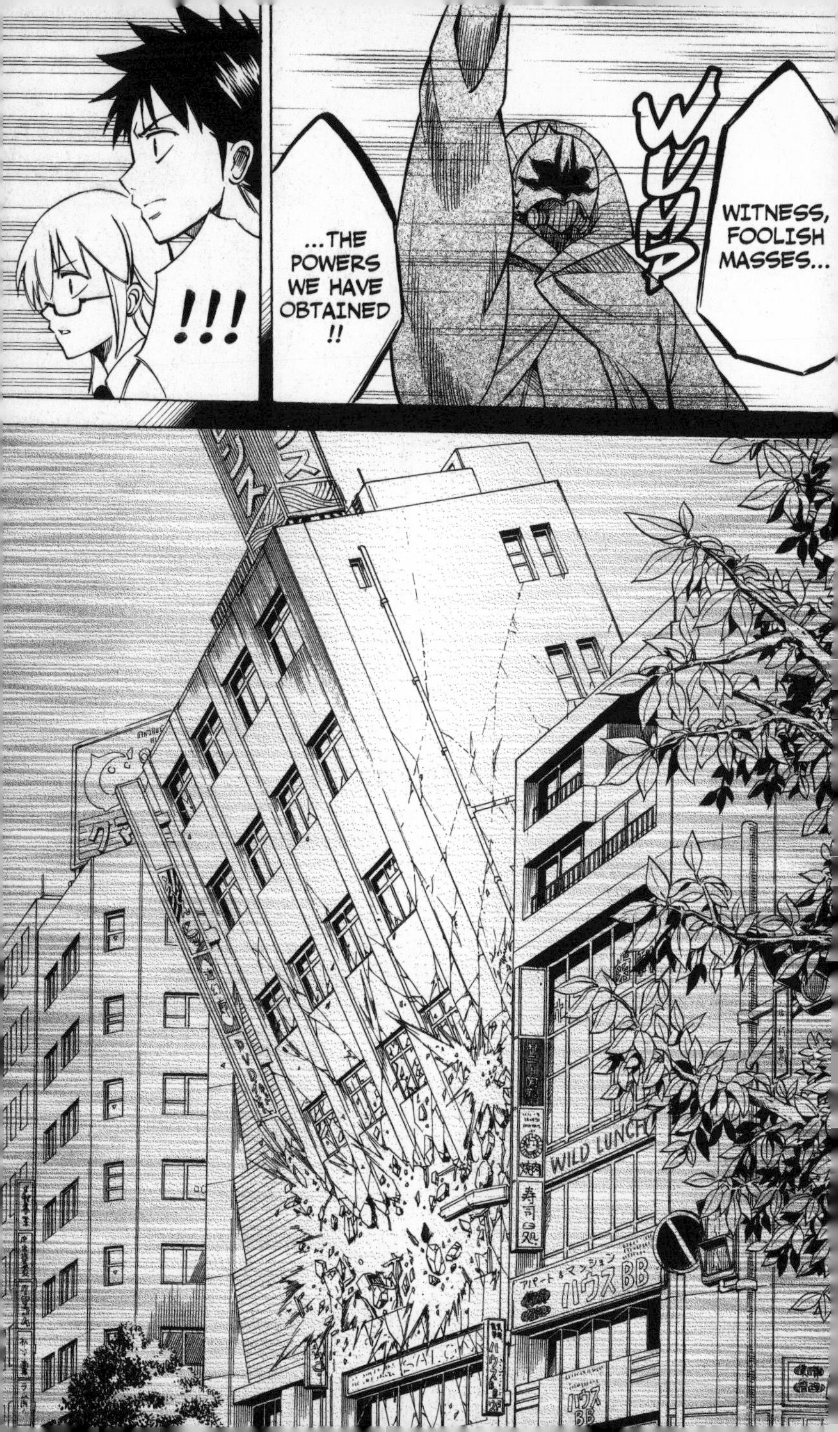
WITNESS, FOOLISH MASSES...
...THE POWERS WE HAVE OBTAINED !!
!!!
DVD
WILD LUNC
焼肉
寿司
アパート＆マンション
ハウスBB

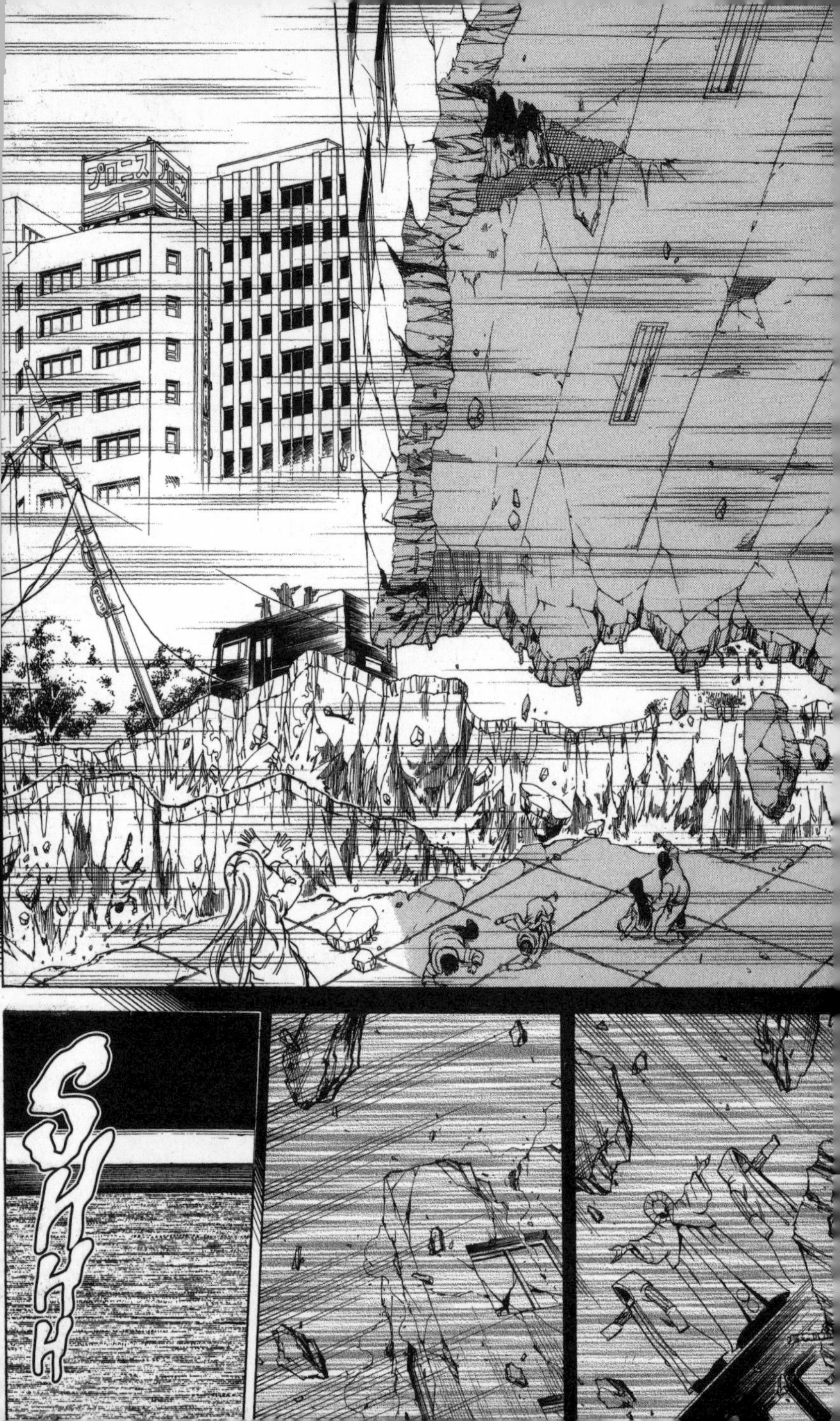
プロニス
P
SHHH

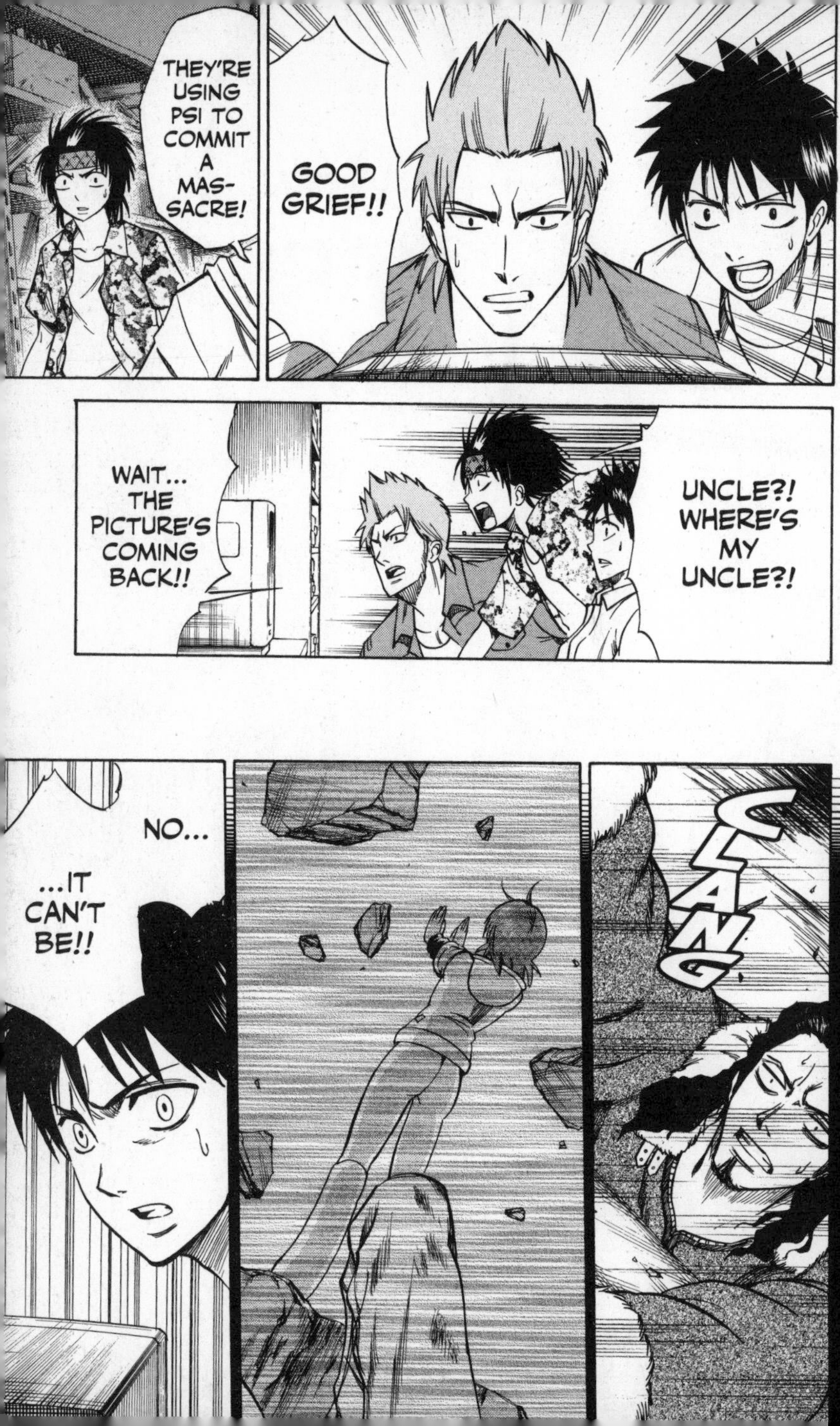
GOOD GRIEF!!
THEY'RE USING PSI TO COMMIT A MAS-SACRE!
UNCLE?! WHERE'S MY UNCLE?!
WAIT... THE PICTURE'S COMING BACK!!
CLANG
NO...
...IT CAN'T BE!!

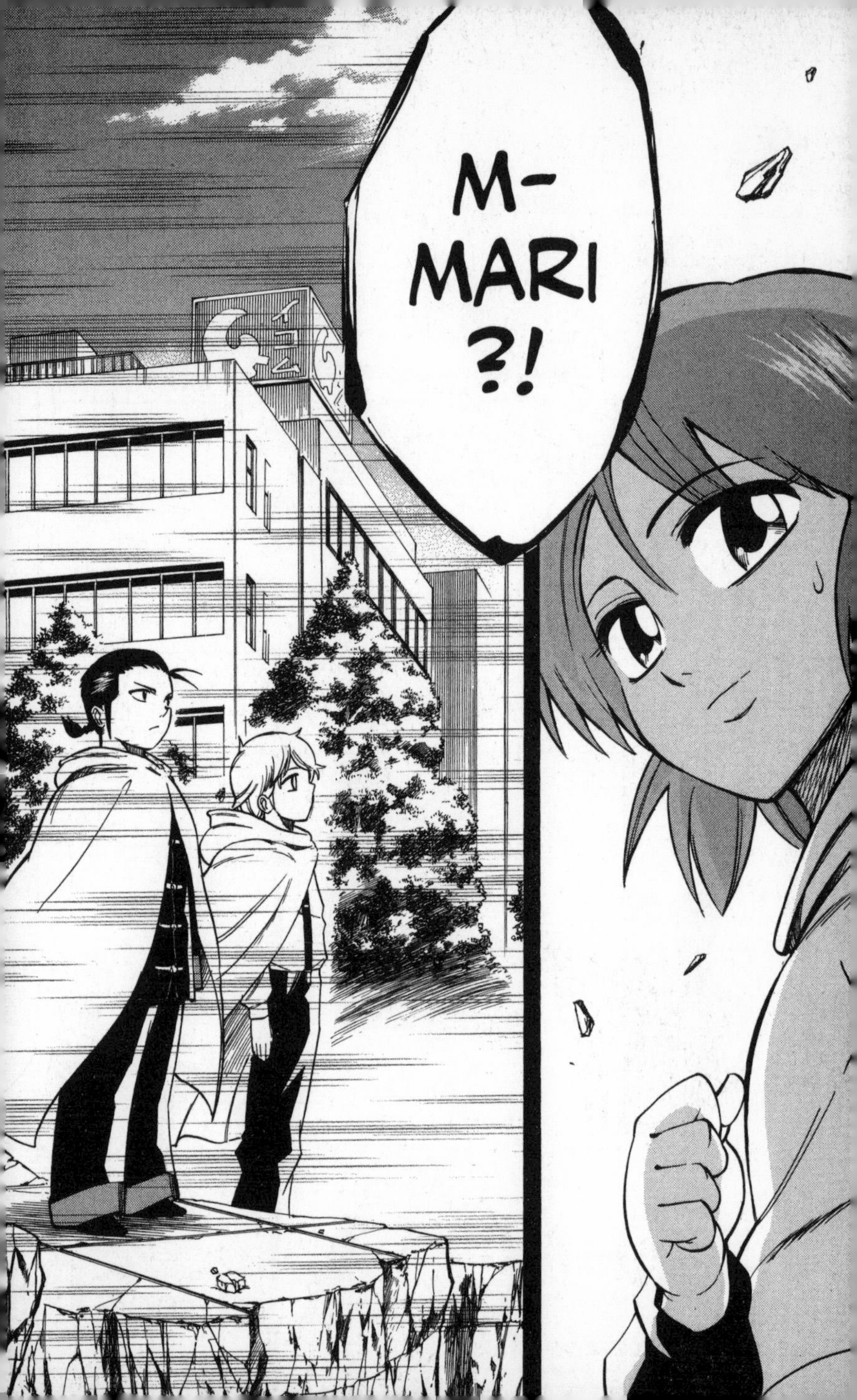
M-MARI?!

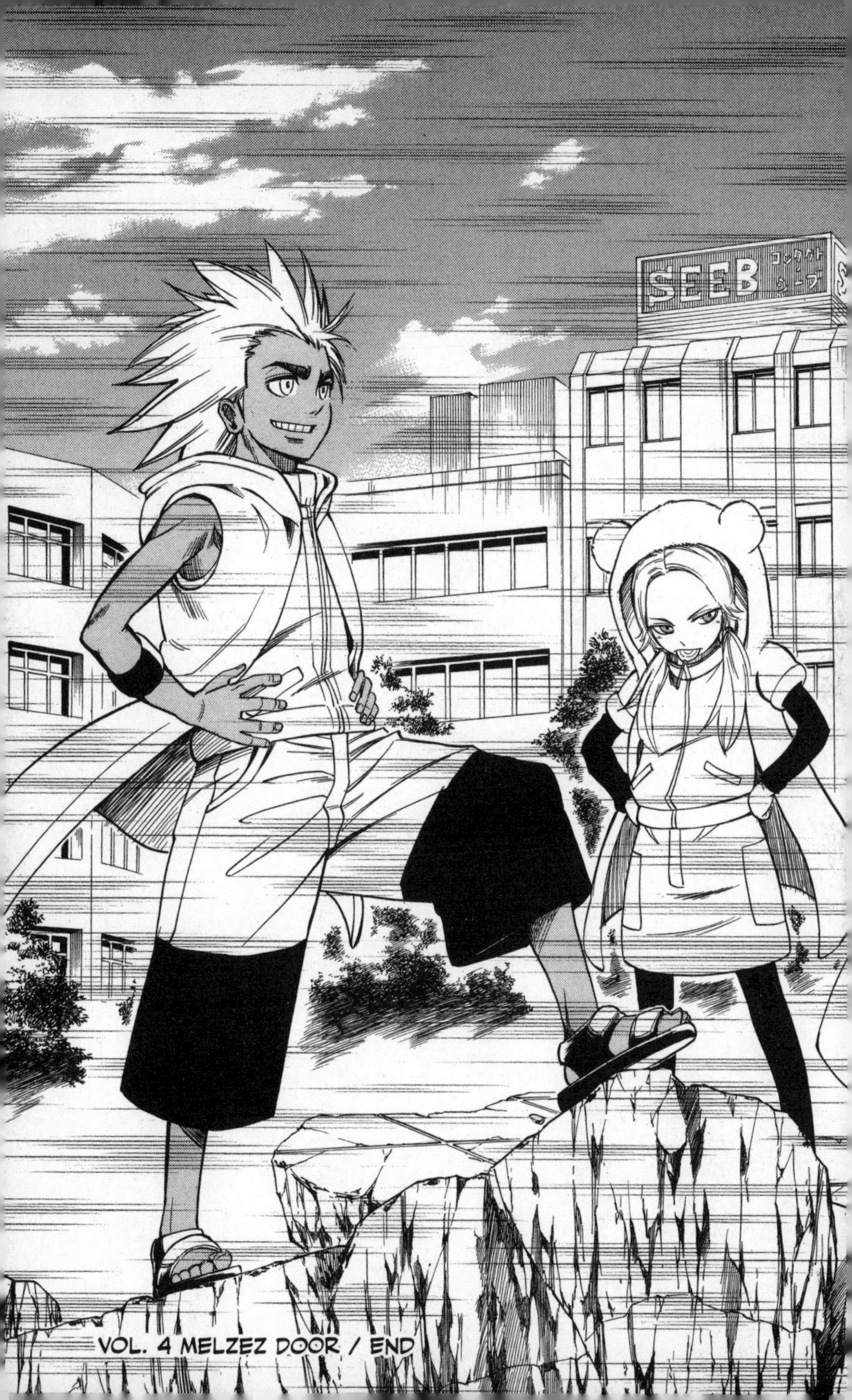
SEEB
VOL. 4 MELZEZ DOOR / END

Afterword

THANK YOU SO MUCH FOR READING *PSYREN* VOLUME 4.

THE SERIES HAS LASTED FOR OVER A YEAR NOW. I'M THRILLED.

IT'S REALLY CRAZY...OF COURSE, MY LAST SERIES LASTED A YEAR TOO...

BUT THIS TIME, I'M BETTER AT HOLDING UP UNDER THE PRESSURE.

IN THE PAST, WHEN I WAS BEHIND ON STORYBOARDS AND WAS SLATED TO WORK ON THE ART WITH MY STAFF THE NEXT MORNING, I WOULD PANIC AND HYPERVENTILATE. NOW, I JUST SCREAM AND PACE AROUND THE ROOM. NOW THAT'S PROGRESS.

THE ATMOSPHERE AT THE STUDIO IS GOOD.

I THINK WHAT MAKES IT WORK IS THAT EVERYONE STAYS POSITIVE EVEN THOUGH THE WORK IS HARD.

EVERYONE'S WORKING HARD TO GET A SERIAL (RENSAI) MANGA.

EVERY DAY I WATCH THEM STRUGGLING AND FRETTING OVER STORYBOARDS FOR SHORT STORY (YOMIKIRI) MANGA.

EVEN THOUGH THEIR SITUATIONS MAY NOT HAVE CHANGED, I CAN SEE THEM DEVELOPING MENTAL STAMINA AND THE SENSIBILITY TO GRASP WHAT MAKES A MANGA COMPELLING.

WATCHING THE PEOPLE AROUND ME PROGRESS BOOSTS MY MOTIVATION TOO.

ANYWAY, SEE YOU AGAIN IN VOLUME 5!

TOSHIAKI IWASHIRO, DECEMBER 2008

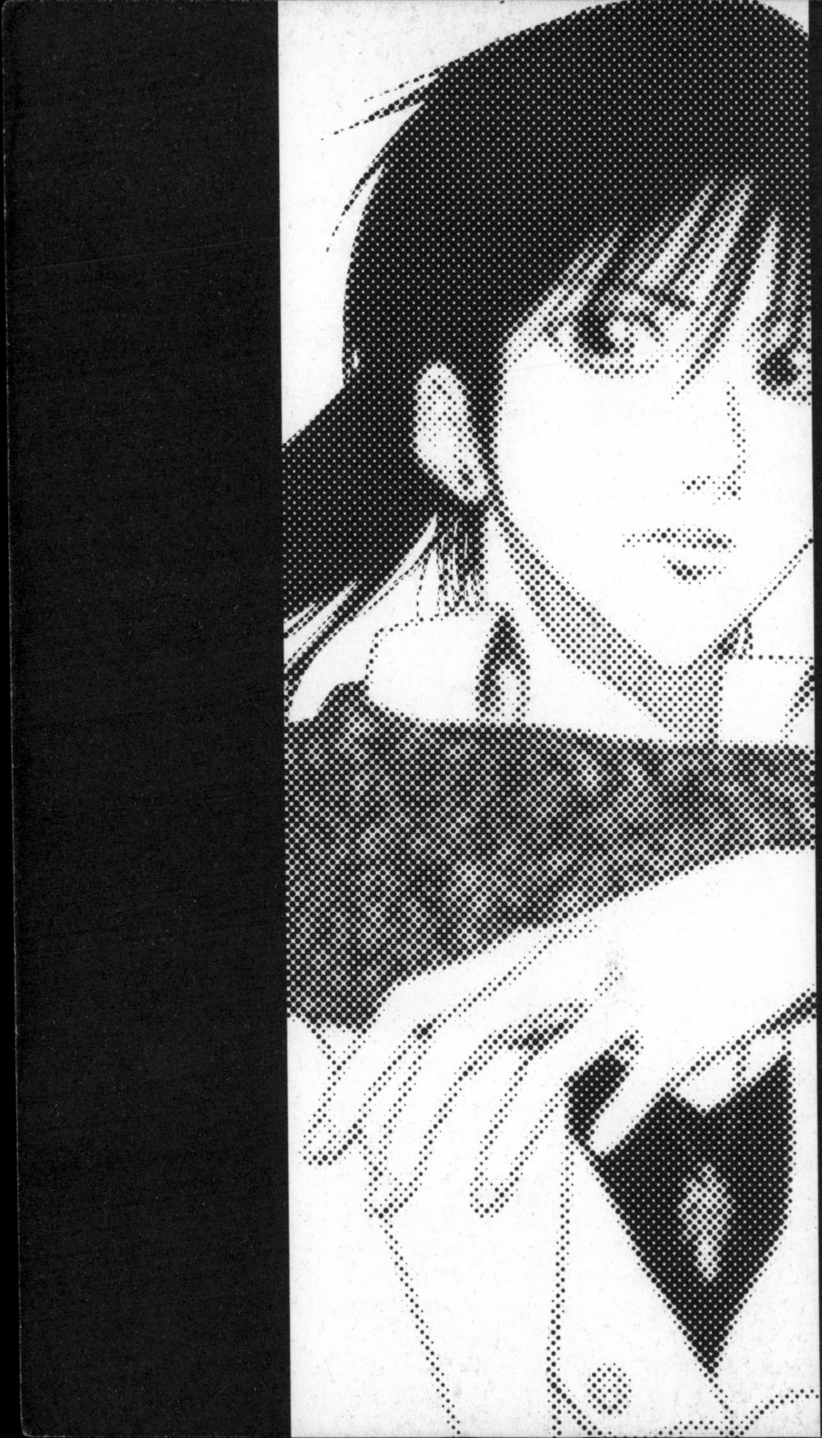

IN THE NEXT VOLUME...

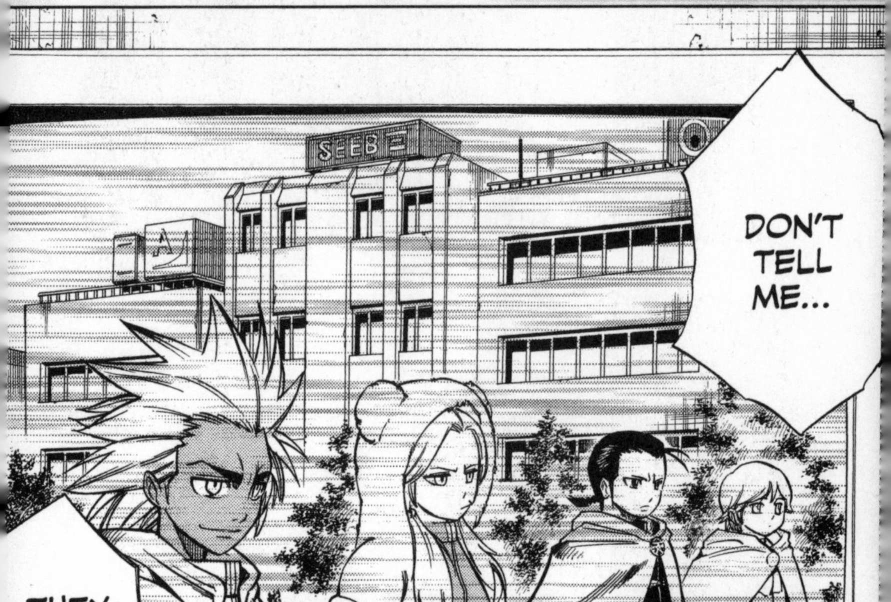
DON'T TELL ME...
..THEY NTEND FIGHT V.I.S.E ?!

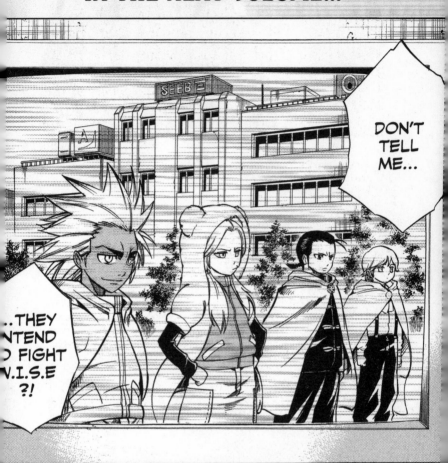

VISIONS

A video recording shows a dark vision of the future, where many of Ageha's friends are ruthlessly killed. To escape the danger posed by the W.I.S.E, Ageha, Sakurako and the others must battle their way to freedom. But even if they escape, can they really fight fate and alter that treacherous future?

Available JULY 2012!

BAKUMAN。

STORY BY TSUGUMI OHBA
ART BY TAKESHI OBATA

From the creators of *Death Note*

The mystery behind manga making REVEALED!

Average student Moritaka Mashiro enjoys drawing for fun. When his classmate and aspiring writer Akito Takagi discovers his talent, he begs to team up. But what exactly does it take to make it in the manga-publishing world?

Bakuman。, Vol. 1
ISBN: 978-1-4215-3513-5
$9.99 US / $12.99 CAN *

Manga on sale at store.viz.com
Also available at your local bookstore or comic store

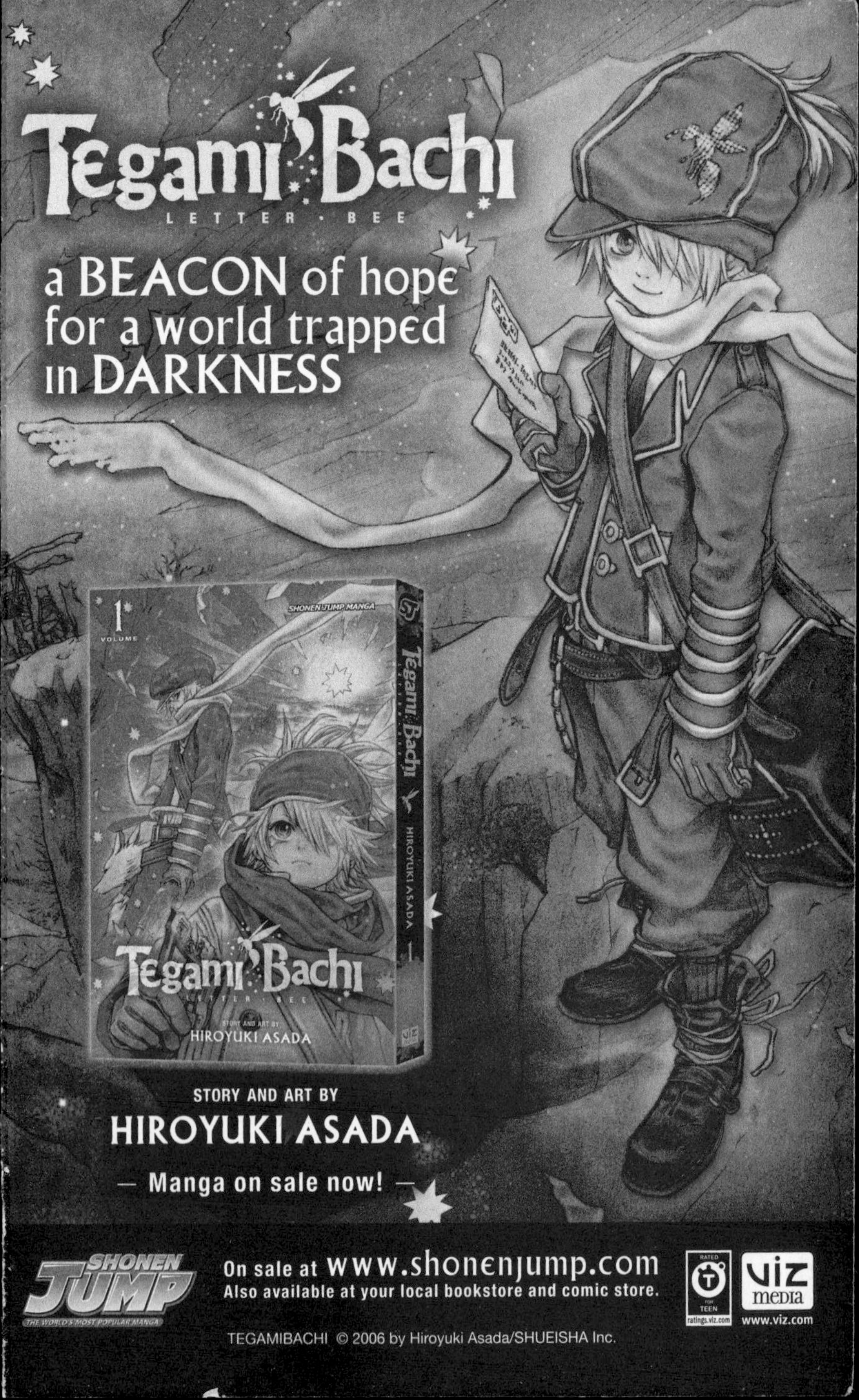

Tegami Bachi
LETTER · BEE
a BEACON of hope for a world trapped in DARKNESS
1 VOLUME
SHONEN JUMP MANGA
Tegami Bachi
LETTER · BEE
STORY AND ART BY
HIROYUKI ASADA
STORY AND ART BY
HIROYUKI ASADA
— Manga on sale now! —
SHONEN JUMP
THE WORLD'S MOST POPULAR MANGA
On sale at www.shonenjump.com
Also available at your local bookstore and comic store.
RATED T FOR TEEN
ratings.viz.com
VIZ media
www.viz.com
TEGAMIBACHI © 2006 by Hiroyuki Asada/SHUEISHA Inc.